GW00645172

Portl

Front Cover: Gav Symonds on *Weakest to the Wall* F7b (page 125)   MIKE ROBERTSON

Front Flap: Danie Rushmer on *Ausfahrt* F6b+ (page 61)   MIKE ROBERTSON

Rear Flap: Lyme Bay sunset from Blacknor   BEN THORNE

Rear Cover: Steve McClure on *The Gates of Greyskull* F7b+ (page 363)   KEITH SHARPLES

Steve Taylor

Maps and photodiagrams by Steve Taylor and Ben Stokes

Bouldering by Ben Stokes and Jim Kimber

Edited by Nigel Coe

Design and layout by Ian Smith

CLIMBERS' CLUB GUIDES TO SOUTH & SOUTH-WEST ENGLAND

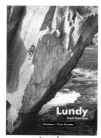

Lundy
2008

Southern Sandstone
2008

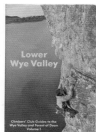

Lower Wye Valley
2007

Forest of Dean
2006

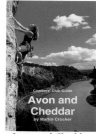

Avon and Cheddar
2004

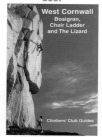

West Cornwall
2001

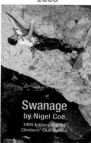

Swanage
1995/2002

Symonds Yat
1999

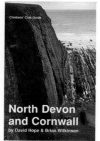

North Devon and
Cornwall 2000

Limestone Climbs on the Dorset Coast 1961
by B Annette

Dorset Climbs 1969 by R C White

Dorset 1977 by R J Crewe

Swanage 1986 by G A Jenkin

Swanage and Portland 1995 by N Coe

 Published by The Climbers' Club

© The Climbers' Club 2008

Taylor, Steve   Portland   (Climbers' Club Guides)

British Library Cataloguing in Publication Data

A catalogue record for this book is available from the British Library

796.522

ISBN 978-0-901601-77-3

Prepared for printing by the designer and author
Produced by 1010 Printing UK Ltd
Distributed by Cordee, 3a De Montfort Street, Leicester LE1 7HD

Maps on inside front cover and page 8 redrawn by Steve Taylor.
Reproduced by permission of Ordnance Survey on behalf of HMSO.
© Crown Copyright 2008. All rights reserved.
Ordnance Survey License number 100047354.

Contents

Climbers' Club Guides

The Climbers' Club

The publisher of this guidebook is the Climbers' Club, which was founded in 1898 from origins in Snowdonia and is now one of the foremost mountaineering clubs in Great Britain. Its objects are to encourage mountaineering and rock-climbing, and to promote the general interest of mountaineers and the mountain environment.

It is a truly national club with widespread membership, and currently owns huts in Cornwall, Pembrokeshire, Derbyshire, Snowdonia and Argyll. Besides managing seven huts, the Climbers' Club produces an annual Journal and runs a full programme of climbing meets, dinners, and social events. Club members may also use the huts of other clubs through reciprocal arrangements. The Club publishes climbing guidebooks (currently 22 in number) to cover most of Wales and Southern England.

The Club is a founder member of, and is affiliated to, the British Mountaineering Council; it makes annual contributions to the Access and Conservation Trust, as well as to volunteer cliff and mountain rescue organisations. In 1999 the Climbers' Club Colin Kirkus Guidebook Fund was set up as a means of distributing some of the profits the Club makes from guidebooks to assist climbing-related projects in keeping with the aims of the Club. Typical projects include ground erosion work and they need not be confined to the Club's guidebook areas.

Membership is currently around 1,300 and at present there are no limits on growth. Members of two years' standing may propose a competent candidate for membership and, provided that adequate support is obtained from other members, the Committee may elect him or her to full membership; there is no probationary period.

Climbing Style

The following policy statement on climbing style was agreed in principle at The Climbers' Club Annual General Meeting on 25th February 1990:

The Climbers' Club supports the tradition of using natural protection and is opposed to actions which are against the best interest of climbers and users of the crags. This applies particularly to irreversible acts which could affect the crags and their environs.

Such acts could include: the placing of bolts on mountain and natural crags; retrospective placing of bolts; chiselling, hammering, or altering the rock appearance or structure; excessive removal of vegetation and interference with trees, flowers and fauna.

The Climbers' Club policy is that guidebooks are written to reflect the best style matched to the ethos and traditions of British climbing.

Guidebook Disclaimer

This guidebook attempts to provide a definitive record of all existing climbs and is compiled from information from a variety of sources. The inclusion of any route does not imply that it remains in the condition described. Climbs can change unpredictably; rock can deteriorate and the existence and condition of *in-situ* protection can alter. All climbers must rely on their own ability and experience to gauge the difficulty and seriousness of any climb. Climbing is an inherently dangerous activity.

Neither The Climbers' Club nor the authors and editor of this guidebook accept any liability whatsoever for injury or damage caused to (or by) climbers, third parties, or property, arising from its use. Whilst the content of the guide is believed to be accurate, no responsibility is accepted for any errror, omission, or mis-statement. Users must rely on their own judgement and are recommended to insure against injury to person and property and third party risks.

The inclusion in this guidebook of a crag or routes upon it does not mean that any member of the public has a right of access to the crag or the right to climb upon it.

Information on all climbing in the area is made available regardless of the access position: for historical purposes; for the sake of completeness; and so that the facts are available if access is permitted in the future.

Before climbing on the crags in this guidebook please read any appropriate access and conservation notes.

The Climbers' Club endorses the BMC participation statement that:

> **Rock-climbing, hill-walking and mountaineering are activities with a danger of personal injury or death. Participants in these activities should be aware of and accept these risks and be responsible for their own activities and involvement.**

Acknowledgements

This guide has been the subject of 10 years of preparation by its authors. Whilst it is heartening to see the guide finally reaching its final stages of preparation, it has been a marathon effort for all involved, all of whom have had to juggle work and family commitments while trying to meet challenging deadlines.

Nigel Coe has been editing this tome throughout its development and has had to suffer my own interpretation of the English language and biased view of local climbing history – thanks for your patience. Ian Smith has been instrumental in pushing CC guides into the 21st century using this guide as his guinea pig, and has put many late nights into developing this simple, effective and attractive design, as well as typesetting the whole thing.

Much of the detail in here is based on the work of previous authors Bob Shepton, Gordon Jenkin, Pete Oxley, Nigel Coe, Mike Robertson and Joff Cook. Special thanks go to Bob for providing me with important historical detail and his own personal topo guide (produced in 1970!), and also being responsible for the Portland and Lulworth sections of Chas White's and Richard Crewe's guides.

Thanks to Ben Stokes and Jim Kimber for their sterling work on the bouldering sections of this guide. Their enthusiasm for local bouldering shines through their work and means Dorset is finally on the bouldering map. Ben has also provided invaluable assistance in the use of the various tools in producing this guide – I'd have struggled without him.

Thanks to Alan James of Rockfax for the technical help given in the early stages of the design, and for the use of the excellent Rockfax database. Thanks also to Rockfax authors Mark Glaister and

Pete Oxley for contributing to our mutual sharing of information when we were clearly working on competitive publications.

Thanks to the many locals who reviewed and helped rationalise grades, descriptions and star ratings. These were Barry Clarke, Joff Cook, Marti Hallett, Neal and Helen Heanes, Mike Robertson, Ben Stokes, Gav Symonds, Rich White, Mark Williams, and all contributors to the Rockfax route database.

Thanks to Simon Spring of Dorset County Council for permission to use their collection of aerial photos, on which the maps are based.

Thanks to the various Portland Rangers, Toby Lowe, Liza Cole and Lyn Cooch, for their good work with the Portland Climbing Forum, excellently chaired by Councillor Les Ames. This forum has been an important vehicle in ensuring access to Portland for climbers.

Many people contributed photos for inclusion in the guide. They are credited next to their photos – many thanks to them all.

Many thanks to Keith Sharples and David Simmonite who commented on the text and also to proofreaders Andy March, Yvonne Jones, Scott Titt and Martin Brice.

A special thanks has to go to my climbing partners over the years. Virtually every day out in Dorset in the last decade has involved visiting new crags, climbing new routes, checking descriptions, taking photos, counting bolts and drawing topos. Well, I can now announce that the 'Steve Taylor Show' is finally over. Thanks to Barry Clark, the late Damian Cook, Joff Cook, Nigel Coe, Guy Dixon, Marti Hallett, Neal and Helen Heanes, Jon Howell, Rob Kennard, Andy Long, Mike Robertson, Dave

Simmonite, Ian Smith, Ben Stokes, Gav Symonds, Scott Titt, and Mark Williams.

Last, but not least, thanks to my wife Karen, and my children Samuel and Eleanor, for being so patient and putting up with me spending so much time working on this guide at weekends and in the evenings. Normality can now be resumed...

Steve Taylor
July 2008

Meilee Rafe on *Bag End* F5+ (page 47).
JON HOWELL

Introduction

This is the only guidebook that covers all the climbs on the Isle of Portland and at Lulworth Cove. Whether it's a sport climb, a trad route, a deep-water solo, or a boulder problem, you'll find it here. The bulk of the guide covers sport climbing, where pre-installed bolts mean that only a rack of quickdraws need be carried. Interspersed between the sport climbs are a number of deep-water solos. The traditionally protected routes are included in topo format for the first time too. And, for ease of use, separate sections of the guide describe the most worthwhile bouldering areas in detail.

Dorset is blessed with a mild climate and a low tidal range. During the winter months, and when the skies are clear, the area is often warm and comfortable for climbing when other parts of the country might be considered out of the question. The location is further enhanced by the beauty of its setting within the serene Dorset countryside; whether for climbing, enjoying one of its many fine walks, exploring the coves and old quarries, or simply lying on the beach it is an area that is a pleasure to visit time and time again.

Approach

While all the climbs in this book are on the Isle of Portland or the Isle of Purbeck neither of these is a true island. Both areas are within easy reach of London and Bristol. A two- or three-hour drive from either city is generally sufficient to get to the crag, though in summer some careful traffic-jam avoidance may be required. Public parking is available, but can be expensive at locations such as Portland Bill and Lulworth Cove. Free parking is always available to those willing to walk an extra mile or so. Remember, however, that by paying to park you are supporting the local community.

The maps and descriptions in this guide will get you to the crags, but you may like to have the local Ordnance Survey 1:50,000 map: Sheet 194 (Dorchester and Weymouth).

Portland

Weymouth is well served by train from London and Bristol coupled with local buses. From London, the South West Trains service from Waterloo to Weymouth runs very regularly. A Wessex Trains service runs from Bristol Temple Meads to Weymouth. Buses from Weymouth train station run regularly to Portland, which is only a 20-minute ride.

Lulworth

From London, most of the Waterloo-Weymouth trains stop at Wool . From here, take the 10-minute bus ride to Lulworth. From Bristol, change at Weymouth to reach Wool (South West Trains). Check the internet for the latest timetables: www.rail.co.uk/ukrail/planner/planner.htm

Chesil Beach
DAVID SIMMONITE

Crag Overview

First on Portland:

West Weares Cliffs
Rock which falls into three categories: soft, weak, and loose. Fortunately the bulk of it is a Sanctuary Zone for birds, with an all-year-round voluntary climbing restriction in place.

The Blacknor Cliffs
A wide spread of grades here; high above the sea and usually in condition. Blacknor North and Central form a major venue, Blacknor South has scope for the chimney enthusiast, and the undercliff is a good spot for beginners, offering many good, bolted routes in the lower (F3 – F4) grades. Blacknor Far South provides excellent mid-grade climbing, and is often far less crowded than neighbouring Battleship Edge.

The Battleship Buttress Area
Battleship Edge is always popular, with technical, fingery sport climbs on clean white rock, all out of reach of the sea. Some of the easier lines on Battleship Block are becoming polished, however.

Wallsend Cove
The northern end of the cove is similar to Battleship Edge, whereas the central section exhibits a split personality: adventure climbs in the VS to E2 range interspersed with a large number of stunning harder, bolted routes.

Coastguard Cliff
A partly tidal cliff with a fine selection of steep, hard routes – many of the island's best flowstone climbs can be found here.

The Portland Bill/Cave Hole Area
A high percentage of short lines – mostly deep-water solos – on high-quality rock. Several of the coves provide good quality bouldering. Calm seas essential.

Beeston, Godnor, and Neddyfields Cliffs
Short, steep routes mainly in the Severe to VS grades, and a fair number of easier bolted routes

(F4 – F6a). The rock sometimes needs care, as do the exits. Only Neddyfields is totally unaffected by the tide. Good, vertical bouldering on the short walls above Neddyfields.

Cheyne Cliff
Hard sport routes on steep flowstone.

The Lost Valley
An inland chasm containing a few short, hard lines (sport and bouldering) on solid rock. Good for a windy day.

The Cuttings
A venue which escapes the full brunt of the prevailing southwesterlies. An inland quarried crag offering the full spectrum of grades, very popular in winter. The boulder field below the crag has over a hundred boulder problems.

Three areas are approached from Lulworth. Climbing is currently banned at all three locations by the landowner, the Weld Estate.

Durdle Door
A few impressive routes on an unusual feature. Some are loose, however. Calm seas required.

Dungy Head
A dozen bolted routes, with variable rock quality.

Lulworth Cove
Sloping roofs (and tourists) abound. Rise to the challenge of a soaring line of bolts, take the plunge on a deep-water solo, or teeter up a terrifying, but nevertheless terrific trad route. Calm seas essential.

The final locations lie within the Lulworth Tank Ranges. These are closed to the public for most of the year. Even when they are open, local byelaws prohibit climbing.

Worbarrow Tout
Almost an island with a few recorded routes on its seaward face.

Gad Cliff
A huge loose cliff visible from Portland, but with only one recorded route.

The Rock
The Portland cliffs are steep and consist of smooth, pocketed faces giving technically hard routes. Unfortunately, the rock itself is sometimes quite weak and the cliffs often terminate with an unnerving band of slatty rock topped by steep earth or grass, usually avoided by the installation of lower-offs on the sport climbs. Interesting features abound, however, such as flowstone-coated walls and conglomerate formations that resemble overhanging scree. These conglomerate structures are formed by rifts filling with rubble, which is then cemented together by the deposition of calcite. You finally benefit from this process when one side of the rift falls away – unless you're attached to it! Friction on the Portland cliffs is generally very good, though the flowstone can be slippery.

At Lulworth the limestone beds tilt down to the north. This gives slabs (and aching calves) as well as some large sloping roofs (and pumped arms). The public can view the tufa remains of ancient tree trunks at the Fossil Forest, a site to the east of the cove, but climbers will see (and use) more of these strange rounded formations on the undersides of many of the overhangs hereabouts. The brecciated limestones of the Broken Beds are another unusual feature here, either to be handled with kid gloves or to be left well alone.

Safer Climbing
The Dorset cliffs see more than their fair share of accidents, so no apologies are made for offering the following recommendations:

• For routes with lower-offs, ensure your second understands whether you are going to abseil or be lowered off. In addition, check you have enough rope to be lowered to the ground safely. All the sports routes in this guide can be climbed and lowered back down from using a 60-metre rope.

• Although it is common practise to lower off the top bolts of a sport climb and the term lower-off is used in this guide, you are strongly advised to check those bolts before deciding what to do. Abseiling puts less stress, and causes less wear, on the ropes than lowering off.

• When belaying, stand close in to the foot of the cliff wherever practical to prevent an outward pull on runners.

• Consider wearing a helmet, but in any event choose belays protected from falling rock.

• *Always* belay at the foot of sea-level cliffs. Ensure there is enough slack in the belay to allow the belayer to dodge any rocks dislodged from above.

• On deep-water solos, check water depth on predicted entry points to ensure a safe splashdown.

• Make sure the rope stays out of the water; several ropes have been lost after being washed around submerged boulders.

• On trad routes, place extra runners before loose exits.

• On sea-level traverses carry gear on bandoliers, which, in the event of a fall, can be easily jettisoned before you reach Davy Jones's Locker.

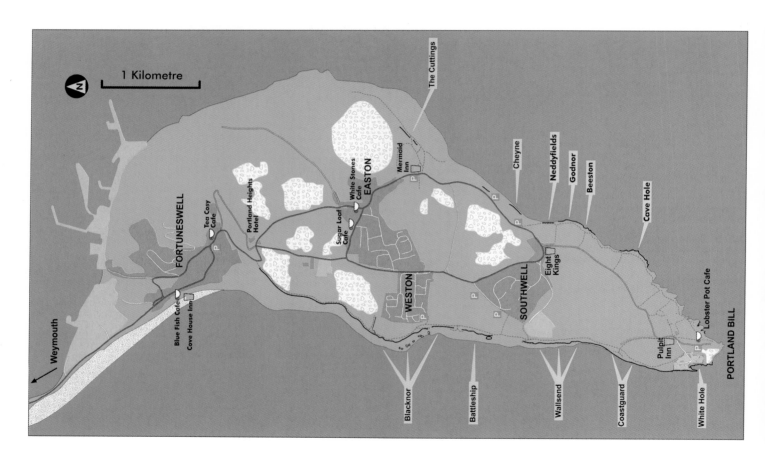

1 Kilometre

The Cuttings

Mermaid Inn

Cheyne

Neddyfields

Godnor

Beeston

Cave Hole

White Stones Cafe

EASTON

FORTUNESWELL

Tea Cosy Cafe

Portland Heights Hotel

Sugar Loaf Cafe

Blue Fish Cafe

Cove House Inn

Weymouth

WESTON

SOUTHWELL

Eight Kings

Lobster Pot Cafe

Pulpit Inn

PORTLAND BILL

Blacknor

Battleship

Wallsend

Coastguard

White Hole

Other Warnings

Portland was once coined the 'Isle of Slingers' by Thomas Hardy as visitors from the mainland were occasionally stoned by locals. Kids still do this! If it happens to you, shout for them to stop and ring the police. As well as stones, other object may be seen flying over the edge of the cliffs. Some Portlanders believe the cliffs to be a convenient rubbish dump. The author has seen (riderless) bikes dumped over the cliff on more than one occasion and empty beer cans are another occasional hazard. Needless to say, severe injury could be caused by such errant behaviour – watch out.

Harvest Mites, locally known as chiggers, are bright red mites that look like tiny spiders. They can be found from March to October around the base of most of the crags. About the size of a pin-head (2-3mm), they inflict an unpleasant bite out of proportion to their size, which only becomes apparent 12-24 hours after the event. The resulting spot will itch severely for a couple of days. They tend to favour warmer parts of the body, such as behind the knees and the groin area. There's not a lot you can do, except keep unworn clothes in your rucksack and watch out for them, although a shower helps.

Brown Tail Moth caterpillars are found on Portland in summer. These are hairy, brown, and about 5cm long. Unfortunately about 50% of climbers have an allergic reaction to them, sometimes severe, with strong irritation, swelling, and a rash.

Adders are a regular sight around Dungy Head and parts of Lulworth Cove. They are up to 60cm long, with a brown/yellow diamond pattern on their

back. They can inflict a very painful, life-threatening bite if they are disturbed.

Terms Used

Flowstone – so called because it looks as if molten rock has flowed down the cliff and then solidified. Generally brown or orange in colour, this forms the basis many of the best routes on the Isle. Routes such as *Sling Shot*, *Reptile Smile* and *Walking the King* typify the flowstone experience – good handholds, poor sloping footholds and pumped arms.

Stal/Conglomerate – a mixture of individual blocks and rocks, welded together by flowstone. Often much more solid than it looks. A good example of a route crossing such terrain is *Captain Klutz...* at Blacknor North.

Chert – a jet-black, flinty rock, often occurring in the base of large pockets, or along horizontal faults/breaks. This can be your friend or enemy, as it provide good resting holds, but can also be very fragile, shattering with little or no warning. Also it has sharp edges, acting like a knife when rope, boots or flesh come near.

Staple – the usual bolt-type used in Dorset. These are marine grade stainless steel, U-shaped anchors glued into parallel holes with industrial resin.

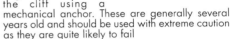

Expansion/Petzl bolt – the original type of bolt. A plate of metal, bent into a right angle and attached to the cliff using a mechanical anchor. These are generally several years old and should be used with extreme caution as they are quite likely to fail

Drilled pegs – pegs which have been hammered into drilled holes, sometimes glued in. These should not be trusted, as they can fail just with the weight of a resting climber.

Stakes – many of the trad routes here need a cliff-top stake on which to pre-place a rope for belaying on. Most of these stakes have now been removed or rusted away. Either place your own, or try to use a bolt belay on a neighbouring sport climb.

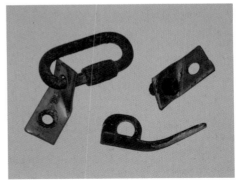

The Sea

The tidal range is very small. The range of spring tides, which coincide with a full moon, is about two metres, that of neaps only just over a metre. However, the actual range can be considerably greater in certain sea conditions. The proximity of the Isle of Wight means that double tides occur, where high tide or low tide may seem to last longer than one would normally expect. The flood tide (incoming) flows to the east and the ebb tide (outgoing) to the west. Strong tidal races occur around the headlands and are particularly dangerous. Swimming is not advised in the open sea in any but the calmest conditions, and then only for strong swimmers. Tide times can be obtained from the internet (www.climbers-club.co.uk), local papers or the coastguard.

The Descriptions

All areas and route descriptions run in sequence from left to right. However, the introduction to each area describes the cliff in the normal direction of approach. Left and right apply as the climber is facing the rock unless stated otherwise.

Read the full route description before embarking on a climb. Some climbs may currently have outdated fixed protection, have had their belay stakes removed, require a pre-placed rope to pull out on or have other considerations to be taken into account before setting off.

Pitch lengths usually refer to the amount of actual climbing and do not necessarily include easy scrambling up grass and earth. The majority of sports routes have bolt belays to lower off from.

R indicates routes which have variable nesting-season restrictions (See the Bird Restrictions section below).

Those routes not known to have had a second ascent are marked with a † symbol; their grades should be treated with caution. Routes and pitches marked †† have had a major rockfall resulting in significant but unassessed change to the climbing.

The Dorset Bolt Agreement

In the last 10 years, sport climbing has gained substantial acceptance nationwide. Bolting in the area is covered by a local bolting agreement worked out at local BMC meetings. The original agreement in March 1993 (modified in March 1996 and April 2005). The agreement was struck in a spirit of compromise and identifies the sections of cliff where, and under what conditions, bolting is permissible. Bolted routes are acceptable on certain cliffs, whilst the remaining cliffs are to be free of any form of drilled protection, whether for runners, belays, aid, or abseil or lower-off points.

The Portland and Lulworth section of the agreement is as follows:

- **Portland** Bolts acceptable

- **Durdle Door promontory** Bolts acceptable

- **Dungy Head** Bolts acceptable

- **Stair Hole roofs** at **Lulworth** Bolts acceptable

- **Intermediate Slabs, Arthur's Mount, and Lulworth East** Bolt free

- **Worbarrow Tout** Bolt free

It was agreed that if retrobolting were considered necessary, the permission of the first ascensionist would always be sought. If permission were not forthcoming then no retrobolting would take place. Where the first ascensionist is unknown, or impossible to contact, suggestions for retrobolting individual routes should be brought up at SW Area BMC Meetings and a vote taken.

If, after a naturally-protected 'first ascent', the line in question is found to have been climbed before, no harm has been done. This is not so with bolt-protected climbs; to bolt up may be to screw up. Particular care should be taken to ensure that any *in-situ* gear is placed as effectively as possible, with the type of placement chosen to be as long-lasting and as unobtrusive as possible. If in any doubt, consult the local BMC Access Rep.

Sport climbs are given a French grade. Traditional routes have an adjectival grade, with deep-water solos also having an S grade and a French grade, as quality of natural protection should not be an issue.

The topos

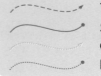

Trad route, top-out

Sport route, lower-off

Crag approach

Project, lower-off

Check the description of projects in the text, as some are regarded as 'open' and others are not.

Route Quality

The standard one-to-three star system is used to indicate the respective quality of each climb. A single star indicates that a climb is of good quality, while three stars denote the very best. Many, many unstarred routes are worthy of attention, however. The hollow stars used for unrepeated routes indicate the star rating is that given by the first ascensionist.

Gear

Some trad climbs have vital runner placements – these are mentioned where known. Some climbs with bolt protection need other protection as well – these climbs are given adjectival rather than sport grades.

> **Although the number of bolts given for a climb is thought to be correct it should only be used as a guide, as it is easy to miscount and some routes may have been retrobolted. As a general rule, take the number of quickdraws stated in the description, two for the lower-off and another just in case – also useful if you drop one.**

After drilled pegs snapped and both home-made and commercial expansion bolts corroded easily in the salty sea air, staple bolts appeared on Portland. Home-made staples, fixed with resin, soon became the protection of choice for most first ascensionists. True, their two holes close together weaken the overall placement, but with unofficial tests showing them resisting an outward pull of 1,800kg, they compare favourably against most *Rocks* on wire, which are rated at 1,300kg.

The corrosion seen with expansion bolts has been notably absent with staples placed as long ago as 1994. Whatever the strength of a newly-placed staple, its performance as it ages must be the main concern. How, when a staple shows signs of corrosion, is one to know when it is seriously weakened? There are no easy answers. Take care!

Bird Restrictions

Certain parts of the cliff on Portland are subject to restrictions during the bird nesting-season to protect species of rare birds. The nesting sites of these birds change from year to year, and therefore the restrictions may also change. Each year, the relevant bird authority consults with BMC representatives to determine the extent of the coming year's restrictions. Signs are placed at the boundaries of the restricted areas and changes are published on the BMC Website, in the climbing press and shown on signs and in pamphlets available at the main access points to the cliffs.

These variable restrictions have proven to be very successful and it is vitally important that climbers respect these restrictions since any disturbances could well have a serious effect upon these colonies. Those climbs which are likely to be included within a restricted area are denoted by **R** in the main text.

Restrictions currently apply to sections of:
• Wallsend Cove: 1st Mar to 31st July inclusive
• Coastguard Cliff: 1st Mar to 31st July inclusive plus a year-round restriction further south.
• Cheyne Cliff: 1st Mar to 31st July inclusive

Peregrine Falcon. STEVE TAYLOR

The Cliff Environment

In 2002, The Dorset Coast from Lyme Bay to Studland was designated a World Heritage Site. This followed many years of effort by local authorities, councils and conservation groups to protect this internationally important environment. It is hoped that this new-found status will not limit climbing in the area.

The **Portland** cliffs are internationally important for their geology and are the Portlandian type section; that is, they are the reference site for these beds of rock. One of the best sites in the world for fossil reptiles is situated on West Cliff; the most important raised beach in Southern England is at Portland Bill and the best British example of rock collapse by slab failure can be seen at Blacknor.

As a result of its situation, rock, and land use, Portland plays host to a large number of rare species. Portland Sea Lavender grows solely on Portland, whilst other rarities are Hoary Stock and Maidenhair Fern, which grows in The Cuttings.

Portland Sea Lavender. BRYAN EDWARDS

Rare mosses and liverworts are basically Mediterranean in character; they include the rare *Eurhynchium Meridionale* (Portland Feather Moss) and *Southbya Nigrella*. The locality is one of the richest coastal limestone sites for lichens in Britain; 210 species have been recorded there, including the rarity *Roccella Phycopsis*.

The nest sites of Herring Gulls are spread throughout the Isle, on roof-tops as well as cliffs. The west coast cliffs provide nesting sites for Fulmar, Guillemot and very small numbers of Razorbill and Puffin. The onomatopoeically-named Kittiwake also breeds here, but its numbers are low and declining. The Isle juts out into the English Channel so many migrants pay a flying visit, Portland being their last stop before they set off for even sunnier climes.

The existence of rare plants on the cliffs lays a special responsibility on the climber. Many of them are very hard to distinguish from more common species, sometimes even for the experts, while others are inconspicuous and easily overlooked. Because of this the 'gardening' of new routes should be kept to a minimum.

Portland Feather Moss. BRYAN EDWARDS

Access

Access to the cliffs depends on many factors, but one of the most important of these is the way climbers conduct themselves. The cliffs on which we climb are owned by a number of individuals and organizations who have one thing in common: climbing is not at the forefront of their priorities. As a result of their unspoilt nature as well as their flora and fauna, the cliffs are of immense worth; virtually all of them have been designated Areas of Outstanding Natural Beauty as well as a World Heritage Coast, and they are all Sites of Special Scientific Interest. With no rights, only privileges, we are on very delicate ground. A whole cliff could be lost to all climbers as the result of one thoughtless act by one person. Especially at The Cuttings, where the general public is nearest to us, the safety of non-climbers is of paramount importance. So, too, is minimizing disturbance, of whatever type. The cliffs, their environs, and their inhabitants deserve both our appreciation and our care.

Any incident concerning access should be reported to the British Mountaineering Council's Access Officer as quickly as possible to prevent deterioration of the situation (telephone number 0161 445 6111). The Access Officer may then refer the matter to the South West and Southern Area Committee to help resolve the problem. This committee is composed of representatives from local and national BMC-affiliated clubs, rescue organizations, and conservation interests as well as other interested individuals. Maybe you could help?

Weather

Generally, the east coast crags (The Cuttings, Cheyne Cliff, Beeston, Godnor and Neddyfields) get the morning sunshine. Blacknor Central and South are the first crags on the west coast to see the afternoon sun, and Blacknor North stays in the shade longest. Obviously, you should choose your venue depending on whether you wish to avoid the sun or chase it. In winter, you can climb in a T-shirt if the sun is on the crag. Summer climbing generally revolves around avoiding the sun, or taking a dip in the sea between routes.

Where and when to climb

Many of the cliffs on Portland provide an excellent suntrap. Whilst this can lead to excellent conditions in the winter, summer days can be stiflingly hot. Following is only a general guide as to where you should climb, based upon the prevailing weather conditions:

Windy Days

The exposed nature of Portland makes it particularly prone to high winds. On very windy days, choose a cliff in the lee of the prevailing wind direction. Therefore climb on the east coast when a strong Westerly is blowing. Apart from the top few feet, the cliff should be relatively still.

Sunny days

In the winter, it is best to follow the sun around Portland, climbing on the east coast in the morning and the west coast in the afternoon. Summer should generally be spent avoiding the sun, especially on the more difficult routes. Climb the west coast in the morning and retire to the shade of the east coast later on. However, the summer months do allow the refreshing alternative of a cool-down swim, especially on the west coast. Note that the intensity of the sun on the west coast can result in sunburnt shoulders in under half an hour – take sensible precautions and plenty of water.

Rainy days

Go to a climbing wall or café. The local caves are an alternative.

Cloudy days

Climb where you like. However, certain cliffs, such as Coastguard and some parts of Wallsend, can seem greasy in humid conditions. Occasionally, routes become so damp they are unclimbable.

Accommodation

For Lulworth:
• Tom's Field Campsite, Tom's Field Road, Langton Matravers (01929 427110) is a popular choice for climbers visiting Swanage, and Lulworth Cove is within easy travelling distance.
• Acton Field Campsite, near Langton Matravers. This site is seasonal.
• Durdle Door Caravan Park (01929 412000). This is closer to Lulworth Cove. It has static caravans for hire and also accepts touring caravans and tents.

Portland currently has no camp sites. Weymouth has many, but these are generally aimed at familes, so groups of more than two climbers may not be welcome. More salubrious accommodation can be found at one of the hundreds of B+B establishments in the area.
• Glen Caravan Park (01305 823548). A static caravan here is the connoiseur's choice.
• Cove Park Holiday Park (01305 821286). Static caravans for rent.
• Sea Barn/West Fleet Holiday Park (01305 782218). Regularly used by climbers.
• Tourist Information offices in Swanage (01929 422885) and Weymouth (01305 785747) can provide up-to-date details of campsites.

Gear Shops

With the closing of Rockies Climbing Shack in 2002, Dorset lost its only dedicated climbing gear shop. However, a number of other outlets exist in the area:
•Parry's Dive Centre (01305 821261) in Castletown on Portland holds a small stock of climbing essentials.
• Portland Sports and Leisure (01305 821398) in Easton Square on Portland sells chalk, boots and even bouldering mats.
• Great Western Camping (01305 266800) in Dorchester has a full range of outdoor gear.
• Cotswold Camping (01202 529123) in Bournemouth has a similarly full range of outdoor gear.

• Outdoor Sports and Leisure (01929 550882) in Wareham stocks a good range of climbing, camping and general outdoor gear.

Cafés and Pubs

On Portland, the *Sugar Loaf Café* is popular with climbers; situated on the north side of the square at Easton it is particularly convenient if one is following the sun from the east to the west coast cliffs during the course of the day. *Church Ope Café* is near The Cuttings, and there is the *Lobster Pot Café* close to Portland Bill (though, strangely, lobster is not on the menu). *The Blue Fish* in Victoria Square has become very popular in recent times, serving fine coffee and voluminous breakfasts. The Bird Watch post in the car-park on the Weymouth-Portland causeway also has a good, cheap *al-fresco* café. The *Mermaid Inn* at the entrance to The Cuttings provides a friendly welcome to climbers, and is handy for the Cove Caravan Park. The *Cove House Inn*, situated at the Portland end of Chesil Beach is a justifiably popular venue to end a day's climbing. At Lulworth, there are a number of pubs in Lulworth itself, and the *Castle Inn* in East Lulworth provides good beer and food.

Mermaid Inn

The Cove House Inn

Sugar Loaf Café

Blue Fish Café

Training

There are very few worthwhile climbing walls in Dorset. These are listed, together with the best walls from further afield.

Fort Purbrook Activity Centre, Portsdown Hill Road, Cosham, Portsmouth, Hampshire (01705 321223) Deep within this old fort are two old magazine chambers fitted out with 5-metre *Bendcrete* bouldering walls. Open 0900 to 2100 weekdays and 0900 to 1300 weekends. Café.

Undercover Rock, St Werburgh's Church, Mina Road, Bristol, Avon (01179 413489) is the best wall in the South West, with bouldering areas and 13-metre leading and top-roping walls (*Living Stone* and *Entre-Prises*). Open 1000 to 2130 weekdays and 1000 to 1800 weekends. Refreshments available.

Calshot Activities Centre, Calshot Spit, Hythe, Hampshire (02380 892077). Excellent leading and top-roping created by *DR Climbing Walls and Walltopia*, including the steepest wall in the South

(equivalent angle to Lulworth Cove, but higher). Excellent bouldering wall too. Café, bar, indoor skiing and Velodrome! Open weekday evenings and weekend afternoons.

Queen Elizabeth Leisure Centre – The Edge, Blandford Road, Wimborne, Dorset (01202 888208). A dedicated area with a 8-metre wall with top-roping and leading sections consisting of panels and bolt-on holds by *Rockworks* and *Merlin*, and a dedicated bouldering room by *Wallkraft*. Open evenings and weekends.

Bournemouth University – Hot Rocks, Wallisdown, Bournemouth, Dorset (01202 595012). A dedicated area with a 6-metre wall with top-roping and leading sections consisting of heavily featured panels and bolt-on holds by *King Kong Climbing Walls*. Open evenings and weekends in term time, ring for availabilty. There is also a good, cheap student bar on campus.

Clubs

The **Wessex Mountaineering Club** draws the bulk of its membership of mountaineers, hill-walkers and rock-climbers from Hampshire and Dorset, but also from Wiltshire and Somerset. They have fortnightly meets in Wales, the Peak, the Lakes, and the South West, and have their own hut in Snowdonia.

New Routes

Please enter details of any new routes as well as any comments regarding this guidebook on the Climbers' Club website www.climbers-club.co.uk. For a new route, please indicate route length and grades, preferably more than one guide to its position, date of ascent, and first ascensionists, as well as an accurate description. If in doubt, it is better to supply too many details rather than too few.

Future Challenges

The text indicates a number of bolt lines which are as yet unclimbed. At the cliff they are often marked by finger tape wound around the lowest bolt. These projects are usually left for their equippers to make the first ascent, except for 'open' projects. Please don't attempt these projects, without direct permission, as a surprising amount of effort is required to clean and bolt these lines in the first place.

Historical

Despite currently being one of the UK's most popular climbing areas, Portland has only a very recent climbing history. The majority of the routes in this guide were put up after 1988 and if you climbed on Portland before 1993, the chances are you would not have met any other climbers. Now, it is estimated that there are one or two hundred climbers on Portland on a sunny weekend. Despite its latter-day popularity, there is a strong history of first ascent adventures, controversial episodes and enough incident to warrant a few pages of narrative.

There is no recorded history of climbing at Lulworth or on Portland prior to 1961. That year, however, saw the publication of Barrie Annette's 'Little Green Book' – a climbing guide to Dorset that covered developments at Swanage but also included preliminary investigations of Durdle Door, Lulworth Cove, and Portland. Southampton University Mountaineering Club published it, and several updated editions were to appear in the next few years. Although containing no information on specific routes on Portland (and few at Lulworth), it highlighted the potential.

In 1962 as a young curate at St John's in Weymouth, the Reverend Bob Shepton thought he had been posted to an area 'bereft of any possibility of climbing'. After reading an article on routes climbed at Malham Cove, he suddenly felt that the limestone in the area might actually be climbable. Instead of holding evening meetings in the church hall, Shepton started taking his youth group off climbing instead — very good for character development.

With a fine sense of adventure he began his exploration at Lulworth and Dungy Head, then moving on to the east coast of Portland in 1963 to develop many short climbs. Modern deep-water solo

devotees will be surprised to find that at this time Shepton dismissed the Cave Hole area as 'useless'.

It was 1967 before any lines were climbed on the west coast that were thought worthy of recording – the first being an incredibly bold ascent of *Vesuvius* at Coastguard South. Ian Kestin took a 13-metre fall on a repeat attempt. In previous years, however, Shepton had climbed (but not recorded) many lines on Battleship Block and the Fallen Slab. It was around this time that an agreement was struck that Shepton had first call on new routes on the west coast, and Ian Kestin and the Whitely brothers had precedence at The Cuttings. Try to imagine such an agreement existing today.

Excerpt from Bob Shepton's personal Portland Guide

Shepton forged his way up the main features on the west coast over the next few years, leading major lines and taking big falls where others had only top-roped before. Others involved in the exploration of the west coast included P Northcote, Murray Hodgson and Chas McCombie — who bagged the impressive *Port Wine* at Blacknor South. We have Shepton to thank for many of the cliff

names on Portland, including The Cuttings, Coastguard Cliff, Wallsend Cove and Battleship Buttress.

The Little White Book?

The new guide, written by Chas White, with Lulworth and Portland sections penned by Shepton, appeared in the shops in the early months of 1969 to mixed reviews. For most climbers it was a welcome and much needed publication and, as White predicted, was soon to be rendered out of date as the fast pace of development continued. Full details of what had been done at Portland and Lulworth Cove were now available, though this stimulus failed to draw the activists away from what was happening on the bigger cliffs at Swanage. Sporadic visits did occur from time to time but little was added. Of note, however, was the addition of some harder lines on the east coast courtesy of Ian Kestin. *Muscleman Direct* was repeated by Martin Crocker 30 years after the first ascent with a mooted grade of E3 5c, not bad at all for 1969.

In 1973, Shepton wrote an article entitled 'Portland Bill' for *Rocksport* magazine — the first national publicity for the island. Portland, however, remained in isolation for the next 10 years or so, and although the Wessex Mountaineering Club climbed there, Shepton, Dutton, Kestin, Northcote and Hodgson were left in peace to explore and make first ascents at their leisure. Some of these ascents were serious affairs, on which steepness and the suspect nature of the rock were given added bite by a lack of adequate protection. A number of the climbs of this period, such as *The Prow, Reunion, Scoup, Wallsend Wall*, and the aptly-named *The Oh-No Variant*, were later upgraded from HVS to the extreme category.

By the mid-70s White's guidebook was hopelessly out of date, some two hundred new routes having been added to the Swanage cliffs alone and the whole of Dorset was in need of a major update. The task of masterminding (and financing) a new guide was taken up by Richard Crewe, who had been quietly compiling the information for nearly five years. The Portland and Lulworth Cove sections of Crewe's 1977 guide were again authored by Shepton.

In the same year, Shepton ended his Portland campaigning with an eventful ascent of *Fond Farewell* — the first attempt ending in a race to the base of the cliff with a table-sized block — luckily the block won.

Despite the significant amount of development that had taken place since the previous guide, development of the area remained a strictly local affair until 1979 when Pat Littlejohn and Chris King added the strong line of *Poison Tip*. Littlejohn returned in 1981 with Hugh Clarke to add Portland's hardest route with *Bad Dream* (E4) at The Cuttings and the impressive *Slice of Life* (E2) in Wallsend Cove. Whilst there, Littlejohn attempted a traverse of Wallsend Cove's high faultline, which would have been one of the longest routes in the country. Unfortunately the attempt ended after 15m when he realised there weren't going to be any footholds. Another reason for Littlejohn to visit was to select routes for inclusion in a new edition of his *South West Climbs* guide, but Portland didn't make the final cut.

The Oxley Era Begins

Late in 1982, a schoolboy introduced himself to Nigel Coe at a Wessex Mountaineering Club dinner. Although he had not climbed a great deal, the youth, Pete Oxley, gave an indication of his ambition by confiding that he wanted to climb *Cima Petite*, which at that time was one of the 10 hardest routes at Swanage. Interestingly, Oxley chose Portland as the location for his first new route —

Two Fingers at The Cuttings in 1983. However, for the following five years he focused on the many great unclimbed lines at Swanage. Oxley's drive, ability, and dedication soon made him the foremost first ascensionist in Dorset, as well as the climber most responsible for the rise in standards in the county. Without Oxley, Portland would not be the ultimate sport climbing arena it is today.

In 1986, Dorset saw its first new guide for nine years, authored by Bristolian Gordon Jenkin. A significant section of the guide was devoted to Portland and Lulworth. However, despite publishing details of over one hundred and seventy climbs at these locations, only one route got any stars. At the time the guide was published, there were no sport routes in Dorset and in Jenkin's own words, Portland was destined to remain a 'backwater'. Oxley was soon to challenge this opinion.

In 1987 Oxley started exploring the Lulworth Cove area, 15 years after Shepton climbed his last new route there. When he saw the East Cave in Stair Hole he thought all of his birthdays had come at once. He climbed *Mark of the Beast*, a contender for the best and most sought-after route in the south, as well as *Lulworth Arms Treaty* and *Grimly Fiendish*. He also began exploration of the Dungy Head area, climbing *Dungeons and Dragons*, the first new route in this area since Shepton's early explorations 20 years before.

A year later Jon Biddle soloed *Anarchy Stampede* on the short steep wall beneath *Mark of the Beast*. Little did he know then that he had climbed the first recorded deep-water solo in the area. Nowadays ropes are rarely seen at Stair Hole, pairs of boots and chalk bags slowly drying in the sunshine being a more likely sight.

The Portland Renaissance

In 1987, Crispin Waddy visited the west coast of

the Isle and made two bold ascents: *Inchworm* was an on-sight solo and *Medusa Falls* took a line up a very thin veneer of flowstone. These ascents lit a slow fuse, and a year to the day later new route activity exploded. In marked contrast to Shepton's earlier ascents, Oxley, seconded by Jon Williams, climbed the first lines on Portland to use bolt and drilled-peg protection. Pegs in drilled placements, as opposed to bolts, were thought necessary on account of the softness of some bands of Portland limestone. In addition, the use of drilled protection meant the possibilities for new routeing on Portland were extensive. Oxley helped himself to several slices of Portland's geological gateau: at Coastguard Cliff, *Superfly Guy* and the impeccably minimal *Nothing but the Groove*; in Wallsend Cove, *Colors*; and then on Battleship Edge, where he climbed *Keyboard Wall* and *Monoculture*, albeit with a rest point on the latter.

Three-quarters of the Dorset new routes in 1989 were on Portland. Scott Titt and Coe discovered The Cuttings New Cliff (conveniently exposed by Hymacs during installation of a sewage pipe). Harry Venables found both the bottle and the right sequence on *Pining for Glossop*, and Brian Tilley burned up *Midnight Oil* at Coastguard Cliff, where a fine soaring crackline was climbed by Ross White to give *Explorator Motivator*. The tops of many of the climbs on Portland's west coast gave cause for concern. This was keenly felt on Titt's *Skateboard to Oblivion*; the possible 15m 'skateboard' back down the steep crumbly earth slope to the top runner and the ground beyond vindicated the use of fixed-rope belays on other ascents.

Tim Dunsby felt the new route tremors too and, starting up *San Andreas*, climbed *High on the Richter Scale* at Blacknor North. But the epicentre of the action was Wallsend Cove with its long bulging wall climbs such as Oxley's *Face the Truth* and *Realm of Chaos*. The Bristol contingent also grabbed a slice of the action. Crocker was drawn to Blacknor Far South for *Ryme Intrinsica* and *Sparkling Bone Chamber*, to Battleship Edge for *Choco Loni*, and to Wallsend Cove for the E6 *ZumZeaux*. On Battleship Edge, Jenkin quickly led *Dripping with Blood* before the crag struck back and a visit to Weymouth General was necessary. For Jenkin this made a change from the Bristol Royal Infirmary.

In 1989, one hundred and twenty new routes were climbed on Portland leading to the urgently needed publication of a Swanage supplement by Jenkin, Oxley and Coe. This guide did a simple and effective job of providing up-to-date information on all developments since Jenkin's guidebook. Suddenly Portland and Lulworth had routes worthy of three-star status – thirteen of them. Oxley wrote an article for *High* magazine shortly afterwards extolling the quality of routes on Portland, its first national publicity for 16 years. Finally, Portland was seeing a slow trickle of visiting non-local climbers.

A year later in 1990, Gareth Jefferies made a bold ascent of *Oscourt* at Wallsend Far North. Oxley was enjoying himself there too, on the likes of *Sweet Smell of Success* and *Ecstasy*. Crocker made an *Infernal Din* at The Cuttings, founded the controversially chipped *The Wax Museum* at Coastguard Cliff, and won the 'heavy route-name' prize with *Saskatchewan Uranium Miner* in Wallsend Central. Later in the year Oxley's attention was drawn to the east coast, where the classic lines of *Hall of Mirrors* and *The Mind Terrorist* were ticked off.

The ceaseless new route boom continued in 1991 when Oxley braved the tides of the southern end of Coastguard Cliff with varying degrees of success (and wetness) to establish a group of climbs such as *Full Fathom Five*. Inland at The New Cuttings, technique reached a new high on his *Pastoral* at

(English) 7a, now given V7. Steve Taylor began his personal new route campaign on Portland with *Fear's Younger Brother* at Blacknor Far South and *Hillman the Hunter* at The Cuttings.

Jon Biddle returned from college at Ilkley and revisited Stair Hole at Lulworth, where he landed *Herbert the Turbot* with an on-sight solo after many an on-sight plunge. The Cook brothers, Jonathan 'Joff' and Damian, also began their deep-water solo new-routing careers with *Captain Bastard Got There First* and *Does Leviathan Plop Float?* respectively.

In 1992 the infamous staple bolt appeared in Dorset. This cheap, long-lasting solution to sea-cliff bolting had an instant impact on the new-route scene. The design of these bolts meant that lower-offs could be installed at the top of all sport climbs, removing the need to preplace lower-off ropes. They also made it possible to back off at any point on a route without leaving gear behind. This invention was to ensure that Dorset was to become the most popular sport climbing destination in the UK.

The Eighth Grade on Portland
New route activity in 1992 was concentrated on Portland, although there was a resurgence of interest in Lulworth. There, the *Mark of the Beast* roof was criss-crossed by Oxley's bolted lines such as the F8a *Adrenochrome*, while an eight-metre rail across a nearby roof was too much for Coe, and went on natural gear to Dunsby: *The Safety Rail*. The F7a traverse of *Horny Lil' Devil*, another bolted line by Oxley, proved popular and was soon receiving more solo than roped crossings. Oxley also climbed all of the major lines in the west cave at Stair Hole with *Animal Magnetism*, *Gates of Greyskull* and *Never Kneel to Skeletor*.

On Portland, Blacknor North enjoyed a renaissance at the hands of virtually all the Dorset activists after Oxley had set the ball rolling with *England's*

Dreaming, taking flowstone next to *Slings Shot*. He climbed another fine line close by, *Reptile Smile*, a three star E1 which, unusually for Portland at that time, became very popular. Also on Portland, Joff Cook climbed *Old Painless* in Wallsend North, where his brother Damian became only the third person to make the E6 grade on a Dorset new route when he savoured *Breakfast of Champions*. Towards the end of the year Oxley finally succeeded in climbing *Freaky Ralph*, then Portland's hardest route, which remained unrepeated until 1997 when Tim Clifford managed to find a way past the huge reach on the crux.

First ascensionists were not alone in hitting the headlines on Portland; local climber Paul Norman was soloing *Persistence* at Blacknor South, protected by a jumar on a fixed rope, when the rope was cut so that his belay karabiners could be stolen. He made it up to the cliff-top and informed the police, but the culprit was never found.

The next year, 1993, saw several new routes provided by non-locals. *Imbolc* was a pumpy E6 addition to the Blacknor cliffs and, unusually, was put up by Nick White from neighbouring Devon. Gordon Jenkin finally returned to Portland and climbed *Fat Falling Pigs*, seconded by none other than Gary Gibson. Mark Higgs popped over from Southampton to add *Fantasy Island* to Coastguard Cliff and Anneka Jende, a Danish chiropractic student, climbed *Apfelstrudel* at Blacknor North. Oxley's *Eternal Spider* featured hard, dynamic climbing and a beautiful-looking line to boot. 'Adopted' local Mike Robertson began his own development of Portland at a determined rate, with *21½ Weeks* and *Actually (Shit) Happens* becoming instantly popular at Blacknor North. Later in the summer, Robertson and Taylor added some of the first deep-water solo lines to the east coast including *Spittle 'n' Spume* — Robertson was now hooked by the deep-water solo habit.

17

Introduction

Battleship Block was bolted up at the end of the summer by Taylor and Mark Williams. The bolting of a crackline first climbed in the 60s on the slab left the previous author of this guide somewhat unimpressed, forcing the comment: 'Four feet from the northern end of the buttress is a solid and perfectly-protected layback crack (Hard Severe 4a). Incredibly it has now sprouted four bolts. What about more for the walk from the car? Sickening!' Coe on-sight soloed the arête right of the crack and named it *Hate the Sin and Love the Sinner* in response.

The cliffs east of Lulworth Cove had been traversed at sea-level in the early days of Dorset climbing, but there were more possibilities than *The Mupe Bay Traverse* alone. Starting beneath the top roofs, facing right, and following their noses, Dunsby and Coe alternated leads on two routes which were the longest in Dorset since *The Boulder Ruckle Girdle Traverse* was climbed at Swanage back in 1969. Unfortunately, the Army then informed the first ascensionists that these cliffs were out-of-bounds to climbers. The House Boulder and Dungy Head became local hot spots for one short period. Taylor added his hardest new route to date with *Turn It On* and Robertson made an adventurous foray into loose rock in the Dungy Head pinnacles to climb *Lost Souls*, partnered by a very young Dave Pickford.

Nineteen ninety three saw the introduction of the Dorset Bolt Agreement. Formulated by local climbers, this agreement defined Portland and most of Lulworth to be a sport-climbing area. Existing trad routes in these areas were agreed to be left unbolted, unless the permission of the first ascensionist was gained. With the formal agreement in place, the Portland Bolt Fund was founded to help with the retrobolting of existing minimally bolted routes. A hastily drawn up left-to-right list of sports routes on Portland was printed out in Taylor's study and sold for two pounds in aid of the fund. In a year well over 300 copies of this list were printed and sold — Portland was soon to sink under the weight of stainless steel.

Nineteen ninety four brought the highest number of new routes on Portland since the boom year of 1989. Some were very good, such as *El Podor de un Coño* by Robertson, and some were unacceptable; while it was a challenging line with a well-positioned crux, Oxley's *Modern Nightmare* shared climbing — and its bolts — with the once committing *Bad Dream*, climbed 13 years earlier by Littlejohn. The same hand was responsible for the retrobolting of *Slings Shot*, without the first ascensionist's permission.

In spring 1994 The Amphitheatre was 'rediscovered' by Coe and Titt. The obvious line was left for later because of the wet rock and Titt's distaste for traverses. A couple of vertical nut-protected lines were climbed. But 'later' proved to be too late, as a month afterwards Robertson added the traverse of *The Great Escape* and the nearby flowstone wall was soon plastered with sport climbs by Dominic Cook, Taylor and Robertson. Cook's *Bay of Rainbows* sported two 'added' holds. These were a small limestone block, glued on to replace one which had been knocked into the sea, and a resin crimp. The replaced block was soon removed by an irate visitor, but the crimp remains...

Cheyne Cliff had been relegated to the minor league after a huge buttress collapsed in the 80s. A decade later, it had settled down somewhat, and although some friable rock remained, half a dozen sport climbs were established by Oxley and Robertson on the flowstone-encrusted faces. Better rock, indeed almost flawless rock, was to be found a stone's throw away from Portland Bill. There, at White Hole, most of the local sport climbing activists contributed a finger-wrecker or two. In contrast, on the other side of the Bill, Robertson took advantage of the watery landings, forsaking the drill in search of a thrill, to carry off a series of on-sight solos in and around Cave Hole.

Oxley was busy with two projects during this period, one a bulging wall on Coastguard Cliff and the other a topo-guide for the sport climbs in the region. *Vespasian*, the hardest climb on Portland, required six days of effort, but success came in the nick of time for inclusion in the Rockfax guide, appearing in late 1994.

At the time that the hardest line on Portland (actually, in Dorset) was F8a+, grades of F9a were being claimed elsewhere in the UK and abroad. Why, then, should Portland be so devoid of cutting edge climbs? Perhaps Nic Sellers summed it up when asked why he hadn't yet visited – 'word is, it's all a bit vertical'. Obviously Nic wasn't aware of the roofs and waves of rock at Cave Hole, but he also had a point. Even today Portland has seen few visits from the climbing 'elite'.

No one would have guessed the huge impact that the Rockfax guide would have on Portland. Prior to publication the only information available on the newer bolted climbs was Taylor's printed list of routes in left-to-right order for each of the major crags — only the name and grade were shown. To find a route one required either a guided tour from a local, or to use the printed list in conjunction with the 1989 supplement and Jenkin's guide to find a landmark route, then work left or right from that point. This error-prone procedure often resulted in F7a+ lines being mistaken for F6a+, and both bruised and flattered egos.

When it arrived, the Rockfax guide sold like hot cakes. Suddenly there were hundreds of well-informed climbers crawling all over the Island, dossing on the cliff-tops, using the shops, drinking in the pubs and getting changed in the streets — one of the few things locals have been complaining about ever since. The rapid growth in traffic meant that a couple from Hampshire thought it worthwhile to open a climbing shop on Portland — Rockies Climbing Shack was born, with Neal and Helen Heanes providing a focal point for the following seven years of development on Portland.

Early in 1995, a huge unexploded world war two bomb was found while levelling a football field on Portland. Shortly afterwards the whole island was evacuated to nearby holiday camps while the UXB squad did its work and Portland was the subject of national news for a while. Taylor named *Portland Exclusion Zone* at Godnor to commemorate the weekend.

Nineteen ninety five proved to be a significant year in Portland's climbing history, due to several events going against the grain of the prevailing British ethical attitudes. In the spring of that year Joff and Damian Cook added some new lines and retrobolted an existing line at Blacknor South left of *Jutland*. These routes sported several drilled and chipped holds. Further south, Damian Cook drilled an undercut into the start of his new line *Bushwacked* at Blacknor Far South, whilst in Blacknor North Joff Cook glued two flowstone holds to ease the difficulty of the final moves on *The Flowstone Shuffle*. Things came to a head shortly afterwards when Oxley removed the glued holds and re-climbed the line as *Unstuck on You*. He also attempted to smash the drilled holds on *Bushwacked*, but unfortunately left the undercut intact, and removed natural holds by mistake. Following this short but unpleasant period in Portland's history, hold improvement virtually ceased.

On a more positive note, the summer of 1995 saw an upsurge in the development of new deep-water solo lines around Cave Hole. Robertson even

bought a canoe to aid with exploration, one result of which was the awesome eight-metre roof of *Crab Party*. Taylor eventually bagged *Aquamarina*, at that time the most technical deep-water solo on Portland, and Robertson ticked *Trashy's Traverse* above a very high spring tide — giving a whole metre of water in which to land. Damian Cook on-sighted several excellent lines including *Ixtlan* and *Reel 'em In*. Later that summer, Joff Cook and Robertson added several difficult link-ups inside the west cave at Stair Hole, the hardest being *El Guapo* — Dorset's hardest deep-water solo first ascent at the time. Ethics soon came back into the spotlight, however, when the Fallen Slab came under the drill. A couple of good new lines were added, and some excellent old lines were retrobolted, *Fallen Slab Arête* being one of them. Strangely the bolters thought it appropriate to rename the original lines — the original names have been used in this guide.

Several climbers were involved in the bolting of some short, hard routes in a bay beneath the beach huts near Portland Bill, including Percival's super-steep *almost* F8a *The Big Blue*. The bolting in this new area, dubbed Sector Pom-Pom, was not welcomed by the owners of said beach huts. All of the belay bolts were smashed and visiting climbers were confronted by angry locals. Luckily, these confrontations have died down, but climbers are still asked to maintain a low profile.

A few months later Taylor added a collection of easy new lines at the Triple Slabs (including a retrobolt of an existing trad route, later de-bolted). This became the first area in the UK where routes of F3 to F5 were available. Add to that the beautiful coastal setting and straightforward access, and the large boulders under Blacknor South suddenly became very popular.

At the end of the summer, Coe's *Swanage and Portland* guide was published by the Climbers' Club.

This guide was a huge personal effort by the author, requiring two volumes to cover the wealth of climbing in Dorset (and the Isle of Wight). The Portland volume was not, however, well-received by some local climbers. Perhaps the guide's most obvious omission was to ignore French grades and use UK grades for both traditional and sport routes alike. Nineteen ninety five was a period of transition for sport climbing in the UK where French grades were becoming the norm. In addition the Dorset Rockfax, published in the previous year, had used both UK *and* French grades for sports climbs, and the CC's approach was perceived to be a backward step.

Those who had given up a significant amount of their time in equipping routes on Portland felt their efforts were distinctly sidelined as the guide took a rather neutral approach to the description of what was already the most popular sport climbing destination in the UK. Coe's preference for trad climbing was somewhat evident in the guide, even though the allocation of stars for certain areas of Wallsend Cove rivalled Paul Williams's star allocation on Cloggy.

Also, the highlighting of certain ethical no-nos such as unapproved retro-bolting and hold chipping/drilling was, with hindsight, very patchy. For instance: *Wax Museum* was highlighted for having a drilled finger pocket, though *Midnight Oil* had no mention of its improved holds; no mention was made of solid holds being removed to make certain routes more consistent. Coe was clearly unaware of these additional indiscretions, (the perpetrators did not make it public knowledge), but those singled-out felt aggrieved nonetheless.

Much of the development in late 1995 was due directly to the appearance of the new guide. Many stand-out lines were previously thought to be existing trad routes, but the CC guide made it clear where the gaps were. Within a few months of publishing Roberston and Joff Cook had plugged several gaps at The Cuttings including *Disobedience Contest*, *Dusty Fred's Winter Collection* and *The Holy Hand Grenade*.

Over the winter of 1995 Robertson decided that there was sufficient interest in the deep-water solos in and around Cave Hole to publish a guide. Very much a personal effort, his guidebook, the first dedicated to deep-water soloing, appeared in the spring of 1996. Whilst the guide was never going to sell in significant numbers, its popularity spurred Robertson, Taylor and Joff Cook to consider a more commercial product. The Climbers' Club soon got wind of the idea and agreed to publish. Much credit must go to the tireless John Willson for his personal belief in the project, and allowing the authors to stray from the usual Climbers' Club writing style to produce *Into the Blue*, an upbeat, slightly irreverent guide to deep-water soloing in Dorset.

All of the locals had looked at the small crag between Battleship Edge and the Back Cliff and wondered if there was any worthwhile climbing. Early 1996 saw Taylor braving a rare Portland snowstorm to bolt up six short lines — the first on Chockstone Cliff's excellent rock. Robertson added a hard and long extension to *The Great Escape* to give *Esmerelda's Monkey*, the longest route on Portland, while Neal and Helen Heanes cleaned and bolted the left side of the Lost Valley. Oxley climbed a collection of fine new routes in Wallsend Cove, including *Genuflection* – one of the best routes of its grade on the island.

Nineteen ninety six also saw the emergence of some new names on the new route scene. Mike Vaicaitis and friends of the Basingstoke Mountaineering Club began developing the previously quiet cliffs on the east coast, with Neddyfields soon being climbed out. Nic Hellyer started his new-routeing career with the unpleasant *Do You Like Our Owls* at Blacknor North, but soon realised that there were much better unclimbed lines elsewhere, including the rather well-named *The Loneliness of the Long Distance Driller* at Blacknor Far South. Local lad Jim Kimber, in an attempt to deter Vaicaitis and Hellyer from bolting some of their more scrappy lines, took to stealing the first ascents of their routes. The naming of one of the lines *Another Stone on the Pile of Choss* was an attempt to make his point. Still – it was someone else's project.

In the summer, Will Jones, an American visitor from Lake Tahoe, climbed a selection of good lines at Blacknor North, the best of which was *Spanner Eyes*, a hard and slightly scary neighbour to *England's Dreaming*. Later that summer Oxley began climbing some of the more obvious gaps in Coastguard South and finished off the year with *Hurricane on a Millpond*, the most technical offering at The Cuttings. Tongues wagged in early 1997 when Dave Henderson stole a project from Luc Percival in the Lost Valley. *Plystalker* was quickly dispatched by the young Devonian, much to the chagrin of Percival.

The remainder of 1997 was a bumper year for Portland, with whole new crags being peppered with bolts. Godnor Far North became the new area for easy-grade sport routes thanks mostly to Vaicaitis and Pete Cunningham, who had the foresight to publish a set of photo-topos describing their achievements, with the proceeds going to the Portland Bolt Fund. Scottish raiders George Ridge and Janet Horrocks added two good, pumpy lines on the left of this crag. Neal and Helen Heanes, along with Neil Burton, bolted up the previously overlooked southern end of Blacknor South with a series of Captain Pugwash inspired route names. At the same time, Oxley and James Dunlop used low spring tides to good effect to gear some excellent short lines in the Hidden Wall area of Beeston, including the photogenic arête of *Sea of Tears*. Gordon Jenkin made a welcome return to the island to add the instantly popular *Monsoon Malabar* and *Bring on the Night* in Blacknor Central. Taylor finally gave in to an expanding waistline and released his Cheyne Cliff project to the more able Guy Dixon, resulting in *Detonata*. Oxley also continued the development of Coastguard South which he began in 1996. The black wall right of *Xavier's Wall* sprouted three good, easy lines, one of which was climbed by Jan Rostron. He also extended the southern limit of the climbing with *Azymuth* and *L'Esprit du Vent*. The remaining gaps on the *Zinc Oxide* wall of Battleship Back Cliff came under Oxley's drill too, with a combination of link-ups and independent lines — *The Racing Line* being perhaps the best of these.

Lulworth saw little in the way of new development in 1997. Damian Cook declared *I Love Eszter* in the east cave, and *Burning Arms* and *Freed from Desire* were added to the roped-up climbing itinerary by Oxley and Kimber.

By now a number of locals began thinking that Portland had been climbed out. However, in early 1998, Dunlop, Oxley and Kimber discovered a new buttress at White Hole. Some fine routes were added in a matter of days to beat the bird ban. Later, in the spring of 1998, others realised that there were some significant gaps on all of the cliffs. Robertson climbed the fingery *Through the Barricades* on Blacknor South, Horrocks and Ridge put up the marvellous *Reality Bites* on Blacknor Far South, and Helen Heanes added the popular *Ocean Drive* a few routes to its left. Oxley took another look at Coastguard South and soon realised much of its unfulfilled potential across the grade range — *Reactor Meltdown*, *New York Dolls* and *Swimsuit Issue*, all high quality routes, were climbed when the tides allowed.

Gav Symonds in beautiful evening light on *Turned to Stone* F7a (page 71) BEN STOKES

Introduction

The arrival of Andy Long in Dorset was soon marked with the difficult *Tennessee* at Coastguard South, a super-steep wall, instantly popular with those capable of climbing it. Another, more temporary visitor was Francis Haden who, with Jenkin, climbed a number of lines in Blacknor Central including the unpleasant *Inbreeding*, though these have resolutely failed to become popular.

In the summer of 1998, Neal Heanes, along with Neil Burton, developed an area of cliff in Wallsend North right of *Streaky*. These routes were all in the F6a-F6b range and destined for immediate popularity. However, a mudslide a few months later coated the new lines in dirt and loose rock. Oxley took advantage of good autumn conditions to fill up the wall left of *The Wax Museum* with a series of sustained and steep lines. *Meridian Line*, *Ming the Merciless* and *Glycerine* now stand proud amongst Portland's hardest. On the right side of the same wall, Chris Cubitt, in search of a rumoured hard project, climbed Taylor's last remaining project to give *Steve's Route*, though 'Steve' no longer has the desire to climb it.

Elsewhere on the Isle, Nic Hellyer enjoyed significant amounts of airtime before completing his hardest new route to date, *Screw the Roses, Send Me the Thorns*. His later addition of an extra bolt ensured less taxing falls for future ascensionists. Damian Cook added the fine line of *Girl Power* to Coastguard South and Bridport lad Gavin Symonds climbed *Castle Anthrax* — his first new route on Portland.

In 1998, Lulworth Cove had little attention from roped climbers. Robertson saw a *Window of Opportunity* with an obvious direct start to *Horny Li'l Devil*, and Joff Cook was the first to succeed on the super low traverse of *Hornier than Thou*. Nineteen ninety nine heralded the inevitable slowdown in new route activity in Dorset. However,

this may have been due, in part, to Oxley's efforts on the second edition of the *Dorset* Rockfax – he only just made it into double figures in his new route tally for the first time since 1986. However, there was still a steady trickle of hard new routes: Oxley cleaned up an old Vaicaitis project on Cheyne Cliff with *Dyno-Mite*; Symonds climbed *ClockWork Orange* on Coastguard Cliff and a fresh-faced Dave Pickford climbed *The Pickford Files* in Wallsend – though he should have removed a deadly loose flake beforehand. Other hard lines ticked in 1999 included Kimber's fiercely technical *Fibonacci Sequence* and Oxley's *Balance of Power* — an F8a project which had been awaiting his ascent for several years.

Taking a very bold approach, Martin Crocker dropped in on Limekiln Cave to solo most of the gaps between the sport routes. Considering the state of the shallow-water landings, this had to be the boldest day's climbing by one person that Portland has ever seen — nine routes all E3 and above, climbed with the absolute minimum of pre-inspection. One of the finest achievements in 1999 was Richie Bingham's outstanding solo of *Adrenachrome* (F8a) at Stair Hole. This was always on the cards, but it took an 'outsider' to succeed on the last great Dorset deep-water solo challenge.

Nineteen ninety nine was also the year in which bouldering began to make itself known. Jim Kimber publicised a 'Nu' School approach on Portland, with a (hopefully) tongue-in-cheek article in *On The Edge*. At the same time, Ben Thorne created an internet chat forum allowing locals to discuss Portland at some length from the comfort of their computer desks. Dorset was quickly adapting to the imminent 21st century.

Ben Stokes, Tim Crawshaw, Gavin Symonds, Thorne and Kimber were re-discovering the boulderfield beneath The Cuttings. Kimber had already extolled

the virtues of the 'Nu Cuttings' in his *OTE* article but made little mention of the Boulderfield. Armed with saws, secateurs and plenty of time to excavate huge piles of rocks, over 100 problems were unearthed. The size of the boulders meant that sit-starts were the order of the day, however, several classy problems were ticked. Problems such as *Lightning Strike*, *Rocky and Diesel*, *Scene Revisited*, *Southern Soul*, *Liquid Sun* and *Cavity Search* would be classics anywhere else in the country. However, even bouldering proved to have an aspect of danger about it. Crawshaw and Stokes had just repeated (after 18 months' working them) some new problems on the Egg boulder when a strange noise was heard. Shortly afterwards, the huge boulder simply toppled over.

The year 2000 saw the publishing of the second *Dorset* Rockfax. Once again, the appearance of a new guide sparked off the new routeing activity to fill in some of the more obvious gaps. Heanes and Symonds climbed *H'Electric Boogaloo* and *American Beauty* at Coastguard South and Oxley added *Pure Shores* and *100% Columbian* to Coastguard North. Dunsby and Titt raised a few eyebrows at Coastguard South by ignoring the 'local ethic' and climbing two new trad routes. Despite being fine lines, *Razor Laugh* and *Hell Razor* have not seen any attention since their first ascents — a lesson to all. Let's hope this isn't the thin end of the trad wedge!

Portland suffered its worst rockfall for years in the winter of 2000. A huge section of cliff collapsed at Coastguard South during a storm in November, taking with it several routes including *Grip '89*, *The Feedback Monster* and the Whitely brothers' fine crack climb *The Lotus Eater*. Bolted sections of rock can still be found in the rubble below.

Two thousand and one heralded the foot-and-mouth outbreak. Knee-jerk government reactions closed down virtually all climbing in Dorset for over a month. Fortunately for locals, the Portland Ranger at the time was sympathetic to climbers and access to the Cuttings, Portland Bill and Blacknor was hastily arranged. Climbers had to follow torturous routes to get to these crags, though they could see Portlanders walk their dogs on the standard crag approaches. As a result, new route activity all but stopped, with the usual activists relieved to be able to climb at all.

However, one very brave soul made a significant effort. Martin Crocker soloed the deadly *Extreme Lives* in The Amphitheatre – with hard, steep moves above a bone-breaking, wave-washed landing.

With the foot-and-mouth epidemic over (without a single case reported in Dorset), Jim Kimber and Ben Thorne came upon the Lunar Boulders beneath Blacknor Pinnacle. They returned with drill, resin and steel to create a good selection of easier grade routes in a very pleasant setting.

In 2002, Portland succumbed to the inevitable attention of Gary Gibson. He had previously dismissed Portland as worthless (remember that he accompanied Jenkin on the first ascent of *Fat Falling Pigs* in 1993), but booked a spring break with his drill. Since then, Gibson has been Portland's main activist. The Gibson machine initially centred on *Downhill Spiral*. A number of good lines were climbed, in particular *Billy Bob's Way*, *Everything's Eventual* and *Wonderful*. However, some lines were not properly cleaned, with repeat ascensionists and their belayers being showered with loose rock.

Gibson also often bolted lines which were seen to be highly eliminate, detracting from the quality of their neighbours. For example, *From a Buick Eight*, if climbed without blinkers, shares a lot of ground with both *New York Dolls* and *Brooklyn Bimbo*. This 'fill the gap' attitude became a pattern of Gibson routes throughout his later Portland campaigns.

Another new name on the Portland roll call was that of Mick Ward. Having made his mark in other areas of the country, Ward settled on Portland early in 2002. He quickly joined the list of first ascensionists with routes in Blacknor Central such as *One Fine Day* and *Valerian* and some significant additions to Cheyne Cliff. However, again, more time spent cleaning would have been beneficial, rather than leaving it for repeat ascents.

It was in 2002 that Portland suffered its first access problem since the bolts at Sector Pom-Pom were flattened in 1995. One of the owners of Blacknor Fort declared that the cliffs at Blacknor North belonged to him and began warning climbers to stay away. Ugly red notices were painted at the base of the cliff stating that climbing was 'prohibited'. The police took an interest at that point and the situation settled down a little. A year later he was charged with shooting the other inhabitant of the fort, and was given a custodial sentence. Thankfully no climbers were ever threatened with weapons.

Later in the year, Andy Long couldn't believe his luck when he checked out the big wall right of *Empire State Arête*. *Beautiful South*, *Rush* and *Dogtown Skate Team* were well-received by those capable of climbing them.

Two thousand and three saw far more traffic than previous years. Ward completed the bolting of Sector Golden Pants, south of Beeston Cliff, with a series of hard, short problems on immaculate rock. He also climbed the tall line left of *The Watchman* to give the necky *Immaculata*, originally graded F6a+, but now a more realistic F6c due to a hard and gripping finish.

Gibson was active up and down the whole length of the west coast. A series of lines right of *Poop Scoop* were quickly dispatched, all of which are very worthwhile (though, strangely, the obvious flake crack remains unclimbed). However, he drilled a pocket on the nearby *Hen's Tooth* to make it climbable — the excuse being Portland's unjustified reputation as an ethical vacuum. Gibson also mistakenly retro-bolted Crocker's *Eyes in your Navel*, *Nigel* at Battleship. His excuse – it wasn't in the guide. Perhaps he should have used the CC's definitive guide rather than the selective Rockfax?

Neal Heanes visited Wallsend South in the early summer of 2003 to climb some fine new lines, including *Vin Chaud* and *Sang Chaud*, with Stokes getting in on the act with the *Parkhurst Dozen* and Helen Heanes climbing *Sans Frontiers*. Symonds became the first person other than Oxley to climb a new route at F8a (though Percival had come very close with *The Big Blue*). *To Hungary for Love* was Damian Cook's old project at Wallsend North, swiftly dispatched by the ever-improving Bridport lad. Meanwhile, down at Coastguard North, Portland's hardest route, *Vespasian*, saw its first repeat in eight years by Liam Halsey, who confirmed the grade of F8a+.

The only significant new route activity in the Lulworth area in 2003 was Barry Clark and Taylor's raid on Worbarrow Tout. The western tip of the Tout offered up a number of strong lines on good rock, which they were quick to exploit.

One of Dorset's greatest characters was lost in April of 2004. Damian Cook — Damo — drowned on a deep-water solo trip to Mallorca. He was responsible, with brother Joff, for coining the term 'deep-water solo' and between them they inspired a whole new climbing sub-culture. Damo's beaming smile and fine attitude is sorely missed. Within a week of the funeral, news came from Iraq that Brian

Tilley had been shot and killed. Brian was a legend in the Dorset climbing scene, appearing occasionally to climb hard routes with Oxley or to solo in the Ruckle between mysterious naval missions and long stints as a personal bodyguard. Brian's background masked a generous and open spirit, and he was an integral part of the Dorset climbing scene.

Two thousand and four was another quiet year for climbing. Ward added some audacious solos to Pulpit Rock at Portland Bill — all awaiting a repeat by anyone brave enough to try. Gibson climbed some fine new lines in Wallsend Cove, though some approach bolts would have been nice for the 10m of choss to get to them. He also added some very tight eliminates at the Blacknor and Battleship areas. Taylor and Williams bolted some mid-grade lines at Beeston, though unknown to them, Ward had soloed one of them two months previously. Over at Stair Hole, Williams nicked a project from Joff Cook to give *Despicable Terrier* right of *Captain Bastard...* Titt returned to Worbarrow Tout for the first time in 25 years with Brian Watson to climb *Pony*, which had an air of the Boulder Ruckle about it.

Taylor kicked off 2005 new route activity with some more easy lines in the Triple Slabs area. Taylor and Titt had both climbed a route each on the Diamond Slab and the Diamond Boulder nine years previously. Taylor returned, new drill in hand, to add three new lines and retro-bolt the existing routes. The newly-christened Blacknor Undercliff now holds more than 20 sport routes of F5 and below — making it unique in the UK, and destined for popularity.

In the spring of 2005, a BMC South West Area Meeting was held in Wareham. One of the topics for discussion was the existence of sport climbs at Lulworth East. The Dorset Bolt Agreement stated that Lulworth East was a bolt-free area, but Oxley and Dominic Cook had been slowly adding bolted climbs to the huge roofs there. The meeting voted strongly for Lulworth East to remain bolt-free. It will be interesting to see if the bolts remain, though new bolted routes have appeared since.

Later in 2005, Gibson returned to Portland to add some worthwhile fillers-in, but once again retroed an existing trad climb — Crocker's *Good Lay* at Blacknor Far South. Later, in Spring 2006 he did it yet again, to Coe's appropriately-named *Hate the Sin and Love the Sinner* at Battleship Block. Despite an official request to Gibson from the BMC SW Area to remove the bolts, they remain in place.

Two thousand and six saw some minor development in Wallsend, where Tom Beaumont began his bolting career on a newly emerging flowstone cliff underneath Wallsend North. However it was Lulworth that saw the most significant traffic. Rob Kennard had been disappointed at the earlier vote for Lulworth East to remain bolt-free. Rather than rebel against the agreement he visited the crag with a fresh view and began climbing (on-sight) new trad lines amongst the bolted roofs. Very soon the likes of Taylor, Hallett, Titt, Stokes and even Dave Simmonite came along to help with the development, resulting in several excellent new climbs on perfect rock – this development continued sporadically throughout 2007, with 20-plus trad routes at Lulworth East now recorded in this guide.

Two thousand and seven was a great year for hard deep-water solos, all from Gav Symonds. In heavy seas, he made the first solo ascent of *Balance of Power* at White Hole. True to the modern way, a terrifying video of his ascent was soon available on YouTube. In much calmer conditions, he spent some time working, and eventually succeeding on *Windowchrome* at Stair Hole, linking *Window of Opportunity* with *Adrenachrome* to give a probable F8a+ — the hardest solo in Dorset, and a contender for the hardest route in Dorset!

In the summer, Taylor added a collection of worthwhile sports routes to Godnor in amongst Shepton's trad climbs, and also gave *Break-over Crack* its first free ascent. Beaumont tripled the number of short sports routes at Dungecroft Quarry, all on flawless flowstone. Steve Muncaster and John Leonard continued in the same vein with the bolting of the short flowstone walls in Sharbutt's Quarry above Blacknor South. The same pair, after a tip-off from Taylor, bolted two new lines at The Cuttings, but their eye for a line was called into question when the lines chosen *avoided* the obvious natural features!

Events over the last 2 years question what the future holds for Portland and Lulworth. An increasing number of visitors to the area believe that Portland should have all of its routes bolted, and the existing trad routes are climbed very rarely indeed. Contrast this with the very recent development of Lulworth East, where hardened sports climbers have been enjoying a return to their more traditional roots, and also the increasing popularity of deep-water soloing and bouldering, which leave no permanent traces on the crag. Worthwhile unclimbed lines remain on Portland, leaving plenty of scope for those still keen on making a name for themselves through new routes. This guide highlights the gaps on both the east and west coasts and will hopefully motivate those with the pioneering spirit to get out and cement Portland's reputation as the best sport climbing destination in the UK.

The Blacknor Cliffs

OS Ref 679 715

Set high above the sea, the Blacknor cliffs offer an assortment of climbs. They are an especially good choice in cooler months, when the afternoon sun reaches them and the bay-shaped walls become sun-traps. These crags are less affected by the greasy conditions experienced on lower crags such as Wallsend and Coastguard.

Approach

Follow the main road onto the Isle and up the hill. On reaching the plateau, turn right towards Weston. Turn right again at a T-junction by a church. Continue for one-third of a mile before turning right onto a housing estate opposite shops. Park and pay in the Climbers' and Walkers' car-park at the estate's southwestern corner by a modern development of flats and a mobile telephone mast.

• For Blacknor Fort bouldering, head towards the cliff-top and walk north along the top of the cliff past Blacknor Fort until you reach the bouldering area on the right.

• For Pit Prop Crag, continue past the bouldering for 30 metres, before dropping down steeply to the left. Walk northwards for 100 metres to reach a 'fallaway'. On the main cliff, opposite the southern end of the 'fallaway' is *Overture Chimney*.

• For Blacknor North and Central, approach as for Pit Prop Crag. After dropping steeply to the left, follow a path south along the base of the cliff.

• For Blacknor South, descend from the cliff-top through the several levels of Sharbutt's Quarry (easily identified by a wall of large, cut blocks along the cliff edge) to the southern end of Blacknor South.

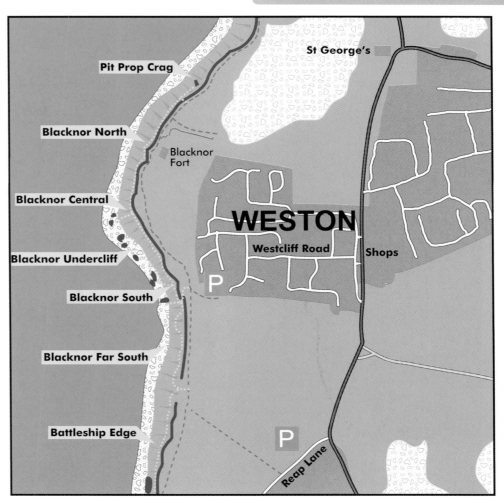

West Weares

OS Ref 685 729 to 682 722

The extensive cliffs at the northern end of Portland's west coast, with shale cliffs and scree slopes beneath them, have a wild, almost mountain-like atmosphere. Unfortunately though, good rock will not be found on them.

In 1998 they were declared to be a 'Sanctuary Zone', with climbers agreeing not to venture in their direction to protect the bird colonies, including peregrine falcons. As such, there should be no climbing on the cliffs north of Pit Prop Crag.

The quarries above West Weares can provide an enjoyable excursion. Tout Quarry, a sculpture park amidst old quarry workings, is situated behind the northern end of the cliff and contains many significant stone sculptures in amongst its maze-like alleys. There is also a limited amount of bouldering for those keen enough to explore.

Pit Prop Crag

The crag lies 150 metres north of Blacknor North and has both unpleasant trad cracks and moderately pleasant sport routes. This area incorporates both the large, loose main cliff and the smaller, solid 'fallaway' block. Approach described on page 25.

The following five routes lie on the western side of the more welcoming 'fallaway'. A grassy base, bolt protection (except for *Enlightenment*) and the fact that it comes into the sun earlier than other parts of the cliff make it a fairly attractive venue. All routes lie on the seaward face.

1 Reinheitsgebot 9m F4 4B   (7.5.95)
Start just to the right of the left-hand arête. Has some doubtful holds.

2 Boiled Lobster 9m F6a+ 4B   (7.5.95)
Climb the bubbly wall. There is a detached block on top of the route, which should be avoided at all costs.

3 Enlightenment 9m HVS 5b †   (12.10.91)
The wide crack on the right-hand side of the 'fall away' crag. Boulder belay on top, or step right to use the lower-off on *Slim Fingers' Revenge*.

4 Slim Fingers' Revenge 9m F7a+ 4B (7.5.95)
Climb the clean wall. The bigger your fingers, the harder this is.

5 Another One for the Pot 8m F6b+ 4B
          (7.5.95)
Pleasant climbing near the right-hand arête of the face.

6 Overture Chimney 24m HVS 5a † (12.10.91)
Big nuts and long slings required. Cross the trench and climb the blocky pillar from the left to gain the chimney proper. An unprotected but enclosed struggle leads to a good ledge, from which a couple of technical moves (now protected) gain the top. Thread belay beneath a large boulder across the path.

7 Resurgent Spirit of Loose 23m E1 5a †
          (12.10.91)
A fine-looking line fatally flawed by the softness of the rock and the off-putting name. Start 12 metres right of the last route. Climb the crack-line, with the psychological crux near the bottom and the technical crux at the top. Since the belay stake is no longer in residence, use the large flake up to the right in conjunction with the thread belay of the last route.

Steve Taylor on Boiled Lobster F6a+.
BEN STOKES

Blacknor Fort Quarry

The quarried walls below Blacknor Fort have been frequented by climbers for many years in anonymity. However, at the turn of the century a topo replete with names and grades appeared on Ben Thorne's Sportland website. Whilst some of the old heads turned their noses up, this was a much-needed documentation of a fine venue. The rock is almost flawless, and the quality of problems first-class. The northerly aspect prohibits the area from being a winter venue and it is best reserved for spring and summer evenings.

Approach

Described on page 25, the approach leads you to a northwest-facing wall easily identified by the rising conglomerate rail of *Mercury and Solace*. North of here the wall steps back to form a small bay filled with quarried blocks. Behind the blocks is the worryingly named *Death Slab*. The left-hand side of *Death Slab* is bounded by the square-cut *Death Arête*. At this point the wall turns inland, extending into a sheltered valley. Surprisingly, the problems in this little valley catch the mid-morning sun. At the far left-hand end of the wall there is the hanging arête of *Teenage Riot*.

There are further boulder and top-rope problems in the valley to the north. These have not been documented due to the amount of glass and rubbish at the base of some of the problems. It appears the area is sometimes used by locals as a shooting alley!

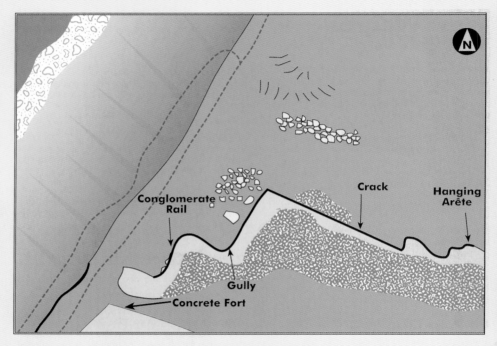

★ 1 **Teenage Riot** **V1** The left side of the hanging arête at the far left-hand end of the wall is a fun problem. Start in the small scoop under the arête. Gain height using slopers either side of the arête and stretch up and left for a jug.

★ 2 **Flaming June** **V0-** The right side of the hanging arête is also a worthwhile problem, particularly if the crack on the right is eliminated.

★ 3 **Downer** **V1** Right of *Teenage Riot* is another, somewhat narrower arête. This provides a worthwhile problem, which if you follow the arête direct is quite technical. Start at a big pocket.

4 **The Groove** **V0-** Immediately right of *Downer* is a wide groove. A little nondescript but a useful down-climb.

5 **Sugar Cane** **V2** At the base of *The Groove* is a low-level slab. Above this is a dark grey wall which, if climbed direct without bridging into the groove, is technical and thin.

the wall direct on good holds. Traverse the top of the wall rightwards to a clean finish.

10 Aero Zeppelin V2 Four metres right of the vertical crack is a blind flake. Start at a hand-ledge beneath the flake. Follow the flake on good holds to a testing stretch for the top.

11 Easy Groove V0- At the right-hand end of the wall is an easy-angled groove, which might interest beginners and those needing an easy down-climb.

James Wharton on *Fiji* V1 (page 30).
BEN STOKES

6 Providence V1 The arête four metres right of *Teenage Riot* is one of the best problems under Blacknor Fort. The small rock at the foot of the arête detracts a little from the fine, balancy climbing.

The next corner can be down-climbed.

7 Firewater V0+ Start one metre right of the corner and follow a rising line of flakes leftwards to the top of the corner.

8 Xpander V2 Two metres right of the arête of *Providence* is a conspicuous full-height vertical crack. Follow the crack with surprising difficulty to a huge hold on the left. Down-climb the corner on the left.

Right of *Xpander*, the bottom of the wall is hemmed in by brambles. Now and again these are beaten back by public-spirited individuals or frustrated boulderers.

9 Theresa's Sound World V0 Start 2 metres right of the vertical crack, above a low ledge. Climb

15 Fiji V1 The rib forming the left side of the gully gives a surprisingly good and balancy problem above a reasonable landing. One of the best problems here.

Right of the gully, the wall turns and faces northeast again.

16 Desperate Death Gully V3 Two metres right of the gully, at threequarter height, is an obvious patch of bright yellow lichen. Start beneath the lichen. Follow a leftward-trending line to a broken edge just right of the big flake. Spurn the flake and reach direct to the top.

17 La Bombe V4 Climbing the wall in line with the lichen is the hardest recorded problem in the quarry. Starting as for *Desperate Death Gully*, tackle the wall direct using chert nodules and small edges.

18 Namistai V0+ In the middle of the northwest-facing wall is a line of jugs and rightward-facing flakes. Start at a good hand-ledge and follow the obvious line of weakness above.

19 Atlanta V2 A metre left of the arête is a thin crack. Climb the crack direct without using the flakes on *Namistai*. Contrived, but worthwhile nonetheless.

20 Sub Rosa Left V2 The left side of the arête is a fine problem.

21 Sub Rosa Right V0+ The right side of the arête is an easier proposition, thanks to the two large letterboxes left by the quarrymen.

The right-hand end of the northeast-facing wall is bounded by a narrow square-cut arête. The rock right of this arête is slabby, faces northwest and receives the last rays of the evening sun.

12 Death Arête V1 The right side of the arête provides unusual climbing above a poor landing. Start from a sitting position in the pit beneath the arête, bearing in mind this is where you will land if you fall off.

Three metres right of the arête is a vertical crack.

Between the crack and the gully to the right is a slab, which provides three problems on superb rock.

13 Death Slab V0+ Starting behind the block, climb the slab using small edges and a wicked mono.

14 Orbitus Teranium V1 Immediately to the right of the large block is a nice problem following left-facing flakes. Start at the foot of the block.

25 Satellite V1 The wide groove right of *Contre le Sexisme* has an easy start on large flakes and a surprisingly hard finish.

26 Ren and Stimpy V1 The pocketed rib just before the grassy bank at the right end of the wall is another good, technical problem.

Mark Williams on *Ren and Stimpy* V1.
STEVE TAYLOR

A metre right of the arête is a full-height vertical crack and a frozen rail of conglomerate. This section is northwest-facing and a lovely spot for a quick bouldering session at the end of a day spent at Blacknor North.

22 Not Sleeping Around V0 The full-height crack is often damp but may appeal to some twisted individuals.

23 Mercury and Solace V0+ The classic conglomerate rail is passed by everyone heading for Blacknor North. Many have stopped, unable to resist the compelling line. Those that haven't climbed it yet should. Start up the crack and follow the rail rightwards to good jugs. Rock-over leftwards to finish.

24 Contre le Sexisme V1 The arête right of the conglomerate rail is a superb technical problem on perfect rock and just as worthwhile as the rail itself.

Approach from Climbers' and Walkers' Car Park

31

Blacknor North

This is the cliff that lies beneath Blacknor Fort, the strange collection of buildings to the north of Blacknor Point. The cliff has a mixture of popular sport climbs and resolutely unpopular nut-protected routes. The extensive sections of flowstone-coated rock give unusual and memorable climbing. This section of Blacknor comes into the sun at around 2pm, so can be a good choice on summer mornings. In the winter, northerly winds can make climbing an unpleasant experience.

Access

In 2002 there were several incidents with local landowners, who claimed to own sections of this cliff. Ugly red 'Climbing Prohibited' signs were daubed at the base of many routes. Contact the BMC for the latest information regarding access to these cliffs.

South of the easy descent are short walls terminated by a corner which offers a rather harder descent route (Difficult). The cliff beyond is much higher and the chimney of *Speleo Joy Toy* is a prominent feature. A pedestal block is the next landmark; this is the starting point for *The Death of Cool*. Two-thirds of the way up the wall above the pedestal is the entrance to Blacknor Hole cave, which would be hard to spot, were it not for the abseil chainset fixed just above it. A recessed face bounded by *The Curler* and *Ximenesque* lies to the south.

Next, past the disaster zone of *Hangman's Loose*, are a vertical conglomerate formation and a large half-height ledge; *Captain Klutz...* clambers up the conglomerate while *Is Vic There?* takes the blunt arête just right of the ledge. To the south again, the surreal *Slings Shot* wall resembles a frozen waterfall. Finally, the wall behind the pinnacle is the venue for *Onto the Icefloe*, with its surprisingly well-attached 'icebergs'. The cliffs at the pinnacle

turn to the southeast; this is Blacknor Point, marked at the top by a concrete lookout-post.

The walls of Blacknor Fort above the cliff should not be used either for abseil anchors or for belays since the owners are concerned about erosion of the bank. Whilst one could top out on many climbs there, the *in-situ* lower-off points on the sport routes allow the bank of the fort to remain undisturbed and the narrow cliff-top footpath to be unobstructed by 'tripwire' ropes. A good thing considering that manic mountain bikers often hurtle along this exposed path.

The Blacknor cliffs are noted for their caving as well as their climbing. Portland has a number of cave-systems, the most extensive being Blacknor Hole (known as 'Ariel' to local cavers). This is a unique outing as the entrance is situated part way up the rockface and is reached by abseil (stakes removed at the time of writing). At over 400 metres, including a link to Sharbutts Quarry, Blacknor Hole provides several sporting and fairly strenuous trips well worth investigating. (Ensure that abseil ropes are tied off in the cave mouth to prevent their being stolen; this has happened.)

The lines of the first five climbs are not shown on a diagram.

Ten metres right of the way down is a crack-line.

1 Deception 10m VS 4b   (5.3.89)
Hardest at the top. Climb the wide crack in the left-facing corner, step right to a ledge, and finish just right of a thin crack to belay on blocks just over the mound.

Right of *Deception* is a wide chimney with a huge, square-cut block wedged across it.

2 Absolute Beginners 8m F2 3B   (2002)
The first bolted line on the way in to Blacknor North, takes the right arête of the chimney with a square capstone wedged at the top.

3 The Black Spot 8m VS 4b †   (2002)
The obvious crack to the right of *Absolute Beginners*. The name says it all. Walk on by...

Right again is a slight bay with two routes.

4 Subterfuge 9m VS 4b †   (31.8.92)
Climb the crack on the left-hand side of the bay; the crack is flaky to start and wide to finish and leads to a block belay.

5 Zeno 9m S   (5.3.89)
The crack-line on the right-hand side of the bay is more difficult than it looks and has an awkward start. Climb the fist-crack to a ledge and the corner-crack to the top. Belay on a boulder far back.

A short walk to the right is a groove/flake on the left-hand side of a much grander cliff. This is graded Difficult and can be used with care for descent, and then:

6 Chin Reaction 16m F6c 7B   (10.05)
Start immediately right of the descent route. Climb the loose wall to the faultline, then attack the rib and roof above to an exposed finish.

Gaz Parry on the classic *Reptile Smile* F6a+ (page 43) DAVID SIMMONITE

7 San Andreas 26m E1 5b †   (6.89)

Good protection from slings and *Friends*. Climb the wide crack just right of the point at which the cliff attains its full height. Block belay.

8 High on the Richter Scale 24m E3 5c
    (25.8.89)

The sustained crack in the upper section is protected by three bolts, though the lower section still needs a trad rack. Climb *San Andreas* for 10 metres, follow a handrail rightwards for 2 metres and move up to a niche. Pull over a small roof and climb the finger-crack to the lower-off.

9 Meltdown 21m F7a 8B   (2.7.95)

Start 2 metres right of *San Andreas*. A good route, providing a direct start to *High on the Richter Scale*. Climb up to the bulge and make a hard reach to the faultline (extremely difficult for the short). Steep moves up and left then lead to a welcome rest in the cherty break. Swing up into the crack-line of *High on the Richter Scale*, which is followed to the lower-off.

10 Quakin' in My Bones 22m F7b 8B
    (4.10.92)

Start 6m right of *San Andreas*. Climb an easy but cherty lower section. Pull strenuously over a pocketed bulge past a horizontal break to a rest beneath a small roof. Fingery moves lead up the headwall to the lower-off.

11 Sellerfield 19m F7b 10B †   (10.05)

Start just right of *Quakin' in my Bones*. Climb the overhanging wall with difficulty and make a long reach to the faultline. Pull over the roof and finish up the headwall to the lower-off.

Emma Madera enjoying *Slings Shot* F4+ (page 43). MIKE ROBERTSON

12 The Taylor Show 20m F6a+   (9.6.07)

The greasy crack is worth the effort to reach the fine flowstone groove above. Start immediately left of the chimney. Climb the steep, scruffy crack to good holds beneath a small roof. Cross it easily to a ledge beneath the flowstone groove. Follow the groove to the roof and traverse steeply left to the shared lower-off.

13 Speleo Joy Toy 26m VS 4b †   (30.10.88)

Start at a short ramp leading to a chimney. Often wet, possibly after the resident of Blacknor Fort flushes the toilet! Not recommended. Climb the chimney passing various obstacles and exit past chockstones onto a dressed-stone capping slab. The belay stakes have been removed.

14 The Death of Cool 26m F7b 10B   (20.9.92)

Right of *Speleo Joy Toy* is a pedestal. The entrance to the cave of Blacknor Hole is above, two-thirds of the way up the cliff. This route, low in its grade, climbs the blunt arête to the left of the cave. From the pedestal, climb to a ledge and up a steep juggy wall, passing a difficult bulge to reach a half-height ledge. Climb a short corner-flake to a horizontal break and the exposed crux, a long blind crack, which leads to a clean-cut exit. The belay stakes have been removed.

15 Drag Racing Underground 26m F6c 10B
    (28.4.93)

A superb, varied pitch that epitomizes the climbing on this section of cliff. Start immediately right of the pedestal. Climb a wide, shallow bay and pass a steep chert bulge with care to reach buckets beyond. Continue steeply to the entrance of Blacknor Hole cave and a welcome rest (and possibly a bemused caver or two). Don't clip the chainset — the cavers wouldn't be pleased if their abseil anchor was fallen on. Bridge into the short, blank groove above (crux) and make an awkward move to stand up in the faultline. Stretch up leftwards (ignore the cavers' bolt up and right) on good holds to the lower-off.

16 Poppadom 26m E1 5a †   (8.7.89)
Start 6m right of the entrance to Blacknor Hole. Climb a corner to its capping roof and go up to another corner. Continue up this, choosing wafer-thin flakes with care, to the second horizontal crack. Turn the roof on its right and move rightwards (scary) to the bolt belay on *Seattle Be the Day*.

17 Seattle Be the Day 24m F6b+ 8B   (4.9.92)
A steep start is followed by a wonderful flowstone headwall. From a recessed ledge, climb through a series of bulges to a conglomerate hand-ledge. Continue more delicately to a mid-height scoop and then technically on flowstone via a slight groove to the lower-off.

18 The Fabulous Bakery Boys 23m F6c 7B   (9.7.95)
Start immediately right of *Seattle Be the Day*. Features some good flowstone climbing. Lower-off shared with the next route.

19 Captain Lob Meets the Nipple Pincher 23m F6b 8B   (9.7.95)
The long arête, with a difficult finish. At the top of the arête, step slightly right and finish direct up a flake.

20 Greasepaint and Monkey Brains 22m F6a 8B   (14.10.96)
The shallow bay immediately to the right of the long arête. Start up the groove left of a rib. Continue up this groove.

21 Indian Summer 21m F6a 7B   (9.96)
An excellent route, with an exhilarating finish. Climb up to a sharp flake, which is followed to a small roof. Pull over this to the lower-off.

To find out more about Climbers' Club guidebooks go to http://www.climbers-club.co.uk/guidebooks.html

To the south is a recessed face bounded by the corners of *The Curler* and *Ximenesque*.

22 The Curler 18m VS †   (3.8.75)
Start on the left-hand side of the recessed face, at a crack with an awkward S-bend near the top. Climb the crack with increasing difficulty to a hard move into the upper section.

23 Blowing Chunks 18m F6c 5B   (14.3.97)
Start 2 metres right of the wide crack, up the blank-looking wall. At the overlap, make some difficult moves up a flake crack to an easier finish.

24 Where's Blue Hippo 18m F7a+ 5B   (15.8.96)
This difficult proposition is similar to its neighbour, although much harder. Climb the thin wall 2 metres right of *Blowing Chunks*. Make a very difficult move to become established above the faultline then continue more easily to the shared lower-off.

25 Beer and Corruption 18m F6c+ 7B   (20.9.92)
The last bolt of this climb is shared with *Henry Rollins for President*. Good, technical climbing. Climb slightly right past a big pocket to a short corner and a jutting hand-ledge. Continue direct with difficulty, just left of the brown streak, until a swing right meets with the steep finish of *Henry Rollins for President*.

26 Henry Rollins for President 18m F7a+ 6B   (12.9.92)
A line of increasing technical difficulty heading for the brown streak high on the wall. Start 8m right of *The Curler*. Pull over a fingery bulge and trend left up the juggy wall past two short cracks. From the second crack, go left to straddle the brown streak and make hard moves to a flake on its left side. Finish steeply up to the lower-off.

27 Shatter My Illusions but Don't Break My Heart 21m VS 4a   (2.7.89)
The chimney in the centre of the recessed face. Climb the chimney past a large flake and then through a constriction at the top. (The flake shifted during the first ascent but is probably safer now.)

28 Wynona's Big Brown Beaver 24m F6b+ 6B   (19.7.95)
Some steep climbing. Start as for *Ximinesque*. At the second bolt of *Ximinesque*, step left and climb the very steep flake crack, coming back right at the top of the flake to a shared lower-off.

29 Ximenesque 24m F6b+ 8B   (5.9.92)
Pumpy! On the right-hand side of the recessed face a wide crack leads to a roof. Start just right of the crack. Climb up on huge holds to meet the crack and follow it to a wide niche right of the roof. Continue steeply up and then left to the lower-off.

30 In Dust We Trust 24m F6c 6B   (3.8.95)
The right hand finish to *Ximinesque* is very dusty and can feel run-out. Move right from the second bolt of *Ximinesque* to climb a steep crack. Finish direct to the lower-off (bold).

⭐ **31 Ironhead** 24m F7a+ 9B   (4.9.92)
An exposed, exhilarating pitch of escalating difficulty up the arête right of *Ximenesque*. The final section poses a difficult technical problem, which requires a rapid solution. Easier (F7a) for the tall. Climb a steep but easy rib straight up to a bulge. Trend left over this on a series of buckets and continue past two breaks. A short layback-edge leading to more good holds is followed by a swing left to a slight groove in the arête. Increasingly strenuous moves lead to a one-shot slap-for-it crux, the top breaks, and the lower-off.

⭐ **32 Meg's Got Leukaemia** 24m F6a 8B
    (10.92)
A much better route than its name would imply, and high in its grade it lies immediately right of *Ironhead*; start beneath the roof. A bucket for each and every move — except the last.

⭐ **33 Cinema Paradiso** 24m F6a 7B   (2002)
Enjoyable — a worthy companion for *Megs's Got Leukaemia*. Start 1 metre right of that route. Climb over a roof and up steep ground to the base of a groove. Follow this to the lower-off.

The large cliff-top block right of *Cinema Paradiso* (shown opposite) fell in 2003.

34 Hangman's Loose 30m HVS †   (10.8.76)
A line which reportedly would clean up with future ascents. Nature has done its best instead; more has fallen off it! Start 7 metres right of *Cinema Paradiso*. Gain the main flake crack from the left, avoiding the loose flakes as much as possible. Continue up the flake crack and pull over the final rock band using a preplaced rope.

Ian Vickers climbing *Wolfgang Forever* F7a (page 41). DAVID SIMMONITE

Further south is a gravity-defying conglomerate formation and then a half-height ledge which has a break leading up to its right-hand side.

⭐⭐ **35 Captain Klutz and the Sailors of Fortune** 21m F6a 8B   (20.3.93)
Fun climbing on the conglomerate to start, and good, steep climbing to finish. Protection includes a thread. Climb steeply onto the conglomerate and up to an earthy ledge. Move left and up a flake before climbing the fine flowstone feature above to the lower-off.

⭐ **36 Major Mushrooms and that Mentally Muffled Mentality** 21m F6c 8B   (9.05.02)
The conglomerate wall right of *Captain Klutz…* Climb the right side of the formation to a higher ledge. A tricky few moves via a shallow groove lead onto the wall and a slim overlap above. Pull over to the lower-off.

37 Is Vic There? 21m F7a 7B   (3.10.92)
The blunt arête just right of the half-height ledge provides excellent sustained climbing right from the start. Step off a flake at 2 metres and climb the wall (quickly) to a lone jug. Continue with difficulty to an obvious block at 15 metres. Finish up flutings just left of the arête to the lower-off.

38 Sanfet Kuss 19m F7a+ 8B   (10.05)
The fine, hard start is marred by an unpleasant finish. Climb the very thin veneer of flowstone to a rest at the faultline and psych up for the loose, dirty and unpleasant finish.

39 Wolfgang Forever 21m F7a 8B   (4.10.92)
Good climbing which becomes more technical and less strenuous as height is gained. Start 5 metres right of the last route. Climb up past a tricky chert bulge to good holds. Move into a shallow groove and then make a committing move leftwards around the blunt rib into an open scoop. Climb this past a calcite formation resembling a water-fountain to a small ledge and the lower-off.

40 French Connection 21m F7b+ 7B   (17.3.07)
This good route has a testing finish on the high prow. Climb the wall and make a hard move to pull onto the prow. Hard, extending moves lead rightwards to the lower-off. An alternative finish (**Popeye Doyle** F7b+(3.07)) pulls leftwards over the prow.

41 Appleturnoverload 21m F7a+ 7B   (11.10.92)
Worthwhile climbing, crossing the right-hand side of the prow; fingery throughout. Climb up, with a shakeout available after the fourth bolt, to the bulge. Use pockets to cross this with difficulty and reach a flowstone rail. Finish more easily up to the lower-off.

42 Very Sleepy River 21m F6b 6B   (12.9.92)
Start 18 metres right of the half-height ledge, at the left-hand of two diverging flake cracks. A good, steep start up the flake, and some fine flowstone in the upper section. Follow the crack to the mid-height break and step right. Continue boldly up past a jutting hold to the sheet of grey flowstone. Climb up rightwards (slightly bold) and cross a small bulge to a lower-off on the right.

43 Edgehog 21m F7a+ 7B   (28.8.93)
Somewhat eliminate in its nature, though with some worthwhile climbing on the black flowstone section. From the top of the conglomerate rubble pile, climb 3 metres up *Klepto*'s 'Krack' and then swing left onto a sheet of black flowstone. Continue up this on small slopers and layaways to a slab. Finish steeply to the lower-off of *Very Sleepy River*.

44 Klepto Krack 21m HVS 4c †   (10.10.92)
Large nuts required. Stolen before it could be bolted! Climb crumbly material to the right-hand crack, and follow it to a high roof. Step left to a flowstone boss and the lower-off of *Very Sleepy River*.

45 Toes Curl 18m F6c+ 7B   (7.96)
A good climb on small holds, spoilt a little by the loose start and proximity to the large crack (which must be avoided for a tick at the grade). Climb the rock and mud to the base of the wall, a metre right of the large crack. Follow crimps on a direct line up the wall to a slight steepening. A few sharp pulls on razor edges lead to a slabby section and the lower-off of *Freaky Ralph*.

46 Freaky Ralph 18m F8a+ 8B   (3.11.92)
The test-piece of the cliff tackles an impressive bulge in the upper section of the wall. Highly sustained climbing with a long reach on the crux, though

Gareth Parry on *Freaky Ralph* F8a+.
DAVID SIMMONITE

those who cannot make the span can make progress with some deft footwork. Climb unswervingly to the start of the bulge at mid height. Power up to a small flowstone undercut and launch rightwards (crux) to a two-finger pocket. Move up past a jug and make hard moves up the front of the bulge to a big ledge and the lower-off.

Further right, past an unclimbed chimney is a very unusual feature, the *Slings Shot* wall, which is composed of flowstone and calcite-cemented blocks.

47 **Aim High, Shoot Low** 20m F6a+ 7B
(4.4.97)

The friable line up the wall immediately right of the chimney. Much better in its steep, upper section.

48 **Downtown Julie Brown** 22m F6c 8B
(12.9.92)

A fine open pitch on unusual rock up the left arête of the *Slings Shot* wall. Climb straight up a blunt rib past a hidden bucket at 6 metres and then slightly right by tricky moves to gain a big undercut at half height. Huge jugs lead to a leftward-slanting ramp which ends at a big hole. Pull up to a projecting ledge and the lower-off.

49 **Reptile Smile** 23m F6a+ 6B
(12.9.92)

The original Portland classic route with beautiful 'pipework' throughout. High in its grade and strenuous too. Start on the left-hand side of the triangular flowstone slab. Climb the flowstone slab to a hand-ledge at 10 metres. Follow a steep shallow groove past amazing tufa formations to a series of good holds leading up a short wall. Lower-off just before the rock deteriorates.

50 **Talking Smack** 23m F5+ 7B
(8.96)

Connects the start of *Reptile Smile* with the finish of *Slings Shot*. Best done on a quiet day to minimise disruption. From the second bolt on *Reptile Smile*, swing diagonally rightwards across the flowstone pipes to the line of *Slings Shot* to finish as for that route.

51 **Slings Shot** 23m F4+ 9B
(31.12.75)

The first route on the Isle to climb a large flowstone formation is an interesting pitch owing to its unusual rock. Controversially bolted to give one of the most popular routes on Portland. Should you choose traditional style for an ascent, please use the lower-off bolts in order to avoid the loose rock and earth on the last 8 metres. (VS to the lower-off, HVS to the top). Climb up the centre of the triangular flowstone slab, moving slightly right to a niche by a tongue of flowstone. Move left and up (crux) to easier ground and the lower-off. Note that the first bolt was removed during bolt strength tests – so please don't write any more letters about failing bolts.

52 **Crocadilia** 23m F6a 9B
(10.05)

The line of bolts right of *Slings Shot*. Good climbing, but requiring blinkers to avoid using holds on *Slings Shot*. Take care with the loose-looking flowstone shelf at the top.

53 **Spanner Eyes** 22m F7b 6B
(8.96)

A difficult addition, rising to the challenge of the flat layaway right of *Slings Shot*. High in the grade, *Petzl* bolts. Start as for *England's Dreaming*. At 3 metres, swing leftwards to the base of a steep flowstone crack. Climb this with difficulty to a small overlap. Span leftwards to the layaway and make some hard moves to a scary mantelshelf onto a sloping ledge. Finish more easily to the lower-off.

54 **England's Dreaming** 21m F7a+ 7B
(4.9.92)

A fine, fingery excursion on flowstone, though its deserved popularity means it is becoming polished. Climb a short corner right of the huge flowstone formation for 3 metres before swinging right and up to jugs beneath a bulge. Stretch for incuts and continue straight up the flowstone, sustained, to a flowstone curtain. Step up and right to the lower-off.

55 **Cakewalk** 21m F6a 7B
(10.10.92)

Worth climbing for its excellent flowstone section, which puts it high in its grade. Climb up just left of *Dirt Track* and join it to cross the bulge. From the flake ledge above, move diagonally left on jugs (run-out) to the base of a dark flowstone 'statue'. Climb this and pull leftwards over a bulge to reach the lower-off of the previous route.

56 **Dirt Track** 26m VS 4b †
(31.7.75)

Start at a wide, dirty crack 10 metres right of *Slings Shot*. The first three bolts of Cakewalk protect the starting moves, if required. Rockfall in 1997 has affected the upper section of this route. Needless to say, it has not been re-climbed since (and probably not before). Climb the crack past an awkward bulge and follow a rightward-leading flake-line to a chimney jammed with loose blocks. Climb this with care to the top and exit to the right. Fencepost belay to the left.

Past *Dirt Track* is the entrance to Sandy Hole Cave down at ground-level. *California Hot Licks* starts from the left edge of the cave.

57 **California Hot Licks** 18m F6a+ 6B
(26.11.94)

An attractive-looking line that unfortunately does not live up to expectations. Rockfall in winter 1997 destroyed some of the finishing moves of this route. Delicate and technical climbing leads up to a crack. Climb the crack and a short blank wall before passing a roof. The final bolt is missing (your belayer is standing on it), making for a reachy, exciting finish to the lower-off.

To the right is a corner-crack leading to a roof with a large, intimidating jammed block underneath: unclimbed.

Blacknor
Pinnacle

58 Doughnuts and Duvets 18m F6b 8B
(10.6.95)
Start as for *Apfelstrudl* and take the line which *Apfelstrudl should* have taken — the thin crack direct! Climb the wall to a recess. Climb the thin crack above direct to a lower-off above the faultline.

59 Apfelstrudel 18m F6a 6B (13.3.93)
Start a short distance right of the corner, beneath a thin crackline. The rock is rather crunchy to start, but an intriguing blind move near the top compensates. Climb the wall easily to the recess. Pull out rightwards and climb diagonally right until it is possible to move up to the lower-off between the horizontal cracks.

60 Dwarf Lops 10m F6b 4B (5.4.97)
A short line taking the blunt arête to the left of *Suck, Don't Blow*. Start just left of the arête. Climb the steep wall on reasonable holds to a row of good crimps. From here, a difficult move leads to a flake and the lower-off.

Beyond, at Blacknor Point, is a pinnacle at the base of the cliff, with two wide crack-lines behind it.

61 Suck, Don't Blow 18m F6c 6B (31.10.92)
Start to the left of the two cracklines. A perplexing crux set amidst enjoyable F6a climbing. Step onto the undercut wall, climb up for 3 metres, and move left into a groove containing calcite-cemented holds. Continue up to the pocket band and go left to a corner, which proves difficult to exit. An easier section above leads to the lower-off.

62 Mother's Milk 18m F6a 6B (8.11.92)
A popular pitch which is easier than its overhanging nature suggests. A good choice when suffering from 'finger fade', but avoid it if your biceps are blown. Would be protectable with Friends/hexes, but

fortunately has bolts. Climb the left-hand crack, with exciting moves over a bulge, to the lower-off.

63 Do You Like Our Owls 19m F6a+ 8B
(27.6.96)
The right-hand crack-line, very steep to start. Climb the flake crack to the roof, which is taken spectacularly on the left using some suspect-looking holds (some of which have now departed).

64 Hot from the Forge 18m F7a 6B (13.2.93)
Start beneath a steep, shallow groove just right of the two cracks. From a hand-ledge at 3 metres, climb the blind crack-cum-groove past a bulge. Follow strange but good holds up to a slight arête on the right. Climb the arête with difficulty and the bulge above to a jug rail and the lower-off.

65 Onto the Icefloe 18m F7a 5B (5.9.92)
Good, steep climbing on strange holds, split by a welcome rest. High in the grade. Climb up past some calcite-cemented blocks and pass a bulge using a flake on the left. Cross the small flowstone roof using a selection from hundreds of holds. If you choose the correct sequence, you'll shortly arrive at a **single, alarmingly placed** bolt lower-off above.

66 Imbolc 19m F7b+ 6B (7.2.93)
A few feet to the right is a tremendous, intricate, pumpy route, which is low in its grade. The bolts are poorly placed for the crux moves. Swing up on a jug and climb the steep, blunt arête to a hard swing right and a grip-clip. Climb the easier scoop to twin breaks beneath a roof. Move left and up the arête to finish as for *Onto the Icefloe*.

Ben Stokes at boiling point on *Meltdown* F7a (page 35). STEVE TAYLOR

Blacknor Central

The junction of Blacknor North and Blacknor Central is at Blacknor Point, marked by a detached pinnacle where the cliff changes direction and character. A series of tall, prominent arêtes form wide bays. Many of the walls in these bays are formed of very shelly rock, though a number of more solid sections exist. In the summer, the undergrowth can make progress along the cliff base difficult and, in the winter, the paths can be treacherous. However, a few of Portland's finest routes are on this cliff and are worth the effort of the approach.

For approach details, see page 25.

The bay nearest to Blacknor Point has an earth mound topped by the chimney of *Bag End* in its centre and *Protein Delta Strip* on its right arête. The climbs in the bay to the south mostly start from a huge earth-covered flake. *Struggling Jim* follows the wide cracks at the back of the bay, but nowadays there is meatier fare on the right wall, such as the fine flowstone pipes on *Twangy Pearl* and the fingery *Boilermaker*. Further on is an open cleft containing a large jammed block; *Nomad's* short chimney is just beyond. Further on lies the huge feature of *Big Corner* with the stunning arête of *Pregnant Pause* on its left, followed by the sharp arête of *The Prow*. Beyond, lies Blacknor South.

1 Dudas Sin Nombres 18m F6b+ 6B (20.3.99)
A good line, spoilt by the fragile nature of the rock. Start 15 metres right of *Imbolc*, 3 metres left of the flake of *Dreamer*. Climb the shelly wall more or less direct to an area of clean rock. Continue to a large ledge and lower-off.

2 Dreamer 30m HVS 5a † (14.5.77)
Start 18 metres south of Blacknor Point pinnacle, at a flake below a small overhang. Climb to the overhang (peg). Move left and up to a wide crack. Follow this and the flake crack above to a small niche. Move left into a small corner and exit with difficulty, taking care with the poor slatty rock.

The next bay has steep earth at its base and the chimney of *Bag End* at its centre.

3 Actually (Shit Happens) 18m F6a 7B (17.2.93)
An enjoyable pitch with some unusual holds. Low in the grade, though style usually goes out of the window at the mantelshelf finishing move! Start 9 metres left of *Bag End* near the arête. Climb easily past a 'welded' boulder to a jutting ledge. Continue steeply past a large, thin, calcite flake and over a bulge. Follow strange holds up to where a tricky mantelshelf gains a commodious ledge and the lower-off.

4 Flowstone Shuffle/Unstuck On You
18m F7b 7B (25.6.95)
Start up the bubbly wall just to the right of *Actually (Shit Happens)* and make fingery moves up to the flowstone overlap. Now make a very difficult, technical move to reach flowstone jugs and the lower-off.

5 21½ Weeks 18m F6b+ 6B (17.2.93)
Start 3 metres left of the chimney of *Bag End*. Unbalanced, with a hard crux following the loss of a hold. Climb easily to a steep groove, which leads to good holds at its top. Make a *long* reach to an isolated hold before following a series of jugs to the lower-off.

6 Bag End 15m F5+ 7B (9.2.75)
Forty metres south of Blacknor Point pinnacle is a chimney in a corner atop an earth mound. Pleasant climbing on stuck-on holds. Climb the chimney, mostly on the left, to a cave. Tricky moves lead left out of the cave and up to the lower-off, though beware of a resident flock of pigeons.

Ben Stokes on *Actually (Shit Happens)* F6a.
STEVE TAYLOR

47

7 Hysterical Solitude 18m F6c 7B   (20.2.93)
A route of two halves; a technical groove is followed by a jug romp. Start 6 metres right of *Bag End*. Climb an increasingly hard shallow groove until a difficult move past the strip roof allows better holds to be reached. Easier climbing up the conglomerate slab leads to the breaks. Above and to the right is a lower-off shared with *Crucifix Kiss*.

8 Crucifix Kiss 18m F7c 6B   (6.3.93)
The blunt arête 10 metres right of *Bag End* may be dusty but has good moves. Climb direct to pockets beneath the bulge at the base of the arête. Make very hard, extending moves past a sidepull out right, culminating in a dyno for a sloping ledge. A mantel from a jug then starts the sustained and delicate climbing up the arête to the lower-off.

9 Choc Speedway 18m F6b+ 8B   (16.8.98)
The honeycombed groove right of the blunt arête. Climb the steep wall to the base of the groove. Climb the groove to the honeycomb section and finish steeply up to the lower-off of *Nothing Is Cool*.

10 Nothing Is Cool 18m F6c 8B   (6.3.93)
Some 15 metres right of *Bag End*, this route climbs the centre of a slightly inset face. A good pitch, slightly marred by its dusty crux. Climb flowstone to a ledge at 8 metres. Make some hard moves past a flowstone undercut to a jug. Follow the crack up to the roof at 15 metres. Reach over the roof and mantel with difficulty onto the ledge above and the lower-off.

11 Protein Delta Strip 18m F6c 8B   (2.93)
This recommended route shares the first three of its bolts with *Nothing Is Cool*. It then branches right, almost to the arête. Here the difficulties start, and it carries on in a great position just left of the arête to the lower-off.

The next bay is recognizable by the huge flake below the wall, with the wide cracks of *Struggling Jim* behind.

12 Kit Kat 22m F6b 6B   (20.2.93)
The thin flake-line 5 metres left of the huge flake. Climb easily to the base of a thin, fragile flake, and follow it to a shallow alcove. Climb over the bulge above on hidden holds to gain a dubious stuck-on jug (still there 14 years later). Trend slightly left on huge holds to the lower-off.

The wall to the right of *Kit Kat* sports an obvious rounded bulge at half height. The following two routes have managed to 'beat the bulge'.

13 While the Cat's Away 21m F7a+ 8B (3.97)
Take the obvious crack-line through the bulge.

14 The Launch 21m F7b+ 8B   (14.9.99)
The harder of the two routes takes a line through the bulge to the right of the crack. Dynamic moves across the steepest section make up the crux. High in the grade since a jug was lost from the crux.

15 Struggling Jim 24m VS †   (23.4.77)
The wide cracks above the mound formed by the large flake. Climb the twisting, wider crack to the top. Care required to exit through the slat band.

Jane Weir on *Monsoon Malabar* F6a (page 51). STEVE TAYLOR

49

16 Fat Falling Pigs 15m F6a+ 5B   (10.7.93)
This safe pitch follows a groove, where a mid-height flowstone bulge increases interest. Can be extremely dusty! Climb the easy but steepening groove to the bulge. Grasp this with determination and grapple with the scruffy flutings above until further good holds lead to a ledge. Use *Twangy Pearl*'s lower-off on the right.

17 Twangy Pearl 18m F7b 6B   (6.3.93)
A fine, varied climb which starts 6 metres right of *Struggling Jim*, epitomising difficult flowstone climbing on Portland. Low in the grade. From a high ledge on top of a large flake, climb up a technical flowstone wall to the base of the organ pipes. Follow these, with difficulty, to the lower-off.

18 Boilermaker 20m F7c 6B   (14.2.93)
A highly improbable line situated 10 metres right of *Struggling Jim*, just left of a black streak in a flowstone sheet. Very fingery, with a steamy crux. From a large calcified jug, trend left over a bulge. Sustained moves lead to a long undercut at the top of a white streak. Move up from the undercut on micropockets to reach a juggy ramp. Continue up a slab and over the top bulge to the lower-off of *Twangy Pearl*.

19 Into The Sun 21m F6c 7B   (24.3.96)
The dusty wall to the right of *Boilermaker* may clean up with time. Climb the wall immediately right of the grey streaks past a stuck-on flake. Lower-off in the shallow groove above.

20 Second's Swing 38m HVS 5a †   (6.77)
Start 13 metres right of *Struggling Jim*. Medium to large nuts are required. Follow the crack on suspect rock at first until more pleasant climbing leads to the overhang. Hand-traverse left (strenuous) to an easing in the angle of the headwall. Climb to the cliff top or use the lower-off of *Into the Sun*.

21 Poison Tip 30m E1 5b †   (28.2.79)
A fine line giving strenuous but well-protected climbing. Follow the crack of *Second's Swing* to the overhang. Step right and make strenuous moves past the roof to gain good finishing holds. A reasonable exit through the earth and slat band gains the cliff top.

John Percy on *Twangy Pearl* F7b.
JUSTIN PETTIFAR

22 Bring on the Night 18m F6c+ 7B   (22.6.97)
The steep wall, rib, and flake left of the sharp arête have some good climbing. Climb up to the base of the rib. Climb this quickly on small holds to the start of a good flake, which is followed more easily to the lower-off.

23 Monsoon Malabar 16m F6a 9B   (22.6.97)
Fine arête climbing at a reasonable grade. Start at the foot of the sharp arête. Climb it on its left side to a good ledge. Tackle the arête on the left, using some pleasingly large holds, to a steep finish.

Eight metres right of *Poison Tip* is an open cleft capped by a large jammed block. This cleft forms the left-hand side of a shallow bay. Sadly, all of the routes in this bay suffer from mud and dust with the exception of *Pregnant Pause*.

24 **Inbreeding** 12m F6b 5B   (16.8.98)
The grey slab on the left of the shallow bay. Don't bother!

25 **Nomad** 40m VS   (14.5.77)
Eight metres right of the open cleft with the large jammed block is a short chimney/crack.
1 20m. Scramble to the base of the chimney before climbing it and its continuation flake to a ledge.
2 20m. Climb up to another ledge and then traverse left into the large cleft. Ascend this to the top and a stake belay.

26 **We Are Not Men, We Are Roto** 18m F7a 8B   (19.8.94)
The tufa line just left of *Mirage*. A low bulge gives the route its hard crux. The lower-off consists of two strange bolt anchors.

27 **The Stal's On Me, Pal** 18m F7a 8B (16.8.98)
The conglomerate line to the right of *We Are Not Men, We Are Roto*, starting as for that route. Very dirty, loose and unpleasant. Still reading? If so, start up *We Are Not Men, We Are Roto* and swing right along the flowstone rail. From the end of the rail, head upwards across some shallow roofs to the lower-off.

28 **Mirage** 29m HVS 5a †   (17.9.77)
Start beneath a crack-line on the right-hand side of the shallow bay. A pleasant climb topped by a slat band — a great deal *less* pleasant — that is best overcome with a long-spiked hammer. Have you remembered yours? Scramble and climb to the crack and follow it to roofs. Gain a ledge on the right and a larger ledge up to the right again. Climb through the shaly slat band to the cliff top. No belay stakes in place.

29 **Toothless Vampire** 23m F7b 6B   (8.8.94)
A fine-looking flowstone line, but don't be fooled — the flowstone is incredibly dusty making this an unrewarding climb. From beneath the crack-line of *Mirage*, climb diagonally right and then up the tufa pillar to the lower-off.

30 **Fond Farewell** 40m E1 †   (4.7.77)
Beneath the right-hand side of the shallow bay is a block that forms a blunt pinnacle. Start 7 metres to the right at a vague arête, close to an occasionally flowing spring. Bold wall-climbing on the middle pitch.
1 15m. 4a. Climb up rightwards into a large bay before moving left to a vegetated ledge.
2 14m. 5b. Step left, climb up, and make a delicate move onto the ledge at the top of a huge flake. Continue slightly rightwards up the wall with increasing difficulty and make a hard move onto a ledge.
3 11m. Trend rightwards through the slat band to the cliff top.

31 **Pregnant Pause** 27m F6a+ 11B   (1993)
A finely positioned route. Climb the left arête of *Big Corner* on its right-hand side to the lower-off. Beware, a 27-metre pitch, so some down-climbing may be necessary, depending on how much your rope has stretched.

Michael Simpson on *Pregnant Pause* F6a+.
ANDY LONG

32 Big Corner 50m HVS   (7.8.72) ☆
This climbs the conspicuous right-facing corner 30 metres south of *Fond Farewell* (120 metres north of *Insistence*). Superb situations; but serious and high in its grade. 'Once beneath the imposing open book the full enormity of the challenge began to dawn... I sent Dave up first' (Bill Birkett).
1 15m. Ascend broken rock to the base of the chimney.
2 15m. 4b. Climb the chimney on flaky holds (but not the huge flake on the left). When near the top of the chimney, step left and move up a flake crack to belay on the ledge above.
3 20m. 4b. Climb up, to arrive at the roof above bridging wide and facing outwards! Pull across onto the wall before making an exposed leftwards traverse to a small corner-ledge. Climb up and left to a larger ledge. Now run it out on easy ground to a worrying finish; walk left along the ledge, step up, and continue back right until a pull through the slat band appears feasible to arrive at the cliff top. Stake belay missing. (An alternative finish has been climbed; this involved a long traverse rightwards from the ledge stance in the chimney, and an inadequate belay before a very loose top pitch.)

33 Suenos de Espana 23m F7a+ 12B †   (4.5.06)
Excellent, steep climbing above the right-hand side of the cleaned ledge (*in-situ* access rope). Climb the pocketed wall to a hard move over the roof.

34 Valerian 24m F5+ 9B   (2002) ☆☆
Breaches the buttress right of *Big Corner*, taking a black flowstone rib in its upper reaches. Superb flowstone on the upper wall, though with a shocking loose and dusty start - take extra care. Climb the left-hand side of a broad rib, trending gently rightwards towards a black flowstone pillar. Finish up this.

35 The Viper's Tale 23m F7a+ 10B †   (5.5.06) ☆
A fine, open route with a real sting in the tail and, therefore, high in the grade. It takes the impressive flowstone-covered wall to the left of *Natural Born Drillers* on superb rock, albeit a little dusty, gained by traversing left along the ledge left of *Natural Born Drillers*. The lower section of the route provides fine, sustained climbing to a hard finale. Would be a classic if not for its dusty nature.

36 Natural Born Drillers 25m F6c 8B   (4.3.95)
Start 5 metres left of *Flake Out* beneath a chossy groove. Scramble with care up the groove to a large ledge. Continue steeply up juggy bands and over a bulge to flowstone. Sustained moves on strangely shaped holds lead to a steep, shallow groove, the breaks and the lower-off.

37 Flake Out 40m VS 4c   (8.8.72) ☆
A compelling but sparsely-protected climb. Start about 30 metres right of *Big Corner*, where a chimney/crack with some large chockstones in it appears to form a huge flake. Climb broken rock to the crack. Follow it past a big chockstone and a beak-like flake to a small platform. Move left to a ledge and then up to the wall again. (The lower-off of *Natural Born Drillers* is here.) Continue to the grass. No belay and little rope friction with the concave top. In an emergency, grab a passing sport climber.

38 The Long Walk 25m F6c 11B   (8.12.95) ☆☆
A long pitch with an exciting finish. Start up the flake of *Flake Out*. At 5 metres, step right and follow the sometimes dusty flowstone to a steep finish past flowstone-cemented blocks.

39 Mexican Stand-off 25m F7b 9B   (4.3.95)
An easy start up the centre of the face left of *The Prow* leads to a flowstone wall. Start 6 metres left of the arête. Climb the easy, horizontally banded wall past a small overhang to a short slab. Sustained, technical moves lead up the wall to a diagonal undercut. Step left, crank up past a strange jug, and follow a blank groove to the breaks and lower-off above.

40 One Fine Day 25m F6a+ 9B   (2002)
The face a few metres left of *The Prow*. Start up a broken wall on good holds. Pull onto the main wall and follow a slight groove leftwards to a dynamic finish.

41 The Prow 40m E1 †   (3.8.76) ☆
The obvious, jutting arête bounding the left side of a bay. Start 3 metres left of the arête.
1 15m. From a short crack, climb up over blocky rock and traverse left to a ledge beneath the smoother upper wall. Peg belay.
2 10m. Move right and follow a crinkly ramp with difficulty to a peg. Step down and continue rightwards to a tiny stance on the very edge of the arête.
3 15m. Make some steep and committing moves up and around the arête to the next ledge above. Continue up and then left before scrambling up the slat band and thence the cliff top.

Blacknor South

A very popular area due to a short walk-in and a collection of easier bolted routes. The harder left-hand section of the cliff gets the sun earlier than any other cliff on the west coast (around lunchtime) and contains a high concentration of good wall climbs in the F6b+ to F7b range. The right-hand section gets the sun about an hour and a half later, but has a good selection of routes in the F4 to F6b range, as well as a few harder lines.

These routes should be approached from the descent through Sharbutt's Quarry (see page 25). In winter, the path beneath this cliff may be treacherous due to the clay-like mud. It gets worse as one moves closer to Blacknor Central due to landslips and the waterfall left of *Gaze of the Gorgon*.

1 Skank Central 27m F6b+ 9B (11.6.95)
The flake in the wall forming the right-hand side of the arête of *The Prow*. Steep climbing up the crack on crunchy holds leads to an exciting finish up the arête.

2 Bob's Big Mistake 30m HVS 4c † (10.10.92)
Not *totally* unpleasant. Climb the chimney on the left-hand side of the bay, with a 'trouser-filler' move up rightwards past the half-height blocks to finish on the cliff top. Belay stake missing.

3 Slim Jim 30m S 4a (31.8.73)
At the back of the bay is a clean-cut chimney with a big chockstone at mid height. A relatively safe route, which is much harder for the overweight. Climb broken rock to the foot of the chimney, where the chief difficulties consist of the entry and the constricted work inside. Come out at the chockstone and continue more easily to the cliff top. Belay stake missing.

4 Last of the Summer Wine 20m HVS 5a (10.10.92)
Enjoyable climbing up well-attached flakes. The majority of this route has been bolted. Climb broken rock to the flake at the foot of *Slim Jim* and step right to a large flowstone-cemented flake (*Go With the Flow* climbs direct to this point). Follow the flake and then move right to more cemented flakes. Gain the horizontal break above, step left, and surmount the overhang. Finish up a short corner and rock steps to the cliff top, or use the lower-off of *Go With The Flow*. Fine climbing, but the proximity of the bolts mean you may as well do the following route.

5 Go With The Flow 20m F6a+ 7B (6.5.95)
A direct start and finish to *Last of the Summer Wine*. In isolation, this would be a three-star route, however, the best sections belong with the previous route. Start at the base of a short black wall. Move up to cemented flakes and follow these up and left to the lower-off.

6 Ocean Rock 20m F6c+ 7B (2002)
Start 2 metres right of *Go With The Flow*. Follow the black flowstone wall to welded jugs. Pull up these to the top faultline and move right to the lower-off.

7 Pedestal Crack 33m HS †
On the right-hand side of the bay is a huge flake forming a north-facing chimney. Follow a vegetated ramp and then climb the chimney to its top. Continue up a crack to the cliff-top. (An easier start can be made up the right side of the huge flake.)

8 Best Destiny 20m F4+ 9B (2002)
Easy and generously bolted. Exposed laybacking up the right-hand arête of the huge flake. Start up a short easy wall, directly beneath the upper reaches of the sharp arête. Move up and right to the base of the arête, which is climbed on its left-hand side to the top. Climb the wall above the flake to the lower-off.

The following three routes share an approach pitch, which climbs a groove in the vegetated breaks up the wall left of the waterfall to a narrow ledge. They should be avoided if the wind is blowing the water onto the routes, since the source of this water is unknown (and smells a little suspect).

9 Aeroforce 27m F7b 4B, 5B (11.6.95)
A fine arête, sustained and on excellent rock.
1 12m F4. *Niagara Wall* pitch 1.
2 15m F7b. Swing up left onto a white rib, which is climbed with difficulty to the lower-off.

10 Blame it on the Drain 27m F7a+ 4B, 5B (19.5.95)
1 12m F4. *Niagara Wall* pitch 1.
2 17m F7a+. Follow *Niagara Wall* to its second bolt and break out left on flowstone and pockets. Cross a bulge and continue to the lower-off.

11 Niagara Wall 26m F7a 4B, 5B (13.5.95)
Start left of the waterfall issuing from a pipe on the cliff-top. Hard for the grade.
1 12m F4. Clamber up vegetated ledges to a grassy ledge and a bolt belay.
2 14m F7a. Climb the steep slab just left of the waterfall to a flowstone-glued jug. Continue up past a flake to the lower-off.

12 Dizzy up the Girl 25m F7a+ 10B (7.2004)
Start as for *Gaze of the Gorgon*. Climb up to a ledge at 10 metres, traverse left 2 metres to a groove and follow this to the top.

13 Gaze of the Gorgon 24m F6a+ 10B (3.10.92)
Start 30 metres south of *Pedestal Crack*. The long, bolted crack-line just right of some overhangs and a cliff-top water-pipe has good climbing in its upper half and is one of the great lines on Portland. Climb a wide scoop and a short leaning corner to a thin crack, which takes you to the lower-off just below the top.

14 Sniffin' Glue 22m F7a+ 9B † (2.5.06)
An interesting pitch on fine rock taking the vague right arête of *Gaze of the Gorgon*, gaining it by the relatively straightforward wall below. The crux section provides difficult climbing with an air of commitment.

15 Insistence 33m HS 4b (13.8.71)
Start at the blunt arête where the cliff swings around to face more to the south. Broken rock on the initial section. Climb up rightwards via a scoop to the foot of a chimney. Worm up the constricted chimney and move out left to an airy finish. Possible stake belay on the left-hand side of the depression above.

Between the conspicuous chimneys of *Insistence* and *Persistence* are a series of fine, difficult wall climbs.

16 Athenian Tactics 26m F7b+ 10B (8.04)
Excellent rock once the scrappy start is over. Climb *Insistence* to a ledge at 8 metres. Step right and climb the bronzed flowstone to a reachy finish.

17 Corinthian Spirit 26m F7b 10B (13.8.95)
Excellent pumpy climbing. Start as for *Cybernetic Orchard*, but move left from the fifth bolt to climb the impending headwall.

18 Cybernetic Orchard 26m F7b 11B (29.5.95)
The steep, uncompromising line left of *Portland Heights*. From a grassy terrace, climb up and follow a long flake/groove. Cross a bulge, moving left slightly to a shallow final groove and the lower-off.

19 I Walk the Line 24m F7b 9B † (4.5.06)
A superb, sustained pitch on excellent rock. Climb a direct line up the wall above the start of *Portland Heights*, with a short intricate lower section and some hard moves centred on the central section of the pitch.

Climbs from *Athenian Tactics* to *Babelicious Redhead* are longer than 25 metres, so a 60-metre rope is required to lower off safely.

20 Portland Heights 27m F7a 9B (14.5.89)
An exhilarating, steep face-climb, which has a bold feel on the initial section. Pockets all the way! Start 6 metres right of *Insistence*, beneath a ledge at 5 metres. Gain the ledge via an easy crack. Climb straight up the scooped, leaning wall with increasing difficulty to better holds (run-out at first). Move up and right with difficulty, then left to the lower-off.

21 Grand Larceny 27m F7a+ 8B (9.99)
The steep prow right of *Portland Heights* which tries too hard to avoid that route. The bolting assumes that you abseil in from the top to a double bolt belay at 8 metres, directly beneath the black rib. Alternatively, start up the dusty wall (unprotected) to the base of the rib. Climb this on small pockets and crimps to the lower-off.

22 Burning Skies 27m F6c 10B (18.6.95)
Fantastic climbing up the grey face right of *Portland Heights*. Start 6 metres left of *Persistence*. Climb the steep wall, trending leftwards to the base of a flake/shallow groove in the grey wall. A series of increasingly difficult moves lead eventually to a slabby section and the short finishing arête.

23 Isle of Slingers 27m F6c+ 10B (18.4.99)
The tight line 5 metres left of *Persistence*. Start as for *Burning Skies*. Good, direct, climbing all the way to a steep and tricky finish.

24 Lord Stublock Deepvoid Breaks the Chain of Causation 27m F6b+ 10B (5.11.88)
Start 6 metres left of *Persistence*. Climb flakes for 10 metres, followed by a scoop on the left to a small ledge on the right. Go leftwards up a slab to finish via a shallow groove and gain the lower-off.

25 Dusty Bedrock in Need of Careful Preparation 28m F7a+ 11B † (4.5.06)
A big, long pitch, one of the longest on the island, taking, in essence, the wall to the left of *Cocteau Phenomena*. Start up the relatively straightforward crack to the right of *Lord Stublock...* The upper wall is sustained and airy with two particularly trying sections. Low in the grade.

26 Persistence 35m HS 4a (13.8.71)
Start below a loose-looking wall with a deep flake/crack above, by some bramble bushes and a tiny stream. Climb a crack, the flake chimney, and the main chimney to a clean exit.

27 Cocteau Phenomena 26m F7b+ 9B (11.5.89)
A wild line on good rock giving sustained climbing up the centre of the towering face. Many blind moves and a difficult, reachy crux to finish, which can be avoided on the right (F7b). Climb *Persistence* for 6 metres (unprotected) and then traverse 4 metres rightwards on ledge bands above a roof. Climb up on wonderful, deep finger-pockets, without deviation, to the lower-off.

28 The Chronicles of Vladimir 28m F6c+ 11B
†   (2.5.06)
The impressive arête left of *Ausfahrt* gained by the
superb roofs below. Take this, first direct and then
leftwards, to gain the main arête. Follow this with
relative ease to a final difficult section. Low in the
grade.

29 Ausfahrt 27m F6b+ 10B   (6.5.95)
Tackles the big wall left of *Port Wine*. Becomes
steadily harder as height is gained. Start as for *Port
Wine*, but swing left across blocky rock to the base
of the face. Climb into a shallow groove with a
difficult exit. Move up to the small roof and make
difficult moves up the thin crack above to the lower-
off.

30 Port Wine 30m VS 4c   (19.5.72)
A good route up the steep corner-crack 8 metres
right of *Persistence*. Climb up to the roof and gain
the crack on its right-hand side. Traverse left and
go up to ledges (peg). A hard series of moves up
the off-width crack allow easier ground and better
protection to be reached. Continue up the groove
to a thread belay.

31 Screw the Roses, Send Me the Thorns
24m F7a 9B   (1998)
Start immediately to the right of *Port Wine*. Blind
moves past the mid-height bulge constitute the crux.
Climb up a slight flake to the bulge and then make
thin moves diagonally right on small pockets. A
lessening in angle provides a welcome respite prior
to the reachy finish.

32 The Shells, The Shells 27m F6c+ 9B
                                                 (16.9.04)
A dusty start and a highly eliminate upper section.
Climb to the overlap and pull over this with difficulty.
Fine face moves above lead to a slabby face and
steep finish.

33 Driven Like the Snow 27m F6b+ 10B
                                                 (14.1.91)
A good route which starts 7 metres right of *Port
Wine* and arcs across the left side of the face. Climb
a steep, thin crack to a ledge and then continue on
jugs to the base of an obvious flake-line. Follow the
flake for 4 metres and break leftwards to a hand-
ledge. Trend leftwards up a technical slab past a
pair of bolts (*not* the lower-off) to a short groove
and the true lower-off.

34 Return to Roissy 26m F6b+ 10B   (13.8.95)
The natural line of the face is unbalanced, with a
very difficult finish. Follow the flake past a bulge,
to finish up a slight groove (crux). Climb past the
lower-off for the full tick.

35 Last Rose of Summer 26m F7a 9B
                                                 (21.8.88)
After starting below and left of the cave, this good
face climb finishes right of the flake-line on the upper
wall. Climb up via a flake to a small roof at 8 metres.
Make thin moves up right to a shallow groove and
continue to a good flake. Move leftwards to more
good holds. Climb up with difficulty to a hand-ledge,
and then to a shallow groove and the lower-off.

36 Through the Barricades 26m F7a+ 10B
                                                 (19.4.98)
Fine climbing on very small holds. Low in the grade.
Start up past the cave entrance and onto the crunchy
wall above. At 15 metres pull left over a slight bulge
into a groove. Climb it on very small holds to a
good flake and the lower-off.

37 Babelicious Redhead 26m F6c+ 8B (1998)
Decent climbing on crunchy rock which is more
solid than it appears. Climb directly past the cave
entrance, and follow the wall above direct on good
pockets.

38 Chasing the Sun 24m F7a 7B   (2002)
Starts right of the cave entrance. Climb the wall
above direct to a crozzly pocket. Move up and
right into a short groove and use small holds to
gain the break and lower-off.

39 Jezebel Spirit 22m E1 5b †   (8.8.88)
Crunchy climbing which starts 5 metres left of the
cleft of *Blockhead*. Climb the crack with steep moves
at its top, and then pull up the block wall to a block
belay.

40 The Angry Sea 24m F6c+ 7B   (23.2.03)
A strange line with easy climbing leading into the
stern crux of *Chasing the Sun*. Start immediately
left of *Blockhead*. Follow the bolts diagonally
leftwards across easy ground. Make a tricky move
into the groove of *Chasing the Sun* and continue
as for that route.

41 Blockhead 20m HS 4b   (30.8.71)
The cleft where the cliff changes direction sports
several insecure-looking boulders, but these need
not (and indeed *should* not) be used too heavily.
Climb the cleft and the piled blocks above to belay
on the topmost blocks. The crux consists of
surmounting the block at the top of the cleft. Luckily,
this one *is* secure.

42 Dirty Cow 18m F7a+ 5B (9.10.93)
Start just right of the cleft. Has a very committing crux. Climb the sea of shells using some good pocket holds to the lower-off.

43 Spontaneous Cattle Combustion
18m F6c+ 4B (2.2.91)
Start 5 metres right of *Blockhead's* chimney. Climb straight up with technical moves at the top of the wall, to the lower-off in the blocks.

44 How Now Brown Cow 18m F6c+ 6B (16.9.04)
The wall and high arête right of *Spontaneous Cattle Combustion* has a fingery finish.

45 Talk 18m F6a 5B (22.2.98)
A direct, bolted start to *Reunion*. Climb directly to the base of the groove containing some yellow flowstone. Layback the groove above.

46 Toe The Line 18m F6b+ 6B (1.12.95)
Start 3 metres right of *Talk*. The moves up to the break are straightforward, those past the pocket in the headwall are an altogether different proposition.

47 Reunion 18m F6a+ 6B (6.72)
Start 10 metres right of *Blockhead's* wide cleft below thin, discontinuous cracks leading to a long horizontal flake. Later, bolt-protected additions to this cliff have effectivly resulted in the retro-bolting of this route. Climb up to the flake, traverse left to a vague groove with flowstone at its top, and climb steeply and delicately to a ledge. Continue delicately up to the block wall and a block belay, or use the lower-off of *Talk*.

⭐ **48 Sacred Angel** 16m F7a 5B (15.4.89/1993)
Very fingery on the headwall. Follow *Reunion* to meet the break at its highest point. Continue diagonally rightwards from a good undercut on small holds into a shallow groove, and up to a large **single-bolt** lower-off.

49 String of Pearls 18m HVS 4c (6.72)
Though the first half of this route is now bolted, the flake remains traditionally protected. Start as for *Reunion*. Climb up and then make a rising rightward traverse to meet the long horizontal flake with relief. Finish up a vertical flake crack. Block belay.

⭐ **50 Pining for Glossop** 16m F7a 5B (8.7.89)
Start at a vague groove 3 metres right of *Reunion*. Climb up to the horizontal crack. Much harder climbing up the shelly wall leads to a large **single-bolt** lower-off.

51 I Love the Smell of Resin in the Morning
16m F6c 6B (25.7.98)
Crosses the *String of Pearls* flake at the point where it moves from horizontal to vertical. Tricky climbing above the flake leads to the lower-off.

The section of cliff to the right has suffered a landslide in recent years. Consequently, it may be difficult to approach the routes up to, and including *Hot Pants Explosion*.

52 The Devil 16m HVS 5b (6.72)
This takes the crack formed by the shallow, curving corner half-way along this face. Swing over to the left at half-height when the crack blanks out and continue via a flake to the top. Block belay.

Jane Weir on *Toe the Line* F6b+.
STEVE TAYLOR

53 Draper's Henchmen 16m F7a 4B (19.8.95)
The wall and difficult groove right of *The Devil* has a very technical crux. Start up flakes 2 metres right of *The Devil*. Follow the groove with increasing difficulty. Pull over the bulge leftwards to good holds and finish up right.

⭐ **54 Oblivion Is Forever** 14m F6c 4B (8.8.88)
Start 5 metres right of *The Devil*. The last move is the crux. As well as the bolts has one drilled peg. Climb directly up into a shallow groove, step right, and go up to the top for the full tick before lowering off.

55 Equinox 15m E2 5c (1.6.88)
The hairline crack 8 metres right of *The Devil*. A hard start due to the landslide. Start up a shallow scoop above the centre of the landslide, traverse right for 1 metre, and climb up to where the crack slants left. Follow this intricately to the top. Block belay.

56 Silent But Deadly 14m F6c+ 4B (19.8.95)
A mediocre start followed by a fingery, difficult finish. Pull left off the grass slope directly above the landslide. Climb the wall on pockets to a very thin move at the top. Often dirty.

57 Hot Pants Explosion 14m F6b 4B (25.7.92)
Worthwhile. Start at the top of the right-hand side of the landslide. Climb up to meet a slight bulge near the top, which gives the crux just before the lower-off.

58 Scoup 15m F5 4B (6.72)
Originally a very bold lead up the rightwards-leaning ramp situated 5 metres right of *Equinox* with a chipped hold high in the groove. Climb the ramp and finish delicately up the left-hand of two short, shallow grooves to the lower-off.

59 Do Ixtlan 14m F4 4B (30.4.95)
Pleasant climbing, but could do with more than the four bolts it currently sports. Bridge up a corner to the ledge at 5 metres, step right and follow the wall past a difficult section to a lower-off beneath the roof-capped groove. More chipped holds.

60 Scoup 14m HVS 4b (6.72)
Climb the wall 2 metres right of the corner to a grassy ledge. Move up and right to finish up a short, unprotected groove. Very bold.

Mark Glaister on *Medusa Falls* F6c+ (page 67). STEVE TAYLOR

61 Imperfect 12m F3+ 5B (30.4.95)
Start just left of the crack of *Jutland*. A difficult first move leads to juggy climbing left of the flake until the lower-off can be reached.

62 Jutland 14m VS 4b (1968)
This climbs the left side of the arête a short distance north of the way down. Enjoyable, with good protection where it counts. Climb the broken wall, step right, and exit steeply up the flake. Large block belay.

63 Lifeline 13m F6b 4B (25.7.96)
A tricky little number just right of the arête. Start steeply past a small roof, then climb right of the arête to a tricky finish and the lower-off. The grade drops to F6a+ if the holds on the left of the arête are used to finish.

64 It's My Life 12m F5+ 4B (30.4.95)
Good wall climbing 3 metres right of the arête. Climb the steep wall and flake to a lower-off just below the top.

Sue Hazell on *Babelicious Redhead* F6c+ (page 61).
MIKE ROBERTSON

The following climbs are located on the wall immediately south of the Blacknor South descent chimney.

65 The Lizard of Oz 14m F6a 6B (24.8.95)
A better line than its companion. Climb the wall 2 metres right of the chimney entrance, then swing left to a white groove. Follow this to steep moves through the flowstone to reach the lower-off.

66 Snakes Alive 15m F6b 4B (16.4.94)
Shares the start of *Lizard of Oz*. Climb the wall 2 metres right of the chimney entrance to gain a small ledge and follow a blank corner to reach up right to a hand-ledge. Continue diagonally right to the lower-off. *Very* bold for the second due to the position of the second bolt.

67 Slither 16m F7a 4B (2.5.06)
An eliminate wall climb taking a direct line between *Snakes Alive* and *Medusa Falls*. A technical start is followed by a good rest and dynamic finale.

68 Medusa Falls 17m F6c+ 5B (8.8.87)
A perfect flowstone rib, don't hang around on the tufas too long or your arms will turn to stone. Start just right of a flowstone rib 5 metres down the slope from the chimney. Climb the wall for 6 metres (small holds, big reaches) and move left onto the rib (the rib direct is much harder: F7a+). Continue up through two bulges to a lower-off shared with *Snakes Alive*.

69 To Wish the Impossible 19m F7a 7B (18.4.94)
To the right of the flowstone pillar is a steep flowstone slab with a slim rib and groove above; fine climbing. Climb the slab into a slight groove. Cross a small overhang and follow the groove above with increasing difficulty to another roof. Continue steeply to an easing of the angle and the lower-off.

70 Psychosomatic Addict 19m F7a+ 8B (16.5.98)
The hardest line on this wall. Start 3 metres left of the central flake-line. Climb the bubbly rock to a faultline and make powerful moves up and left into a groove. Steeper climbing leads to the high faultline. A couple of hard moves lead to a good pocket. Pumped? The crux lies above to reach the lower-off!

Mick Cooke enoying a rare Portland trad ascent on *Blockhead Hard Severe* (page 61). CHRIS LODGE

Tim Emmett on the crimpy crux of *Loose Cannon*
F7a. MIKE ROBERTSON

71 **Crack My Bitch Up** 19m F6c 8B   (6.98)
Pleasant climbing up the central flake-line, though with a
finish much harder than the rest of the route. Bridge up
the corner, past a bulge to a juggy flake. Climb this to a
roof, taken on jugs, which run out just as the lower-off is
in sight. Imagine some holds, and use them to gain the
lower-off.

Immediately beneath the outfall pipe on the cliff-top is a
shallow bay, climbed centrally by *Kamikaze Moped*.

72 **Kamikaze Moped** 19m F6c+ 6B   (10.7.94)
Enjoyable and technical climbing. Climb the middle of
the bay with difficulty to a chert band at 10 metres. Above
the band, climb up on the left to the roof. Cross this and
the perplexing bulge above to reach a **single-bolt** lower-
off beneath the outfall.

73 **The Oldest Profession** 20m F6c+ 6B   (10.7.94)
A delicate and technical climb, which starts on a boulder-
pile on the right-hand side of the bay. Climb up through a
slight groove formed by flowstone. Continue up, and cross
a bulge at half height to reach a resting-position. Climb
the scoop on the right and finish steeply up a short,
undercut corner.

74 **Loose Cannon** 20m F7a 7B   (7.98)
The black rib between *The Oldest Profession* and *Turned
to Stone* provides a technical start and a steep, juggy
finish. Much harder if not chalked. Climb the black wall
on pockets to the base of a flowstone pipe at mid-height.
Step left and climb this on wonderful jugs to the break
and the lower-off above.

*Guy Dixon making an early repeat of Chasing the
Sun F7a (page 61).* STEVE TAYLOR

75 **Turned to Stone** 20m F6c+ 8B   (22.4.89)
This wonderful, highly photogenic flowstone route is a must-do for anyone operating at the grade. It takes the black pillar bounding the bay, and is low in the grade. Start just right of the boulder-pile, slightly left of the arête. Move up and right to a flake and then go leftwards and up on 'welded' jugs. Make more difficult moves to gain a relaxing-spot. Follow dramatic steep flutings to the break and finish more easily up flowstone curtains.

76 **Skids of Mark** 20m F7b 8B   (24.8.02)
A good route taking the smooth-looking upper wall immediately right of *Turned to Stone*, though it shares some holds with this route in its upper section. Start 5 metres to its right. Climb the wall with difficult moves over a bulge to gain a good resting area. Continue directly via holds on the left up the flowstone headwall and pull right to a nose. Pull over this and continue direct to the lower-off.

77 **Bum Droplets** 20m F6b+ 7B   (23.4.89)
Steep climbing with a high crux. Start 6 metres right of *Turned to Stone*. Better than the name suggests. Climb fairly easily for 8 metres and mantel a flowstone protrusion with difficulty. Move up and then very slightly left to a horizontal break. Step right and climb the slim groove and the layback flake above (difficult) to breaks below a bulge. Step left and finish up flowstone curtains to the lower-off.

78 **Cut Throat Jake** 20m F6b 7B   (4.9.97)
This route provides some good climbing, especially in its upper reaches. Start 7 metres right of *Turned To Stone*. Climb the wall past some fragile pockets and up to a ledge. Make balancy moves past thin cracks to the lower-off.

79 **Cute Ass** 20m F7a 7B   (10.7.94)
Start 10 metres right of *Turned To Stone*. A route of contrasts; a disconcertingly shelly wall leads to some very hard climbing up a smooth wall, where height is a distinct advantage. The crucial clip is not made easily, and a ledge awaits a falling leader. Climb the shelly wall with care to a chert ledge. Continue with difficulty to a small ledge and the lower-off.

80 **No Ifs, No Butts** 18m F6c 6B   (15.9.04)
Climb the wall right of *Cute Ass* to a slim finishing groove and headwall.

81 **Seaman Staines** 18m F6c 5B   (23.7.97)
A dangerous clip at the third bolt! Climb the wall on small pockets, and make a rockover to easier ground.

82 **Kite Marks** 16m F6c+ 8B †   (10.05)
The groove left of *Master Bates*.

83 **Master Bates** 18m F6a+ 5B   (1.8.97)
Start at the top of the mound. Move up and left to the base of a short, blank corner. Avoid it on the left (harder direct) and climb the flake above to the lower-off.

84 **Hello Sailor** 16m F6c+ 8B †   (10.05)
The wall and roof left of *Captain Pugwash*.

★ 85 **Captain Pugwash** 18m F6c+ 6B   (29.7.97)
A good route up the centre of the wide groove. Climb over the bubbly bulge to a resting point. Climb the flake to the breaks and make a series of steep pulls, followed by a hard reach to the lower-off.

★ 86 **Roger the Cabin Boy** 18m F6b+ 6B   (1.8.97)
Good climbing again up the right hand side of the wide groove. From the top of the mound, swing right to a curving overlap. Pull past it to beneath a steep, dodgy-looking flake. Gain the flake (crux) and follow it though the roof to the lower-off.

★ 87 **Black Pig** 20m F7b 8B   (4.10.97)
The right arête of the wall is high in the grade. Step down the slope to a bolt belay. Climb the lower arête to the faultline. Make a difficult move to get established on the arête above, which is followed with difficulty past the breaks to the lower-off.

88 **Still My Bleeding Heart** 23m F6a 6B (26.1.97)
This flake-line bounds the right-hand side of the cliff. Doubts have been expressed as to the soundness of the lower-off in a large, seemingly detached flake at the top of this route. Not shown on topo.

To the right is a set of holes belonging to an unfinished project. There are two bolt lines up the large wall further to the right that share a common start. These have never been claimed/climbed.

Blacknor Undercliff

Many of the boulders beneath Blacknor Central and Blacknor South are large enough to attract climbers. The Fallen Block was a popular top-rope venue decades before the sport climbing revolution began. However, during that revolution, these large boulders were not overlooked. Generally of a slabby nature, they have become a honeypot for novices. This is due to a generous collection of climbs in the F3 to F4 range and their location by the waters-edge – the swimming and snorkelling in this area is wonderful in the summer. The attraction of these easy routes is, however, tempered by the sometimes difficult approach down steep mud and scree slopes beneath the main cliff.

Approach

From Sharbutt's Quarry on the Blacknor South approach (see page 25) the top of the Fallen Block is visible looking down and left, easily identified by a pointed pinnacle perched above it. One hundred and fifty metres north are the closely stacked Triple Boulders. A 50-metre boulder-hop north leads to the Jacuzzi Boulder, with the big white Diamond Boulder 40 metres further on. Another 150 metres of boulder-hopping northwards leads to Lunar Park.

Lunar Park

This is a collection of low-graded sport climbs on two large sea-level boulders below Blacknor Pinnacle. They can be approached from Blacknor North, dropping down grassy scree slopes 40 metres south of the pinnacle, directly underneath *Boilermaker*. Alternatively, a long boulder-hop from the Fallen Block will get you there eventually.

The first two routes lie on the northernmost of the two boulders (The Solar Boulder). Belay bolts are on the top of both boulders. There are also two V0 problems on the extreme left side of the boulder.

LUNAR BOULDERS

DIAMOND SLAB

DIAMOND BOULDER

JACUZZI BOULDER

TRIPLE BOULDERS

5 Walking on the Moon 10m F4 3B (2001)
From the ammonite, move up and traverse the boulder rightwards at half-height to finish up *Half Moon*.

6 Dark Side of the Moon 8m F4 3B (2001)
Climb the centre of the wall on slopers.

⭐ **7 Lunar Eclipse** 8m F2 3B (2001)
The line of pockets up the right-hand side of the boulders – excellent.

8 Half Moon 9m F2+ 4B (2001)
Start up *Lunar Eclipse*, step right after 2 metres to traverse the lip of the cave, and finish up the scoop.

9 Full Moon 7m F3+ 3B (2001)
A direct start to *Half Moon*.

1 Solar Flare 7m F3 3B (2001)
The line of small pockets up the left side of the boulder.

2 Sun Spot 7m F5 3B (2001)
The slight groove on the right side of the boulder.

The next seven routes lie on the larger Lunar Boulder, which contains a large ammonite fossil. Note that the starts of *Dark Side of the Moon*, *Lunar Eclipse* and *Half Moon* are tidal.

3 Sea of Tranquillity 8m S (2001)
The left-hand line – a solo on crimps and ripples

4 Moonshine 8m F3 5B (2001)
Climb the wall above the ammonite on crimps, tending left into a groove to finish.

TRIPLE BOULDERS

JACUZZI BOULDER

The Triple Boulders Area

Down by the sea, beneath *The Prow*, is a group of three large boulders that have a few short but good routes and, 100 metres north of them, is a huge white diamond-shaped boulder, which leans against the earthy undercliff. This boulder has three bolted lines on its slabby south face. On the overhanging seaward side of this boulder is a bolted project (F8a+).

1 Diamond Geezer 20m F4+ 7B　　(27.2.05)
Start at the bottom right-hand corner of the huge white boulder beneath the left-hand bolt line. Pull onto the boulder and climb up to the third bolt. Step left across the giant flake and climb a short steep wall to a ledge. Progress more easily to the shared lower-off.

2 Diamond Boulder 18m F4 8B　　(26.3.94)
Start as for *Diamond Geezer*. Climb directly up the steep slab to a pocketed steepening and a ledge. Follow the short wall to the shared lower-off.

3 Diamond Edge 19m F4 7B　　(27.2.05)
Start immediately right of *Diamond Geezer*. Climb the boulder, keeping a metre left of the arête, to the lower-off, with some tricky moves to finish.

Ten metres south of the Diamond Boulder is a smaller boulder with a clean slab on its seaward side containing two bolted lines.

4 Diamond Solitaire 9m F3 4B　　(9.4.95)
Start at the base of the slab. Pad up the left-hand side of the boulder to the lower-off.

5 Portland Snowshine 9m F3+ 4B　　(27.2.05)
Start as for *Diamond Solitaire*, but climb the right-hand side of the slab to the lower-off.

Heather Chapman on *The Bolt Factory* F4+ (page 79). STEVE TAYLOR

75

Blacknor Undercliff

Slightly further south, above a tidal pool, is the Jacuzzi Boulder – home to a set of excellent deep-water solos.

6 Twisting by the Pool 8m XS 5c S1 (8.5.95)
Start on the left, climb up towards the centre of the boulder then slightly leftwards towards the top. Don't hit the boulder you've just stepped off!

7 Shades of the Deep 7m XS 5c S0 (1.5.95)
The best line on the face. Traverse the first 2 metres of the previous route; then follow the pockets diagonally rightwards all the way to the top.

8 Jaws 6m XS 5c S0 (8.5.95)
The arête/groove on the right. Can be done using a number of methods.

9 Reservoir Dogfish 6m XS 5b S0 (8.5.95)
The low traverse.

Ben Stokes on *Diamond Geezer* F4+ (Page 75). STEVE TAYLOR

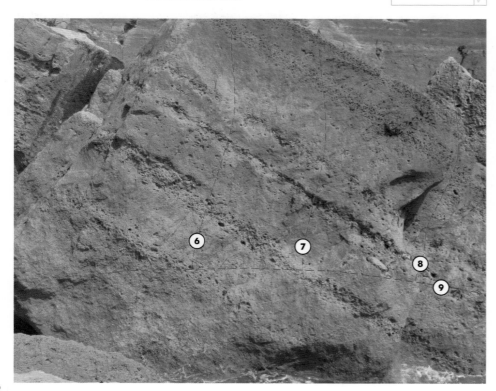

11 Retraction 7m VD
A short solo starting beneath the right side of a vague overlap. Unprotected.

12 My Little Buddha 8m F2 2B   (8.95)
The first bolt line from the left. Very straightforward climbing.

13 Sunday Swing 9m F3 3B   (8.95)
The second bolt line from the left has a roof to start. Once the roof has succumbed, the climbing becomes very straightforward.

The following three routes all start from a boulder near the end of the trench.

14 Suburban Dave 10m F2+ 4B   (8.95)
Pull off the boulder and step 2 metres left. Follow a direct line to the top.

15 Sketchtastic 10m F2+ 4B   (8.95)
Pull off the boulder and climb straight up.

⭐ **16 The Mystical Gill** 11m VS 4b   (10.8.88)
An unprotected climb left of the wide crack, though the bolts on the neighbouring route are never *that* far away. Pull onto the slab, step right and follow a direct line just to the right of *Sketchtastic*. Use the nearest bolt to belay on the top of the slab.

17 The Erogenous Stone 11m VS 4b (14.7.94)
Another unprotected climb, which looks a tight line until you are high on it and have 'crunched' a foothold! Start 2 metres left of the wide crackline. Climb straight up the slight depression and pass a steepening near the top.

Ten metres to the south is a north-facing boulder with a useful pool at its base and one climb.

10 Limpet-Fest 8m XS 5b S0   (8.7.95)
The traverse. Drop down to the water-line from the left and traverse rightwards, tapping on the limpets prior to crimping them. This makes them clamp to the rock surface to repel outside attack. It has the added advantage of making them suitable for cranking on!

The remaining routes described here are on The Triple Boulders themselves, which lie directly beneath the waterfall.

The largest of the three boulders, the closest to the main cliff, has become popular due to its collection of very easy bolted routes. **Single-bolt** belays for these routes are on the ledge at the top of the slab, useful for those looking for the top-out experience. Alternatively, the sports routes have standard lower-offs.

Gavin Symonds soloing *Portland Snowshine* F3+ (page 75). STEVE TAYLOR

The following routes are on the seaward boulder, reached by scrambling through a hole at the lower end of the large trench. The top of the boulder has a **rickety single-bolt** belay – useful if you like a view while belaying, though standard lower-offs are available too.

18 **A Nugget of Purest Green** 10m F4 4B
(2006)

The first line reached after scrambling through the gap.

⭐ 19 **The Vertical Thrill** 10m F4 4B (15.10.88)
Start below the left-hand side of the less-than-vertical slab. Climb straight to the top, finishing just left of the highest point at the lower-off.

⭐ 20 **The Bolt Factory** 11m F4+ 4B (26.8.93)
The central line on this boulder has thin starting moves.

21 **The Last Suitcase before the Holocaust**
9m HVS 5a (28.8.93)

Unprotected. Climb diagonally rightwards from the start of The Bolt Factory to finish halfway along the seaward-slanting top.

The Fallen Block

From the bottom of the descent through Sharbutt's Quarry (see page 25), follow a small path down to a massive fallen block with a pointed pinnacle on its top, down by the sea.

The Fallen Block is a suntrap, composed of good rock, and at a friendlier angle than the main cliffs with some excellent swimming to be had in summer. These elements combined with relatively easy access make it a popular top-roping venue for beginners. Three cemented stakes have been placed at the top for this purpose. Some of the lines are now bolted, with bolt lower-offs.

On the seaward side of The Fallen Block are two vertical chert bands.

1 Crack Minuit 30m HS
Take the cherty crack on the left. Go right at the top and over the bulge before finishing easily. Cemented stake belays.

⭐ 2 Six Good Biceps 15m F4+ 4B   (28.5.95)
The left-hand bolt line on the seaward face. Fine climbing on sharp holds. Climb the slab to a steepening, where the holds get much bigger. When the angle eases, move diagonally right to a poorly positioned (for this route) lower-off, shared with the next route.

3 Losing My Sad Tomato 15m F6c 3B
(27.5.95)
Very hard moves on blank rock — technically challenging. Climb the slab to a stuck-on hold. Make a couple of big reaches, and then pull blindly past a small bulge on non-holds to easier ground and the lower-off.

4 Broken Trail 23m VD
Very poorly protected. Climb the right-hand chert band. At the top, traverse right and scramble up to the lower-off of the next route.

5 La Cranium Cassé 18m F6a+ 6B   (27.5.95)
A bolt is always there when you don't need it – *after* each difficult move. Climb the nerve-wracking white groove to the top of the boulder and a lower-off.

The south-facing slab of The Fallen Block has four routes:

6 Arête Route 18m F3+ 7B
Start at the lowest point of the slab, on its extreme left-hand side. One of the best routes in Dorset and highly photogenic. Climb the exposed left edge of the slab. Lower-off shared with *La Cranium Cassé*.

7 Fallen Slab 14m VD
Somewhat artificial in line, but worthwhile. Starting 4 metres up the slope, climb the pitted slab, keeping about a metre right of the arête and moving slightly right near the top. Use the lower-off of *Arête Route*.

8 Intermediate Route 13m F4 6B
Start 2 metres higher again. Climb straight up the centre of the slab to the lower-off.

9 Right-Hand Route 11m VD
Start just below the point at which the boulders bounding the slab start to overhang. Step left and climb up pockmarks to the top. Cemented stake belay, or swing left to the lower-off of the previous route.

Simon Nadin cruising up *Arête Route* F3+ in perfect conditions. MIKE ROBERTSON

Blacknor Far South

Blacknor Far South shares the same approach as Battleship Edge (p 92). It is reached from a path beneath a line of large blocks across the cliff-top path. Drop down this path to the southern end of the crag.

Generally quieter than Battleship Edge, but providing longer, often better, routes (especially in the F7a to F7b range).

The cliff varies between 10 and 20 metres in height and is 200 metres long. Walking north from the southern end of the cliff, you pass beneath the short, cheekily-named *Enema Within* buttress. Next is a long, flat wall; the two short conglomerate pillars mark the start of *Paint a Black Picture*. Past this wall is a U-shaped formation of bubbly flowstone tackled by *Great Barrier Reef*, and then the protruding flowstone shelf of *Slumberland Direct*. Twenty metres further north is the curved conglomerate and flowstone line taken by *Ocean Drive*. The short, wide chimney marks the end of the climbing here.

Jason Pickles on *Kendo Nagasaki* F7a+ (page 85). ANDY LONG

Barry Clarke on *Reality Bites* F6b+ (page 87). STEVE TAYLOR

1 **Where's Me Washboard?** 11m F6b+ 6B
(4.98)

Start at the northern end of the cliff from the top of a vegetated bank, beneath a blunt flake. Straightforward laybacking up the blunt flake leads to the faultline. Psyche up and make a difficult pull around the roof for a flat hold, before hauling yourself up to the lower-off. Originally graded F5+!

The following two routes share a common start from the base of the vegetated bank.

2 **Castle Anthrax** 14m F7a+ 6B
(5.98)

Perform a difficult mantelshelf to gain the ledge at 4 metres. Swing up the left-hand flake to the faultline. You are now faced with a massive reach (or leap) for an obvious flat hold up and right. Go for it!

3 **An Arse With a View** 14m F7a+ 6B (4.98)

Harder than its companion. After mantelshelfing, follow the right-hand flake-line. Make a series of difficult moves over the bulge above to arrive gasping at the lower-off.

4 **The Singing Bush** 15m F7a+ 6B (2.6.96)

The superb flowstone rib; sustained, but never all *that* hard. It has a drilled pocket at the start.

5 **Bushwhacked** 15m F7a+ 6B (1.6.95)

The line through the wave of black flowstone, with some great climbing in its upper half. Some natural holds were destroyed in 1995, but a drilled undercut remains.

6 **Chaos UK** 18m F7a+ 6B (19.5.89)

A route of character, giving steep and fairly well-protected climbing. Start below the black, bulging groove in the overhanging wall 10 metres left of the curved flowstone line. Climb up on fragile rock, cross the bulge, and climb the groove to the breaks. Finish up the flowstone above to the lower-off.

7 **AKA UK OK** 18m F7b 6B (9.5.03)

A route sharing many of its moves with its neighbours. Climb the easy wall to the bulge. Good holds gain access to the upper wall, which provides a fingery finale.

8 **UK Subs** 18m F7a+ 6B (2.2.91)

Start 5 metres left of the curved flowstone line. High in the grade. Climb fairly easily past small ledges to the horizontal scoop. Gain a flowstone rail with difficulty and make hard moves followed by a long reach rightwards to the breaks. Trend rightwards up flowstone to the lower-off above.

9 **The Unknown Soldier** 16m F6b+ 5B (1996)

So-named because it has never been claimed. Start 3 metres left of the conglomerate. Climb the wall to the base of an orange flowstone groove. Launch up this on sharp jugs to reach the lower-off at the break.

10 **Read the Small Print** 20m F6b 7B (17.5.95)

A good climb. Start just to the left of the conglomerate. Climb up to the base of a flake crack. Climb this for 3 metres to a small ledge and step precariously left into the base of a white groove. Make some technical moves up this to a bulge, which is taken using good pockets to the lower-off.

11 **Fear's Younger Brother** 19m F6a 7B
(2.2.91)

Climbs the curved conglomerate and flowstone line, with some strange formations higher up. Climb the flowstone-cemented blocks, step left, and follow a short flowstone groove. Make difficult moves past a small undercut to gain a good spike and step left to a constricted rest. Continue up past a large 'fang' to the lower-off.

12 **Ocean Drive** 19m F6a+ 7B (4.98)

Good climbing up the right-hand side of the conglomerate pillar. Climb up the pillar on excellent holds to half-height, where the climbing becomes more absorbing (that is, difficult) on small flowstone holds. Make your way quickly to the lower-off (with a slight detour to the left) and resist the temptation to grab the quickdraw before clipping the rope in.

13 **Kendo Nagasaki** 20m F7a+ 6B (7.5.89)

A power-packed climb, which starts just right of the base of the curved flowstone line. Protection includes one peg. Climb a shallow groove on peculiar rock to meet a flake crack. Climb the flake, swing out right along a short handrail, and make fierce moves straight up the bulging rib to a good break. Pull straight over the roof, moving slightly leftwards, to the lower-off.

14 **Ryme Intrinseca** 20m F7b 8B (26.3.89)

One of the best routes on the crag, and a classic for the grade. Very strenuous. Start 5 metres right of the curved flowstone line. Climb the wall with a tricky move to gain a hand-ledge at 5 metres. Move up a shallow groove to gain a cherty break. Swing right to a resting point on the faultline. Gather your wits, step left to a thin crack, and move up into a short groove, where a lurch leads to a break above the bulge. Pull up to another break and continue to the lower-off. High in the grade if the rest is spurned.

15 The Strobolising Scyphostoma 20m F7a+ 6B (26.3.89)

Arduous climbing, a little bold in places and quite sustained, which takes a rounded rib above a chert roof at two-thirds height. Long arms required for the clip at the crux and for the hard finish. Start beneath the chert roof. Climb the wall to a good hand-ledge above a tiny roof. Make hard moves up and left to reach good holds at the chert roof, and pull over on buckets. Climb the rib to the deep break, stretch for the break above, and finish with a long reach to the lower-off.

16 Kill a Gent's Tart 20m F6c 6B (12.6.94)

Varied climbing. Climb the left side of a large flake. Pull direct through the steep bulge and make hard moves to enter the shallow groove above. Climb up to the roof and pull strenuously up right, making a long stretch to the shared lower-off.

17 Rag 'n' Bone Man 20m F6b 5B (14.10.90)

A suitable warm-up for the other routes here. Climb carefully up the right-hand side of the large flake and then go over the bulge into a scoop for a delicate rest. Move up leftwards to good holds below the roof. Pass it on the left and push on to the lower-off.

18 Steptoe and Son 20m F6c 7B (7.5.03)

Pleasant climbing with an impressive finish. Climb the wall with tricky moves to the roof. Take this head-on to finish.

19 Sparkling Bone Chamber 20m F7b 6B (27.3.89)

A good pitch on excellent rock, though with a brutal crux. Start at the toe of a short flowstone ramp. Climb straight up the steep wall on good fingerholds until a complex and reachy sequence leads slightly leftwards to a chert hand-ledge and a rest. Proceed more easily up a thin crack in a slab to the breaks and the lower-off.

20 Reality Bites 20m F6b+ 7B (6.4.98)

Excellent climbing, sustained at the grade. Start to the left of the small protruding ledge at 6 metres. Climb the slight groove on very small holds to a small ledge. Step left and continue more easily up the wall above to gain a large ledge at mid-height. Follow the left-hand groove and launch up the steep wall on good, hidden holds to the lower-off.

21 Slumberland 21m F6a+ 7B (15.4.89)

Start to the right of a small, protruding flowstone ledge at 6 metres. Three resting-ledges make the route low in its grade. Now bolted, and superseded by its neighbours. Climb up for 6 metres and move left to the flowstone ledge. From here, gain a short groove, step left again and go up to ledges. Climb the corner and turn the roof on the right.

22 Slumberland Direct 20m F6b+ 7B (10.6.95)

Takes the direct line on *Slumberland*, without recourse to the steps left at the ledges. Entering the groove below the main fault line is difficult for the short.

23 Nobody's Hero 20m F6c+ 7B (19.5.89)

The wall right of *Slumberland* offers some absorbing climbing. Start 3 metres left of some vertical conglomerate. Climb straight up on good holds and trend left past the left-hand end of the massive calcite 'reef'. Move up left below the flowstone, and surmount the bulge to get established in a slim, white groove. Climb steeply up this past a good hidden jug to reach the breaks and the lower-off.

24 Great Barrier Reef 20m F7a+ 8B (30.4.89)

Amazing rock. Start as for *Nobody's Hero*. Climb up on good holds to the calcite 'reef'. From its right-hand end, climb a thin groove with difficulty, move left at the break, and finish straight up the fine flowstone headwall.

25 Crown of Thorns 19m F7a+ 6B (26.2.95)

A sustained climb, which starts 3 metres right of *Great Barrier Reef*. After a short conglomerate wall, climb up to a large flake beneath a blind crack in the white headwall. Fingery laybacking up the seam leads to the breaks, followed by steep moves on flowstone to the lower-off.

26 Wax on Wheels 20m F7a+ 6B (7.5.89)

An undistinguished start but with brilliant climbing above half height. Start at a wide flake crack which forms the right-hand side of a vertical conglomerate formation. Climb the crack and amble up to the top of the pedestal. Reach up to 'coral' crimps beneath the smooth wall and gain a leftward-slanting flowstone rail with difficulty. Pull up to the roof and finish on fine flowstone to the lower-off.

27 Cerebellum 19m F7a 7B (26.2.95)

Very height dependent. Climb easily to the top of the pedestal as for *Wax on Wheels* and then continue to a good ledge. Climb steeply on 'coral' undercuts and up a thin flake before making a long reach to a good hold (shorties should move left on small crimps). Finish left up steep flowstone 'organ pipes' and a flake.

28 Hollow Ground 20m F6b+ 7B (22.3.02)
The 'wheat-thin' flowstone flake — nerve-wracking. Belayers should stand to the right, and be prepared for avoidance action. Start just right of a large ivy patch. Follow the conglomerate for 3 metres and pull past a grey bulge on small holds to a resting point below another bulge. Battle past this to the start of the flake, which should be climbed with extreme care.

29 So Special 19m F7a+ 6B (23.4.89)
Worthwhile. Climb straight over a bulge to good holds. Traverse left and move up to the ubiquitous shale shelf. Surmount the bulge and make a precarious move to reach a hand-ledge and flowstone. Climb the slippery flowstone and finish up the short wall above and the lower-off.

30 Mechanoids 19m F7a+ 6B (23.4.89)
A first-rate pitch on good rock. Low in the grade. Start right of *So Special*. Climb straight over a pocketed bulge and continue up to the shelf. Pull over a bulge onto the headwall, which is climbed on small holds to a straightforward finish.

31 Cliché upon Cliché 19m F6c+ 7B (7.5.89)
An absorbing wall climb. Start 3 metres right of *Mechanoids*. Climb the lower wall to the shelf. Pull up on jugs and follow the line of weakness on good flowstone finger-ledges until a very thin sequence leads to the break. From the wider break above, finish boldly leftwards up the short, steep wall to the shared lower-off.

32 Senseless Thing 19m F7b 7B (19.5.89)
This would be an amenable route, were it not for a 'frustrating sod of a move'. It climbs the fine grey wall 6 metres left of a conglomerate pillar. Climb easily to a flake and move up slightly left to the shelf. Pull up left to jugs over the bulge and reach a good finger-ledge on the wall. Move up, step right, and go up to the breaks.

33 In on the Kill Taker 19m F7b+ 7B (28.5.93)
The bulging black wall 3 metres left of the conglomerate pillars. Sustained, with the main technical difficulty just below the twin breaks. Climb up past a small ledge to the shelf. Mantel past the bulge to a big hold and continue straight up the bulging rib to the breaks. Continue easily up to the lower-off.

34 Think Black 18m E6 6b (23.4.89)
Follow *In on the Kill Taker* to a mid-height ledge. Move right and make fingery moves up a shallow groove (scary) to reach the breaks and the lower-off. Will be F7b when it is eventually bolted.

35 Paint a Black Picture 18m F7b+ 7B (28.5.93)
Start between two conglomerate pillars, below a smooth black sheet. Climb straight up the wall, without laying a finger on the conglomerate, to the midway shelf. Cross the bulge above to reach a flake under the black sheet. Gain a sloping edge and then pull out something special to reach the next holds. Continue slightly leftwards to the lower-off of *Think Black*.

36 Look on the Bright Side 19m F7b 8B (1999)
Not for the vertically challenged. Follow *Paint a Black Picture* to the half-height bulge. Pull over and start a difficult rightward hand-traverse until it is possible to pull onto a good ledge at the base of the black wall, beneath some flowstone undercuts. Pull into these and make a huge reach to the break above. Easy climbing then leads to the lower-off.

37 Boom-Boom Boom Box 18m F7a+ 7B † (30.4.06)
The wall left of *Carlos Fandango Belay* has a difficult move low down and a desperate crux from the half-height ledge.

Steve Golley on *The Loneliness of the Long Distance Driller* F6b (page 91). NIC HELLYER

The following seven routes provide some excellent easier climbing.

⭐ 38 **Carlos Fandango Belay** 17m F6b 7B
(16.3.02)
A good route which tackles the groove on the right-hand side of the long grey sheet. Start below the groove and climb the initial white wall on good, but spaced holds. From the ledge, pull into the off-balance groove and climb it to the fixed-krabs lower-off.

39 **Ghetto-Blaster Master** 18m F6b 7B
(30.4.06)
The wall right of *Carlos...* has two hard moves low down and an easing off in standard as height is gained.

40 Paying it Forward 17m F6a 8B (16.3.02)
Steep to start, then delicate then steep again. Start 4 metres right of *Carlos...* Climb the grey wall with difficulty to the ledge. Pull into a shallow groove above and tip-toe up it to a steepening, where a couple of long pulls lead to the lower-off.

41 Escape from the Dwaffee Room 17m F6a 8B (8.4.99)
A good line, starting just left of *Punter's Way*, which climbs the excellent grey rib.

42 Punter's Way 18m F6a+ 7B (2.5.97) ⭐
Good slab climbing in its upper reaches. Climb up to a small roof at 3 metres. Move over this onto the tricky wall above. Pull past the faultline on good holds to reach the slab (yes, a slab) which is climbed delicately to a steeper finish.

43 Blackthorn Winter 20m F6b+ 7B (28.5.96)
A steep start is followed by good, occasionally difficult, groove climbing. Start 3 metres left of the black fang. Climb carefully up and right, and follow the shallow central groove to the faultline. Make a couple of steep pulls into the clean groove above. Follow it with difficulty to a series of long reaches to the lower-off.

44 Master of the Rolls 20m F7a 8B (23.4.89)
A pitch with varied climbing on good rock and a spectacular finish. It takes the groove in the white wall and the prominent roof above. Start at the foot of the descent slope. From a black chert 'fang', climb trending slightly leftwards to a shelf. Gain the white groove above and follow it to the roof. Pull over with difficulty on an enormous bucket to the lower-off.

Project 20m F7c
A blind crack on the right-hand side of the blunt rib has yet to see a successful ascent. If climbed on the left it is very escapable, so keep to the right of the flake. All suitors are welcome.

45 The Loneliness of the Long Distance Driller 18m F6b 5B (7.12.96)
The wall and groove to the right again. A difficult start up the initial wall leads to a stiff pull over the bulge. Climb the tricky flake above.

46 The Sponginess of the Wrong Mixture Filler 18m F6b 6B (10.05) ⭐
Good climbing up the groove with a tricky finish. Climb the lower wall to a hard move up and left to leave the faultline. The groove above requires a considered approach to ensure success.

47 If You Should Go Skating... 17m F6c 6B (19.10.96)
This takes the overhang and the blunt arête. Pulling over the bulge is a bit gripping due to a low bolt, but the upper flake is straightforward.

48 Pulling Daisies 14m F6a+ 4B (10.05)
Climb up to the flowstone curtain and make a butch pull to pass it. Climb the wall above absolutely direct to a steep, juggy finish. Using holds on *Skating on Thin Ice* reduces the grade to F5+.

49 Skating on Thin Ice 14m F5 5B (1996)
A better finish to *Spare the Fern*. Step left at the third bolt of that route and pull over the small bulge to the lower-off.

50 Spare the Fern 13m F4 4B (30.7.96)
The groove just to the right of the dodgy-looking flowstone. A poor route in its original form. It is improved greatly by stepping left into *Skating on Thin Ice*.

51 Desireless 14m F4+ 3B (13.5.89)
Start near the bottom of the descent slope below a conspicuous detached flake. Climb up via the right hand side of the flake to the lower-off.

The following four routes take the compact, white buttress at the southern end of the crag.

52 Good Lay 12m F6b 4B (27.3.89)
A dynamic little route taking the layback-edge just right of *Desireless*. Climb carefully up to undercuts, assume an heroic layback pose and go for the top break and lower-off.

53 The Enema Within 12m E4 6b † (27.3.89)
The 'bumcheek slit' in the centre of the white buttress. A key hold was ripped off during a later top-rope attempt; now certainly a great deal harder than the grade given. Gain the slit and overcome the bulge with some gut-wrenching moves. Continue direct past breaks to a straightforward exit and a block belay.

54 Shoobedoobahbahda 10m F6c 4B (16.6.95)
This problem takes the 'peapod' groove on the right of the buttress.

55 Blood and Chocolate 10m F6c 3B (27.3.89)
Start by the right arête of the crag; quite technical. Climb the groove and go up past two horizontal cracks to hidden flowstone finishing holds. Lower-off above.

Gav Symonds on *Margaret on the Guillotine* F6a+ (page 99). STEVE TAYLOR

The Battleship Buttress Area

OS Ref 680 711 to 678 706

When the Portland sport climbing boom began, these were the most popular cliffs, though new guides have assured that climbers are now more willing to explore other areas. Simple access, fine climbing, excellent rock and a good range of grades have ensured a steady stream of visiting climbers. This crag suffers very little from seepage.

Approach

Follow the main road onto the Isle and up the hill. On reaching the plateau, turn right towards Weston. Turn right again at a T-junction by a church and continue one-third of a mile before turning right onto a housing estate opposite some shops, following signs for the 'Climbers and Walkers Car Park'. Park considerately in a small car-park at the estate's south-western corner near a mobile telephone mast and follow a path to the cliff-top.

• For Battleship Edge, walk south along the cliff-top. 40 metres beyond a line of blocks at right-angles to the path a small path leads down to the northern end of the cliff.

• For Battleship Buttress, approach as for Battleship Edge and then walk south beneath the edge to reach it. Alternatively, follow the cliff-top path south for a further 180 metres and descend a gully with a chockstone jammed across its top. Care is required near the base of the gully, and this descent is not recommended in damp conditions. Battleship Buttress is 50 metres to the south.

Barry Clark on *Eyes in your Navel, Nigel* F6b+ (page 97). STEVE TAYLOR

Battleship Edge

This is the 150-metre stretch of short, clean cliff to the south of the Blacknor Cliffs. The rock is of excellent quality and the cliff offers fine technical climbing. The majority of the routes are bolted and have double-bolt lower-offs. Although several of the traditional climbs may be finished by scrambling up steep grass and slat bands, an alternative is to use the lower-off point of the nearest sports climb to prevent any erosion of the cliff top vegetation. Note that there are no longer any cliff-top stakes above the Portland cliffs to pre-place belay ropes on.

1 Another Trojan Horse 14m F6c 4B

(14.9.04)

Start 5 metres left of *The Misanthrope*. Climb the wall with a reachy move to the break. A long reach above gains the lower-off.

2 The Black Pariah 14m F7a 4B (14.9.04)

Climb the wall immediately left of *The Misanthrope*, with a technical move from a ledge and fingery moves to reach easier ground slightly right.

3 The Misanthrope 15m F7b+ 4B (1.4.89)

A very hard and strenuous pitch up the overhanging white wall at the northern (left-hand) end of the edge. Climb up and right to layaways then up and left over the small roof to a good break. Cross the roof on jugs to finish.

4 Silage Clamp 14m F7a+ 4B (1.4.89)

Hard, enjoyable climbing on excellent rock. Start at the base of the flake crack. From the foot of the flake, climb straight up thin cracks in the rib to gain a small ledge in a shallow scoop. A reachy move up the short groove then hard moves left out of the scoop lead to the breaks and the lower-off shared with *The Misanthrope*.

5 The Sheer Weight of Prague 14m VS 4c

(10.12.88)

The prominent, wide crack formed by a flake is high in its grade and a better climb than it looks. Climb the off-width crack and the short wall above. Lower off a rope preplaced on a large cliff-top block.

6 Kicking Steps 17m E1 5b (10.12.88)

Start 3 metres right of the wide crack. Climb a wall, a thin crack, and a corner. Swing right at the top of the corner (a step has already been kicked) and finish over a bulge onto a ledge. Lower off a rope preplaced on the large cliff-top block, or shuffle carefully right to the lower-off of *Never Drive....*

7 Never Drive a Car When You're Dead
15m F6a 5B (17.4.93)

A good route. Start 2 metres right of *Kicking Steps*. Climb the bulge and thin crack to a hard move to reach the high break and pull diagonally right.

8 Wind in the Riggin' 14m F6b+ 5B (1.4.89)

An enjoyable, attractive pitch. Start beneath a rounded flake at 3 metres. Gain the shelf and pull over the bulge via a thin crack. Climb the shallow groove and short headwall to the shared lower-off.

9 Bawdy House 12m F7a 5B (1.4.89)

Start halfway up the left side of the grassy mound. The second bolt is difficult to clip and *many* people fail on this route. Gain the shelf and surmount the bulge (hard). From the small ledge, climb a thin crack delicately to breaks and move up left to a lower-off shared with the last two climbs.

10 The Ghost of Saturday Night 12m 5+ 4B

(6.1996)

Start on the left side of the grassy mound. Worrying for your second at the start. Move leftwards along the low break to the base of a shallow groove. Climb this delicately to a steep juggy finish.

11 Sugar 'n' Spikes 12m E1 5a † (17.12.88)

Start on the left-hand side of the grassy mound. Step left, climb up past a spike into a corner, and continue to the break. Pull over the top of the short wall (two poor microspike runners) and climb grass for 3 metres to a peg on the right-hand side of a large block. From here, lower-off a rope pre-placed on a large cliff-top block. Alternatively, but avoiding the crux, swing right to the lower-off of *Borstal Breakout*.

12 Borstal Breakout 12m F6c 4B (17.12.88)

A difficult finish above easy climbing. Start as for the previous route, beneath a short groove at 3 metres which has a square-cut left side. Gain the groove and climb it to the break. Surmount the blank top wall direct to the lower-off. Using the holds to the left of the headwall reduces the grade to F6a+.

13 Stripped for Action 11m E1 5b † (10.12.88)

A poor line which starts on the left-hand side of a wide, shallow bay, at the top of the grassy mound. Climb the leftward-slanting flake and continue to the second horizontal crack. Move 2 metres right and go up to a ledge and the lower-off of *Citizen Dust*, or top out.

14 The Kane Mutiny 12m F6b 4B (3.5.06)

The shallow scoop and tricky wall left of *Citizen Dust*. Keep direct on line.

15 **Citizen Dust** 11m F6a+ 4B (9.4.89)

Start on the right-hand side of the shallow bay, beneath a blind flake crack at 3 metres. Climb to the crack and use friable 'crozzles' in the groove on the right to move up and left. Step left above the crack and continue to a rounded finish and the lower-off. The parallel cracks provide a difficult left hand variant. (**The Best Men** F6c+ 1996).

16 **Eyes in Your Navel, Nigel** 12m F6b+ 4B (9.4.89)

A good line up the thin crack just right of *Citizen Dust*. Now bolted with an independent finish, and high in the grade. Climb a short groove. Balance up to reach small crimps and gain the crack with some difficulty. Proceed direct, past a pocket to the lower-off.

17 **Bilboes** 12m F6c+ 5B (9.4.89)

The shallow groove 2 metres left of the calcite-flecked wall. Climb steeply to gain the groove and follow it with difficulty to 'Thank God' jugs in a break. Pull up to the next break and finish boldly rightwards up to the lower-off of *Keyboard Wall*.

18 **Keyboard Wall** 12m F7c 5B (10.12.88)

Hard and good climbing though, thankfully, short on the crux. A very popular choice for those aspiring to this grade, with a good line and excellent climbing. Climb the calcite-flecked wall to the shared lower-off.

19 **Choco Loni** 14m F7b 4B (9.4.89)

This fine wall-climb starts 6 metres right of *Bilboes*; high in the grade (if you *don't* like crimps). Gain a shelf and move up a shallow groove to jugs. Climb straight up the smooth, white wall above to the deep break. Finish more easily straight up.

Steve Taylor attempting *Norfolk Coast* F7a+ (page 99). MIKE ROBERTSON

20 **Wurlitzer Jukebox** 15m F7a+ 6B (9.4.89)

A sustained line with a strenuous finale. Start 5 metres left of the roof-capped corner. Gain the right-hand end of a shelf. Make hard, fingery moves up the wall to chert jugs and an easing of the angle. Intricate technical moves leading to the break are followed swiftly by pumpy moves on deep holes and a long stretch to the lower-off.

21 **Evening Falls** 15m F6a+ 4B (17.12.88)

Start beneath a corner capped by a roof at three-quarters height. Feels bold, and becoming polished. Climb the corner. Turn the roof on its right, using a steep flake to arrive at the lower-off. An alternative finish is to turn the roof on the left and climb to the lower-off on *Wurlitzer Jukebox*: F6c+.

22 **Victims of Fashion** 15m F7a+ 5B (10.5.89)

Enjoyable, flowing climbing straight up the white arête right of the roof-capped corner. Popular with those pushing their grades, but no soft touch. Climb up, making a difficult move to reach pockets. Continue straight up the rib and make a tricky reach for the breaks. Use the final flake of *Evening Falls* to reach its lower-off.

23 **Barbed Wire Kisses** 15m F7a+ 5B (13.11.88)

The long, white groove right of the roof-capped corner. Easier for the tall. A long reach to gain the groove is followed by easier moves to the breaks. Pull over the right side of the roof and trend rightwards on big pockets to the lower-off shared with *Monoculture*.

24 **Monoculture** 15m F7c+ 6B (12.88)

The perfect, pocketed sheet 5 metres right of *Evening Falls*. Sustained all the way, with some very difficult moves up the smooth wall and powerful pulls on one-finger pockets to finish.

25 **Rêve d'un Corbeau** 14m F7a 5B (19.11.88)

Start on the right-hand side of the smooth sheet taken by *Monoculture*. Low in the grade. Climb the blunt arête, scoop, and layback groove, before heading diagonally leftwards to *Monoculture's* lower-off.

26 Lazy Days and Summer Haze 14m F6a+ 4B
(8.5.89)
Some fine climbing protected by bolts and an in-situ thread. Start 8 metres right of *Evening Falls*, on the left-hand side of the smooth, grey wall. Climb the scoop on small holds to gain the obvious flake-line, which leads with improving holds to the breaks. Move up on flowstone past the thread to a lower-off.

The next four climbs are situated on a smooth, grey, 80-degree wall in a shallow bay.

27 Norfolk Coast 13m F7a+ 4B
(4.5.03)
The grey slab right of *Lazy Days and Summer Haze*, requiring a myopic approach in parts, but with good, hard climbing nonetheless. Climb the holdless grey slab, avoiding holds on the neighbouring routes, to a tricky flowstone finish.

28 Pinch an Inch 12m F6a 4B
(21.8.88)
Start beneath a shallow groove in the centre of the wall. Four bolts. A good introduction to the edge's fingery walls. Climb the groove on good, spaced holds and continue up, bearing slightly rightwards to a short crack and the lower-off.

The original route of the cliff starts on the right side of the smooth grey wall.

29 Inchworm 12m F6a+ 5B
(8.8.87)
This was climbed on-sight solo prior to the placement of any bolts, a bold effort. Now protected by bolts belonging to the neighbouring routes. Start 2 metres to the right of *Pinch an Inch*. Climb the shallow groove to two finger-ledges at the same height, and then move up leftwards before continuing as for *Pinch an Inch*.

30 Inch Perfect 12m F6b 4B
(21.8.88)
Excellent technicalities with overhead protection. Start as for *Inchworm* to the finger ledges, then continue direct with difficulty into a shallow groove and follow it to the lower-off of *Pinch an Inch*.

31 Serious Music 12m F6c+ 4B
(19.11.88)
A stimulating, technical pitch. Pull over the bulge right of *Inch Perfect* to good ledges. Step rightwards onto the grey rib and continue up it to a lower-off shared with the next route. Can be started direct at F7a+.

32 Margaret on the Guillotine 12m F6a+ 5B
(22.4.89)
Takes the left-hand and more pronounced of two grooves. Start below and left of the disconcertingly high first bolt. Climb up right to the first bolt and then left into the groove. Move up past a slight ledge and follow a flake to the breaks. Finish straight up on small flat holds.

33 Gratuitous Lies Here 14m F7a 4B (22.4.89)
Takes the right-hand of the two grooves which feels very bold on the bulge. Start as for *Margaret on the Guillotine*. Move up and slightly right to the groove and climb it delicately to the breaks. Reach over the bulge and finish boldly up the short headwall to the lower-off.

34 Keelhaul 14m F7b 6B
(16.2.93)
A desperate eliminate taking the next arête. Two metres before the break it bows to the inevitable and finishes rightwards up the following route's final wall.

35 Out of Reach, Out of Mind 14m F6c 5B
(13.11.88)
The pocketed groove 8 metres right of *Inchworm* and 12 metres left of *Eighth Wonder*. A fingery start and a reachy finish, all following a natural line! Climb quickly *past* (don't pull on!) an ancient bed knob to better holds. From here, use a network of good pockets to gain the breaks. The headwall succumbs to a long reach and leads to the lower-off (a single staple and a Petzl bolt).

36 No Me Comas el Coco 14m F7a 5B (7.2.93)
This is a good, direct line just to the right. Climb up a slight groove and across chert bands to a bulge. Overcome the bulge and move over the roof with difficulty.

37 Come Armageddon, Come 12m F7a 5B
(22.4.89)
This steep climb up the ribbed wall has a very blind start. Layback on fins to reach the breaks. Pass the roof via a loose-looking flowstone undercut to gain good holds. Lower-off shared with the next route.

38 Def Con One 12m F6c+ 4B
(17.7.90)
Takes the blunt arête and the slight corner just before the black streaks. Dynamic climbing on surprisingly good holds. Climb a shallow groove to good layaways. Pull up to flowstone jugs on the right. Now GO straight for the breaks: the crux. Finish slightly leftwards to the top of the last route.

★ 39 **Blood Simple** 10m F7a 5B
(4.5.03)
Tackle the bulge right of *Defcon One* from the right and pull up to a tricky move in the scoop. The finale requires invention.

40 **Eighth Wonder** 14m HVS 5a
(19.11.88)
The obvious flake bounding the black wall on the left. Start at a finger-crack in a slight corner with a black left wall. Well protected, naturally. Haul over the bulge and climb the crack to a block. Move left to the lower-off of *Blood Simple*, or top out.

41 **The Barton Fink** 14m F6c+ 5B
(14.9.04)
The wall right of *Eighth Wonder* has desperate moves at half-height. Easier for the tall.

42 **Hipnition** 12m F7a 4B
(22.4.89)
Start 3 metres right of *Eighth Wonder*. A vicious start leads to positive holds and then a jug. Continue up a flake/groove to reach the breaks. Finish slightly right to the lower-off.

Unknown Climber on *Judge Jeffreys* F6c+ (page 103). GAV SYMONDS

⭐ 43 **Master of Ape Science** 12m F7a+ 4B
(22.4.89)
Perfect rock, great moves. Start 5 metres right of
Eighth Wonder. Layback over the roof to reach
good holds in the concavity. Reach up left onto the
grey wall and follow the slight scoop-line (crux) to
breaks above. Finish fairly easily up the short
headwall to the lower-off of *Hipnition*.

44 **Dripping with Blood** 12m F6c 4B   (5.8.89)
The difficulties on this route are short lived, and
quite height dependent. Surmount the initial bulge
to gain a hand-ledge. Make hard moves up onto
the ledge followed by a deviation to the right before
climbing the crackline above to a good ledge. Go
up a flowstone groove over on the right to the lower-
off.

45 **Skateboard to Oblivion** 12m HVS 5a
(9.4.89)
Start on a slight rise beneath a thin crack in a
shallow groove. Climb the groove to a good ledge
on the left and then move up right to the last route's
lower-off.

46 **Maud in Memoria** 12m F6c+ 4B (20.10.90)
Good moves; start immediately right of *Skateboard
to Oblivion*. Climb a line of small layback edges to
a ledge on the left. Now layback up a blind flake
and move diagonally leftwards to the base of a
short flowstone groove leading to the lower-off.

⭐ 47 **On the Wall** 14m F7a 3B   (26.11.88)
High in the grade. As well as the bolts there is a
drilled peg. Climb the lichen-streaked wall 5 metres
right of *Skateboard to Oblivion*. Finish by moving
rightwards to the lower-off.

48 Trance Dance 14m F7a 5B   (8.11.88)
Start 8 metres right of *Skateboard to Oblivion* below an enticing small pocket in a slight right-facing corner. Make hard moves past the pocket and follow a shallow groove to a lower-off shared with *On the Wall*.

49 Judge Jeffreys 14m F6c+ 5B   (19.11.88)
Once a necky lead, this route has moved with the times and is now bolted. Start 12 metres right of *Skateboard to Oblivion*. Climb two layback edges and then go rightwards to a hand-ledge. Continue direct to the lower-off.

50 Humanoid 14m F7a+ 3B   (19.11.88)
Classy climbing up the very sustained wall 2 metres left of *One for the Gipper*. Protection includes two drilled pegs. Climb the wall, swing right to a jug, and trend left past the breaks to the lower-off of *Judge Jeffreys*.

51 One for the Gipper 12m F6c 4B   (8.11.88)
Start at a shallow groove 15 metres left of the southern descent gully and 5 metres right of *Trance Dance*. Elegant technical climbing. Climb the groove and continue up to the lower-off.

52 President Elect 12m F6c 3B   (19.11.88)
Start beneath the face 3 metres right of *One for the Gipper*. Also has a drilled peg. Climb past a slot at 3 metres before stepping right and up just right of a hairline crack. Make thin moves to the breaks and finish more easily (but quite boldly) leftwards to the top of the last route.

53 Chappaquiddic 11m F6a+ 4B   (6.90)
Start just right of *President Elect*, beneath a rightward-leaning ramp at one-third height. Climb direct on positive finger-ledges to a ramp. Continue to the breaks and lower-off above.

54 Coastguard Ron 11m F7a 3B   (26.4.98)
Technical climbing up the wall right of *Chappaquiddic*. Start 2 metres right of *Chappaquiddic*. Pull up left to a series of layaways, which are climbed until it is possible to reach right on small holds to gain the break and lower-off.

Ten metres further south, at the end of Battleship Edge, is a descent gully capped by a jammed boulder, followed by Chockstone Cliff. This short cliff has a scoop in its centre and a short chimney at its southern end. Immediately beyond is Battleship Buttress and Battleship Back Cliff.

Mark Williams repeating his own route, *Coastguard Ron* F7a. STEVE TAYLOR

Chockstone Cliff

As the base of these routes is a sloping grassy ledge, belay bolts have been placed. All routes are on perfect rock and pack a lot of climbing into their short length.

1 Flickhead Goes Boing Boing 11m F7a 5B
(2.96)

The open scoop on the left-hand side of the cliff. Entering and leaving the scoop provides the meat of this route.

⭐ 2 Hats off to the Insane 11m F6c 4B (2.96)
The face right of the scoop provides the best route on this section; sustained. Pull steeply onto the wall and follow a series of small crimps.

3 Trashcan Man 11m F6a+ 4B (2.96)
The thin flakeline in the centre of the cliff, left of the central groove. Climb the steep wall to the base of the flake, which is followed to the lower-off.

4 Setting the Date 9m F6a+ 4B (2.96)
The central shallow groove line. Follow the groove and pull through the capping roof to reach the lower-off. Stepping left to avoid the roof reduces the grade to F6a.

⭐ 5 Champagne Supernova 9m F6a 3B (2.96)
The tight, shallow groove right of *Setting the Date*. Good climbing on excellent rock. Pull into the constricted groove and leave it with difficulty to reach the lower-off.

6 Andy Wallhole 8m F6a 2B (2.96)
The short, blunt arête on the right-hand side of the cliff. Climb the rib with interest to the lower-off.

Steve Taylor repeating his own route, *Setting the Date* F6a+. GAV SYMONDS

Battleship Back Cliff

To the south of Battleship Edge and Chockstone Cliff lies an enormous 'fallaway' block, detached from the main cliff and shaped rather like a listing battleship. The slab is popular due a number of easier, bolted slab climbs. More substantial, however, are the climbs on Battleship Back Cliff.

The first three routes share a common start up to a ledge at 10 metres.

1 The Sex Cauldren 24m F7b+ 8B   (2.5.98)
The left arête of Battleship Back Cliff. Start below a ledge at 2 metres. Climb the wall above to the ledge at 10 metres, above which the wall steepens. From the ledge, swing up and left to climb the left side of the arête. A massive reach from a small pocket is the key to success.

2 Even Better than the Beatles 24m F7a+ 8B
                                                        (19.4.97)
The wall and groove left of *Arc of a Fridge*. Climb to the ledge at 10 metres, plan your assault and then climb the technical groove above. The initial moves to a thin break are height dependent. The moves from the thin break are strength dependent. Finish more easily to the lower-off.

3 Arc of a Fridge 24m F7b 7B   (1.12.91)
Some very extending moves above half height. Climb to the ledge at 10 metres before pulling up and right underneath an open scoop. Climb with difficulty through a bulge to a big sidepull and an even bigger sidepull above. Continue up the pocketed scoop to deep pockets, whereupon a short rib leads to the lower-off.

4 Dreams Burn Down 24m F7a+ 7B (27.1.91)
Start beneath the first hanging corner at the top of the cliff (5 metres right of *Arc of a Fridge*). High in the grade. After a strenuous start, climb directly up the wall on good holds to the faultline. Move up with difficulty and then left (crux) into the base of the corner. This leads to the twin horizontal breaks and the lower-off.

5 Nihil 25m F7b 7B   (16.4.93)
A fine route tackling the arête right of *Dreams Burn Down*. Climb to a break at 5 metres, over a slight bulge, and up to a small half-height ledge. Surmount another (harder and bold) bulge and follow the arête to a large pocket on the front face. Continue up to the lower-off.

6 No Man's an Island 25m F6c 8B   (10.7.90)
After a very strenuous start this aims for the long flake on the left-hand side of a wide bay in the upper half of the cliff. Start below the prominent strip roof at 5 metres, some 5 metres right of *Dreams Burn Down*. Climb up to the right-hand end of the strip roof (*in-situ* thread) and go leftwards over it. Continue on jugs and cross the wide chert band to a ledge beneath the flake-line. Follow this to roofs formed by leftward-pointing flakes and trend leftwards to a good flake and a lower-off shared with *Nihil*.

7 Always Have the Edge 25m F6c+ 9B
                                                        (10.7.90)
This route starts at a flake 3 metres right of *No Man's an Island* and finishes up the right-hand side of the upper bay. Halfway and fading? It's easier higher up! Move up and cross the roof using distant jugs. Continue up and leftwards, crossing a fingery bulge to reach a ledge beneath a rightward-trending groove. Layback strenuously into the groove and follow it to the breaks. Reach for the deepest pocket in the world (unfathomable!) and go leftwards to jugs and the lower-off.

8 Pump Hitler 25m F7a+ 10B   (14.4.93)
A stamina climb with tricky route-finding on the crux. Climb over a roof and up to a band of pockets. Stretch left for smaller pockets and continue up the wide white pillar to the breaks. Use two huge holes to swing over the top roof to the lower-off.

9 Buoys Will Be Buoys 25m F6c 8B (10.7.90)
A classic sustained, pumpy route with a high crux waiting for tired arms. Start beneath a jutting ledge at 3 metres. Climb past the ledge and the wall into a short corner. Continue up a blind crack and make a long reach to the breaks. Swing up rightwards onto a small foot-ledge and climb up rightwards to the lower-off shared with the next climb.

10 Jurassic Shift 24m F7a 8B   (16.4.93)
Finds its way up the wall and the wide scoop above. Quite 'go-ey' on the crux. Climb a juggy lower wall to a ledge beneath a shallow groove in the wide scoop. Climb the steep groove to a slot on the right, and layback with difficulty to a flake. Make steep moves to the top breaks and finish leftwards past an enormous porthole.

Alex Dennis on *Price of Silence* F6a (page 111). STEVE TAYLOR

⭐ **11 The Fun Factory** 23m F7b+ 8B (4.6.97)
More like F7b for the tall. The groove-line bounding the left of the white face has a monster reach to finish and is very technical in the groove. Follow *Info Freako* to the ledge at its third bolt before following the groove.

⭐⭐ **12 Info Freako** 25m F7b+ 9B (18.7.90)
This searing test-piece is centred around a blind flake on the impending white headwall. Start 5 metres right of *Buoys Will Be Buoys* and 5 metres left of a broken flake-line. Climb the easy lower wall to a ledge beneath a chert roof. Continue up and climb the bulging flake-line to the breaks. From a large pocket, make a monstrous stretch to the final jugs and the lower-off.

In recent years a number of variants on the following routes have been reported. These have not been included as they are essentially connecting the start of one route with the finish of another and involve very little, if anything, in the way of new climbing.

⭐⭐ **13 Trance Mission** 23m F7c 9B (1.7.97)
The one variant with a reasonable amount of new climbing! It takes in the crux of two other routes. Start up *The Racing Line*, step left above the shelly bulge and move into the seam of *Info Freako*. Finish as for that route.

⭐⭐ **14 The Racing Line** 23m F7b+ 9B (4.6.97)
It almost joins *Zinc Oxide Mountain* at one point, but despite this, has excellent climbing all the way. Start up the wall just to the right of the large flake crack. Difficult moves lead to the crux crossing the shelly bulge. The headwall above is only *slightly* easier. **Single-bolt** lower-off.

⭐⭐⭐ **15 Zinc Oxide Mountain** 23m F7b+ 8B (25.7.90)
'High octane finger-damage'; a sustained line on the right side of the impending wall. Start behind a block. One of the best routes on Portland. Climb up past a tiny slanting roof to good pockets. Span a blank band to 'crozzly' holds on the white headwall. Move leftwards and climb up just right of a blind crack to the breaks and **single-bolt** lower-off above.

16 Lost Army Expedition 19m F6b+ 4B (1992)
Climb the wall to a flake crack and continue to the often-dusty niche. Lower-off on the left.

Kev Fearney on *The Racing Line* F7b+ (page 109).

17 Scapa Flow 19m F6c+ 6B   (6.90)
Start on top of a grassy mound. Some excellent thin bridging. High in its grade. Climb up to a band of pockets. Step left to a blind flake at the base of the blank groove, and climb the holdless groove to the breaks (crux). Move rightwards more easily to a huge pocket and the lower-off.

The next large scoop in the upper wall has a shallow groove up its middle. This is taken by *Raising the Titanic*, and the rightward-leading flake to its right by *Price of Silence*.

18 Raising the Titanic 18m F6b+ 7B   (4.9.93)
The left-hand groove above the ledge at 6 metres. Climb the steep wall to the ledge. Follow the shallow groove above to the break. Step left and continue up to the lower-off of *Scapa Flow*.

19 Price of Silence 18m F6a 6B   (1993)
Excellent climbing at an amenable grade, taking the right-hand groove above the ledge. Climb to the ledge, continue up to meet the rightward-slanting flake, and follow it to the breaks. Swing left and pull up to the lower-off using a hidden pocket.

20 Wave Dodging 16m F7a 5B   (25.9.93)
Start 10 metres right of *Scapa Flow*, just left of a small roof at 4 metres. Climb past a pocket and then past a slot at 5 metres to the second bolt. Move left and climb up over two bulges to a lower-off above the twin horizontal cracks.

21 Sink the Bismark 17m F6c 5B   (11.7.89)
Open climbing which starts as for *Wave Dodging*. As well as the bolts there are two drilled pegs. Climb past a pocket to a slot at 5 metres and continue to a scoop. Move right and up into a wide shallow depression and follow it to a ledge and shared lower-off on the left. (Originally, this route finished up the wall above to a lower-off in a band of rock – however the expansion bolt protecting this hard move is now in a poor state.)

Gavin Symonds on *Zinc Oxide Mountain*, possibly the best F7b+ on the island (page 109). MIKE ROBERTSON

22 **Big Fish** 16m F7a 6B   (14.9.04)
The slim pillar right of *Sink the Bismark* has three hard sections, but good rests in between. Unfortunately ,the final headwall is avoided by a necky traverse right and back left for the lower-off.

The next two routes climb either side of the large white flake/pillar.

23 **Wiggy and Mopokes Excellent New Hilti** 12m F5+ 6B (28.8.96)
The dirty crack forming the left side of the pillar. Pull into the flake and climb it to the top of the pillar. Make committing moves up and right to the shared lower-off.

24 **A Dream of White Porsches** 12m F5 6B   (28.8.96)
A better route than its companion. Climb the flake crack on the right side of the pillar before pulling up and right to the lower-off.

⭐ 25 **The Sound of One Hold Snapping** 11m F6b+ 5B   (5.4.97)
A good route, taking the slight groove 3 metres right of the large flake. Climb the groove with difficulty and move right to reach the lower-off shared with the next route.

26 **Electrically Injected Shed Head** 11m F6c 5B   (16.12.90)
The shallow leftward-leaning groove 5 metres right of a huge flake. Climb a frictional scoop and move slightly left around a bulge and up. Use a two-finger pocket to reach the high break and cross easier ground to the lower-off.

27 **Splat the Cat** 9m F7a 3B   (16.12.90)
Start half-way up the grassy mound, opposite the southern arête of Battleship Buttress. This is a very difficult problem. Somehow climb a short scoop to the breaks and a **single** lower-off bolt.

28 **The Shallow End of the Gene Pool** 12m F6c 3B   (3.11.97)
Start at the top of the grassy slope. A difficult boulder problem leading out of a scoop is followed by much easier climbing above.

29 Project A 12m F6c+ 5B (25.6.95)
This tricky route starts from the right side of the grassy mound. Climb the faint rib on layaways.

30 Searing Tunnel of Re-Injury 15m F6b 4B (11.7.90)
Delicate climbing up the shallow groove, 3 metres right of a broken, easy-angled area. The final section involves some rounded earthy holds; these lead to two lower-off bolts which are in **poor condition**. Climb the groove with sustained difficulty to gain, and stand up on, the break. Finish easily up to the **rotting lower-off**.

31 The Cones of Stress 15m F7a+ 6B (16.1.94)
A poor eliminate, which starts right of the shallow groove. Climb up and move leftwards with difficulty until close to the groove of *Searing Tunnel of Re-Injury*. Move 2 metres to the right, up to the horizontal breaks, and then leftwards to that route's **rotten lower-off**.

32 Psychic EMF 15m F7a+ 5B (11.7.90)
Hard, puzzling moves up the centre of the white wall. Low in grade. Climb up into a short layback corner. Power up the blind crack to the breaks and gain the lower-off.

33 God Told Me to Skin You Alive 14m F6c+ 4B (11.7.90)
Three metres right of *Psychic EMF* is a blind crack-line which, although only short, packs a punch. Climb up past a faint rib, and continue up the crack above to the breaks. Finish up a short arête to reach the lower-off.

34 Roadkill on the Information Superhighway 9m F6b 4B (16.3.97)
The left-leaning groove. Some difficult moves in the groove.

35 Error 404 8m F6a+ 3B (26.1.97)
Start at a low ledge on the right-hand side of an arête. Surprisingly difficult, considering its lack of height.

Battleship Buttress

The following routes are on the landward side of Battleship Buttress. Iron stakes, a boulder, and wide cracks provide the belays on top for the traditional routes.

1 **U-143** 8m HVS 5a   (c.1979)
The knife-edged, southern arête. Climb the crack, and continue on when its left-hand side disappears!

2 **Coming Unstuck** 9m F6a+ 3B   (18.9.93)
Start just right of the low roof. A short difficult section puts this high in its grade. Climb up and move left past a bolt runner. Use very small pockets to reach a crack and the lower-off.

3 **Block 1** 10m VD
Climb the left-facing corner to finish up flakes. Stake belay.

4 **Block 2** 10m D
The easiest way onto the top of the block. Start on the right hand side of a bulge. Climb the groove on good holds and step left onto a ledge. Follow flakes to the top. Stake belay.

5 **Block 3** 10m VD
Start up the previous route. Instead of stepping left, move slightly right and climb the groove (unprotected). Stake belay, or reach right to the lower-off of the next route.

6 Braer Rabbit 9m F4 3B   (18.9.93)
The faint polished groove.

7 This Is This 8m F5 3B   (22.7.90)
The slab 6 metres right of the arête is surprisingly easy. Climb twin cracks to the horizontal crack and continue on positive holds to the lower-off.

8 Wake Up, Time to Die 8m F6a 2B (22.7.90)
Start 2 metres right of the last route. Follow a short groove to the horizontal crack. Layback up to good pockets and rock over for the final jugs and the lower-off.

9 No Smears Here 8m F6a+ 3B   (3.5.06)
Go straight up the wall right of *Wake Up, Time to Die*. Harder than it looks.

10 Block 4 10m S
Climb the crack in the centre of the block. Good protection all the way. Stake belay.

11 Block 5 10m HS
Start immediately right of the previous route. Make a bold pull up to the faultline and continue more safely up a flake to the top. Stake belay.

12 Like a Drowning Man 8m F5+ 3B (22.7.90)
Start 9 metres from the northern end of the buttress. Climb a large flake and then a tricky layback edge to the lower-off. Following the bolts more closely is a touch easier.

13 Hang On to Your Ego 8m F6a+ 3B (18.9.93)
Thin moves up the slab.

14 She's Going Down! 8m F6b 3B (22.7.90)
Start below a faint line of weakness near the right-hand end of the block. Jump for a good hold in the horizontal crack and continue up a pocketed crack to the lower-off.

15 **Listing Badly** 9m F6c+ 3B (22.7.90)
Start beneath the vague arête left of a layback crack. Climb over the bulge to a pocket and an undercut, where tenuous moves on tiny holds lead to a jug. Above, the ochre scoop also gives pause for thought.

16 **I'm Doing it Anyway** 9m F4 3B
The obvious flake crack 2 metres left of the arête. Polished and pumpy.

17 **Hate the Sin and Love the Sinner** 8m F4+ 3B (6.11.93)
The once protectionless northern arête of the block. Note that the route was bolted outside the bounds of the Dorset Bolt Agreement, and may be debolted.

The following routes both lie on the seaward face of the block and are not shown.

18 **Another Stone on the Pile of Choss** 10m F6c+ 5B (4.8.96)
The steep wall and arête left of the central arête.

19 **Welcome to the Gravity Programme** 10m F6c 4B (28.9.97)
The wall and arête right of the central arête.

Right again is a solitary bolt awaiting two more to make a route.

Dave Pickford setting up for the bold section on *Useless Generation* F7b (page 129). STEVE TAYLOR

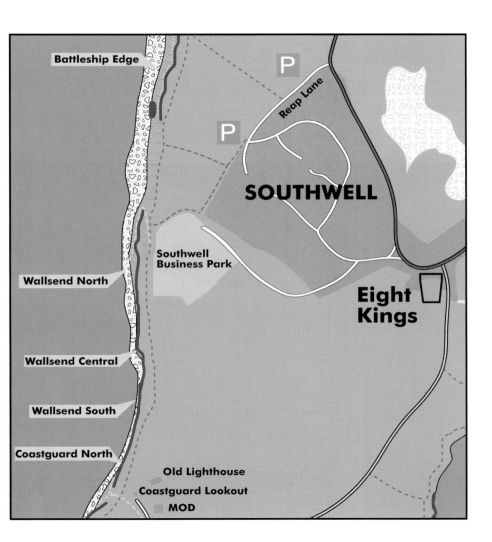

Wallsend Cove

OS Ref 677 703 to 676 694

The most extensive of the west coast cliffs, Wallsend Cove is probably the most impressive area to climb on Portland. Grades range from F6a to F8a, with a liberal sprinkling of traditional routes. It is steep, serious (particularly when climbing the traditional routes) and certainly big in atmosphere.

The cliff lies beneath and continues some distance south of the large, white, securely-fenced building on the cliff-top. The building once housed a secretive Defence Research Agency establishment, but is now a more mundane business park.

The lower half of the cliff has many nodules and bands of chert. It is on the upper reaches, with their smooth, white and often pocketed rock that the quality climbing is invariably found.

Although Wallsend Cove is a long, continuous cliff, it has been split into five distinct sections to aid location of the climbs. Each section has its own character.

• **Wallsend New Cliff** is a newly emerged flowstone cliff beneath the Wallsend North descent path. Only two routes exist currently, though more are likely to appear in the future.

• **Wallsend Far North** is a stretch of low cliff similar in nature to Battleship Edge. It is situated high above the sea, from which it is well-protected by a boulder beach and grassy slopes.

• **Wallsend North's** climbs also start from the top of earth and grass slopes, but these are less secure, and progress is made along this section by boulder-hopping down by the sea.

• **Wallsend Central** is the fully 'marine' part of the cove, with longer climbs rising straight from a boulder beach. The traverse along these boulders may be hampered by several wave-washed sections when the sea is rough. A high tide forces one to traverse a steep wall for a short way to reach Wallsend South.

- **Wallsend South** is protected by a large boulder beach and is approachable in most seas.

Part of Wallsend Central is subject to nesting-season restrictions from March 1st to July 31st inclusive (see page 11). This restriction may vary from year to year. Please consult the climbing press, the BMC, or on-site notices for details. Also, please do not pass through restricted sections during this period.

Approaches
1. For the routes on Wallsend Far North and Wallsend North, follow the main road onto the Isle and up the hill. On reaching the plateau turn right towards Weston and right again at a T-junction by a church. Drive on for a mile, turn right into Reap Lane, and park at its end by a modern housing estate. Take a footpath to the fence around the Business Park, turn right and follow this to the cliff-top. A path leads gently down the grassy bank to the northern end of the cliff. Note that the path beneath the 'Slapper' routes is narrow and very close to a long drop. Take special care when traversing this section.

Graham Lynch eyeing up the finishing moves of *Unsung* F6a+ (page 125).
STEVE TAYLOR

2. For Wallsend Central and South, approach Portland Bill along the A354, passing The Pulpit public house. Park in the large public car-park (fee charged) and walk north for 400 metres up the grass to reach the cliff-top by a Coastguard Lookout. (Do not park next to the Wireless Station, or in the closely guarded pub forecourt). Drop down the grassy bank to the cliff-top at a point where a tall, earthy buttress meets the cliff. Scramble carefully down the bank and walk north (beneath Coastguard North) for 150 metres to reach the southerly end of

Wallsend South. Alternatively, one hundred and twenty metres north of the Coastguard Lookout are a pair of earthy gullies which divide Wallsend Cove from Coastguard Cliff. The southernmost of the two faces north and is more pronounced. Care is required descending this gully.

Warning: this gully should not be confused with another, north-facing gully 70 metres further north, which ends in space halfway down the cliff.

Wallsend New Cliff

Wallsend New Cliff has slowly emerged from the earthy undercliff beneath the Slapper routes at Wallsend Far North. Originally unnoticed, as people watch their step at this point on the approach, recent attention has shown there to be some worhwhile climbing. The rock quality varies from pristine flowstone to shattered, loose flakes. Fortunately the existing routes stick to the former.

Approach as for Wallsend Far North (page 119). After passing the clean wall of *They Walked in Line*, drop rightwards down a steep slope to arrive at the southern end of the cliff. The routes are both within the first few metres of the cliff, starting by a flowstone bollard.

1 **Faith, Hop and Charity** 8m F6a 3B (5.9.06)
The left hand line up the fine flowstone.

	✓

2 **Short 'n' Sexy** 8m F6a 3B (12.12.06)
The right-hand line up equally fine flowstone.

	✓

Wallsend Far North

Wallsend Far North consists of 100 metres of short cliff between the descent path and a pillar/flake to the south. The cliff lies high above the sea, protected from the waves by grassy slopes and a boulder beach. The rock is generally of excellent quality.

The approach is described on page 119.

After a couple of small bays containing *Left* and *Right Little Slapper* and *So Hardcore*, a larger expanse of rock is climbed centrally by *The Right Mix*, with its easily-spotted calcite rail. The bay to the right contains several easier lines such as *Unsung*. To the south again is a wide chimney containing two huge blocks. All that remains south of here are a few microlines, such as the arête of *Mr Angry*, before the ground cuts away at the start of Wallsend North.

In the first bay below the descent path is a black-streaked prow. The following two short sport routes take lines up this prow and share a common start and lower-off.

1 Left Little Slapper 9m F7b+ 2B   (28.4.96)
Take the left-hand side of the prow, the crux being a dyno from a one-finger pocket.

2 Right Little Slapper 9m F7a+ 2B   (28.4.96)
The right-hand side of the prow.

3 Black 12m E1 5b †   (11.5.89)
This has a serious finish on loose rock and may well be undergraded. Start immediately right of the prow. Climb a shallow scoop and trend left to a collapsing exit slope. No belay, though it *may* be possible to teeter leftwards to the previous route's lower-off.

4 **They Walked in Line** 9m F7b 3B (5.7.92)

Start on the left-hand side of the second bay south of the descent track. The crux involves a long reach. Climb the hairline crack to the ledge. Drop back down and lower off the **final bolt**.

⭐ 5 **So Hardcore** 9m F7c 2B (11.5.89)

Desperately thin, containing no obvious holds on first inspection. Start in the centre of the bay which is stained black. Boulder out the crinkly wall to reach a sidepull, and make a strenuous rockover to gain the only jug for miles. A surprisingly hard crank is required to reach the **single** lower-off bolt.

6 **Layback Chimney** 7m HS † (11.5.89)

The wide crack to the right of *So Hardcore* is devoid of protection, and also possibly undergraded. A layback — or can you fit inside? Lower off a rope pre-placed on a stake (not in place) near the descent path. This route is not shown but is just off the topo.

Gav Symonds on *They Walked in Line* F7b.
STEVE TAYLOR

Fifty metres south of the descent track is a buttress, which is climbed by a series of sustained routes. This is followed by a bay, which is the setting for *Unsung* amongst others. Ten metres further south, a wide chimney is a good landmark. Use of this chimney, whether for descent or ascent, is not recommended.

7 RP Screamers 9m F7a 4B (6.5.89)

A technical route up the twin, thin cracks on the left side of the buttress. Start 15 metres right of *So Hardcore*, just past an S-shaped flake on the left arête of a shallow groove. Gain a good hold in the groove, and move left with difficulty around a blunt rib to a good sidepull. Stretch up for more sidepulls and then move rightwards to the shared lower-off.

8 Alpenglow 9m F7a+ 3B (22.7.03)

The rapidly fading groove up the right-hand crack. Start as for *RP Screamers*, but climb the groove. A pleasantly intricate sequence, though the climb shares holds with its neighbours.

The next two routes veer rightwards up the smooth white buttress.

9 Topsy Turvy Land 15m E6 6b 6B † (6.5.89)

A sustained line across the top of the pocketed sheet. Start at a shallow groove just right of *RP Screamers*. Make one move up the groove and swing right to a shallower groove. Follow this, and make a very long stretch for finger-pockets in the break. Traverse right boldly (useful empty peg slot) to a step up onto the small ledge in the centre of the headwall. Move up to a short drilled-peg runner and up again to the lower-off.

10 Weakest to the Wall 15m F7b 3B
(10.5.89)

A superb pocketed sheet giving very fingery climbing. Start 2 metres left of a flowstone handrail, beneath a blank, leaning face. High in the grade. Climb up using two pockets at 3 metres and slap up on edges until a rightward crucifix move gains a 'mono' hole. Reach up for another pocket and step right for a jug. Continue on better holds past a big hole to the lower-off.

11 Resisting Mutiny 15m F7c+ 2B
(12.95)

There are *two* difficult routes using a pair of eye-bolts, left of the blunt arête. For the F7c+ tick, stay on the bolt line. Climbing to the left of the bolt line gives a reachy F7b+.

12 The Right Mix 15m F6b+ 2B
(6.5.89)

Contrasting bold climbing up the blunt arête. Start left of the arête at a flowstone handrail. Also features one *in-situ* thread. Swing right along the handrail and make a bold reach (lunge) to flowstone jugs. Use these to gain a ledge around the arête. Step back left to the edge and climb the arête to the shared lower-off. The direct start up the blunt arête warrants F7a.

13 Never Lose That Feeling 13m F6a+ 5B
(2.7.92)

An innocuous-looking warm-up on the slab. The hardest move is an intriguing mantelshelf to start, before better holds lead up past the breaks to the lower-off.

14 Sing Something Simple 12m F6c 4B
(20.5.04)

The wall immediately left of *Unsung* has a hard move by the second bolt.

⭐ 15 Unsung 12m F6a+ 3B
(18.8.92)

Start on the left-hand side of the back of the bay. Climb up and turn a bulge on its right to reach a shared lower-off.

Marti Hallett on *RP Screamers* **F7a** .
STEVE TAYLOR

⭐ 16 **Come In Alone, Go Out Alone** 12m F6b
3B   (6.5.89)
Start 3 metres right of *Unsung*. After a hard start, climb a leftward-trending line to join *Unsung* at its third bolt.

The right-hand side of the bay plays host to the next six routes.

17 **No Soft Option** 11m F7b+ 2B   (10.5.89)
Start at a white scoop. Probably only F7b for the tall. Step up a short ramp beneath a bulge. Crank fiercely from a mono up to positive edges and make further hard moves to the breaks and the lower-off.

18 **Dial-a-Cliché** 11m F6c+ 2B   (6.5.89)
Start in the centre of the buttress at a grass-bedecked flake. Fairly dangerous: the route has seen several inverted falls and only *just* warrants a sport grade. Climb up to a small roof and a bolt above. Move rightwards over the roof (hard) and make another hard move back left to a welcome bolt on the left side of the groove. Make a long reach for the breaks and the lower-off.

Sergeant Ford's Roving Truncheon 40m E3
5b,6a † (1994) is the first route on the Isle to follow the twin horizontal cracks near the top of the cliff. It starts as for *The Web*, belays on *The Right Mix* and descends *RP Screamers*. It uses the fixed protection of the routes it crosses, so some runners are spaced.

19 **The Web** 9m F6b 3B   (8.5.94)
Start a metre right of the grassy flake. Climb up to a rib and follow it past the twin breaks to the lower-off.

20 **Oscourt** 10m E3 5b †   13.7.90)
Bold climbing up the short scoop left of the wide
chimney. Lower off a preplaced rope (or reach left
to the lower-off of *The Web*).

21 **Can't Stop the Bosch** 9m F6c 2B   (8.5.94)
Trends up rightwards from the base of *Oscourt*.

The next four routes are on the short wall between
the wide chimney and the point at which the grass
slope reverts to earth and drops away.

22 **Mr Angry** 8m VS 4b   (1990)
The unprotected arête which forms the right side of
the boulder-choked chimney. Escape down the
chimney with care.

23 **Twistin' My Melon, Man** 8m E2 6a (17.7.90)
A reachy problem starting 3 metres right of the arête,
just left of a slight rib. Avoiding easier ground near
the arête, climb past a two-finger undercut directly
to the breaks, and then slightly right to a clean-cut
exit. Lower off a preplaced rope.

Five metres right of the arête is a blind crack,
Screaming Toilet Fish 6m E1 5c (13.7.90), and 2
metres right again is **The Price of Potatoes** 7m
HVS 5a (13.7.90). This finishes rightwards onto a
chossy ledge. For both of these, lower off a
preplaced rope tied to an imaginary stake.

**Marti Hallett making the unprotected lurch
on *The Right Mix* F6b+ (page 125).**
STEVE TAYLOR

Wallsend North

In Wallsend North the base of the cliff is protected by boulders and banks of earth, though these are not as substantial as in Wallsend Far North. Progress beneath the cliff is made along the boulders. This section of cliff starts where the slope cuts away and changes from grass to earth. The first climb, *Sniper in the Brain*, takes the wall left of a pillar just to the south, with the big wall to the right of the pillar containing some of Portland's finest testpieces. Some 200 metres further south, the stunning orange-coloured streak climbed by *Sweet Smell of Success* is an obvious landmark to all but the colour-blind. Finally, the arête of *The Bigger Piece* marks the start of the 'marine' section of the cove (Wallsend Central).

The approach is described on page 119.

The earth bank beneath the section of cliff from *Sniper in the Brain* to *Acid Jazz Disco* is receding. The routes in this sector may therefore become more difficult, longer, or at least very bold up to the first bolt. Take notice!

A few climbs to the south, the earth slope from the pillar of *The Watchmaker's Hands* to *To Hungary, for Love* was always a precarious proposition; it has slumped recently and is still far from stable. Some bolts have been placed to safeguard the approach to the (not quite so) high earth ledge from its northern end, though it is recommended that one approaches via the knotted rope at the southern end of the high ledge. Approach these routes with caution and be prepared to contend with an extra few metres of climbing.

The following four routes share a common tricky start up a groove above the extreme left-hand end of the mud slope. Note that in 2008 the mud slope receded further, rendering them unclimbable.

24 Sniper in the Brain 13m F7a 4B †† (17.10.03)
Climb the groove. At the second bolt, step left to a ledge and climb the wall above, with a hard move to the lower-off.

25 Holding the Zero 13m F7a 4B †† (27.9.03)
Low in the grade. Climb the groove direct to the breaks and the lower-off.

26 Dead Man's Click 13m F7a 4B †† (10.03)
Climb the groove. At the first bolt, swing right along a cherty fault, moving across *Stay on Target* to finish up a short easy groove. High in the grade.

27 Stay on Target 17m F7b+ 3B †† (28.4.94)
A poor route which starts between the point at which the earth falls away and the pillar. It may now be reached by stepping right from *Holding the Zero* at about F6c+. After a problematic layback move up the very smooth wall, continue with difficulty up the centre of the wall to the lower-off. (No sneaking off into the right-hand corner to bypass the top section!)

28 **Eternity's Toothpaste** 17m VS 4c † (27.12.89)
This poorly-protected route tackles the flake on the right side of the pillar, with a deviation left onto the pillar at half height to avoid loose rock. At the grass, lower off a rope pre-placed on a stake (not in place).

29 **Old Painless** 18m F7a+ 4B (30.5.92)
Start 3 metres right of the pillar. Pumpy, with a technical upper section. Climb a ramp formed by a flake and the open groove above past three bolts to a high ledge and the final bolt. Continue up, quickdraw in your teeth, and clip the lower-off.

30 **Useless Generation** 20m F7b 5B (12.4.92)
One to cheer up the moodiest of teenagers! High in its grade and feeling very run-out on the crux section. The wall 5 metres right of the pillar gives a superb, sustained, fingery exercise, with hard moves all the way to the breaks. A very long reach then gains a hole and the lower-off.

31 **My Love of This Land** 20m F7b 4B (14.5.89)
A technical route on excellent rock. Start 6 metres right of the pillar. Gain a cherty ledge and climb a layback edge with difficulty with a hard undercut move to a chert sill and a grip clip. Move rightwards along a pocketed section. Continue to the breaks and go up a fossil runnel to the lower-off.

32 **Going Blank Again** 20m F7a+ 4B (12.4.92)
More superb stone 3 metres right again, in the form of a vague pillar. Climb to cherty ledges, where thin moves lead rightwards to a hidden finger-ledge above the second bolt. Mantel the ledge and move up slightly left on pockets to the breaks. Finish up the runnel of *My Love of This Land* to its lower-off.

33 **The Treacle Factory** 20m F6b 5B (30.5.92)
The system of vague scoops and flakes 3 metres right of *Going Blank Again*.

Twenty metres to the right of the pillar and just left of two short, south-facing chimneys is a rounded corner with an arête on either side. *The Montreal Protocol* and *Acid Jazz Disco* climb these arêtes.

34 **The Montreal Protocol** 20m F7b 7B (20.5.89)
The blunt left-hand arête is an elegant but difficult proposition. Climb up ledges and a short wall to the base of the arête. Climb it on its right with some difficulty to the breaks and the lower-off.

35 **Cosa Nostra** 20m F6a+ 9B (24.4.94)
The corner between the two arêtes offers some good bridging. Climb over broken rock (slightly better on the left of the bolts) to a ledge at the base of the groove. Follow the groove to the lower-off.

36 **Acid Jazz Disco** 20m F7a 6B (20.5.89)
A broken start detracts little from a tremendous, sustained climb. Start beneath the right-hand arête. Climb easily up left and back right to a slot. Proceed up on chert to the base of the arête proper. Follow the arête, mostly on its right-hand side, to a ledge near the top and the lower-off.

37 **Eight Bar Blues** 17m F6c+ 6B (1995)
The technical blue wall to the right of *Acid Jazz Disco* gives an excellent outing on immaculate rock.

The following routes lie 13 metres above a high earth ledge, above the boulder beach. They are reached by pulling up a knotted rope at the southern end of the ledge. They see little traffic and have

Jim Kimber on *Resisting Mutiny* F7c+ (page 125). STEVE HARDY

become very dirty since they were first climbed. Be prepared to do some cleaning en-route. If these routes *were* clean, you could add a star or two to each of them.

38 Precious to the Last 18m F7c 6B † (11.5.90)
Hard sustained climbing on excellent rock. Start 12 metres south of the two short, south-facing chimneys, on the high-level terrace. Make searing pulls to good sidepulls below a shallow groove which extends to half height. Desperate palming and smearing followed by a dyno now lead to a jug. Go leftwards on pockets to the headwall. Move up to the breaks and exit up a slight groove. Stake belay (not in place).

39 Ecstasy 18m F7a+ 6B (27.3.90)
The wide groove 15 metres right of the two short chimneys is a joy to climb: white rock, white-hot moves *but* the bolts are in a poor condition and need replacing. Start from the high-level terrace. Layaways and pressure moves afford entry to the groove. Easier climbing leads to an overhang at the breaks. Bear right to the next route's lower-off.

40 Live Now Pay Later 18m F7a+ 6B (5.7.92)
Varied moves up the arête and face. Start just to the left of *John Craven's Jumper Contest*. Climb steeply and then layback the rounded arête on the left, using sidepulls on the left to assist, to reach a break. Trend left up the blank headwall past a pocket to the horizontal cracks. Shared lower-off.

41 John Craven's Jumper Contest 18m F6b+ 5B (7.6.92)
Start at a groove 5 metres right of *Ecstasy*. Interesting, reachy climbing but with a grip-clip and some filthy rock. Use two whopping great jugs to enter the groove, and follow it strenuously to the twin breaks. Mantelshelf up to the lower-off.

42 The Watchmaker's Hands 18m F7c 6B † (8.7.92)
A hard sequence up the white pillar. Starting just right of *John Craven's Jumper Contest*, gain a big layaway and use opposing sidepulls to surge powerfully up to a ledge at half height. Make more hard moves to the breaks before trending left more easily to the shared lower-off.

43 Breakfast of Champions 19m F7b+ 7B (29.8.92)
Just 3 metres right of *The Watchmaker's Hands*, some choice moves and an exquisite crux make for a delicious route. (The left-hand option has not yet been tasted on lead.) 'Drag hungrily past the initial hump and unswervingly past two bolts to vantage jugs by a third. Veer up into the furrow and check out the menu. Either munch through the rounded left-hand layback (the original, but not the best, due to an unpalatable topping), or savour the ambrosial right-hand course, with the finest ingredients of wide pinches, smears, and pocketed edges. Just after the fifth bolt, a reach left will bring you satiated to a further selection of pockets and edges (bolt). Take one last gulp before an agreeable amble to the two lower-off bolts.' (First ascensionist). A pleasant surprise awaits you at the lower-off.

44 Youth Body Expression Explosion 20m F7b 7B † (15.8.92)
The groove 10 metres right of *John Craven's Jumper Contest* proves harder than it looks. From a jug, rock up right and climb the wall to the groove. Hard pressure moves up the left arête lead to better holds where it bulges near the top. Reach for a large hidden hold and make the precarious crux moves for the breaks and the lower-off.

45 To Hungary, for Love 24m F8a 7B † (6.9.03)
The desperate arête to the right has a hard, bouldery crux. Amble up the warm-up wall to a semi-rest beneath the upper arête. Extending moves with few footholds lead to an excruciating pull on a small crimp to gain improving holds, which lead to the break. A last balancy rock-over gains the lower-off. Top conditions are required for the footholds to work.

46 So Shoot Me 24m F7a+ 7B (8.5.94)
The slim white groove near the right-hand end of the earth terrace is a rather misconceived route, on which four pockets have been drilled. These may now have been filled in, invalidating the grade. Climb through poor chert bands and up a steep groove to the lower-off.

The next two routes take the tremendously imposing hanging buttress, starting from the beach. A 60-metre rope is required to reach the ground safely.

47 Lolita 28m F7b+ 12B (17.5.99)
A tremendously intimidating line breaking out left from *Teenage Lust*. Swing left from the third bolt on *Teenage Lust* (apparently it is a good idea to stick-clip this). Trend left up the steepening face until hard moves gain a large blind flake. Layback this in heart pumping exposure to the roof and cross it to pockets and the lower-off.

48 Teenage Lust 28m F7b+ 9B (12.4.92)
The direct line up the huge buttress, with an orgasmic crux at the very top on monos. Not exactly safe sex though, despite the bolt protection; the third clip is very poky. Start just right of centre, beneath two high roofs, by scrambling 6 metres to a bolt belay on top of a pillar. Climb the steep lower wall direct to a flake-line. (A hidden pocket right of the third bolt makes a big difference — so now you know!) Follow the flake to the first roof, which has a rail on its lip. Swing 2 metres left onto a blunt arête and climb on pockets to the breaks. Cross a short wall to the lower-off.

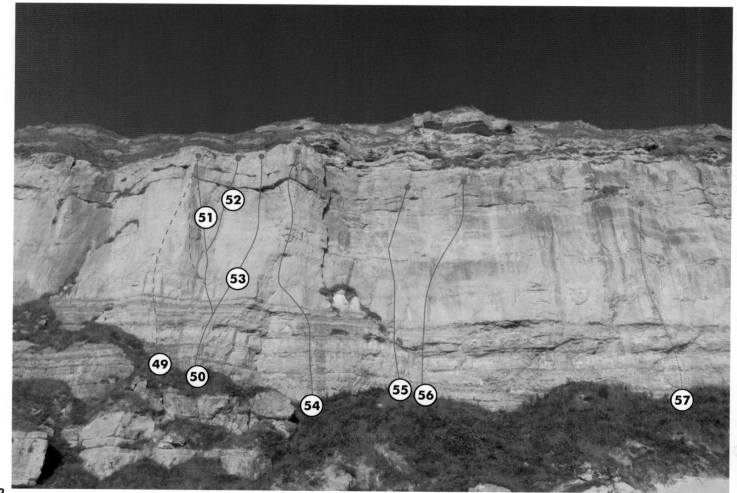

One hundred and fifty metres south of the start of Wallsend North (with some excellent unclimbed rock on the way) is a rounded pillar of perfect light-grey rock – this is the fine line of *My Dog's Got Fleas*. Beneath this pillar is a promontory of boulders at sea-level.

To get to the base of this route, continue southwards for 50 metres until beneath a beautiful orange-streaked buttress and scramble up to a comfortable grassy depression. The routes between *My Dog's Got Fleas* and *Jungle Drums* may all be reached from this point.

49 My Dog's Got Fleas 20m E6 6b † (12.8.89)
The rounded left-hand edge of the grey pillar is a superb pitch featuring some dynamic manoeuvres. Start from the extreme left-hand end of the terrace. Climb past a peg at 3 metres, to get established on a thin foot-ledge (failed bolt). Clip the drilled peg above and gain a layback edge on the left, around the rib, with difficulty. Continue past a bolt, with an almighty leap for a resting-ledge. Climb straight up the rounded rib (manky bolt) on improving holds to good breaks and the lower-off of *Yikes Shaggy*.

50 Poop Scoop 20m E4 5c † (12.8.89)
A better climb than the name suggests. It takes the right-hand edge of the pillar, unfortunately with a step in from the right. Start up *Yikes Shaggy* to the base of a long crack. Climb the crack to a sloping ledge where it kinks. From there, traverse out left around the arête to good holds on the face (drilled peg). Follow the arête and make a bold move to reach the breaks. Finish easily up to the lower-off on *Yikes Shaggy*.

51 Yikes Shaggy 20m F6c 6B (27.5.03)
Pleasant climbing, though extremely close to the line of *Poop Scoop*. Climb easily up to the flake

right of *Poop Scoop* and stand up onto a sloping ledge. Step left and climb the groove in the right-hand side of the arête in a fine position to the lower-off.

52 Pixie and the Milford Powerhouse 18m
F6b 5B (29.1.07)
The full-height flake crack, starting as for *Poop Scoop*.

53 Scoobydoobydoo 20m F6b 5B (25.5.03)
Excellent. Climb rightwards up the slab from the foot of *Yikes Shaggy* onto the slightly steeper wall. Climb straight up its middle, pulling over the top bulge to the lower-off.

54 Scooby Snacks 20m F7a 6B (25.5.03)
The striking arête right again. Climb the straightforward lower wall to a hand-ledge. Step up and move left onto the arête proper. Fine open climbing leads to the lower-off.

Marti Hallett on *Up on the Hill* F7a (page 135). STEVE TAYLOR

55 The Heanous Quest 20m F6a+ 7B (5.03)
The groove immediately right of the gully is slightly dusty. Start up a flake crack and then step right into the groove, which is climbed to the lower-off.

56 Hen's Tooth 20m F7b 7B (27.5.03)
A controversial route with a drilled pocket. Tackle the bulge to gain the scoop and use two positive holds and a very long reach to gain easier ground. The bulging rib on the right provides the finish. Harder for the short?

57 Project 16m F7c †
This takes the impressive square-cut arête to a chain lower-off. Start directly beneath the arête and climb the steep wall. Follow the right-hand side of the arête above with difficulty.

133

58 So You Want to Be Happy?
23m E5 6a/b † (17.7.90)
The blank-looking wall and scoop 5 metres right of the square-cut arête. Not recommended, as the hangers are no longer in place. Start at a shattered flake. Carefully pass the friable flake to a good sidepull and cross a chert bulge. Make difficult moves up the blind crack above and go left to a resting-flake. Make more tricky moves up a slight groove to a resting-place. Continue up the left side of the scoop on good holds to a small overhang. Swing right to the shared lower-off, or top out.

59 Up on the Hill 20m F7a 6B (25.5.03)
A super little route taking the wall and blunt rib left of *Hallelujah* onto the face above. This eases considerably before the lower-off is gained. An airy third clip.

60 Hallelujah! 23m F7a 6B (17.7.90)
An excellent outing on good rock. Start 10 metres left of the orange streak, below a triangular roof at 12 metres. Climb slightly rightwards with a long reach to a hand-ledge. Move to the base of a groove and follow it to a short flake. Swing boldly leftwards onto foot-ledges astride a blunt arête. Continue straight up to a big jug and the lower-off.

61 Old Speckled Hen 20m F7a 7B (27.5.03)
Another worthwhile pitch, low in the grade. Climb the wall just to the left of *Stone Cold Sober* to gain a prominent flake hold. Enter the thin crack above with difficulty and follow it, soon easing to the slabby wall. Lower-off shared with *Stone Cold Sober*.

62 Stone Cold Sober 22m F7a+ 7B (18.8.98)
A fine and varied route, taking the wall, groove and bulge to the left of *Stay Golden*, sharing the first two bolts of that route. Climb the steep initial wall on good pockets past a rust streak. Continue

direct into a contorted groove, with some difficult moves to exit. The wall above is somewhat easier!

63 Stay Golden 24m F7b 8B (17.7.90)
High in the grade due to its sustained nature. A fantastic pitch taking a strong line up the bulging buttress, 3 metres left of the orange streak. Climb straight past an undercut pocket to the chert band and pull strenuously rightwards. Layback precariously into a short, left-facing corner and gain a good flake. Continue straight up on small pockets to a small, clean-cut ledge and the lower-off.

64 Sweet Smell of Success 25m F7b 8B (11.5.90)
One of the best climbs of its grade in Dorset, taking a super-sustained, natural line direct up the centre of the orange streaked arête. Not to be missed, with a crux at half height and hard climbing above! Start just left of the streak and take a direct line to follow a groove. Step rightwards onto the streak after the sixth bolt and go up on better holds to a lower-off.

65 Frazzled 24m F7b 7B (9.94)
The right-hand side of the arête, up thin cracks. Almost as good as its northerly neighbours, with a succession of difficult sections and a technical crux.

To the right of the orange-streaked arête is a 40-metre-long recess in the upper wall. *Streaky* starts beneath the left-hand end of this recess.

66 Streaky 24m F7a 7B (5.8.94)
Technical steep slab climbing. Some tense clips! Climb steeply to a ledge at 6 metres. Continue up a grey slab, trending leftwards, to the crux, a series of delicate moves up from a line of horizontal slots. Finish up a slight groove to the lower-off.

67 Das Boot 20m F6c+ 9B (27.5.03)
A good face climb. Climb the short steep wall right of *Streaky* to gain the blackened upper face. Intricate climbing up this leads to a bulge and big jug above. Finish up the scruffy groove on the left.

Meilee Rafe on *Short 'n' Sexy* F6a (page 121). STEVE TAYLOR

135

68 Falling with Style 18m F6b+ 8B   (16.8.98)
Good climbing. Start from the top of the grassy mound. Pull up the steep wall to ledges. Move up and left, crossing a flake crack to the base of a short groove. Climb this on small holds to reach the lower-off.

The routes from *Screw You, Hippy* to *Beefcake, Beefcake* are often dirty due to runoff from the mud-slopes above. Be prepared for some cleaning en-route, especially after rain.

69 Screw You, Hippy 18m F6a 8B   (16.8.98)
Start as for *Falling with Style*. From the ledges, move directly up the orange face into a groove which leads pleasantly to the lower-off.

70 Tanya's Sex Pot 18m F6a+ 7B   (16.8.98)
A somewhat loose route, starting 2 metres right of *Falling with Style*. Pull steeply onto ledges and climb the wall carefully to the lower-off.

71 Gay Dog 18m F6a+ 7B   (16.8.98)
Start part-way down the grassy slope. The climb features some 'go for it' moves from a fragile flowstone undercut. Climb the steep wall carefully past some loose holds. Move up into a flake-line and layback it to a welcome rest. Continue more easily to a shared lower-off.

72 Lay Back and Take It 18m F5+ 7B (16.8.98)
The left-hand side of the huge flake. Start beneath the flake. Climb the loose, muddy rock to the flake and layback it to the lower-off. Unpleasant.

73 Blackwind Fire and Steel 20m F6b+ 7B   (16.8.98)
Worthwhile. The ubiquitous steep start leads to a groove in the centre of the massive flake, which is difficult to exit. Follow the good flake above to the lower-off shared with the following route.

74 Beefcake, Beefcake 20m F6a+ 8B (3.8.98)
The big, butch layback flake on the right-hand side of the wall is reached by steep climbing up some suspect rock.

75 Jungle Drums 23m F6c+ 6B   (29.8.92)
The discontinuous layback flakes on the buttress just south of a ridge of boulders down by the sea (30 metres south of *Sweet Smell of Success*). Challenging and strenuous but feeling bold despite the bolts. Climb a loose cherty wall to a square-cut ledge. Make a hard pull to gain the flake above the right-hand side of the ledge and swing rightwards with difficulty to a second flake. Continue up the wall above to the breaks and the lower-off.

76 Aaron the Aardvark 24m F6c 8B (6.5.95)
Good wall climbing 6 metres right of *Jungle Drums*. Climb a juggy wall, a steep, sustained series of flakes, and a problematical groove to the lower-off.

☆ **77 Bladerunner** 24m F6b+ 9B   (6.5.95)
From above the last route's flakes, climb rightwards to a sharp, hanging arête for a weird, rock-hugging finish!

Guy Dixon on *Scooby Snacks* F7a (page 133). STEVE TAYLOR

To the right of the *Bladerunner* arête is an unclimbed chimney. The black-streaked faces right again are home to a selection of newer climbs. The ground underneath these routes is generally steep and does not provide good stances for belayers, but an access rope and belay bolts are available. The easiest approach leads direct from the boulder beach to the foot of *Downhill Spiral* – the original route on this section of cliff.

78 Fatal Fibre 15m F6c+ 4B (4.5.02)
From a high ledge and bolt belay, climb the left-hand side of the wall by fierce moves to gain good holds. Continue direct up the easier, yellow-coloured wall to a lower-off slightly to the right.

79 Billy Bob's Way 13m F6b+ 5B (4.5.02)
Climbs the prominent blackened streak left of a wide corner line. A difficult start leads to lovely, sustained climbing up the black rib and a shared lower-off.

80 The Man Who Wasn't There 15m F7b 7B (3.5.02)
The rounded arête has many dubious holds. Climb very carefully up the wall to reach the left-hand side of the arête. Continue up this to reach a good chert hold and then swing up and right onto the face. This leads directly to the lower-off.

81 Hate Crime 15m F7a+ 7B (9.5.98)
The left-hand groove of the open, yellow bay. At last — a route which is harder for the tall. Unbalanced, but good climbing nevertheless. Climb up from a low belay bolt to a steepening. Rock over into the groove with difficulty and continue up the pleasant groove to the lower-off.

82 Lefty Hoot 'n' Annie 15m F6c 8B (2.5.98)
The right-hand groove of the open, yellow bay. Fine bridging up the wide groove. Follow the groove with increasing difficulty to a good undercut. From it, make a long hard reach to small calcite holds and finish easily.

83 And the Boat Sails By 18m F7a+ 8B (30.3.02)
The fine open face left of *Downhill Spiral* saves hardest till last. Sustained moves directly up the lower calcite-encrusted wall via overlaps and flakes leads to a good resting-place on a large calcite frieze. Hard moves lead to the main upper break. Move slightly left to gain the lower-off.

84 Downhill Spiral 19m F7b+ 5B (19.4.92)
The original route on this wall is arguably one of the best. Start at a sheet of flowstone-cemented conglomerate to the right of the black streaks. A very run-out pitch. Climb the flowstone to a ledge at 6 metres. Increasingly hard and reachy moves lead up an open white groove to a chert break with a big sidepull on the left. Continue over a bulge and up to a ledge and the lower-off.

85 Everything's Eventual 20m F6c+ 8B (1.4.02)
Start immediately left of the right-hand calcite sheet. A dusty start that improves greatly as height is gained. Move up rightwards to good holds in the calcite, and then pull up left to a flake, which is followed through two bulges to a layback flake. Pumpy.

86 By Mistake 20m F7b+ 7B (2005)
The line branching left from *More Than a Legend* has some thin moves on the headwall.

87 More than a Legend 20m F7b+ 7B (1.4.02)
A desperate technical sequence since the demise of an important hold. Climb straight up the centre of the calcite frieze right of *Everything's Eventual* to a ledge. After a technical and forceful crux a faint crack gives an easier but pumping finish.

88 Under Crimson Skies 19m F7a+ 7B (1.4.02)
Climb the next calcite-encrusted line with care to gain a ledge. Fine technical moves lead onto the upper wall, where further hard moves gain a good edge and difficult moves left to the shared lower-off. Surprisingly sustained.

89 My Figure Head 18m F6c 7B (11.5.02)
Climbs the groove containing the large, horizontal spike. From 8 metres right of the last route, climb over unpleasant ground to a ledge. Hard moves via a finger-crack lead on to a slab and a bulge above a protrusion. Pull over and climb up to the lower-off.

90 The Shipping News 19m F7b 7B (3.6.02)
Follow *My Figure Head* to the ledge, step right and climb the desperate wall by fingery moves to gain better holds. Continue straight up the wall, which gradually eases, past the wide break to the lower-off.

91 Five Easy Pieces 18m F6c+ 6B (3.6.02)
Technical face climbing above the ledge. Climb the wall 10 metres right of *My Figure Head* to a ledge. Make intricate moves up the steep slab to an angled ramp. The headwall above provides steep and juggy climbing.

92 Laid Black 18m F6c+ 6B (11.5.02)
Take a belay 12 metres right of *My Figure Head*. Climb over cleaned ledges to below the obvious black wall. Tricky moves over the bulge lead onto the wall. Climb it leftwards to the lower-off.

The last two routes on this cliff are worth the effort to get there. They should be approached with care along the earth slopes south of *Laid Black*. There is a high bolt belay at the start.

93 Wonderful 16m F7a+ 5B (1.6.02)
Excellent rock situated 30 metres right of *Laid Black*. Climb a thin intricate wall via a faint crack until hard moves lead slightly leftwards to better holds. Continue direct, easier now, to a ledge and awkward finish.

94 Wonder-Bra 16m F6b 6B (1.6.02)
Trend rightwards from the start of *Wonderful* and climb the scooped wall past an obvious ledge to gain the upper breaks. Pull up to reach the lower-off.

Graham Lynch on *Never Lose That Feeling*, belayed by Nick Colton. F6a+ (page 125). STEVE TAYLOR

Ben Stokes warming up on *No Place for Mambas* F6b+ (page 145). STEVE TAYLOR

Wallsend Central

This is the best crag on Portland. Towering, steep lines, heaps of atmosphere and little change from a 60-metre rope mean that time spent on the 30-minute walk-in will always be rewarded.

Wallsend Central is very much a sea-cliff when compared with the northern parts of the cove. The southern limit of this section is 20 metres north of *Sea Saga*, where progress at high tide can be made only by traversing the wall. To the north is *McKenna's Cleft*, the second of two north-facing corners. This marks the start of a bulging wall packed with high-quality, hard sport routes (F7a to F7b+). At the end of this wall the rock platform gives way to boulders near the south-facing chimney of *The Gash*, with its vegetated ledge at half height. On its left side is *Wallsend Wall* and other wall climbs at more amenable grades (F6a+ to F6c+).

Thirty metres from *The Gash* the huge flakes of *Laceration* are an obvious feature, though only when viewed from the north. The ledge jutting from the cliff at a height of 3 metres some 60 metres further on marks the super-steep *Troll Team Special* buttress. Forty metres to the north, past a shallow bay climbed by *ZumZeaux*, an earth cone rises to an unclimbed chimney. Above the next earth mound are two wide chimneys/gullies. The left-hand one is choked with mud and has two large jammed boulders: Double Boulder Gully provides a useful landmark. The buttress to its left is climbed by *The Bigger Piece*.

The approach is described on page 119.

The routes from *Halfway to Heaven* to *Walking on Sunshine* are subject to a variable nesting-season restriction (see page 11).

Marti Hallett in the perfect finishing groove of *The Watchman* F6b (page 156).
STEVE TAYLOR

1 Slice of Life 35m E2 † (1.5.81)
A good, varied route. This climbs the buttress left of Double Boulder Gully, which is one of the most obvious features along this stretch of cliff. The climb finishes up a prominent, thin crack on the left side of the buttress. Start just left of the arête of the buttress.
1 21m 5a. Move up onto the wall and climb diagonally right to the arête. Follow this to a horizontal weakness, traverse left, and move up to belay below the crack.
2 14m 5b. Use finger-jams in the crack until it becomes choked. Continue on, using the right arête of the groove to layback up to better holds and a ledge. Move up leftwards and follow cracks to a clean exit. Belay immediately.

2 The Bigger Piece 30m F7b 12B (13.8.89)
Safe and technical climbing in superior situations. Start above the arête of the buttress. Take the arête directly and with little difficulty for 15 metres. Make a short traverse left to a horizontal crack. From here, pull straight up the chert bands onto white rock and a good rest on the left-hand side of the rib. Make hard moves up and right across the rib (desperate clip) to some short flake cracks and then climb straight up the front of the arête to a deep break. Pull up the short wall to the lower-off.

3 No Place for Mambas 29m F6b+ 12B (2.5.92)
Well-bolted fine face-climbing. Start below a corner. Climb up the corner then slightly rightwards to a ledge. Step left and move up and left to the bulge below the grey face. Surmount the bulge and continue direct on pockets to a small foot-ledge. Move up a shallow groove to deep horizontal breaks and climb to the shared lower-off.

4 Opposites Attract 29m F6c 12B (2.5.92)
Superb technical pocket pulling on the refined side of vertical. Climb *No Place for Mambas* to the ledge at 13 metres. Take a groove on the right to a bulge and pull over onto the grey face. Follow a thin crack, step left, and go up the pocketed face using a small groove on the left to deep horizontal breaks. Step right and finish up a thin crack to the square-cut top of the buttress.

5 Mick Lovatt Stole My Trousers 29m F6b+ 13B (2.5.92)
Start as for *No Place for Mambas* and follow it to the ledge at 13 metres. Swing right to the base of the curving flake crack and follow this to a thin finish and the lower-off.

The following eight routes are all approached by scrambling up to a grassy terrace from underneath Double Boulder Gully, using an *in-situ* rope.

6 Cool to Be Uncool 15m F7b+ 3B (2.5.92)
The left-hand arête of Double Boulder Gully; perfect moves otherwise found only on grit arêtes, but with a serious section below the first bolt. Scramble up the gully and move to ledges on the left at the foot of the arête. Climb this direct, with an intricate crux, to finish at the jammed boulder. **No lower-off.**

7 Coconut Milk 24m F7a+ 6B (16.7.89)
Superb though rather short-lived face-climbing up the ultra-white face. Start just left of the arête below a threaded pancake of flowstone. Climb up to the ledges below the white face. Follow the thin crack with increasing difficulty to a break. Swing right and, from the next break above, step right to a ledge and short corner. Climb the corner to a good ledge and the lower-off.

8 On a Desert Island Beach 24m F7b 6B (16.7.89)
The blunt, white arête on the right side of the wall is a stunning climb. From the pancake of flowstone, climb a short flake and rib to ledges below the white face. From below the thin cracks, traverse right onto the arête. Sustained climbing up the arête leads to a ledge and the lower-off.

9 Vin Chaud 22m F7a 6B (16.6.03)
The flake-line just to the right of the arête gives fine, sustained climbing. Start as for *Accordions...* At the second bolt, step left from the ledge to climb the right-facing flake.

10 Accordions Go Crazy 22m F6b+ 6B (15.7.89)
The open central groove is high in the grade. Climb easily up left to a projecting ledge. Make a long stretch to reach the flake-line, which thins out, forcing some difficult moves to the break above. Reach up to the next break and stretch to the lower-off.

11 Basra Blues Band 22m F6c 6B (14.6.03)
The groove and slab just right of *Accordions...* Start up a dirty flake. Step right and follow an open groove through the roof above to the lower-off.

12 Laughing Peter 24m F7b 5B (15.7.89)
This takes the thin cracks in the steep, brownish face left of the right-hand gully. Very strenuous and sustained, though low in the grade. Gain a flat ledge at 3 metres, below an overhung, open groove. Bridge up the groove and pull straight over the bulge. Climb direct, with assistance from holds in the thin crack on the right, to the horizontal cracks. Finish up a crack and a prow to the lower-off.

13 Sans Frontiers 24m F6b+ 5B (23.6.03)
Climb the fine crack and arête, mostly on the left. One hard move at mid-height, followed by sustained climbing to a reachy finish.

To the right of the arête is an unclimbed gully, bounded on its right by a clean, white wall containing several fine routes.

14 Charlton Mackeral, the World's Strongest Fish 20m F6c 6B (10.6.06)
Not shown on topo. The left-facing flake just right of the gully. Climb the flake to a hard reach to the first break. From here a hard pull leads to the next break and the finish.

⭐ **15 The Parkhurst Dozen** 24m F6c+ 6B (20.6.03)
The stepped, sustained, 20-metre crack, 5 metres right of the gully. Climb boldly to a ledge at 4 metres. Move left into the crack and climb it all the way.

⭐⭐⭐ **16 Sang Chaud** 24m F7a+ 6B (14.6.03)
The flake-line in the centre of the white wall has excellent climbing from start to finish and is hard for the grade. Follow the blind flakes to the flowstone headwall.

⭐ **17 Son of Mustang Ford** 24m F7a 6B (26.4.92)
Move up steeply to the first bolt on *Mr Natural* before climbing direct up a slight juggy groove to two ledges. Make thin moves up the white wall to reach the base of a tongue of flowstone. Start off up the flowstone using sidepulls on the left and climb tufa pipes to the lower-off.

⭐⭐ **18 Mr Natural** 24m F7b+ 8B (19.4.92)
The thin crack in the white sheet 25 metres south of the right-hand gully is high in its grade. Climb steeply to gain better holds, and at the second bolt swing right 2 metres. Continue up to a ledge at the base of a narrow crack. Follow the crack, make a thin crank, and grasp the breaks. Climb a calcite curtain to the lower-off.

⭐ **19 Catatonic** 26m F6b+ 7B (19.4.92)
Sixty-metre rope and a steady head required. Delicate rather than strenuous, this run-out route climbs the slabby face right of *Mr Natural* and is a touch bold to start. Gain easily a ledge at 5 metres. Climb slightly left on good holds to a semi rest beneath

the white upper slab. Balance up to a scoop and then gain the breaks, where a short corner leads to the lower-off.

20 Random Texter 24m F6b+ 8B   (6.06)
A companion route to *Catatonic,* though somewhat less bold. Start 3 metres right of *Catatonic* and take a line more or less direct to the shared lower-off.

21 Gravity Epiphany 23m F6c+ 8B   (23.09.06)
The steep groove in the arête left of the wide, snaking crack. Move right from the second bolt of *Random Texter.* May contain some loose rock.

22 Family S 35m VS †   (9.8.76)
This south-facing snaking crack 40 metres south of Double Boulder Gully is a prominent feature.
1 15m. Unprotected. Gain the chimney and follow it to a block belay in a more clean-cut section.
2 17m. Continue up the chimney to the top. Belay in the poor rock band, or carry on up the grass to easier ground.

On the south-facing buttress between the chimney of *Family S* and an unclimbed chimney above an earth cone are two routes:

23 Moan, Moan, Moan 21m F7b+ 7B   (20.4.92)
The elegant slim groove in the blunt, undercut arête with a high crux. From the foot of a flake, step left and climb the wall before moving right to the shattered chert band. Cross the roof (hard for the tall) and move into to the base of the groove on the arête - follow this (sustained) to the lower-off.

24 Injury Encyclopedia 18m F7b 5B   (25.4.92)
A forceful pitch of escalating difficulty up the solid white wall left of the unclimbed chimney. At the top of the grade, with one peg as well as the bolts. Climb a fairly easy groove to the foot of the white wall. Pull onto it with a long reach. Proceed directly up the centre of the wall to horizontal breaks and a succession of jugs that leads to the lower-off.

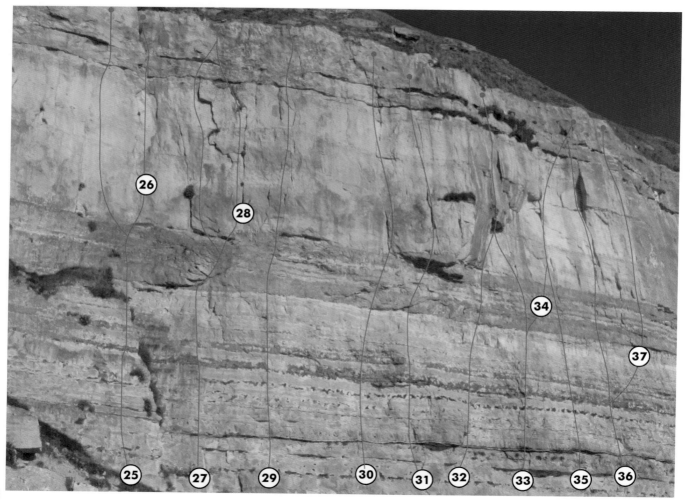

25 Will 16m F7b 7B (4.4.06)
Climb the wall left of the scruffy flake to a ledge. Step left and follow the elegant, technical groove above.

26 Michèle 16m F6a+ 7B (4.4.06)
The *Consommé* of Wallsend? Climb *Will* to the ledge (extend the third clip). The hanging groove and flake crack above give some excellent climbing.

The next two routes share a common start. Of obvious concern are the dangerous hanging flakes they climb above the half-height ledge. These flakes may be removed, hopefully as part of a pre-planned manoeuvre.

27 Shape of Tomorrow 16m F6c 7B (4.4.06)
Start a metre right of the scruffy flake. Climb a steep wall to the halfway ledge, move left and head for the scary flakes (shared lower-off).

28 River of Dreams 16m F7a 7B (13.4.06)
The obvious crack left of *Spinal Tap*, with a short sharp crux. Start as for *Shape of Tomorrow* with hard moves to gain the right side of the scary flakes.

29 Cloud Atlas 24m F7b+ 9B (7.06)
The steep wall and blind flake is powerful in its first half then technical in its upper reaches.

30 Spinal Tap 26m F7b+ 8B (26.4.92)
The next wall climb is not a particularly pleasant proposition, being pumpy all the way and quite bold high up. Start on a ledge just right of the earth pile. From a jug, make hard moves straight up to good holds at 10 metres. Stretch to reach the left side of a bulge and run it out steeply up a series of flakes to a ledge. Gain the breaks and the lower-off.

31 Million Watt Marshalls 26m E5 6b (F7b) 10B (26.4.92)
A sustained and strenuous effort which takes in a wall, a roof, and a finger-crack. Start 8 metres right of *Spinal Tap*. Ageing bolts. Climb the crack-line to steep moves through the left side of a bulge. Fingery climbing leads to good slots beneath the roof. Make a long reach and pull around the lip. Follow a crack with increasing difficulty to the breaks. Lower-off above.

32 Ariane V 23m F7b 10B (9.5.96)
Start directly below the roof of *Million Watt Marshalls* and climb the slight groove to the base of a black bulging groove. Move up and use jugs on the lip of the roof before strenuously laybacking to the breaks and lower-off.

33 Disintegration 24m F7b+ 9B (25.9.89)
No respite but reasonably protected. Superseded by its adjacent routes. Follow *ZumZeaux* to just after the fourth bolt (at mid height). Trend leftwards into *Ariane V* beneath the roof and finish as for that route.

34 ZumZeaux 24m F7b+ 10B † (16.7.89)
Has a peg as well as the bolts. A tremendous route with a strenuous, bulging lower section coupled with a dynamic and committing finish. A no-hands rest renders this pitch low in its grade. Start on the left-hand side of a shallow bay. Climb a corner and power up through the bulges to a jug. Hard moves above lead to a break and a traverse right to a rest at the base of a long, thin crack. Climb the crack to below a fin arête and launch up to reach good holds above. Move up, and rightwards across the headwall to the shared lower-off.

35 Magnetic Pull 24m F7c+ 11B (14.9.96)
A direct and difficult start to *Zum Zeaux*, starting immediately to its right. High in the grade and taking an uncompromising line. Power up the unrelentingly steep wall to half height and finish as for *Zum Zeaux*.

36 Realm of Chaos 24m F7b+ 12B (24.9.89)
One of the best sport routes in Dorset, this sustained climb tackles the vague shallow groove above the right side of the shallow bay midway between the earth cone and the jutting ledge. Climb on the right of a large flake to jugs. Attack the leaning scoop on positive holds to reach jugs at half height. Follow the slight, left-facing corner above until it overhangs. Layback to the breaks and continue up to the lower-off.

37 Hombre Solaire 24m F7c 10B (6.9.96)
The original bolted direct start was abandoned. This fine route now starts as for *Realm of Chaos*. From the fourth bolt, swing right for 4 metres, climb the steep wall to a ledge, and follow the thin crack above.

38 Face the Truth 25m E6 6c (F7c) † (1.9.89)

Initially very steep, it then relents to climb a right-facing groove. Some serious clips remove this from the sport-climb category. Start 3 metres right of *Realm of Chaos*. Climb to a vague ledge and pull up to a good hold and a drilled peg. Boulder out the next 6 metres past two more drilled pegs with several dynos. Continue on better pockets to jugs and large runners at half height. Climb up the pocketed groove and then go right to the lower-off of *A Shadow on Mankind*.

39 A Shadow on Mankind 25m E5 6b (F7b+) (27.3.90)

A direct line starting below the left-hand end of the jutting ledge. Good moves, but run out in places and high in the grade. Climb to the left-hand end of the ledge at 6 metres, beneath a bulging rib (drilled peg). A strenuous crux past three drilled pegs leads to better holds. Continue up a blind crack on the left (peg) to jugs at half height. Swing rightwards to a flake and good wires, and then go back leftwards to a slight groove (peg). Layback onto a good flake and climb twin cracks to the break. Continue on deep pockets to the lower-off.

40 Saskatchewan Uranium Miner 24m F7c 10B (23.9.90)

A first-rate pitch with an especially good upper half. Climb to the ledge and up the bulging rib as for *A Shadow on Mankind*. Move right and continue with difficulty up the groove and white wall to good ledges at the break. Enter the slim groove and climb it directly, without respite, to the upper breaks. Continue more easily to the lower-off beneath the grass slope.

41 Troll Team Special 25m F7b 11B (13.7.89)

A fine pumpout, unrelentingly strenuous, with good positions and following a strong line. Start at the flake above and just left of the widest part of the jutting ledge. Surge up the flake to an undercut before powerful layaway moves gain a hand-ledge. Make an awkward mantel to a jug on the left. Step right, go over juggy bulges to a crack-system, and continue to a good resting-ledge. Follow the twin cracks by wild moves straight up to the top breaks and the lower-off.

42 The Pickford Files 25m F7b+ 10B (9.99)
Break left at 6 metres from *Breakbeat* and climb direct through bulging rock past a very dangerous flake to a half-height shake out. Pull through onto the final, blank headwall and climb it on superb micro pockets with difficulty to the top. Lower off on the left as for *Troll Team Special*. If the flake can be stabilised it would deserve two stars. Large amounts of cement would work!

43 Breakbeat 25m F7b+ 10B (19.8.90)
A highly sustained, well-protected route with a particularly sensational upper groove. Start from the right-hand end of the jutting ledge. Trend diagonally rightwards past a flake to enter a shallow scoop. Pull around the right-hand side of the roof above – the crux. Climb via a thin crack to the break. From the projecting chert ledge above, use a pocket to start an intricate sequence across the bulge and so reach a resting-ledge in the main open groove. Attack the grooved roof and continue quickly to the breaks and the lower-off.

44 The Mask 25m F7b 10B (30.4.90)
Very steep climbing through the tiered bulges 3 metres right of the widest part of the jutting ledge. Climb easily via a vague, shattered flake and step left at 18 metres to a jug. Move over a bulge into a scoop and stretch past the first roof to a good pocket. Violent undercutting up and right gains a good short crack. Reach a sensational rail over the next roof and stand on it with difficulty. A thin crack in the headwall leads to the breaks and the lower-off.

45 Trent Reznor 25m F7b 9B (14.10.95)
An exposed alternative finish to *The Mask*. From the fifth bolt on *The Mask* move up steeply rightwards and pull around the blunt arête rightwards to finish up a short groove.

151

46 Kraken 30m HVS † (4.8.75)
Sustained climbing. Ten metres south of the jutting ledge and 50 metres north of *Lacerations* is a tilted boulder on its own raised platform. Start there.
1 15m. Climb the rightward-slanting line of weakness to a poor stance below and right of a vertical groove with a crack at its back.
2 15m. Follow the groove and move around to the right at the top. Belay well back on a stake and an earth bollard.

47 Bevis 25m F6b 9B (19.06.04)
The wall and soaring cracks right of *Trent Reznor* provide relatively easy access to spectacular territory. Start up a short triangular groove. Climb up to a chert ledge and move left into a bottomless groove. Follow the clean crack leftwards in exposed positions to the lower-off.

48 Moonfleet 25m F6b 8B (19.06.04)
Interesting and sustained. Follow *Bevis* to the chert ledge. Climb past a projecting block and follow the flake above to a short final wall and the lower-off.

49 Divine Madness 30m E1 5a/b † (1.5.81)
Start 15 metres south of *Kraken*, setting off from the left end of a grass terrace 6 metres up. Very enjoyable. Move left onto the wall and climb flakes before bearing left to ledges and a junction with *Kraken*. Follow *Kraken* pitch 2 to the top.

Gavin Symonds contemplating the crux of *Vin Chaud* F7a (page 145). STEVE TAYLOR

The unclimbed ramp and block-filled chimney to the south looks like a dice with death. There are three routes starting from the base of the ramp, sharing their first bolt in the initial wall.

50 Gossip and Drool 20m F7b 7B   (13.8.89)
The black-streaked groove in the upper wall gives a strenuous and sustained pitch with plenty of variety and excitement. Climb to a vegetated ledge. From the left-hand end of the ledge, climb up easily and mantel boldly into the base of the groove; follow this until it closes. Pull up the slanting crack, make a rib-wrenching span up right to a good slot, and gain jugs above by the lower-off.

⭐ **51 Heatstroke Groove** 20m F7a 7B   (7.9.89)
The obvious, white groove in the upper wall just right of the previous route. From the vegetated ledge, climb up to jugs at the base of the groove. Make a difficult move to another jug, and continue by fine bridging. Pull into the right-hand section of the groove for a no-hands rest; then teeter upwards to beckoning jugs and the horizontal cracks. Use a big hole up right to make a long reach to better finishing holds and the lower-off.

⭐ **52 Summer Babe** 20m F7b+ 7B   (2.5.92)
Very technical climbing up the pillar just right again. From the vegetated ledge, trend right to beneath a slight groove below bulges. Make a desperate move to a jug and contorted reaches to incut holds. Carry on straight up the buttress to a lower-off above the breaks.

Right of *Summer Babe* is a series of broken ramps, bounded by a buttress right again. The original route of this buttress, *Lacerations*, follows a series of cracks in the front face.

53 Dark Play 22m F6b 9B †   (4.10.03)
The wall, prominent ledge, and hanging groove left of *Lacerations*. Climb the loose wall to the prominent ledge at 11 metres. From this ledge, step left and follow the clean groove past the breaks to the lower-off.

54 Eternal Peace 22m F6c 9B † (4.10.03)
Climb *Dark Play* to the prominent ledge. Pull onto the hanging arête and follow this, with some difficulty, to a lower-off beneath the faultline.

55 Lacerations 40m VS † (8.70)
Some 150 metres south of Double Boulder Gully is a huge flake up against the face, which is only visible from the north. There is a lot of loose rock about but the holds are mostly firm. Pegs required.
1 16m. Follow cracks to the half-way ledges, and belay with a thread at the bottom of the continuation crack.
2 24m. Climb the crack and the big flake to its top. Gain the ledge up and to the left (steep and awkward) before exiting to the right. Continue a long way up the earth and grass until a reasonable ledge is reached on the left. Place pegs to belay.

56 The Bog Man 22m F6b+ 7B (17.7.03)
Start on a raised ledge, 4 metres right of *Lacerations*. Climb the loose wall, overlap and flake crack left of the high arête, with a long, scary reach to make the lower-off.

57 Garstang 22m F6c+ 8B (5.7.03)
Starts immediately right of *The Bog Man*, 2 metres left of the ramp of *Ferocity*. Feels bold most of the way. Climb the loose wall, slight groove, and overlap on the right-hand side of the buttress. Another long, scary reach to finish.

Five metres south of the towering buttress a wall is split by an earthy ramp leading to a clean cleft high up – this is *Ferocity*.

58 Bolder Crack 40m HVS † (29.8.74)
Above the start of *Ferocity* is *Bolder Crack*, a vertical crack-line guarded by a large block half-way up. Pegs required.
1 20m. From the earth ramp, move up and left onto the wall and climb to a belay ledge.
2 20m. Follow the crack, past an old wedge, to the block and gain a ledge above and to the right. Continue slightly left up the headwall. Place pegs to belay in the rock band well above.

155

☆ 59 **Shibumi** 22m F7a+ 8B † (6.7.04)
Pleasant, technical climbing. Scramble up onto the grassy ledge and climb the wall, big overlap, and faint groove left of *Slavestate*.

★ 60 **Slavestate** 21m F7b+ 7B (2.5.92)
The leaning white wall above the earthy ramp is sustained and pumpy. The third bolt is a grip-clip, and a *Rock 6* provides some peace of mind after the fourth. From the earthy ramp, climb steeply on buckets to the centre of the white face. Follow the vague crackline past a big undercut on the left. Some unlikely but good holds are then used to reach the breaks and the lower-off.

61 **Ferocity** 40m VS † (8.70)
A strenuous route, high in its grade and poorly protected. Pegs required.
1 20m. Follow the earth ramp up to the rock on the right and belay at the base of the chimney.
2 20m. Climb the chimney to a classic earth-axe exit. Place pegs to belay in blocks 6 metres higher up.

★ 62 **Immaculata** 26m F6c 8B (31.3.03)
The wall and fine groove left of *The Watchman*. Start 6 metres right of *Ferocity*. Climb the wall, taking a direct line. Step right into the clean-cut groove and follow this to the faultline. Summon some commitment and pull over the roof to finish with a grip-clip at the lower-off.

★ 63 **The Watchman** 26m F6b 10B (31.12.89)
An excellent route, picking the easiest line through some impressive territory. Ten metres right of the start of *Ferocity* is a short right-facing corner with a short, scooped slab to its left. Climb the technical scoop (crux) and the bulging wall to a mid-height ledge. Follow twin corners and make a tricky move to gain the horizontal breaks. Finish up the short scoop above to the lower-off.

⭐ **64 Peace in the Nineties** 26m F6c 9B   (31.12.89)
A fine pitch on good rock, easier in its top half. Start 2 metres right of
The Watchman, up the short right-facing corner. The original start,
across the roof 2 metres to the right, was much more difficult than the
rest of the route. Pull over the roof at 3 metres and trend right to the
flake above. Climb straight up to a rest by a hollow flake (bold) at half
height. Follow the groove/crack, finishing straight up to the lower-off.

⭐ **65 The Enchanted Path** 25m F6c 11B   (13.7.89)
Start just left of a sentry box. A hard start for the short (or weak). Climb
up and pull around the roof via a jutting ledge. Continue up on good
holds to the left-hand of the two corners above. Finish as for *Wallsend
Wall* by turning the bulge above on its left and gaining a ledge on the
left. Finish steeply up the headwall to the lower-off.

⭐ **66 Best Fingers Forward** 25m F6c+ 9B   (11.7.89)
⭐ Exhilarating climbing tackling the wall right of *The Enchanted Path*,
followed by a finger-crack on the white headwall. Climb up the right
wall of the sentry-box, over a bulge, and up an unlikely bulging rib to
juggy ground. Follow the steep crack (difficult all the way) to the top.

⭐ **67 Blue Faced Booby** 25m F6c 8B   (13.8.89)
⭐ The impressive square-cut arête provides engrossing climbing in its
steep upper half. Start 2 metres left of the large arête. Climb up, pull
over the roof with difficulty, and move up easily, but with spaced bolts,
to a short, steep wall. Pull up right across the wall to a big ledge below
the upper half of the arête. Summon up the courage to climb the
committing square-cut edge, using good pockets around the other side,
to a juggy ledge. Climb a short, pocketed crack to breaks. Finish
straight up the arête to the lower-off.

68 Wallsend Wall 32m E1 † (23.8.72)
The original route on this wall; a wandering line, but steep and exposed nonetheless. The first half can be climbed with a mix of trad and bolts; the second half is fully bolted.
1 20m. Climb the corner-crack to the roof and traverse left to gain the wall proper. Continue up, across leftwards, and up again, taking the most reasonable line to reach a stance and peg belay at the foot of the first corner on the left.
2 12m. Traverse left into the next corner. Climb steeply up to the bulge and step left around the corner to gain a ledge on the left. Finish steeply up the headwall to a clean-cut ledge. Lower-off above.

69 The Gash 35m VS † (8.69)
This is the unmistakable south-facing chimney in the centre of Wallsend Central. Pegs required.
1 13m. Follow the chimney/flake to the vegetated ledge. Place pegs to belay inside the chimney.
2 13m. Climb the chimney, passing on the right of a large flake to reach a ledge. Belay over to the left.
3 9m. The steep grass soon gives way, only figuratively one hopes, to an earthy bay on the right.

The following stunning climbs are situated on the smooth, impending wall between *The Gash* and *McKenna's Cleft*, the north-facing corner 25 metres south of *The Gash*. This wall is one of the greatest sectors of unbroken face in Dorset, offering a selection of routes of most grades, though particularly F7a to F7b+. Many are classics of the area – make sure you do at least one of them.

★ **70 Teacakes Calling** 25m F7a 10B (21.5.96)
A good route with a boulder-problem crux. Start just right of *The Gash*. Climb the groove, with a hard move at 5 metres, to fine steep climbing up the crack above.

★★ **71 The Jewel of the Isle** 25m F6c 10B (25.6.95)
The slight rib and crack starting 2 metres right of *Teacakes Calling*. Pull up to the rib and make thin moves slightly rightwards past chert crimps. Pull into the crack, which provides excellent climbing to the lower-off.

72 Stalker's Zone 25m F6b 10B (30.4.89)
Fine wall climbing which takes the thin crack in the upper wall 6 metres right of *The Gash*. You will struggle to find a better sport route at this grade in the UK. The first bolt is missing (the eagle-eyed will spot it in the boulders below). Climb straight up the lower wall on positive holds to gain the pocketed crack, which is followed to a ledge. Step right, and continue up a good flake to the lower-off.

73 Trad Free World 23m F6a+ 8B (7.11.92)
Start on the left-hand end of a perched ledge. A cracking good route offering sustained climbing. Climb a slight rib and the wall above to a thin crack. Follow this to the breaks. Two pulls up the flake above, and the lower-off is within grasp.

74 Genuflection 23m F7b 9B (11.5.96)
A more recent addition, and a quality one at that. Climb the groove of *Reverence* for 5 metres, before stepping left to launch up the pristine white wall and juggy bulges to the lower-off.

75 Reverence 23m F7a+ 9B (5.7.89)
Start from the left-hand end of the huge block. On excellent rock but often damp on the crux section, this route climbs the shallow bay and the groove above. Climb the shallow bay to a big jug at 15 metres. Continue, using a hold on the right to reach better holds. Follow the hanging corner with difficulty and so gain the breaks above the capping roof. Continue straight up to the lower-off.

76 Outside the Gate 23m F7b 8B (5.7.89)
Start at the right-hand end of the huge block for a continuously steep pitch up the central prow. Protection includes two poor drilled pegs. Boulder up to a jug and climb to a flake. Continue up past a good slot to jugs at mid height. From the last of these, make technical moves to a shallow scoop.

Continue to a hands-off rest beneath the roof and superb pockets on its lip. Use a thin flake with difficulty to reach the breaks and finish more easily.

77 Halfway to Heaven 23m F7b 7B (29.4.89)
★★★ R
A magnificent outing. Start just right of the huge block, beneath a hole at 4 metres. Three poor drilled pegs. Make a difficult move to a flat hold and continue up to a large ledge at mid height. Move up a hollow flake and span leftwards to a jug at the base of a flake/groove. Layback steeply to deep pockets; trickier moves then lead to the breaks. Continue straight up with difficulty to the lower-off.

> The routes from *Halfway to Heaven* to *Walking on Sunshine* are subject to a variable seasonal restriction (page 11). Do not climb on them from 1st Mar to 31st July inclusive

Gav Symonds on **River of Dreams** *F7a (page 149).* STEVE TAYLOR

★★★ **78 Organic Snail Farming** 21m F7b 12B
(29.4.89)
R Fantastic climbing above half height. Start from a raised ledge at 2 metres positioned 3 metres right of *Halfway to Heaven*. Climb layback flakes to big chert holds. Reach up right and continue to the half-height ledge. Above is a slim groove topped by a flake crack; gain the groove from the right and follow it to the break. Continue up the sharp flake to a ledge on the right. A small scoop leads to the lower-off.

★★ **79 Wave Graffiti** 22m F7b+ 10B
(27.7.89/24.9.89)
R Brilliant climbing on the curling upper sheet, starting just left of a leftward-slanting ramp. Climb up to the easy but friable ramp. Follow this to the chert band and a rest on the left. Pull over the roof to a rail, and climb to a sloper. Rock up rightwards to a jug before undercutting the bulge and making a monstrous reach to catch a finger-rail. Carry on slightly leftwards to the shared lower-off.

★ **80 Hawaiian Pipeline** 22m F7a+ 9B (13.7.89)
R Follow *Wave Graffiti* to the chert band at half height and a rest on the left. Step back right and follow the long, blank groove with increasing difficulty to the breaks. Trend rightwards to the lower-off.

★★★ **81 Running Down a Dream** 23m F7b 8B
(1.9.89)
R An ultra-sustained line which gives tremendous climbing throughout when dry in summer. Starting at the leftward-slanting ramp, this aims for the streaked groove. Move up rightwards from the base of the slanting ramp to a big flake hold. Continue with difficulty to jugs leading over a bulge to a no-hands rest (just!) beneath the groove. Climb the groove to a pocketed break. Press on blindly to the twin horizontal cracks and climb a flake to the shared lower-off.

82 My Two Left Feet 23m F7c+ 11B (19.6.98)
Start just left of the base of the ramp which leads to the chimney. Extremely sustained all the way. Crank up the wall on small holds, staying 3 metres right of *Running Down A Dream*, to reach a rib at half-height. Follow the tenuous and sustained rib and just when completely pumped, begin the bouldery crux straight up the final wall. Step left to finish up *Running Down a Dream*.

83 Bob's Gold Run 23m F7a+ 5B (1.9.89)
A good climb which takes the shallow, leaning groove just left of *McKenna's Cleft*. Spoilt slightly by the pegs on the difficult moves. Follow *McKenna's Cleft* for 7 metres and then swing leftwards to gain the groove. Climb this on positive holds to exciting moves up a 'tips' flake just to the left, which leads to the break and lower-off.

84 McKenna's Cleft 37m VS † (4.70)
This is the chimney in the large north-facing corner 25 metres south of *The Gash*.
1 23m. Climb the chossy ramp to the chimney. Go inside and continue more easily to a belay ledge higher up at the back.
2 14m. Climb up to the grass on the left and belay in an earthy bay 10 metres to the left.

Steve Taylor on the stunning *Stalker's Zone* F6b (page 159). BARRY CLARKE

The section of cliff from *McKenna's Cleft* to Wallsend South is impassable in rough seas, and requires a paddle at high tide in calm seas.

R **85 Fleshworld** 26m F7b+ 12B   (8.8.91)
Some good climbing spoilt by sandy holds and an easy top section. Start 10 metres right of *McKenna's Cleft*. Climb up a short, steep corner-crack and then rightwards to the left edge of the strip roof at 8 metres. Pull over the roof on the right and step back left to a jug. Fingery moves up the leaning wall lead to a large, half-height ledge. Trend slightly right on water-worn flakes before going up past a deep hole to the lower-off.

86 Colors 25m F7b+ 11B   (8.11.88)
A blinding route taking a dominating line heading for the central crack in the headwall. Very sustained climbing, but low in the grade. The quality of the rock in the top half could be straight from the Verdon. Climb past two wide horizontal cracks to the strip roof. Move around to better holds and swing right. Continue on small pockets to the juggy break and follow a thin crack on the white headwall to a thin break. Deep pockets lead to the shared lower-off.

87 Olympus Mons 25m F7b 11B   (6.7.03)
A magnificent sustained effort with a sting in the tail, which just merits the grade. Climb the wide crack and wall right of *Colors* to the overlap. Pull through and make a fingery move to gain good jugs and a chert band. Continue up the shallow groove and crack until a final bulge and short wall give a splendid finale.

R **88 The White Unconquerable** 25m F6b+ 12B (1.10.95)
The unpleasant corner and muddy groove; only the last 5 metres are worth climbing – not recommended. Start at the foot of the corner. Climb up the corner and step right into a muddy groove. Climb this carefully to the base of a thin finger-crack. Clean the grime off your boots and launch up the crack to the lower-off.

89 Gedge 26m F6b+ 9B (8.8.91)

The slight groove which starts 3 metres left of *The Worm*. Climb into a sentry box at 5 metres and pull around the roof to jugs. Follow the vague groove direct to large flakes. The flake-line leads up leftwards to a ledge and the lower-off.

90 Black'll do Nicely 26m F7a+ 10B † (10.5.03)

A magnificent sustained pitch up the fine wall to the right of *Gedge*. Climb the initial bulges on jugs and meander up to a half-height ledge. The fine thin crack/groove above provides sustained moves to a chert lump and a technical finish.

91 The Worm 40m VS † (5.8.72)

Twenty metres south of *McKenna's Cleft* is a crack/chimney in a north-facing corner. 'An absorbing line at a reasonable standard' said the first (and only known) ascensionist. Pegs required.
1 18m. Climb the crack, keeping outside to avoid the rubble. Belay at the bottom of the chimney.
2 18m. Dodge the overhanging section by climbing inside the chimney and coming out only when forced to. Continue up and place pegs to belay on the right.
3 10m. Go over the broken rock band and continue to where the angle eases.

92 The Empire State Arête 25m F6b 10B (27.9.94)

The right arête of *The Worm* is an impressive, towering line with fine climbing in the upper half. Climb up past two short vertical cracks and pull rightwards around the arête onto its right-hand side. Continue up on cherty rock, and trend rightwards on jugs to the base of an open groove. Climb the groove past a small ledge and then the left rib to the horizontal breaks. Lower-off above.

Rob Lamey on *Beautiful South* F7c (page 164). ANDY LONG

163

The impressive wall to the right contains three routes, all starting from the stack of large blocks. It is possible to belay at the top of the stack (belay bolt in place), but a 50-metre rope is sufficient to lower off if belaying from the ground.

93 Dogtown Skate Team 24m F7a+ 8B † (2002)
The left-hand line from the blocks. Move delicately leftwards across the wall and pull over a small overlap. Follow the slab above to a larger overlap. Difficult moves then lead up the headwall to a high lower-off.

94 Rush 24m F7b+ 7B † (2002)
Start straight up from the blocks. At the third bolt, move left to follow the crack and flake leading leftwards to the lower-off.

95 Beautiful South 24m F7c 7B (2002)
Start as for *Rush*, but continue direct to the square roof above. Pull over the roof and climb the difficult headwall.

Ammonite's Tooth was a prominent feature south of *The Worm*, but it has been extracted; a pile of boulders is all that remains. To the right of the rockfall area, immediately right of a shallow left-facing corner, is a bulging wall, which has a light covering of flowstone.

96 Tarquil's Trollies 17m F6c 5B (2.5.98)
The left-hand side of the flowstone wall. Climb the flowstone wall, keeping 3 metres right of the arête, to a lower-off just below the grassy ledge.

97 Flipper's Revenge 17m F7b 5B (29.3.02)
A route with a desperate crux, though it may only be F7a+ for the tall. The lower-off is just below the grassy ledge.

98 Walking on Sunshine 17m F7a 6B   (5.8.94)

The first bolt is missing, so use a long extender on the first bolt of the neighbouring route. The direct line up the right-hand side of the flowstone is sustained but has positive holds. Cross a strip roof at 3 metres and continue up steep rock to the lower-off.

Twenty metres further south is a short section where a hand-traverse is necessary at high water (hardest at its southern end).

Wallsend South

The earth and grass slopes beneath the descent gully stretch northwards for 30 metres to where the cliff attains its full height. This, the southernmost buttress in Wallsend South is split in two by the wide chimney of *Halfway House*. The far side of the buttress is defined by a large, low-level, diagonal roof, which provides some exposure for *Stylus*. The next wall is initially of poor quality but is smoother and cleaner at its northern end, where *The Bad Seeds* have taken route. Thirty metres further north is the chimney of *Sea Saga*, while the easier-angled but vegetated walls 20 metres further on again are passed at high tide by traversing the wall; this marks the start of Wallsend Central.

The approach is described on page 120.

1 **No Victory in Europe** 15m F6c † 5B (7.5.95)
An isolated line taking the centre of the high triangular wall left of *Sea Saga*. Not shown on the topo. Approachable using an *in-situ* rope, which is now in poor condition.

2 **Sea Saga** 45m HVS †   (14.8.73)
Start on a large, smooth rock platform beneath a wide, north-facing chimney-ramp. Pitch 1 appears to be in a state of flux.
1 12m. Climb the crack to the right of the chimney and belay on the first large ledge.
2 18m. Move up to the next ledge and step rightwards. Climb the crux wall above, move left and continue up the crack-system above to a reasonable ledge near the top.
3 15m. Traverse left across the void to the bigger ledge; then climb the wall to the grass. Go up left then right and continue until the angle eases.

Joff Cook running it out on *The Great Pretender* F6c+ (page 170). STEVE TAYLOR

The next trio of routes climb the prominent pillar to the right of *Sea Saga*.

3 Critical Mass 22m F6b 7B †   (9.5.03)
Pleasant climbing with a boldish finale. Climb the left-hand arête of the wall with relative ease to the upper pillar. This gives a technical move and sprint finish via the left arête.

4 Rapid Response 23m F7a 7B †   (9.5.03)
The central line of the wall. Easy ground leads to a stand up to the base of the groove. A very technical sequence gains a slabby wall and thin crack to finish.

5 Chert Noble 23m F7a+ 7B †   (10.5.03)
The right-hand pillar/face gives the best route of the three. Climb over easy ground to a bulge. This is bypassed on the left with difficulty, whereupon sustained but easier moves up and then right gain the slabby face and lower-off above.

Right of the prominent pillar a large broken slab leads up to a corner.

6 End of the Pier 35m E2 5a †   (21.10.90)
Start just left of the slab. Loose, not recommended, and not shown on the topo. Follow the diagonal crack, move left at the twin cracks, and continue up to the jutting overhang. Belay on a rope preplaced on a stake (removed).

167

7 Face in the Chert 20m F5+ 6B   (6.5.03)
A slight climb, which feels runout. It takes the obvious flaky crackline to the left of *Glamour Cat*, gained direct via a juggy wall and chert ledge. Shared lower-off.

⭐ **8 Glamour Cat** 21m F6b 8B   (25.7.96)
Good climbing up the left-hand side of the grey slabby wall. Start under the left-hand side of the high roof. Climb steeply up to the base of a shallow groove, which is followed slightly rightwards to the lower-off below the roof.

⭐ **9 1789** 24m F7a 8B   (11.7.89)
A clean wall climb, which follows very shallow indentations in the face. Start under the right-hand side of the high roof. Climb to a large flake at 5 metres and then on small holds to a deep slot on the left. Move rightwards and then directly up on incut holds to the upper face. Pull up right to a big, hidden pocket and continue by hard pocket moves to a good flake. Continue up past the right-hand side of the roof (difficult) to the high lower-off on the left.

⭐⭐ **10 The Bad Seeds** 24m F7b 7B   (23.9.90)
A continuously rewarding face climb. Protection includes two drilled pegs. Start 3 metres right of *1789*. From good holds above a very small roof at 2 metres, pull up slightly rightwards. Climb straight up to jugs and follow thin disjointed cracks (sustained) to the lower-off.

⭐ **11 Magical Mr Mephistopheles** 24m F6c 9B   (1.11.94)
Almost a slab in its upper half. Start by a step in the ledge at the base of the cliff (3 metres right of *The Bad Seeds*). Climb over a bulge and up the wall on spaced jugs, keeping to the left of a vegetated ledge. At half height, trend steeply rightwards to a black open groove. Climb the sustained groove on small incuts to the first break. Swing left to the shared lower-off.

The next two routes climb the flowstone up and right of *Magical Mr Mephistopheles*. There is a bolt belay at the top of a grassy ramp beneath these routes, above a huge detached flake. The approach to this belay, up grass and loose rock is, frankly, terrifying.

⭐ 12 **Calcichew** 24m F6b 6B   (22.5.04)
Slightly lichenous. Climb the left-hand line via a prominent dripping pillar of flowstone.

13 **Calcite Compliment** 24m F6c † 6B   (22.5.04)
The right-hand line is on good rock and has a trying central section.

The middle of the high-level triangular face just north of the large, low-level, diagonal roof is sleek, smooth, and sheer. The following two routes use a knotted rope to gain a belay on a vegetated ledge.

14 **Jazz it Up** 15m F7a+ † 4B   (22.5.04)
A worthwhile line to the left of *Razzamatazz*, with a very short hard section.

⭐ 15 **Razzamatazz** 15m F7b 5B   (6.11.94)
Great rock and technical climbing make this route worth the effort of the approach. Delicate climbing in line with a blind crack leads to easier moves up flakes to the lower-off.

Between *Razzamatazz* and *Stylus* is a low platform, which is awash in heavy seas.

16 Stylus 35m HVS   (24.8.73)
Immediately right of a large, low-level, diagonal overhang is a short corner-crack above a cherty wall. Not recommended if the crux, which is just above the belay, is at all damp.
1 18m 4b. Climb the wall to a large flake. Step right and continue up to the 'stylus', a large spike of rock.
2 17m 5b. Climb the corner past a jammed block to solid but small horizontal chert holds. Continue up past a flake to a grassy ledge. Thread runner behind a blunt flake. Scramble carefully rightwards up the grassy arête to a stake belay (removed).

⭐ **17 The Great Pretender** 21m F6c+ 6B   (5.8.94)
The wall and rounded arête a few metres right of *Stylus* are 'sportingly bolted'. From a high ledge, climb the wall via a 'mono' move to the chert break. Move up leftwards to below the clean arête, then rightwards and finally leftwards again to reach the arête. Climb this in a great situation, trending leftwards to the lower-off.

⭐ **18 After the Goldrush** 24m E2 5c †   (16.9.90)
Good, well-protected climbing which is harder than it looks. Start at the bottom of a rightward-leading ramp, as for *Half-Way House*. Climb up and cross the cherty roof to a tiny slab. Follow the thin crack to a ledge and the corner-crack to grass. Stake belay (removed).

⭐ **19 Totally Foo to You** 22m F6c 8B †   (22.5.04)
The prominent arête 10 metres right of *The Great Pretender*, immediately left of *Half Way House*. Climb up to an overlap and make hard moves to gain the arête. Fine, open climbing on the left-hand side of the arête leads to the lower-off.

20 Half-Way House 33m HS †† (8.70)
The wide cleft 30 metres north of the descent gully. An earth-fall at the top has left this route very dangerous and harder than the (first-ascent) grade given above.
1 18m. Climb rightwards up the earthy ramp and continue up the chimney to a belay at its top. (No worthwhile protection.)
2 15m. Follow the continuation chimney to a ledge on the left. Exit up the right-hand crack and belay to stakes.

South of *Half-Way House* is a large flake. There are five routes on the wall beyond.

21 Tunnel Vision 23m F7b+ 8B (2.4.99)
A parallel line left of *Hong Kong Phooey*. Blinkers are required at the grade given, as it seems natural to stray off-line onto easier rock.

22 Hong Kong Phooey 23m F7c 10B (20.3.94)
Sustained yet varied climbing up the blunt arête 5 metres right of the large flake. A dominating line offering superb hard climbing, with the crux just where it should be – at the top. Steep climbing leads up to a slight corner. Cross the smooth bulge above and continue to the lower-off.

The next two routes share a starting-point halfway up the grass slope, beneath a large scoop.

23 Doolittle 20m F6b+ 7B (13.2.94)
Low in the grade. Climb up into the scoop and follow the crack to a roof, which is turned on the left. Continue to the lower-off.

24 Jane Says 20m F6b+ 7B (1994)
High in the grade. Climb up into the scoop as for *Doolittle*. Continue rightwards over slabby rock and follow the crack to the lower-off.

25 Relax 19m F6b+ 7B (10.99)
In the middle of the grade. Start 5 metres further up the slope. Follow the line of weakness up and leftwards to the lower-off of *Jane Says*.

Coastguard Cliff

OS Ref 675 691

The cliff lies below the Coastguard Lookout on the west coast of the island, three-quarters of a mile from Portland Bill. Flowstone abounds here, with Coastguard South hosting some of the best routes on the island and Coastguard North containing two stunning walls, including Portland's hardest route – *Vespasian*. Unfortunately, these cliffs are very condition-dependent, with the rock often feeling soapy when there is no wind or the humidity is high. Late summer evenings generally offer the best conditions.

The southernmost three bolt lines have a variable nesting restriction. The unclimbed cliff beyond is a bird sanctuary subject to **a year-round climbing restriction** (see page 205).

Approach Drive towards Portland Bill along the A354 to its conclusion at the large Portland Bill car-park (expensive). Walk back north up the road to reach the cliff-top by the Coastguard Lookout.

1. At the bottom of the grass bank below the Coastguard Lookout is an earth ridge. Scramble down and rightwards to the boulder beach. The stake at the top of the ridge may become useful, as this descent is suffering from erosion.

2. For the northern end of the cliff only, and to be completely avoided in damp conditions. One hundred and twenty metres north of the Coastguard Lookout are a pair of earthy gullies, which divide Coastguard Cliff from Wallsend Cove. The southern, more pronounced gully gives the easier descent, but care is required and a rope on the nearby stake may be necessary.

Warning: do not confuse this gully with another 70 metres further north, which ends in space halfway down the cliff.

Unknown climber nearing the finish of *Superfly Guy* **F7a+ (page 180).** ROB KENNARD

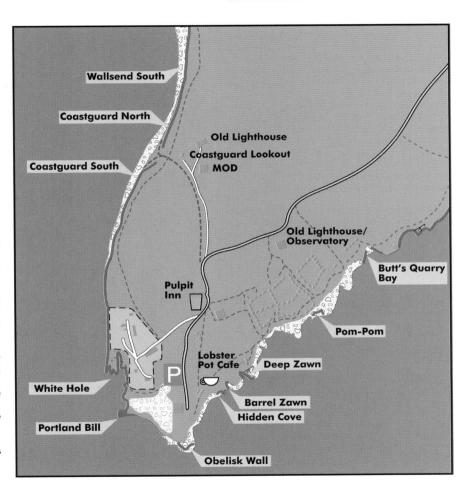

Coastguard Cliff North

As one descends the earth ridge beneath the Coastguard Lookout, the shallow groove of *Midnight Oil* is the first climb to strike the eye. The smooth wall to the left, tightly packed with hard routes such as the very shallow runnel of *Nothing but the Groove*, leads after thirty metres to a pinnacle behind which *No Lion, No Tiger* resides. Fifty metres of bulging rock further on, just before a prominent earth mound, *The Wax Museum* exhibits its colourful challenge. *Boys from the Loose Stuff* and the remaining routes are clustered on a wall south of the earth gully, which signifies the northern end of the cliff. This section has no tidal problems but can be affected by heavy seas.

At the northern end of Coastguard Cliff North (120 metres north of the earth ridge descent) lies the descent gully mentioned above, which is also used for access to the southern end of Wallsend Cove. A big prow forms the retaining wall of this gully. Its seaward face has six routes and an isolated block beneath gives a short problem:

The smooth slab on a boulder below and a few metres north of the descent gully is **Cunning Lingo** (7m E3 6a 6.89). Protectionless, sustained and over a leg-breaker landing! Both arêtes of this boulder go at a scary 5a/b.

1 **El Poder de un Coño** 21m F6c+ 8B (5.2.94)
Start 5 metres right of the prow, at a calcite stain in the lower wall. Delightful sustained climbing leads to a welcome rest before a steep finish. High in the grade. Climb the wall and the groove above. From the top of the groove, use a short crack to reach the arête. Swing back right and follow a tube to the lower-off.

2 **Explorator Motivator** 24m E3 6a   (5.89)
The soaring finger-crack 7 metres right of the prow
gives an outstanding route – though only when it is
in condition. Climb the crack to a peg at its top
and move 3 metres left on sloping holds. Pull up the
wide, hanging crack formed by a tube in the rock
to the shared lower-off.

3 **100% Columbian** 21m F7b 7B   (19.3.00)
One desperate move spoils this otherwise good
route. Start 2 metres right of *Explorator Motivator*.
Climb easily up to the base of a rib and make the
desperate move to gain a flake on its right-hand
side. Follow the flake to the faultline, where a long
but straightforward reach gains the lower-off.

4 **China White** 21m F6c+ 6B   (11.7.89)
Start 3 metres right of *Explorator Motivator*. Good
sustained climbing, though highly condition-
dependent. Climb a short wall, and then a blind
crack using holds on the left. Continue on better
holds to a horizontal crack and the lower-off.

5 **Boys from the Loose Stuff** 21m E3 5b †
    (5.89)
Start 5 metres right of *Explorator Motivator*. Climb
the wide rightward-slanting crack. Continue up a
flake (bolt) and then straight up, past a peg in the
upper band, to the top. Lower off a rope preplaced
on a stake situated on the far side of the descent
gully.

6 **Pure Shores** 21m F6c 8B   (1.5.00)
The wall to the right of *China White* is better than it
looks. Climb a flake easily and the wall above to a
steep finish.

Theo Elmer styling up *Shining Heart* **F7c**
(page 182). RICHARD HORN

To the right is a rightward-leading ramp above a grassy mound, and then a series of huge flakes abut the cliff. *Headwall Emptiness* starts on the right-hand side of the first flake. Unfortunately, this wall is highly condition-dependent: low humidity, a breeze and sunshine is the key. The grades given assume optimum conditions, during which this wall is one of the best areas for hard sport climbing in the UK.

7 Meridian Line 23m F7c 7B   (3.10.98)
Start from the top of the first large flake leaning against the cliff. Follow a thin crack with difficulty to join *Ming the Merciless* near the top.

8 Ming the Merciless 23m F7c+ 6B   (7.11.98)
Start on the right-hand side of the first flake. Pull onto the headwall at a short flake with some difficulty. Climb the thin veneer of flowstone above.

9 Headwall Emptiness 23m F7b+ 8B
                                    (12.7.92)
'A stamina test which soars away to pumpsville.' Climb the large flake and pull out right to a big undercut beneath a short corner. Layback with difficulty to a good tufa hold and make more thin moves to a finger-ledge. Continue direct to a thin flake and the lower-off.

10 Glycerine 23m F7c+ 8B   (17.10.98)
Start beneath the right-hand end of a small roof at 6 metres. This is an extremely pumpy pitch. Climb up to the roof and continue more or less direct to a long reach for the lower-off.

11 Sandcastles 23m F7a+ 5B   (9.7.95)
Start immediately left of *The Wax Museum*, beneath the right-hand side of a half-height roof. Beware the flexi-flake at the crux and some big run-outs!

Climb flakes, cross the small roof, and carry on up flakes to the lower-off.

12 The Wax Museum 23m F7b+ 8B   (1.4.90)
A contender for the best route of its grade on the island — a demanding power climb up the orange flowstone-veneered wall some 40 metres south of the descent gully. Unfortunately, a hold was created low down on the route; no ascents which have avoided it have been reported. From a raised ledge at 5 metres (on the second huge flake), launch up the flake and move right using the drilled pocket to the base of a flowstone fluting. Layback up this and go left to a huge resting-jug. Continue straight up flowstone and reach left to a pocket. Finish with a big stretch up the headwall to the lower-off.

13 Dr Phibes 21m F7b 6B   (28.4.93)
Steep, insecure climbing on flowstone flakes. Start from the same raised ledge as *The Wax Museum*, at a bolt belay near a step in the ledge. After the barn-door start, follow flakes up the right-hand side of the orange flowstone to the lower-off.

14 Clockwork Orange 21m F7c 7B   (4.99)
Climb to the raised ledge, 2 metres right of *Dr Phibes*. Climb the thin crack to the breaks. Further hard moves above lead to the lower-off.

15 Project 21m F8a
When complete, the project right of *Clockwork Orange* will be a severe test of stamina.

16 The Nth Degree 21m F7c 9B   (4.6.98)
Start up an easy scoop in the lower wall. From the ledge, step right and climb the groove past a flake. A dynamic approach is required to reach the breaks and the lower-off.

17 Wasted 21m F7b+ 7B   (28.3.99)
Start below a notch in the large flake leaning against the wall. Climb up to the notch and step onto the headwall from the highest point on the ledge system. Climb the right-hand side of the scoop above to a large undercut, which is often damp. Follow it left and finish up a flake to the lower-off of *The Nth Degree*.

18 Last Orders 21m F7c 6B   (10.5.99)
The right-hand finish to *Wasted*, avoiding most of the damp undercut. From the large undercut, move up and right to the lower-off of *Bar Room Brawl*.

19 Bar Room Brawl 23m F7c+ 6B   (23.4.95)
A physically demanding route with laybacks and knee-bars. Scramble up *Vespasian's* starting scoop. Step left and climb the grey-streaked wall and groove above. Continue with difficulty to the top break and the lower-off.

20 Vespasian 23m F8a+ 8B   (1.10.94)
A ferociously sustained line up a streaked wall; aesthetic as well as athletic. Portland's hardest route. Many of the UK's climbing elite have failed on this. Climb via the scoop to the base of the wall. Make hard moves up to tiny holds in a short rightward-facing groove. Layback onto poor undercuts, and attack the bulging wall above to reach improving holds and the twin cracks. Lower-off above.

A short distance right, above a drop in the height of the huge flake, is a crack in a shallow rightward-facing corner.

21 Sale of the Century 23m F7b 7B   (8.9.96)
The often-soapy crack. Pull up to the ledge and make a couple of hard moves to gain the crack. Follow it to where it steepens, with reachy moves to gain the breaks.

22 Zero Tolerance 23m F7b+ 8B   (23.9.98)
Difficult climbing which connects the start of *Sale of the Century* to the finish of *Mid-Strife Oasis*. From the first hard moves of *Sale of the Century*, pull up and right to gain the ramp which is followed to the lower-off of *Mid-Strife Oasis*.

23 Mid-Strife Oasis 23m F7c † 7B   (18.9.94)
The bulging wall 3 metres right again has a very good first half. Climb easily rightwards up the huge flake to a ledge. An unremitting series of hard moves in line with a blind crack leads to a hard reach for the mid-height ledge. Follow the short groove and bulging wall, easier now, to the top breaks and lower-off.

24 Eternal Spider 22m F7c+ 7B   (18.4.93)
A powerful and good-looking line up the white wall just north of the pinnacle; sustained and high in its grade. Climb easily leftwards on calcite up the huge flake to a ledge on its top beneath a twin opposing layback line. Dynamically overcome a bulge and continue up the twin seams to the lower-off.

25 Project 22m F8b 8B
Open to all contenders. A difficult proposition moving right from the starting ledge of *Eternal Spider*. From the high ledge, climb up slightly right to a large sidepull, and then explode for miles up to catch a mono. A short pocket traverse left and up gains a good edge. Continue slightly right with escalating difficulty to searing pulls below the breaks. Finish directly with ease.

26 Happy to Go Blind 23m F7b+ 8B
                                       (12.12.97)
Start below a steep corner. Climb the flowstone-streaked corner to a grassy ledge. The groove above looks straightforward, but appearances are often deceiving.

27 No Lion, No Tiger 38m E1 5a †   (6.7.86)
Start behind the conspicuous pinnacle. Large nuts needed. Climb up just to the right of a flake. Continue up the off-width crack above to twin cracks, which lead steeply to a ledge on the right. Continue leftwards to steep earth and pull out on a rope preplaced on a stake (removed).

28 Spare Rib 23m F7b 7B   (6.5.95)
Quite obviously, the rib behind the pinnacle. Perfect rock and escalating difficulty make this a route to remember. Climb the lower wall to the left-hand side of the rib. Climb it with increasing difficulty to a pocketed bulge. A series of hard pulls leads to easy ground and the lower-off.

29 Girl Power 22m F7a+ 8B   (1998)
This reachy number takes the right-hand side of the aforementioned rib. Climb the right-hand side of the rib, with a long reach to gain the thin faultline. Continue to the lower-off.

30 Steve's Route 22m F7b 7B   (1998)
The very shallow groove to the right of the rib. High in the grade. Not yet climbed by 'Steve', though many others have succeeded where he has failed. Start below the orange stains on the wall. Climb a short corner to the base of a slabby wall. Make thin moves up to the overlap. From a pocket, climb the groove above (crux) to the breaks and the lower-off.

⭐ 31 **Retaining the Ashes** 22m F6b+ 7B (7.3.93)
A strenuous route which starts 3 metres right of the pinnacle. Low in its grade. Climb a short steep wall to a ledge. Follow a thin crack, which has some tricky moves before the break is reached. Finish steeply past a pocket to the lower-off.

⭐ 32 **Into the Groove** 22m F6b+ 6B (2000)
This alternative start to *Nothing but the Groove* avoids that route's demanding start. Start up *Retaining the Ashes* until it is possible to break out right past a lone *Petzl* bolt to gain the groove. Finish as for *Nothing but the Groove*.

⭐⭐ 33 **Nothing but the Groove** 21m F6c+ 8B
(8.8.88)
A tricky start and superb upper groove should put this on everyone's tick-list. Start 6 metres right of the pinnacle. Climb a flowstone-decorated scoop and go leftwards with difficulty to jugs. Continue up into the very shallow, blank runnel and gain a ledge. Step up rightwards before going back left and up the groove to the lower-off.

⭐⭐ 34 **Running It In!** 22m F7c 8B (10.6.90)
A highly sustained and fingery test-piece. Gain an obvious pocketed bucket at 3 metres and climb straight up to a thin crack, which is overcome by an intricate and strenuous sequence. From the resting-place above, follow the continuation crack more easily rightwards to the break, and then bear leftwards to the shared lower-off.

⭐⭐ 35 **Superfly Guy** 18m F7a+ 7B (8.8.88)
Yet another excellent climb – never *that* hard, but it may leave you grasping for non-holds at the crux. Start at a tiny undercut shelf at waist height, 3 metres right of *Nothing but the Groove*. Climb the grey streaks past three pockets to a larger one, and continue to a jug at the base of the slab. Go straight

up slight grooves to better holds just below the breaks. Lower-off on the left.

36 Lost in Rock 20m F6c 6B   (17.7.92)
A succession of bouldery moves between good holds. Start 2 metres right of *Superfly Guy*. Climb up to jugs and then rightwards over the chert bulge to a ledge (shared with *The Man…*). Step up left and make thin moves up an open scoop to a hidden bucket above a slight bulge. More tricky motions lead strenuously to the breaks. Swing 2 metres right and up to the next route's lower-off.

37 The Man Who Never Found Himself
19m F6a+ 6B   (15.8.88)
Wet for some of the year. Start 3 metres right of *Superfly Guy* (6 metres left of the earth slope). Climb up the wall past a pocket, and go rightwards over the large chert bulge to a ledge. Follow the shallow groove above (ancient *in-situ* thread) to the horizontal breaks and a lower-off.

38 Van People 19m F6c+ 5B   (20.8.89)
Worthwhile, solid climbing on the dark streaks 3 metres right again. Climb directly up a black streak over two slight bulges to a shallow groove bounded on its left by a rib. Climb delicately up the groove and make a hard lunge for the breaks and the lower-off.

John Fletcher nearing the finish of *Nothing but the Groove* F6c+. KEITH SHARPLES

⭐ 39 **Fantasy Island** 22m F6c 7B   (28.5.93)
The flaky, acute-angled groove gives unusual climbing and is much better, and harder, than it looks. From conglomerate, climb over a bulge to the groove. Climb the groove to big incut holds at its top, and move up rightwards to the lower-off of *Shining Heart*.

40 **La Usurpadora** 18m F7c 8B   (25.5.00)
Start between *Fantasy Island* and *Shining Heart*. Climb the steep wall above, until it is possible to join *Shining Heart* via a series of desperate pocket moves. Finish as for that route.

41 **Heartland** 18m F7c 8B   (17.5.00)
The link between the eliminate line of *La Usurpadora* and *Shining Heart* is useful as an alternative start to *Shining Heart* if the starting undercuts are damp. From the second bolt on *La Usurpadora*, move right to gain the pinch on *Shining Heart*.

⭐⭐ 42 **Shining Heart** 18m F7c 6B   (20.8.89)
A super power climb up the hanging (and overhanging) rib 3 metres past *Fantasy Island*. Very photogenic. Start beneath a small roof at 5 metres. Move leftwards to incuts and then up to undercut a small roof. An outrageous move gains a pinch in the flake on the left. Climb precariously up the thin crack above to twin horizontal cracks. Finish slightly leftwards to the lower-off.

⭐ 43 **Frenzied Detruncation** 18m F7b+ 5B
    (27.7.89)
A ferocious test-piece climbing a leaning groove. Start beneath a small roof at 5 metres. Fingery lock-offs allow a jug over the roof to be reached. Contorted bridging then leads to the horizontal cracks. Continue via a faint flake to good jugs and the lower-off.

44 Prison Sex 15m F7c 5B   (28.5.93)
The blunt white arête is a sustained and fingery pump protected by five bolts, if you can stop to clip them. Starting with a very hard rockover, climb the arête to the crux: gaining the horizontal break. Finish up the hanging groove of *Midnight Oil* to the shared lower-off on the left.

45 Midnight Oil 15m F7a 4B   (5.89)
Start 10 metres up the grass slope at a leftward-slanting groove. Swing steeply into the groove and continue with further difficulty to the roof. Move left and go up the hanging groove to the shared lower-off on the left.

46 Gunbarrel Highway 17m E6 6a   (5.89)
Start up *Midnight Oil* but move right past a very rusty peg to finish on the lower-off of the next route.

47 Hang 'Em High 16m F7b 5B   (19.3.00)
Strenuous climbing on good rock. Start up a difficult corner right of *Midnight Oil*. Climb over the bulge and past horizontal bands to finish right of the large roof.

48 Gun Runner 12m F6a 4B   (19.3.00)
The open groove on the right-hand side of the cliff. Climb the groove past breaks to the shared lower-off.

Tim Emmett pulling into the groove of *Nothing but the Groove* F6c+ (page 180.
MIKE ROBERTSON

183

Unknown climber on *Walking the King* F6b+ (page 200). KEITH SHARPLES

Coastguard Cliff South

Coastguard Cliff has many excellent routes. Were it not for the tidal problems outlined below, it would be one of the more popular cliffs on Portland. There are several strong, hard lines, interspersed with walls of a more amenable nature.

The approach is described on page 173.

A pinnacle supports the earth ridge which forms the easy way down. Grass slopes at the base of the cliff prevent it from reaching its full height until 80 metres south of the pinnacle. At this point is the conglomerate start of *Biscuits for Smut*. Fifty metres further (past an area often awash at high tide) is the south-facing chimney of *Easy Cleft* and the long flake of *Vesuvius* a few metres south again. The chimney of *Lucky Dip* is 80 metres to the south, 10 metres beyond a low tidal ledge. Just right of *Lucky Dip* is the thin, disjointed crackline of *What Gives My Son?* Twenty metres south is the large, impossible-looking roof of *Wharfedale Boyz*. To reach *Smashing Orange* and to explore the remainder of the cliff often necessitates a steep, low-level traverse (or a paddle) beneath a buttress which has some scaffolding in its upper reaches, unless the tide is low and the sea is calm. Several hundred metres further on, a deep zawn with smooth walls bars further progress towards Portland Bill.

As described, there are a number of areas at the base of the cliff that are awash at high tide and in rough seas. Keep a careful eye on the state of the tide to prevent the need to wade or swim out. In rough seas, the lower ledges are extremely hazardous.

Nesting-season restrictions apply here, although the area in question has only three climbs at present. Ten metres south of the arête of *Existenz* is a shallow bay. Restrictions apply from the right-hand side of a cave at the northern end of this bay southwards to the start of White Hole. Except for the three existing routes on the *Down to the Wire* buttress, there should be no climbing at any time in this area. The restrictions on the existing routes run from the 1st of March to the 31st of July.

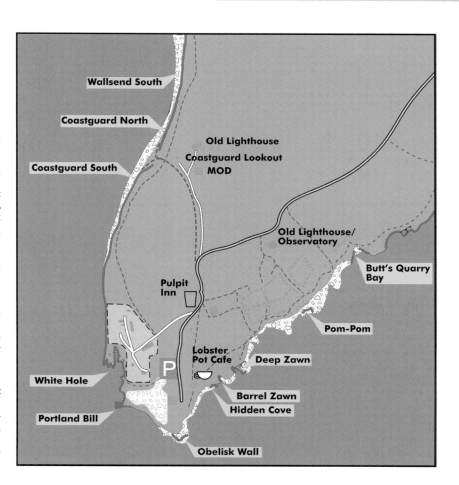

The first four routes on this cliff start at the base of a conglomerate tongue, which reaches a height of 8 metres.

⭐ 1 **Seat of Learning** 21m F7c 7B   (27.5.98)
This is an impressive route. Scramble up the left side of a conglomerate feature behind a large flake (bold). From the second bolt, climb diagonally left through a slight scoop and up the headwall.

⭐ 2 **The Font of Knowledge** 21m F7c 7B   (18.5.98)
Start as for *Seat of Learning*. From a point level with the top of the conglomerate, fire directly up the impending headwall to a difficult finish.

⭐ 3 **Biscuits for Smut** 21m F7b 8B   (30.9.94)
The lower section is easy, and more solid than it looks. Climb the right-hand side of the conglomerate to a dark groove which is shallow and wide. Layback the right side of the groove, and make a hard stretch for a large undercut. Jugs now lead to a final hard move up the headwall.

⭐⭐ 4 **Reactor Meltdown** 21m F7b 8B   (27.5.98)
The best of this collection of four routes. Start up *Biscuits for Smut*. Move right at the top of the conglomerate to a flake and then climb the arête on its left side.

The very wide groove/corner right of the conglomerate formation used to contain several sport and traditional routes. A huge rockfall in the winter of 2000 destroyed *The Lotus Eater, Given to Fly, Broadcast Emotion, The Feedback Monster, Grip '89 (Audi 80 v. The Law), Junk Gun Fever, Come Hell or High Water* and *Snorkelling amongst Sharks*, the bolts for which can still be seen in the large boulders strewn around the base of the cliff. The starting bolts for *Snorkelling amongst Sharks* are still in place, however.

To the right of the rockfall is a tall face, streaked with flowstone in its lower reaches. A short finger-crack on the left terminates abruptly at a rubble-strewn ledge, and marks the southern reaches of the massive rockfall. Eight metres right of the crack is a striking arête.

5 Guardian Angel 20m F7b+ 10B (2.5.98)

The steep face 6 metres left of the striking arête. Climb fairly directly up flowstone patches to a ledge. Attack the thin crack above — sustained.

6 Brooklyn Bimbo 20m F7b+ 11B (29.6.91)

Two metres to the right of *Guardian Angel* is a magnificent arête which is reached by difficult climbing up an orange flowstone wall. Start 4 metres left of the arête's undercut base. From a small finger-flake, crank up left to big flowstone holds. Move up and right to an overhung ledge at 7 metres which boasts a big sharp jug. Reach up and make hard moves into a shallow niche. Further taxing moves allow a rest to be taken on the arête. Climb the arête to a ledge and continue to the lower-off. A direct start a metre left of the arête has been bolted, making the route even more sustained and F7c.

7 From a Buick Eight 20m F7b 10B (26.8.02)

Immaculate rock and climbing, taking the undercut arête then the right-hand side of the sharp arête of *Brooklyn Bimbo*. Unfortunately it gets very close to the neighbouring routes. From a block below the start of *New York Dolls*, swing left and up the nose of the arête, initially with fingery moves but slowly easing, to a ledge. The upper, right-hand side of the arête gives extremely technical and sustained climbing though it is all too easy to step left to the finish of *Brooklyn Bimbo*.

8 New York Dolls 20m F6a+ 8B (9.5.98)

The pleasant groove to the right of the arête. Start at the base of the flake and follow it with continued interest to the lower-off.

9 The Devil's Work 20m F6b+ 8B (6.10.96)

The unattractive, dirty flake right of *New York Dolls*. Start 3 metres right of *New York Dolls*. Pull onto a ledge at 2 metres and continue to the large flake above. Climb the scruffy flake to a lower-off between the faultlines above.

⭐ **10 Marshalling Amps** 20m F7b 8B †   (15.9.02)
The impressive pitch taking the wall left of *Broadway* is high in its grade. Climb the overhanging finger-crack 5 metres left of *Broadway* with tricky blind moves and pull over a bulge onto a good resting ledge. The wall above gives a very hard sequence up blind cracks to reach good holds, from which a step left and a fingery move gain the lower-off.

⭐ **11 Broadway** 20m E3 5c †   (10.11.91)
Strenuous to start. Fifteen metres right of the arête of *Brooklyn Bimbo* is another undercut arête, which has a crack 'decorated' with four aging in-situ threads on its left-hand side. Follow the overhanging crack to a cherty ledge at 10 metres. Continue up the crack past two chockstones to a jug, whereupon a slanting crack leads rightwards to the arête and a ledge above. Step right to the lower-off of *Skyscraper*.

⭐ **12 Manhattan Skyline** 20m E4 6a   (10.11.91)
Good climbing throughout but especially exhilarating near the top. From a raised ledge just to the right of the arête, step left and move up (peg) to a horizontal slot (*Friend 2* and *Rock 4*). Pull over the bulge on jugs to a horizontal break (in-situ thread). Move up a thin crack (*Rock 1s*) and step left to the arête (in-situ thread). Now climb straight up the very edge of the arête (drilled peg and bolts) to the ledge of *Broadway*. Use a lower-off shared with the next route.

⭐ **13 Skyscraper** 20m F7a 7B   (26.8.02)
Another route in the wall-climbing mould. Start just right of *Manhattan Skyline*. Climb the wall moving slightly left past the initial overlap and continue up to the main overlap bisecting the wall. Using a flake on the right, swing up and left to a respite at the chert break. The fine wall above is taken initially via a faint crack and then more directly on positive crimps.

14 H'Electric Boogaloo 16m F6b 6B   (6.00)
Start in a shallow cave. Climb out of the cave on its left-hand wall. Swing right over the roof of the cave and follow the groove above to the lower-off.

⭐ 15 **The Bronx** 20m F6c+ 7B † (7.5.02)
Start 2 metres left of *Easy Cleft*. Climb leftwards up the relatively easy wall above the overlap to a good ledge. The square-cut arête above provides the main entertainment.

16 **Easy Cleft** 30m HS 4a
Not *that* easy. The south-facing cleft. Check that the stake is in place before setting off. Thrutch up to the top of the cleft and step left to a ledge. Climb a wall past an over-corroded peg and finish up the grass above. Belay to the left on a stake in the depression (which may have been removed).

The consequences of not watching the tides carefully! STEVE TAYLOR

⭐ **17 American Beauty** 17m F6c+ 7B † †   (5.00)
The fine white arête between *Easy Cleft* and *Vesuvius* would appear to be buckling under it's own weight. Until the pillar stabilises, or (more likely) collapses, this route should not be climbed. The description remains for historical purposes only. Climb the easy wall to the base of the arête proper. Climb steeply on flakes to the right of the arête to a slight overlap. Use a hold on the left arête to make a difficult move to the lower-off.

18 Vesuvius 40m VS ††   (8.67)
A sustained route starting at a short corner 5 metres right of *Easy Cleft*. Pegs required. Note that if the pillar of *American Beauty* collapses this route will also be affected.
1 18m. Climb the preliminary corner and follow the right-hand flake crack to the roof.
2 8m. Traverse left under the roof past a small platform to the jutting ledge. Place pegs to belay.
3 14m. Climb 6 metres of steep earth and rock before the angle eases. Belay as for *Easy Cleft*, a long way to the left.

Past *Vesuvius* the boulders give way to a low, wide platform, usually awash at high tide.

19 Californian Dreams 20m F6b+ 6B   (5.00)
The dusty, blunt arête 5 metres to the right of *Vesuvius*. Start up a difficult corner and pick your way carefully up the blunt arête.

The next two routes breach the long roof right of *Vesuvius*.

20 **September Mourning** 23m F7b 9B †
(15.9.02)
A hard fingery start leads to open climbing above. Start 15 metres right of *Vesuvius*. Pull over an overlap and trend leftwards then straight up to the break. Step right and pull leftwards through the central, narrowest point of the roof to a ledge. Move right again to reach the base of a thin crack in the upper wall and follow it to the top.

21 **Wharfedale Boyz** 23m F7c 10B (30.4.95)
The roof and groove starting 3 metres right of *September Mourning*. Climb up to and rightwards over the strip roof (*in*-situ thread). Follow a groove to a tricky finish.

22 **Screaming Skulls** 23m F7c 11B (10.12.99)
Seven metres right of *Wharfedale Boyz* is an ominous bulge; this route takes the excellent groove to its left. Climb the narrow wall and move left into the hanging groove. Hard, contorted moves between good holds will leave you breathless at the shared lower-off.

23 Tennessee 23m F7c 11B   (7.98)
Another fantastic route taking the bulge which *Screaming Skulls* avoids. Start as for *Screaming Skulls*. Attack the bulge direct to gain the leaning headwall. Pumpy climbing leads to the lower-off.

24 Darkest Before Dawn 23m F7b 9B   (23.5.97)
Start under the left-hand side of a long, low roof. Pull over the roof with difficulty, climb the wall above, and follow an easier long rib to the lower-off.

25 Actions Speak Louder 23m F7a+ 8B   (21.9.94)
A sustained line with a wild start. Start beneath the middle of the roof on the right-hand side of the platform. Gain the ledge at 3 metres. You will now be rather constricted by the roof above, so get over it! If you managed the stretch, climb steeply up to jugs at mid height, and follow a slabby rib and groove to the lower-off above the horizontal cracks.

26 L'Odyssee Noire 23m F6c 8B   (7.5.02)
Climb the dusty wall to an overlap. Pull over and climb the shallow groove directly above to good holds. Move right to the lower-off.

27 Xavier's Wall 21m F6a 7B   (21.9.94)
Sustained yet varied. Start on the left-hand side of the black-streaked face left of the north-facing chimney. Climb a short flake and a shallow groove to foot-ledges beneath a small half-height roof. Follow a flake and the left side of a rib to the twin horizontal cracks.

The following four sport climbs provide amenable climbing at the heart of one of Portland's hardest cliffs, and make the effort of the approach worthwhile. They start out of reach of a high tide, though it would cause problems on the approach.

28 Coming of Age 21m F5+ 8B   (8.9.96)
Great, varied climbing with exquisite technical moves in the upper groove. Climb a flake crack on the left extremity of the black wall until forced right into an angled flowstone groove. Continue up this groove on small holds to the lower-off.

⭐⭐ **29 Underage** 21m F6a 8B   (5.97)
The crack to the right of *Coming of Age* has fine, intricate climbing in its upper reaches, making it one of the best F6a's on the island. Climb the crack 3 metres right of *Coming of Age* (originally climbed by *Light Relief*) to a difficult steep section and the lower-off just above.

30 Light Relief 40m HS †   (12.8.72)
An interesting line sharing the left-hand exit of *Lucky Dip*. Start 6 metres left of *Lucky Dip*. Pegs required.
1 24m. Climb the crack to a ledge at 12 metres (as for *Underage*). Move rightwards along the ledge, diagonally right, and up the corner-crack. Place a peg to belay on the right.
2 16m. *Lucky Dip* pitch 3.

⭐ **31 Xavier Zoo** 21m F6a 7B   (8.5.03)
A pleasant little route. Start 4 metres left of *Lucky Dip* and take a direct line up the wall left of *Young at Heart* to finish via a shallow groove.

⭐ **32 Young at Heart** 21m F6a+ 8B   (6.97)
Takes the right-hand side of the black wall. Somewhat wandering in line, but balanced by pleasant climbing. Start a metre left of *Lucky Dip*. Follow the line of least resistance above to the strange 'Vulcan' belay bolts which make for a quick lower-off, but may twist your rope.

33 Lucky Dip 40m HS †   (8.68)
Start at the right-hand side of the black wall, at a north-facing chimney. Pegs required.
1 12m. Climb the chimney and right-hand arête.
2 12m. Go left awkwardly and follow the corner-crack above. Place a peg to belay on the right.
3 16m. Ascend the broken rock and grass above.

Variation
2a 24m VS †   (5.73)
Take the rightward-slanting line past some large blocks, and finish up steep earth and rock.

193

34 What Gives My Son? 23m E3 5c (13.4.91)

The finger-crack 7 metres right of *Lucky Dip* provides an enjoyable trad route. Climb the lower crack to a ledge. Move left and follow the sustained continuation crack to the top. Scramble carefully right to the *Wavewatch* lower-off.

35 Wavewatch 23m F7b+ 8B † (9.5.02)

This is a fine pitch. Start 10 metres right of *Lucky Dip*. Climb the relatively easy wall to a final steepening. A hard sequence of moves eventually gains the lower-off.

36 Full Fathom Five 23m F7b 7B (13.4.91)

Twelve metres right of *Lucky Dip* is a superb pitch of escalating difficulty, which has a hard crux and a blind finish. Climb up the wall to a horizontal break. Continue up a scoop and over fingery bulges to the top break.

37 Bad Moon Rising 23m F7a+ 8B (12.4.91)

Commendable climbing up the blunt, deeply-pocketed arête just right of *Full Fathom Five*; a bold finish. From a high boulder, climb a slight ramp on good holds to a ledge. Follow the deep pockets above, and then layback steeply to a good flake. Sustained moves lead to a break and the lower-off above.

38 A Ship Load of Moonies 21m F6c+ 8B (15.9.02)

A very fine pitch. From the first bolt on *Bad Moon Rising*, step right and pull through the bulge to reach a ledge. Continue up the faint crack-system above to a bulge and pull through it using a prominent flake crack to reach the lower-off.

39 **Dead By Sunset** 21m F7a+ 9B   (28.9.96)
Steep climbing all the way. Start in the trench 4 metres left of the raised
ledge. Climb into a flake, then pull out of it on the left (hard). Follow the
shallowest of grooves up the wall above.

40 **Witchdoctor** 21m F7b 7B   (3.5.98)
This route is quite bold. A grade of E6 6b may be more appropriate.
Start in the trench, immediately left of the raised ledge. Pull onto the wall
and pass a 'rust' stain low down. Climb the blunt crozzly rib above.

41 **Vampire Killers** 21m F7b 8B   (23.5.97)
An isolated pitch offering slightly dirty, but good climbing. Start by a
right-facing flake. Climb the steep wall on good holds and pull over a
roof to enter the high groove with difficulty. Technical moves lead up the
groove to the lower-off.

To the right is a large roof breached by the following three routes.

42 The Lost Buoys 21m F7c+ 8B †   (14.9.97)
Easily identified by the 'lost' buoy hanging from the lower-off. The hardest route hereabouts, skirting around the left side of the large roof. Climb the amenable lower wall left of the roof and then boulder desperately up the crimpy rib. Finish up the easier crack to a safe harbour at the buoy.

43 No Survivors 21m F7b+ 10B   (15.9.96)
Climb up to the roof, 4 metres from its left-hand end. Make a series of powerful pulls to gain a good hold on the headwall. Move up to a ledge and climb the deep groove above.

44 A Meeting of Minds 21m F7a+ 10B
   (15.9.96)
The centre of the massive roof goes at a surprisingly amenable grade. Climb up to the roof, take a deep breath, and swing across on jugs. Pull onto the headwall and move up and left to climb a groove.

The following pair of routes share a common start just to the left of the tidal trench.

45 Lip Service 21m F7a 9B   (15.9.96)
This route takes in some impressively steep rock, generally on good holds. Climb the steep wall to a small roof. Swing diagonally left across it and move up to a protruding ledge. Climb the wall and move left to a flake to finish.

46 Bermuda Triangle 21m F6c 8B   (8.9.96)
A worthwhile pitch with a wonderful top slab, tempered by a difficult initial wall. Climb the steep wall as for *Lip Service*. At the roof, pull up and

right with difficulty. Follow the thin crack in the slab above to the lower-off of *A Bird in the Hand*.

47 A Bird in the Hand 21m F7a+ 7B †
   (14.9.96)
Start immediately left of the tidal trench. Climb the difficult bulge to a suspended flake at 5 metres. Move up and left to a grooved slab containing a wide flake; climb this to the shared lower-off.

★ **48 Hasta la Vista** 21m F6b+ 8B   (4.5.03)
A fine start leads to a good finish, unfortunately with a big ledge in between. Better than its neighbour. Climb the wall to the right of *A Bird in the Hand* (high clip) to the bulge which is crossed on jugs. The upper rib gives an excellent finish.

Beyond this point is a tidal trench – the scene of many a wading expedition. In calm seas, this trench is dry for about 2 hours at low tide (though not during neap tides).

★ **49 Small Talk Costs Walls** 21m F6c+ 8B
   (27.5.98)
Start on a square ledge above the centre of the tidal trench. Pull out across the low roof/bulge rightwards to flakes. Climb these, past a patch of flowstone, to the lower-off.

Unknown climber on *Bad Moon Rising* F7a+; a stunning climb (page 194).
KEITH SHARPLES

The magnificent wall beyond the tidal trench offers a unique area of superb flowstone, supporting a series of sustained grade sevens. It's well worth the effort of the approach!

50 Smashing Orange 21m F7a 7B   (11.5.91)

A pitch up the flowstone-coated buttress right of the tidal trench. Start on the left edge of the buttress, at the left end of a ledge-system. Climb steeply past a large pocket and move rightwards to gain a flake. Pull back left to 'welded' jugs and follow the finger-crack above to finish.

51 Drive Blind 21m F7a+ 7B   (11.5.91)

An easier upper section than *Smashing Orange*, climbing some spectacular calcified conglomerate in relative safety. Start just right of *Smashing Orange*. Boulder up to a large pocket, continue on more pockets, and make hard moves up the bulging rib. Climb a shallow calcite groove which steepens towards the top.

52 Forensic Scene 21m F7a+ 8B   (14.5.95)

Climb a steep crack for 6 metres and go left over a bulge to a bucket. Climb the arête and continue to the lower-off.

53 Quick as Rainbows 21m F7b 7B   (17.7.91)

A stunning stamina climb with its crux at the top. Start beneath the scooped, leaning wall 5 metres right of *Drive Blind*. Climb a short groove and a bulge to a jug. Make a hard rockover to reach coral buckets. Layback the right side of a flake to a huge thread. Surge up the flowstone headwall to the lower-off.

⭐⭐ **54 Red Medicine** 21m F7b+ 8B   (14.5.95)
Very sustained. Climb up and over two bulges. Follow a slight groove and gain a calcite jug on the right. Climb a rib and a flake before finishing up tufa on the right.

☆☆ **55 Aeon Flux** 21m F7b 6B †   (17.7.91)
Start 3 metres right of *Quick as Rainbows*. Climb pockets to a shallow alcove. Haul over the bulge above to a half-height resting-scoop. Follow calcified jugs straight up to a flowstone corner.

The next three climbs are based around an overhanging arête and the half-height roof.

⭐⭐ **56 Under the Sky, Inside the Sea** 21m F7a 7B
    (17.7.91)
The overhanging arête at the right end of the wall. Climb the arête direct to a big hold at 6 metres. There are hidden holds on the seaward side of the arête; use them with difficulty to gain an open groove. Climb the groove on huge flowstone formations to the lower-off.

☆☆ **57 Taking Advantage** 18m F7a+ 6B †   (6.06)
An alternative finish to *Under the Sky, Inside the Sea*. Climb that route and move right over the lip of the roof to finish up the flowstone wall.

⭐⭐ **58 Forget Columbus** 18m F7a+ 6B   (6.6.93)
Start 5 metres right of the overhanging arête at a blunt rib. Also has two *in-situ* threads. Spoilt a little by the difficult start, but the second half is stupendous. Climb steeply up the rib and cross a small roof with difficulty. Layback up to the 'dripping' tufa crack above. Finish steeply on large holds in the tufa.

⭐ **59 Buried Violence** 20m F7b+ 8B   (2.11.93)
Seven metres right of the overhanging arête is a raised ledge; its left-hand side is the starting-point for this steadily overhanging climb. Make a hard move to a flake and pass it rightwards to reach a pocketed break. Continue with difficulty to undercuts, and stretch left to two hidden buckets. Follow tufa pipes to a jug before swinging left to the shared lower-off.

⭐⭐⭐ **60 Walking the King** 20m F6b+ 7B   (20.4.93)
One of the best routes in Dorset. Fantastic and strenuous climbing up flakes and flowstone above the right-hand side of the raised ledge. Follow a flake easily, undercut leftwards at 10 metres, and swing steeply up to buckets. Make a trickier move leftwards to the left-hand side of a strip roof before continuing strenuously up over a bulge to the lower-off.

The grey wall right of *Walking the King* provides several very good routes characterised by steep starts and technical headwalls.

⭐⭐ **61 An Ideal for Living** 20m F7a+ 7B   (21.8.95)
Start 4 metres right of *Walking the King*. Climb the initial wall on crozzly holds to the base of a well-defined groove. Technical moves follow, up a groove in the left side of the grey headwall to the shared lower-off.

⭐⭐ **62 Time Bomb** 20m F7a 7B   (21.8.95)
The central line of the grey headwall. Start 3 metres right of *An Ideal for Living*. Climb the crozzly wall to a seam in the grey headwall, which is not as blank as it looks.

☆☆ 63 **Winning at Rodeo** 20m F7a 7B (21.8.95)
How long can you stay on? Low in the grade. A steep start leads to a short corner on the right side of the grey headwall and the lower-off above.

☆☆ 64 **Chevette de la Mer** 20m F6b 7B (9.5.98)
The deep groove is sometimes damp. Start up a short flake and continue up the wall to the base of the groove. Climb it on its left-hand side.

☆☆ 65 **Swimsuit Issue** 20m F6c+ 7B (9.5.98)
The arête right of *Chevette de la Mer*. Pull onto the arête just left of the deep flake. Climb up to a ledge and slap up the square edge above to finish.

To the right lies a deep unclimbed flake/corner, with an impressive unclimbed wall and fine arête to the right again.

☆☆ 66 **Existenz** 20m F7a+ 8B (5.7.97)
The clean-cut arête is taken direct and features fine climbing and exciting positions. Start at the base of the arête and climb it!

Both the following trad routes share a lower-off maillon on a sling around a large block near the top of the crag. This lower-off was not in place at the time of writing, so go prepared.

67 Razor Laugh 20m E1 5b   (2.7.00)
The left-hand of two striking cracks. Climb up a chimney to reach a recess under a roof. Pull out of this and climb the fine crack to a large ledge. Lower off a sling threaded around a large block.

68 Hell Razor 20m E3 5b/c   (2.7.00)
The right-hand crack. Climb to a ledge at 6 metres and then through a shattered area to the jamming crack. Follow it to the large ledge and lower off as for *Razor Laugh*.

69 Space Shanty 20m F6b 7B   (23.5.97)
Often damp, but a great line with some good climbing. Climb up the centre of the wall right of *Hell Razor* to a jutting flake. Pull around this and follow the flake above to the top of the rib and a lower-off shared with *Astra Blaze*.

70 Astra Blaze 20m F6c 6B   (23.5.97)
The central line up the broad arête. A rewarding climb. Climb the short arête just left of a flake. Move up and left to a small sloping chert ledge, where intricate moves lead to a slight groove in the arête above.

Craig Smith climbing *Biscuits for Smut* F7b (page 186).
KEITH SHARPLES

71 Come in and Burn 20m F7b 8B   (5.7.97) R
Start up a short flake just right of *Astra Blaze*. Move
up to a halfway chert ledge and climb the shallow
groove above with some difficulty to the lower-off.

72 Azymuth 20m F7a+ 7B   (23.5.97)
Start just right of *Come in and Burn*. Climb a short
wall to a roof at 5 metres. Attack the blunt rib above,
which is very sustained and has an air of boldness
about it.

73 L'Esprit du Vent 20m F7a+ 8B   (28.5.97)
Four metres left of a deep cave is a wide groove.
Climb the right wall of the groove and move left to
a triangular ledge. The wall above provides the
main interest.

To the south is a shallow bay containing a large
cave. **Nesting-season restrictions** apply from
here southwards (see page 11).

The following three lines are on the imposing white
pillar right of the cave. It has excellent rock, but the
lower-offs are amongst some impressive guano
deposits.

74 Down to the Wire 20m F7b+ 7B †
(12.2.00)
Start up a flake crack on the left side of the grey
wall. At 6 metres step left and power up the steepest
part of the pillar, past an undercut, to a fingery
finish.

75 Dawn of a New Age 20m F7b+ 7B †
(26.1.00)
Climb the easy wall 2 metres right of the flake crack.
Pull over a roof at 6 metres and climb the difficult
wall above.

76 Project 20m F7b+ 7B †
The shallow groove bounding the right side of the
pillar is a neglected project. Start 5 metres right of
the flake crack. Climb the grey wall to a flake, step
left and follow the blank-looking groove above.

Guy Dixon on the now-defunct *Grip '89*
F6c+ (page 186). **KEITH SHARPLES**

To the right of the white pillar
is an agreed bird sanctuary
— no climbing at any time.
This sanctuary stretches all
the way to the climbs at
White Hole.

The Portland Bill Area

OS Ref 675 686 to 687 691

What the cliffs around the Bill lack in stature they make up for in rock quality, being composed of a solid and relatively flawless limestone. The micro-routes here are technical and fingery, and with water beneath some of them, several have been soloed.

The climbs are spread across two distinct areas. The first area reached is a short, west-facing wall directly beneath the QinetiQ fence. These routes are generally short and intense and usually seem hard for their grade. The second area is around the promontory, which provides atmospheric situations and some committing climbing. Pulpit Rock, the stack at the tip of the Bill, has also been climbed (by routes other than the tourist slab), and there are some interesting solos in and around the zawns.

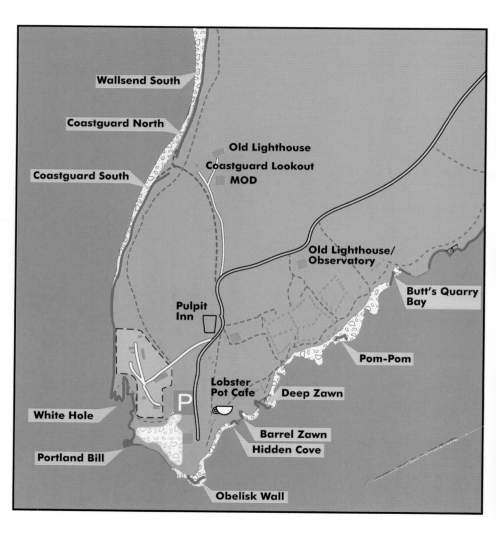

White Hole Promontory

Approach

Park at Portland Bill (parking fee charged). To the west of the car-park is a QinetiQ compound. Walk clockwise around the compound to reach White Hole, a deep zawn with a geologically important raised beach above it. The original approach to this cliff is barred by an unsightly fence and tangle of razor wire. Nowadays, one must take the harder alternative of stepping across the back of the zawn, beneath the razor wire, and climbing a short (unless you look down!) wall to the top of the eastern buttress. A rope may be required.

White Hole Promontory consists of three distinct buttresses in a roughly east to west configuration. To the north of the promontory is an agreed bird nesting sanctuary zone — no climbing allowed at any time. All the climbs are approached by abseil and require calm seas.

The western buttress is reached by traversing carefully westwards across the top of the central buttress and making a short zawn-jump under an impressive earth bridge to the top of the western buttress. Traverse carefully left and abseil from bolts to a ledge 3 metres above the sea. The first route climbs a groove up the front of the buttress.

Portland Bill. MICHELLE IRELAND

1 Second Attention 11m F6c+ 4B (7.8.98)
From the centre of the ledge, climb the central groove to a lower-off.

2 Crossing the Boundaries of Affection 11m F7a+ 5B (28.2.98)
Terrible name, good route. From the right side of the ledge, pull into a recess on the arête and swing left onto the face. There is a belay bolt on the ledge above.

3 Kinaesthesia 11m F7a+ 5B (7.8.98)
Start as for *Crossing the Boundaries of Affection*. From the recess, pull right and climb the blind flake with difficulty. There is a belay bolt on the ledge above.

For the next two routes, abseil to a hanging belay on a low ledge just above the sea beneath the arête of *Crossing the Boundaries of Affection*.

4 Intricacies of Dreaming 14m F7b 5B (24.8.98)
A boulder-problem start. There is a belay bolt on the ledge above. Pull over the bulge above the belay with difficulty, and then climb the crack to the ledge.

5 Memories 15m S2/3 F6a+ 7B (28.2.98)
From the hanging belay, swing right to the corner-crack. Climb it (it is possible to bridge across the zawn) to the ledge. There is a belay bolt on the ledge.

The following routes are on the central buttress, with the first five being approached by abseil from bolts to a hanging belay beneath a prominent boulder.

6 Hung, Swung and Zawned Out 19m S2/3 E2 5b (10.1.99)
Traverse strenuously left for 10 metres until beneath a groove opposite the corner of *Memories*. Climb the groove to the ledge. A high-tide deep-water solo.

7 Paraphilias 17m S3 E6 6a (2.2.00)
Traverse left for 7 metres to reach the base of an arête. Climb it on its left-hand side. Another high-tide deep-water solo, with a high crux.

8 Aphasia 11m S2/3 E3 5b (8.99)
Traverse left for 5 metres and move up to a triangular ledge. Climb the groove above. A deep-water solo at high tide only.

9 The Drill Sergeant 11m F6c+ 5B (11.1.99)
Swing left and climb a thin crack on the left side of the arête. There is a belay bolt on the ledge above.

10 Until the End of Man 11m F7a 6B (1998)
An exhilarating route up the right side of the arête, beneath the prominent boulder. There is a belay bolt on the ledge above.

The next two routes are reached via abseil from the prominent boulder down the front of the central buttress to a good ledge on the right (facing in). They share a belay bolt at the top.

11 Karate Kid 11m F6a+ 5B (25.2.98)
Climb the groove in the centre of the buttress directly above the ledge.

12 Bar Bar Black Sheep 11m F6c+ 5B (25.2.98)
From the ledge, move right and cross a roof (using a knee bar) and climb the wall to the left of an arête.

13 Excalibur's Edge 11m F6b+ 5B (25.2.98)
An isolated route up the right arête of the central buttress. Fantastic positions and highly photogenic. Abseil from a **single bolt** to a small ledge just above the sea on the right-hand side of the arête. Climb the right-hand side of the arête.

The next route is on the eastern buttress, and is reached by abseil to a ledge beneath the left arête.

14 The Labyrinth 11m F7b 8B (8.00)
From the belay, swing left on jugs past a corner. Pull onto a ledge at the base of the wall at the back of the zawn. Move left past a roof and climb the honeycombed wall to a belay bolt on the ledge above.

There is a hard project up the wall three metres left of the arête, up the centre of the face.

To reach the routes from *One Life* to *The Skin Trade*, abseil from bolts down the face of the eastern buttress to a ledge 3 metres above the sea.

15 One Life 13m F7b 5B (9.5.00)
The left arête of the eastern buttress. There is a bolt belay on the ledge above. Swing left from the ledge and climb the arête on its left-hand side. A better, direct start (15 metres F7b 9.6.00) is possible from the low ledge, below and left of the arête.

16 Faceache 11m F7b 4B (16.7.94)
A finger-destroyer! Traverse left from the ledge and climb the sustained, pocketed face right of the arête.

17 The Codebreaker and the French Teacher 11m F7a+ 4B (26.6.94)
The groove on the abseil line is sustained, blind, and technical, with the crux kept back till the last possible moment.

18 Obscene Gesture (Part 2) 11m F7b 4B (13.6.94)
Also starting at the groove, and utilizing the first bolt of the last route, this route swings right into a niche before finishing up the wall.

19 The Skin Trade 11m S3 F6c+ 4B (26.6.94)
A varied and interesting line starting from a double-bolt belay just right of the groove. Easiest if tackled to the left of the bolts. Swing right and use a short diagonal crack to reach a small ledge up to the right. Continue with difficulty to the top. A high-tide, high crux deep-water solo.

The east wall of the eastern buttress is undercut at its base. Most of the obvious lines have now been climbed, some of them only as solos. The bolted lines are at the left-hand end of the wall and have belay bolts at their start and finish. The two cracks are taken by *Splendid Isolation* and, to its right, *Mirthmaid*.

20 Sad Young Biscuits 8m S3 F7a+ 3B (13.6.94)
A finely positioned climb, taking the short, overhanging groove just right of the arête. From the belay on the ledge shared with *The Skin Trade*, make powerful moves up past bolts to the top.

209

21 Dead in Europe 11m S3 F7a+ 4B   (6.8.94)
Start from a hanging belay on a small ledge, which is both undercut and overhung. Climb up leftwards to a projection by a short slabby corner. Continue diagonally leftwards, close to the arête, to the top. A high-tide deep-water solo. It is possible to take a line up the wall to the right of the projection, but this is F7a.

22 Splendid Isolation 11m S3 F6c 5B (26.6.94)
Isolated only in the sense that it is difficult to escape from; you may have an audience by the time you top out. Start from the jutting ledge, as for *Dead in Europe*. Climb over two small roofs and up to the crack, which gives balancy climbing and a high crux. Take a bow. Single-bolt belay on the ledge above. A high-tide deep-water solo.

23 Just for a Day 12m S3 E5 6a   (15.6.00)
A pumpy high-tide deep-water solo up the rib to the right of *Splendid Isolation*. Start as for *Splendid Isolation*. Traverse for 2 metres rightwards along the pocketed break above the roofs and climb the rib on layaways.

24 Mirthmaid 12m F7a+ 4B   (6.94)
Start from the jutting ledge used for the last three routes and take the longer of the two cracks. Move rightwards over the roof to gain the crack with difficulty. Beware the krab-snapper second bolt!

25 Nightmirth 13m F7c 7B   (7.4.96)
Start as for *Mirthmaid*. At the lip of the roof swing airily rightwards for 3 metres and ascend the crack.

The following three routes are in the middle of the face and are approached by abseil to the ledge 10 metres right of *Mirthmaid*. They were soloed on their first ascent on a very high tide and are **not** bolted.

26 Sister of Night 13m S3 F7a+ †   (24.6.00)
Takes the curving groove to the right of *Nightmirth*. Traverse from the ledge left and downwards for 8 metres until beneath the groove, which is then climbed direct. High spring tide required to warrant the deep-water solo grade.

27 Any Last Requests 13m E5 6a †   (7.00)
Traverse the ledge leftwards for 3 metres until beneath a slabby groove. Climb the groove, with a hard rockover to finish. Insufficient water to warrant a deep-water solo grade.

28 Spanish Air 13m E3 5b †   (24.6.00)
Climb the groove directly above the ledge. Insufficient water to warrant a deep-water solo grade.

29 Tiny Smiles 13m F7a+ 3B †   (24.6.00)
The short wall at the back of the zawn. Step across the gap from a ledge and move left to the base of a groove. Climb it past the bolts.

Dave Pickford on *Second Attention* F6c+ (page 208). ROB KENNARD

White Hole South

The landward face of the zawn has a number of solo lines, but only attempt them on a high spring tide, as they have tricky finishes. The first line is at the back of the zawn.

1 Totally Stoked 8m VS 5a †   (24.6.00)
Not shown. Down climb left of a corner to the beach – there is no water beneath this line. Swing left and climb to a groove and the ledge.

For the next two solos, abseil to a small ledge 4 metres right of the corner.

2 Pedriza 8m S2 F6b+ †   (24.6.00)
Climb the wall directly above the small ledge.

3 Siurana 8m S2 F6b †   (15.6.00)
Pull up and right from the ledge and climb the groove above.

To the right of the small ledge is a large roof. It is possible to descend easy rock steps further to the right (facing in) to reach a ledge beneath this roof. The next four routes start here.

4 Get Some Air, Fatso 16m S1 F6a †   (9.03)
Move left along a break for 8 metres and pull up leftwards, to finish up the groove of the previous route.

5 On With the Games 8m S1 F6c †   (15.6.00)
Swing left and climb up onto the face for 4 metres before making a difficult pull up to the top.

6 Unnamed 5 8m S1 F6b †   (15.6.00)
From the left side of the ledge, pull out left and climb a slight groove to the top.

7 True to the Game 8m S1 F6c † (15.6.00)
From the right side of the ledge, swing over the right side of the roof, move left, and finish directly above the apex of the roof.

8 Dragon's Lair 22m VS 4a † (7.00)
The deep chasm behind the previous routes should only be attempted in calm seas. It is very similar to *Camel Filter* at Swanage. Scramble down ledges to the rock-pool, enter the wide chimney, and bridge along it for 16 metres until you can move up into the daylight.

The following three solos are in a bay just to the south, above a deep rock-pool. Whilst the rock-pool is deep, it is also narrow, so don't fall off. The first two climbs swing onto the wall above the rock-pool from the left.

9 Chorro 6m E2 5c † (24.6.00)
Traverse in from the left and climb the left side of the wall.

10 Penon 6m E2 5c † (24.6.00)
Traverse in from the left and climb the centre of the wall up a slight groove.

11 Sella 6m E2 6a † (24.6.00)
Traverse in from the right, move up beneath the stepped roofs, and climb the rib above.

There are several bolted climbs on the short cliff below the QinetiQ fence on the approach to White Hole. Low tide and calm seas are required for your dry enjoyment of the routes on the left side of the cliff, which start from a small cave between two low ledges. Approach via the northern ledge and belay on a single bolt in the cave. Belay on top using threads around the concrete below the fence. The first bolt line, breaking through the left-hand side of the cave's roof, is the hardest route hereabouts.

★ ★ 12 **Balance of Power** 9m F8a 6B (21.11.99)
The blunt arête, with photogenic climbing, hard from the start and condition-dependent due to the smallness of the holds.

The next three climbs start on the right-hand side of the cave.

13 **The Pipers of Portland** 9m F6c 5B (16.9.94)
Worthwhile and strenuous. Pull over the roof of the cave and climb a steep, shallow groove straight to the top.

★ 14 **Funnel Web** 11m F6a+ 5B (16.9.94)
The easiest route of the area. Swing out rightwards from the cave and climb a sustained shallow groove just right of a drainage streak. Finish right of the cause of the streak: a large pipe.

15 **End of Season Sale** 12m F6b 6B (16.9.94)
A well-positioned route. Traverse 5 metres rightwards past two bolts shared with *Funnel Web* and climb up a hidden groove.

Close to the southern end of the QinetiQ fence, scramble down ledges and a short north-facing corner to a spacious lower ledge, which has a trench between it and the cliff. This ledge is accessible at all states of the tide, but calm seas are needed. Just left of the descent corner is a flake-line (*The Cruel Sea*) and then a low cherty overhang crossed by *The Feather*. Three climbs start at the northern end of the ledge, beneath a slanting series of three roofs. They belay on threads around the concrete below the fence.

16 The Reign of Steel 11m F6b+ 5B   (16.9.94)
From the end of the ledge, traverse left, clipping the first bolt of *Red Raw*. Follow a groove past a huge jug to the top.

17 Red Raw 10m F7a+ 4B   (5.9.94)
From the end of the ledge, swing leftwards to pockets on a blank rib. Continuously difficult moves lead straight to the top.

18 Tickled Pink 9m F7c 3B   (5.9.94)
A desperate, fingery pitch. Climb a short, steep groove to layaways. Hard and increasingly powerful moves lead over the leftmost two roofs to the top.

19 Wafer Thin 8m F6b 2B   (5.9.94)
The name probably refers to the state of the two old pegs by the flake. Three metres before the end of the ledge is a black sloping ledge on the wall. Gain the black ledge, follow a layback flake, and finish with difficulty. Single belay bolt.

Dave Pickford on-sight soloing *Splendid Isolation* S3 F6c (page 211). JOFF COOK

20 Run, Rabbit, Run 8m F6c 3B (5.9.94)
Pull over a bulge and climb a slight groove. Move up to an undercut and finish up the blank wall. Two belay bolts in the short wall.

21 Staple Diet 8m F6a+ 3B (1.10.94)
Start just left of the low cherty overhang. Climb up to a high hand-ledge and stretch for the top. Two belay bolts in the short wall above.

22 Painted Lady 8m F6a+ 2B (9.8.03)
Good climbing between jugs on the faint rib. Pull over the cherty overhang on incut holds to gain a flat jug. Mantel the jug and stretch or jump to a good flake, to finish at the lower-off.

23 The Feather 8m F6c 3B (1.10.94)
A poor route. Climb over the cherty overhang on friable holds and continue up the blunt rib. Two belay bolts in the short wall above.

24 The Cruel Sea 8m F5+ 2B (1991)
The leftward-leaning flake bounding the right-hand side of the wall. From the base of a short chimney (the approach to the ledge), climb to the flake and follow it with difficulty to the lower-off.

25 **Adonis Blue** 8m F6b+ 2B   (15.8.03)
The centre of the steep wall right of *The Cruel Sea* has a gritstonesque crux. Using a good undercut, reach to a flat hold. Mantel with difficulty to gain a flake. A tricky stretch leads to the lower-off.

26 **Chalk-hill Blue** 8m F6a 2B   (15.8.03)
The innocuous-looking wall starting 4 metres right of *The Cruel Sea*. Make a long reach to a good handrail. A longer reach (or some improvisation) leads to easier ground and the lower-off.

Pulpit Rock

The short stack at Portland Bill is Pulpit Rock. Annette's 1963 guidebook mentioned a 10-metre Very Difficult climb up its seaward face, which needed a low-tide approach. In 1997, a bolt line was added to the seaward face of the Rock. Due to its extremely visible location and the inherent risks of attracting 'cowboy climbers', the route was quickly de-bolted. All would-be bolters, please think for at least 10 seconds before making your mark.

There are a number of other lines, which were all soloed (with the exception of *Swirling Pool*), on the Rock. They are approached by bridging across the gap beneath the fallen slab (long legs useful). Currently there is an abseil bolt on top of the pedestal, but it may be removed. The first line takes the northern arête. There are no topos for these climbs.

27 **Tombstonin'** 10m S1 F6b+   (25.6.00)
Good climbing up the arête and the thin crack above, following a steep start. Deep water beneath, but watch out for the tidal flow.

28 **End of the Land** 10m S2 F6b+   (7.00)
The south-west arête, approached by an anti-clockwise traverse from *Tombstonin'*. Start right of the arête and step left to climb the prow to the top. A serious solo.

⭐29 **The God of Sleep** 10m XS 5a (13.5.04)
Not a deep-water solo. The rib right of *End of the Land*. Ascend the vague rib via flakes and nodules on wonderful rock. A fragment of the Verdon in Dorset.

⭐30 **Chymerie** 10m HVS 4c   (12.5.04)
Not a deep-water solo. Start just left of the arête bounding the south side, immediately right of *The God of Sleep*. Climb the shallow, hanging groove, again on wonderful rock.

31 **Edge of Beyond** 10m S2 F5   (16.5.04)
The faint groove line on the east side, just right of the arête.

32 **Bleeting Nincompoops** 10m S1 F4+   (27.6.06)
Start immediately right of *Edge of Beyond*. Amenable climbing up the slight groove.

33 **Rapture of the Deep** 10m S0 F6a (17.5.04)
Start just right of *Bleeting Nincompoops*. Follow the overlap, slab, and short hanging groove in the centre of the wall. A well-positioned crux.

34 **Swirling Pool** 10m XS 5a   (19.5.04)
This climb has been soloed, thought the consequences of a fall are too messy to contemplate. Climb the obvious crack on the east side. The crack can be protected with natural gear.

Unknown 'tombstoner' risking arrest off Pulpit Rock. STEVE HARDY

Portland Bill to Cave Hole

The craglets, boulder-filled bays and interesting caves northeast of Portland Bill are short and sometimes difficult to reach. Don't be deterred though, as boulder problems, deep-water solos, and traverses make the most of the area's excellent rock.

Approach

The approach to this stretch of coastline is best described in terms of the three 'jib' cranes along its length, now used for launching lobster-potting boats, but originally designed to load the quarried stone onto boats.

1. In the car-park at Portland Bill (parking fee charged), turn your back to the lighthouse, cross the road, and walk towards the cliff edge directly behind the café. The small cove here is Hidden Cove (p. 222), which contains some wonderful bouldering from V2 to V5. Walking 20 metres northeast brings you to the narrow Barrel Zawn (p. 226) which has some good, hard bouldering up to V8. Northeast from there is the first crane, beneath which is the compact, south-facing wall of Deep Zawn with a selection of high-quality deep-water solos (p.228).

Continuing northeast you enter an area of beach huts. To your right is Sector Pom-Pom, a cove with a pinnacle in its centre, containing several sports routes on impeccable rock, including the test-piece *The Big Blue*. From there, the cliff-top path turns generally northwards. At the last of the beach huts a deep inlet lies to your right. This is Butts Quarry Bay, containing *Once Were Warriors* and *Too Funky (for Me)*. Three hundred metres north is the second of the jib cranes, sitting above a huge cave (Cave Hole). An unsightly ladder allows easy access to a few deep-water solos below.

The prow of rock 20 metres to the north is traversed by *The Big Easy*. Fifty metres north of the second crane is a jutting prow climbed by *Up the Grotto*, and reached by an in-situ 'pirate' rope. Walking a few metres north (above the cave containing *Crab Party*) brings one to a flat ledge above a clean, wide wall traversed by *Bare Reputation*.

A collection of large square boulders further north marks the top of Waterfall Cave, home to *King of the Swingers*. The last few of the boulders lie above the *High Klicks* routes. From here, the coastline forms a large, wide bay, containing the last of the three cranes, directly above the *Octopus Weed* cave. To the north is Beeston cliff (p.244).

2. The climbs at Cave Hole itself can also be approached from the north. (Both approaches are about a kilometre long.) From the pumping-station just south of *The Eight Kings Inn*, follow a track to the cliff-top. Continue southwards to the northernmost crane, which sits atop the *Octopus Weed* cave.

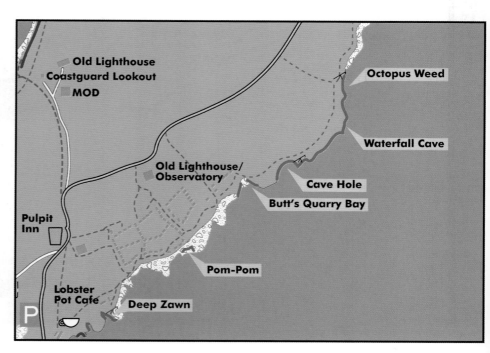

Gav Symonds on *Barrel Arête LHS* V4/5 (page 227). STEVE TAYLOR

Portland Bill

At the very tip of Portland Bill is the Trinity House obelisk (and lots of tourists). This 7-metre-tall white obelisk was built in 1844 as a warning to sailors of a low shelf of rock extending 30 metres south into the sea. Directly under the obelisk is a vertical wall of the finest dark-grey limestone. Whilst the Obelisk wall never exceeds four and a half metres in height, the flat rock platform under the problems makes a bouldering mat essential. The close proximity of the aforementioned tourists means you are rarely without spectators. This may be seen as a good or bad aspect of this area, depending on your point of view. The best time to climb there is late spring through to early autumn. At other times of year the ledges beneath the problems are covered in very slippery seaweed.

Approach

Park at Portland Bill (parking fee charged). Follow all the tourists along a concrete path past the lighthouse to the white obelisk. Descend to the problems immediately right (looking out) of the obelisk, down rock ledges. At the base of the down-climb is a rock-filled bay. Looking out to sea, the Obelisk Wall is to the left (east) and is reached by a short scramble over small boulders and ledges.

The Swiss Cheese Wall

To the right of the down-climb is a short heavily-featured wall. The climbing there is a complete contrast to the technical highballs on the Obelisk wall. In general the landings are not brilliant, but the climbing is fun and unusual. The problems have not been described due to the transient nature of the boulders at the base of the wall. One day a problem will start from bedrock at the base of the wall, the next day it will start from the top of a metre-high pile of boulders.

The Obelisk Wall

The first feature you pass as you walk eastwards along the base of the wall is a large jutting roof. Beyond this are a short wall and a roofed alcove. Up to this point the base of the wall is strewn with boulders that provide rather unpalatable landings. Eight metres further right a stepped arête defines the right-hand edge of the area.

1 Terror Tactics V0 The crack immediately left of the jutting roof is rather nondescript.

2 Kiss and Tell V2 Follow *Terror Tactics* to a downward-pointing fang and stretch rightwards to a large pocket on the lip of the roof. Swing out, wave to the crowds, and pull over the roof to more good holds.

3 The Poxley Pocket V3 The direct line through the jutting roof proves less difficult than appearances suggest which, considering the landing, is just as well. Start on good edges beneath the roof. Climb up to a conspicuous pocket in the centre of the roof. Use this and an edge to the left to reach jugs over the lip, which is surmounted in the usual thrutching manner.

4 Penny Lane V0 To the right of the jutting roof is a full-height crack above a terrible landing. A bouldering mat offers some comfort but is unlikely to be much benefit in the event of a fall. Follow the crack on good holds and exit just right of the roof. Named after the semi-embedded penny halfway up the problem.

5 Stake Through the Heart V1 Climb the wall immediately left of the roofed alcove. Again the landing is terrifying.

Right of *Stake Through the Heart*, the flat ledge at the base of the wall is no longer covered by boulders and offers a far better landing.

6 Groundhog Day V2 The moves around the lip of the roofed alcove and onto the upper face are surprisingly amenable. Get established on the good ledge below the roof. The face and crack above the roof are reached by virtue of a deep leftward-facing slot on the lip.

7 Willow's Crack V0 Bounding the right side of the roofed alcove is a niche. Start at the niche and follow the continuation crack to a ledge. Thankfully, the mantel is easy.

8 Angel Dust V0 Low down, a metre right of the alcove is a tiny roof – start here. The line of good holds above lead to the finishing ledge of *Willow's Crack*. A superb problem that rewards a positive approach.

9 Buffy's Groove V0 The shallow groove and narrow corner offer one of the finest low-grade boulder problems in Dorset, with superb technical moves on perfect rock. Not to be missed.

10 Blade V3 The slight rib right of *Buffy's Groove* is overcome by a series of technical moves cumulating in a committing long reach for the top.

11 Vampire Killers V1 Between the rib of *Blade* and the stepped arête at the right end of the crag is a slight groove. If the ledges on the right are ignored, the groove is a nice technical problem.

12 **Silver Bullet** V0- The stepped arête is a useful ⭐ down-climb.

13 **Sea Spray** V0 The little arête right of *Silver Bullet* is very photogenic – what other reason do you need to climb it? Start from the higher ledge and follow the arête direct.

More bouldering can be found in the boulder-filled cove to the east.

traverse of low bulge

Rock steps

The Hidden Cove

The Hidden Cove is a pleasant little venue with some of the best bouldering in Dorset. The cove walls offer a variety of climbing styles from steep, pumpy traverses to technical highballs.

Approach
Park at Portland Bill (parking fee charged). On the mini roundabout facing the car-park entrance is the Lobster Pot Café. Walk past the café on its south side to reach the cliff edge. Follow the cliff edge northwards to a white stone hut. A slight gully leads seawards from the stone hut to rock steps at the back of the cove.

Standing at the water's edge facing inland, one can see from left to right: a long low bulge, a large roof jutting from a deep corner, a low strip roof, the descent ledges, a series of shorter walls, a stepped ramp, a tall vertical face, a large jutting roof, and a rock-fall area. The cove is tidal and you should plan your visit for mid to low tide. Being tidal, the level of the beach, and hence the difficulty of the starting moves, may vary. The left side of the cove is only kissed by the sun during the morning hours. The right side of the cove faces south and is a veritable suntrap, giving superb conditions on fine winter days, but you will find it too hot in the summer.

The left side of the cove (looking in) is not blessed with the same immaculate rock as the right and is slightly broken in places. However, there are a number of traverses along the long, low bulge, the difficulty depending on which holds you chose to be in or out of bounds.

To the right of the long, low bulge is a deep corner, capped by a large jutting roof with a handrail on the lip.

1 **Once More for the Camera** V1 Make a sit-down start on good edges beneath a small vertical crack three metres left of the roof-capped corner, where the low bulge is less pronounced. Gain a good edge at the top of the crack before stepping left onto the jutting ledge.

2 **Cut, It's a Wrap** V3 Two metres left of the roof-capped corner is a vertical face. Start in the lowest break and climb the face on small edges.

3 **The Scary Roof Traverse** V2 Hand-traverse the lip of the roof from left to right, starting and finishing on the beach. A spotter is essential.

The rock to the right of the roof-capped corner is rather broken and offers little of interest to the boulderer. At the back of the cove, immediately to the left (looking in) of the descent steps, is a low strip roof. A number of worthwhile eliminates exist in this section. All are relatively short and start from a sitting (or even lying) position.

4 A Local Problem for Local People V5 Two metres left of the low strip roof is a blunt undercut arête. This eliminate problem starts from a lying position on good edges directly under the arête. Crank up to a good edge over the bulge and again to the sloping ledge on the arête (the juggy part of the ledge is out of bounds). Use a side-pull on the arête to slap for the top.

5 Country File V0 A metre left of the low strip roof is a groove and a flake crack. Climb the flake crack, starting at the lowest jug.

6 Marsh Beauty V1 From a crouching start, climb the wall between the groove and the low strip roof using a series of small flakes.

7 Marshmallow V0 Start at a low jug under the right-hand side of the low strip roof. Move out to a sloping ledge in the middle of the roof and thence to jugs over the lip. Swing left along the lip of the roof and pull over using a thin flake.

8 Adam's Triumph V2
Start as for *Marshmallow*. From the jugs over the lip, pull over rightwards onto the descent ledges.

Immediately to the right of the descent ledges is a small cave. Whilst there is little of interest to be found here, the short wall to the right again provides some worthwhile climbing.

Neal Heanes on *The Hidden Wall* **V4** (page 224). BEN STOKES

9 **Skid Mark** V2 A traverse of the short wall to the right of the small cave at the level of the brown streak. Start 3 metres to the left of the arête.

10 **Guru Pete** V1 Start in the lowest break at pockets a metre left of the arête. Two positive edges lead to a sloping edge and the top.

The following problems are situated directly under the stepped ramp that defines the left edge of the tall vertical face.

11 **Youth of Today** V0 Starting in the lowest break, follow a leftward-trending line of good holds.

12 **Loaded Questions** V1 Start in the lowest break at a threaded pocket. Follow a series of sloping holds to finish at the top of the stepped ramp.

13 **Hip and Trendy** V1 The arête direct, from a sit-down start in the lowest break. A tricky finish on sloping holds.

The tall vertical face of immaculate rock to the right of the stepped ramp is the showpiece of the cove. The landings are good, which when you consider the height of the wall is just as well. Low tide is preferable if you don't want your mat to get wet. The stepped ramp provides an easy down-climb.

14 **The Hidden Traverse** V5 A traverse of the low break from left to right. Start at the base of the stepped ramp. Imagine there are footholds and follow the break ever rightwards until you can finish up *The Hidden Roof*.

15 **The Hidden Wall** V4 A technical line just right of the stepped ramp. A series of small edges leads directly up to a tiny roof. This is passed with a long reach to yet another small, but hidden edge. Very photogenic.

16 **The Hidden Niche** V3 To the right of *The Hidden Wall* is an obvious niche at half-height. Good holds lead up to the niche. Move slightly leftwards with difficulty, pass the niche, and finish two metres right of *The Hidden Wall*.

17 The Hidden Eliminate V4 An eliminate style problem between *The Hidden Niche* and *The Hidden Crack*. Start from a good hand-ledge. Move straight up to a jug and make a hard rock-over to gain distant edges. The top is gained by a final big stretch, which will be locked by the strong and jumped by the brave. The weak and scared will mince around looking for non-existent holds. The niche to the left and the crack to the right are out of bounds.

18 The Hidden Crack V3 The crack is tricky to start, and depending on the level of the beach, sometimes needs a jump to reach the first break. The crux is getting your feet on the first break.

To the right of the flat wall is a large jutting roof at half height. Thankfully, the top of the crag is lower in this section.

19 The Hidden Escape V1 Start under the left side of the roof. The first holds may require a long stretch or a jump. Turn the roof on its left side using not-too-generous edges.

20 The Hidden Roof V1 Start up *The Hidden Escape* and traverse under the jutting roof on jugs. Pull around the right side of the roof. An absolute classic and one of the best boulder problems on Portland.

21 The Hidden Jump V1 Start under the right side of the roof. Jump to jugs and finish as for the previous problem. Harder if the beach is low.

The section beyond here is subject to regular wave damage, rendering the recording of problems pointless.

Pete Oxley on *Hip and Trendy* **V1**. STEVE TAYLOR

Barrel Zawn

With its steep problems and interesting sloping holds, this is a splendid venue. Conditions depend greatly on the temperature and amount of sunshine on the wall – too little sun and it will be greasy. The tide also adds another dimension, as do the fluctuations in height of pebbles in the bay, which change from year to year. Currently the beach is low and this makes some starts very difficult for the short!

Main Face

1 **Eranu** **V5** The overhanging bulge is the most difficult to reach and most affected by the tide. Try using Zen and levitation to reach the first holds, or alternatively, and more usually, get a bunk up.

2 **Uvarvu** **V4** Somehow reach the now-high break and climb the groove.

⭐3 **Barrel Roll** **V3** A jump-start leads to more amenable climbing.

⭐4 **Barrel Groove** **V2** Jump to the break and climb the groove direct.

5 **Cooper Trooper** **V3** From the break, climb the crack-line.

⭐6 **Half Measures** **V3** Starting in the break, climb the flake and cracks.

A **Barrel Zawn Traverse** V7 A long and sustained traverse from *The Barrel* to exit up *Eranu*. Probably the easiest way to reach *Eranu* without the aid of a human ladder!

7 **The Barrel** V6 Sit start on the lowest pod and make long powerful moves to exit up *Half Measures*.

8 **Over a Barrel** V2 The slabby face is tricky.

9 **Rampline** V1 The superb rising flake-line.

10 **Corner Layback** V0- The corner-crack.

11 **Deviant** V3 Break rightwards out of the corner-crack to climb the face.

Barrel Buttress

12 **Corner Flake** V0- Sometimes used as an escape route when the tide comes in.

13 **The Flake Escape** V5 From the low part of the main flake, break out right using long arms to climb the main face.

14 **Barrel Arête LHS** V4/5 From a low start, climb the arête on its left-hand side. The grade depends greatly on how much of the ledge you allow yourself to use.

15 **Barrel Arête RHS** V1 Climb the right-hand side of the arête with some initial difficulty.

Deep Zawn

Only two minutes walk from the car-park, Deep Zawn contains the most accessible deep-water soloing on Portland. Whilst its problems are short (most only getting V grades), they are certainly worth a visit or two. The zawn is below the southernmost crane.

The first two problems are reached by scrambling down a short corner on the southern side of the zawn.

⭐ 1 **White Pony** **V2** SO The hanging flake crack, starting from the ledge at the entrance to the zawn.

⭐ 2 **The World's Best Mono** **V5** SO Traverse the faultline rightwards for 4 metres under the prow, then pull over the bulge using a single mono.

The following problems are on the northern wall of the zawn, reached by down-climbing a convenient rusty ladder (much easier than the chain of old days).

⭐ 3 **Salty Sea Dog** **V5** SO From the base of the ladder, traverse left for 6 metres to a lone sidepull. Hard moves on slopers lead to a slab and a final difficult move to finish.

⭐ 4 **Sugar Daddy** **V4** SO From the base of the ladder, traverse left for 4 metres and climb the slight groove, though it is difficult to leave the comfort of the ledge.

5 **All Things Being Relative** **V1** SO Climb the slight rib 2 metres left of the ladder – easier than it looks.

6 **Relativity** **V1** SO A tight line immediately right of *All Things Being Relative*.

⭐ 7 **The Red Crane Traverse** 18m F5 SO (25.6.00) From the base of the ladder, traverse the break rightwards past the arête. Top out on the east-facing wall beneath the crane.

The next two routes are approached via the *Red Crane Traverse*, and are worth the trip.

⭐ 8 **Wall of Squares** 12m F5+ SO (2000) The face between the quarried cut-outs is taken on pockets and edges.

⭐ 9 **Red Crane Wall** 14m F5+ SO (2000) The face right of the quarried cut-outs, using the right side of the right-hand cut-out.

Andy Long on the Waveband V10 (page 230). CHERYL EVANS

Sector Pom-Pom

Best approached from Portland Bill, this small bay contains a collection of compact, difficult bolted problems. There have been access difficulties here in the past, so a low profile is best adopted. Most of the routes are tidal, and the height of the beach varies, sometimes requiring a jump, or assistance, to reach the first holds.

The first four routes (not shown on the topo) are on a jutting prow on the southern side of the bay.

El Scorchio 7m F6c 3B   (23.1.00)
Start right of a cave, on a ledge beneath the left side of the prow, below a hanging corner. Climb the bulge and then move leftwards. Lower off the third bolt.

Maximum Grr... 7m F7b 2B   (23.1.00)
Start as for *El Scorchio*, but blast straight up with difficulty to a short flake. Lower off the second bolt.

L'Eau Profile 7m F7c 4B   (4.4.96)
Start just to the right of *El Scorchio*. Pull around a roof (hard) and climb the wall above, right of the arête. Lower off the fourth bolt.

Private Dancer 7m F6b 3B   (4.4.96)
The slight groove on the right-hand side of the jutting prow. Lower off the third bolt.

The remaining climbs are on the impeccably clean walls on the north side of the bay.

1 **Thirty Years Young** 6m E3 6b   (4.4.96)
A scary solo up the blunt arête, with a committing finish to a small ledge. Mat required.

⭐ 2 **Burbage Belle** 7m F7c 2B   (27.3.96)
An excellent, hard boulder problem. Jump to the break and power up the bulging wall on sloping pockets, staying right of the small ledge. Single bolt lower-off.

⭐⭐ 3 **The Big Blue** 7m F7c+ 3B   (26.10.96)
A compelling line up the steep central groove. Long reaches make this F8a for shorties. Lower off the third bolt.

⭐ 4 **Ninth Wave** 7m F7a+ 3B   (6.95)
The hanging crack right of the prow. Jump to the break and climb the crack.

5 **Zimmerframe With Attitude** 7m F6c 3B   (6.95)
The difficult corner. The final bolt is missing.

⭐⭐⭐ 6 **The Waveband** V10 'The best boulder traverse on the Isle'. From the hand-ledge below *Zimmerframe...* traverse the break leftwards to the ledge by *Burbage Belle*. Note that the start has suffered from rockfall recently, though the grade remains unchanged.

7 The O'lympets 7m F6c+ 3B   (6.95)
The twin, thin cracks are hard to reach, but worth the effort. Lower off the third bolt.

8 Honorary Froggatt 7m F7b+ 4B   (19.3.96)
Mantel onto the left-hand side of a ledge and climb the difficult ramp line. Lower off the fourth bolt.

9 Pocketful of Shells 7m F7b 4B   (19.3.96)
Rockover onto the right-hand side of the ledge and bridge tenuously up the groove above.

Andy Earl bouldering at Sector Pom-Pom.
ANDY LONG

231

Butts Quarry Bay

When approaching from the south, continue past the first of the three cranes on the cliff-top, and descend into a large boulder-and-pebble-filled bay in front of the three northernmost beach-huts; this is Butts Quarry Bay. *Memory Lane* traverses the south wall of the bay and *Too Funky (For Me)* climbs steeply up just to the right of the large roof on the bay's northern side.

1 Memory Lane 40m XS   (6.8.94)
A leftward traverse out of the bay along its southern wall, where a loose cliff-top prevents upward escape. The grades are for high tide; at low tide easier options are possible.
1 20 metres 4c. Climb on good holds to the far side of an inset section of the wall.
2 20 metres 5b. Continue across blank-looking walls to the large platform on the promontory.

The following routes are on the northern wall of the bay.

2 Up, Up and Away E2 6a/b (1995) is an extended boulder problem up the bulging rib/arête just left of the cave.

☆ **3 Once Were Warriors** 13m F7c †† 6B (16.9.95)
The impressive large roof on the northern side of the bay. Start at the back of the cave. A large block (and attached bolt) have gone missing. Pull up on good holds to the start of the cramped seam in the roof, which is followed with difficulty to the top.

☆ **4 Penny Lane** 15m XS 5b   (20.8.94)
Start under the large roof; usually soloed. Climb up to the horizontal crack a metre below the roof. Traverse rightwards, keeping below the roofs and crossing *Too Funky (For Me)* halfway, to a large ledge.

The routes from *Too Funky...* to *Makin' Bacon* require a high tide for them to be even considered as deep-water solo climbs. With the highest of spring tides, there will only be 1.5 metres of water beneath you.

☆ **5 Too Funky (For Me)** 8m S3 F6c+ 3B (6.8.94)
A steep problem up the wall on the seaward side of the large roof. Low tide required for the bolt clipper, high spring tide and a traverse in for the soloist. Gain the undercut wall, cross a small triangular roof, and move out rightwards: 5 metres up and 2 metres out! Finish up the short headwall. Stake belay well back.

6 The Big Boss E5 6b †   (8.98)
A low tide is required to start this serious solo. Pull onto the wall as for *Too Funky (For Me)* and move right for 2 metres. Cross the large roof and headwall above. Powerful.

7 Marine Boy 8m S1 XS 5c (F6a+) (10.6.95)
From the *Penny Lane* traverse, make some rather blind moves on good holds to negotiate the left-hand side of the capping roof. Crank and make a long reach for the break. The bolted direct start is F6c+.

8 Godzuki 7m S0/S1 XS 5c (F6a+) (9.6.95)
Start from the promontory to the right of the wall. Swing leftwards around the arête; then climb the pockets immediately left of the arête.

☆ **9 Makin' Bacon** 6m S0 XS 5c (F6a+) (5.8.95)
The short arête immediately right of *Godzuki*, taken direct, provides an entertaining solo.

The next route traverses the lip of the cave immediately north of the beach.

10 Trashy's Traverse 11m XS 5c (11.8.95)
A long, involved traverse, requiring a high level of commitment to hang the numerous huge hollow flakes. From the lower ledge at the south-west side of the cave, climb up high to start (large triangular

flake); then drop down slightly and continue the traverse rightwards across the lip of the entire cave. At least one hands-off rest if you can find it. The highest of tides only provides a metre of water beneath!

11 Eight Inches 7m S1 XS 6a (F7a)   (22.7.05)
Traverse in, with difficulty, from the right side of Trashy's cave and make hard moves from an undercut to gain a hand-rail in the roof.

Cave Hole

North of Butts Quarry Bay is a 100-metre section of cliff that is riddled with small caves. This section forms a very shallow bay, at the northern end of which is a south-facing wall beneath Broad Ope crane, the second of the three cranes. *Temporary Lifestyle* climbs this wall, and is approached by an unsightly ladder and some old iron rungs. The southern end of the bay has three deep-water solos. They are reached by down-climbing from the promontory at the southern end of the bay and making a low-level traverse along a seam of shallow pockets.

12 Psycho Man 11m S1/2 XS 5b (F6a+) (10.6.95)
An entertaining solo through intimidating roofs, with reasonable water. Traverse rightwards on *Desperado* to the start of its crux traverse; then climb directly up on jugs to the roof section. Make a reach up to a huge conglomerate jug and swing out on it to sloping finishing holds in a lichenous V-groove in the roof, and a crux mantel. All good fun. Note that there is a nasty little pointed boulder below the crux. Not a problem at high tide, but if you fall off at anything less than high tide, make sure you do it sideways.

13 Mike's Free Willy 11m S0/1 XS 6a (F6b)
(23.7.95)
An eliminate starting on the initial traverse of *Desperado* and taking the harder line left of the *Desperado* finish. A very committing roof finish.

14 Desperado 18m S0 XS 6a (F6b)   (9.6.95)
An exciting introduction to long 'cavey' routes, with a fingery traverse just above the sea to start. Traverse northwards into the cave, traverse the pocketed break-line low down with some difficulty, and continue to jugs. Continue diagonally rightwards past an old rusty peg and move up to a large break-line; then trend rightwards to top out on rock that is significantly better than it looks! Atmospheric.

15 Lick of the Cat 10m S1/2 XS 5c (F6b+)
(9.6.95)
The obvious overhanging 45-degree arête. Approach down *Pirates of the Black Atlantic*. From the bottom ledge, traverse south at 5a until you reach the base of the arête. Swing underneath it. The route climbs the left-hand/south face of it, so is less formidable than it looks. But it's pumpy! A superb line, and littered with excellent holds. A must-do.

16 Pirates of the Black Atlantic 9m S2 XS 5b (F6a)   (9.6.95)
The middle of the three arêtes was originally down-climbed to reach *Lick of the Cat*! Abseil from the 'P'-embossed square limestone block next to the path. At the bottom is a useful ledge to sit on or abseil to. Don't fall onto it though… A pleasant route with good holds all the way.

233

17 **Surface Tension** 10m S0/1 XS 5c (6c+)

(4.8.95)

The northernmost square-cut arête in the Desperado Cave has a grossly overhanging upper section. The base is accessible only by boat or swimming! A daring and committing finish, direct over the roof right of the V-groove.

18 **Underlife** 13m S0 F7a 4B †

(2003)

An exciting footless traverse beneath *Temporary Lifestyle*. Start as for that route and swing up left to a handrail. Follow this to finish as for *Temporary Lifestyle*.

19 **Temporary Lifestyle** 12m S0 VS 4c (F4+)

(31.7.94)

The best introduction to deep-water soloing on Portland, very safe, though best to avoid at dead low tide. Upward escape is possible before the roof and the technical grade depends on the exact starting-point. From the rungs, climb a few feet leftwards and then up into a shallow corner. Traverse leftwards on the brink of the large cave, moving around an arête and under a roof. At the far end of the roof, climb to the top.

For the next three climbs, descend rock steps 12 metres north of Broad Ope crane.

20 **Babes and Bedsheets** 8m E5 6a

(6.8.94)

Above the centre of the large overhung shelf is a hanging groove, the start of a serious solo. Even at high tide, failure on the crux would mean an inverted fall into only 2 metres of water. Use a tiny undercut pillar to gain the groove. Traverse left under the roof to a bottomless corner and finish diagonally left to the arête.

21 **Foxy Chicks** 6m S1 XS 5c (F6a+)

(6.8.94)

Start near the right-hand side of the large overhung shelf situated above a low sea-arch, beneath a hanging crack. High tide required for clearance over the submerged boulders. Reach up to a sidepull (there is a good handjam too) and commit yourself to a thuggy move up over the roof. Continue up horizontal slots to the top.

22 **Reel 'em in** 6m S1 XS 5c (F6b)

(21.5.95)

From the right-hand side of the overhung shelf, pull out over the roof from a good diagonal jug and follow a series of good holds to the top. Usually climbed footless. Wait for high tide.

23 **The Big Easy** 18m S0 XS 5c (F6a+)

(6.8.94)

High tide and calm conditions are desirable for this solo traverse. Start on the left side of a small east-facing wall. Traverse rightwards to the overhung shelf. From the right-hand end of the shelf, committing and technical moves above fairly shallow water lead to the arête. Swing around the arête and continue rightwards past an overhang to a ledge. To escape, reverse the pitch or take to the sea! Better still, finish up *Ixtlan* for a thrilling finale.

24 **Aquamarina** 6m S1 XS 6b (F7a)

(11.8.95)

Only safe at mid tide. Traverse rightwards out of the overhung shelf to a jutting jug. From here, climb the wall above on small slots and crimps.

The Big Easy has proved popular with first ascensionists, who have used it to reach the following solos. High tide is required if you intend to fall off! At low tide, however, there are a number of bouldery traverses along and under the arch that are quite entertaining.

⭐ 25 **The Little Hard** 7m S2 XS 5c   (15.5.95)
Climb a groove above the initial wall of The Big Easy.

26 **The Route With No Name** 7m HVS 4c (1994)
The right-hand arête of the initial wall of The Big Easy. Can be used as a downclimb but has shallow water underneath.

Ixtlan Wall

27 Massive Amounts of Strength 7m S2 XS 6c (F7b) † (1996)
Climb the impressive arête to the right of *The Route with No Name* via the overhanging scoop.

28 Huge Reaches 7m S2 XS 6b (F7a) † (5.10.96)
The steep groove to the right of the arête. Beware of submerged boulders.

⭐ **29 Mad In Me** 7m S3 XS 6a (F7a) † (5.10.96)
High spring tide is essential for the steep line above the end of *The Big Easy*. Start 6 metres left of *Ixtlan*. Undercut left to a jug in a niche. Reach out over the roof to finger jugs leading left; then pass the top roof to step left to the finish of *Huge Reaches*.

30 Lunge or Plunge 7m S1 XS 6b (F7b) † (1996)
The excellent and obvious steep line starting 4 metres left of *Ixtlan*. Take the break in the roofs to the left, traverse back right, and float straight over the final roof.

⭐⭐ **31 Ixtlan** 9m S1/2 XS 5b (F6a+) (4.95)
Continue rightwards past the end of *The Big Easy*. Climb a flowstone groove and the roof above to a terrifying (though relatively safe at high tide) mantelshelf exit, the scene of many a grovel.

32 Karma 9m S2 XS 5c (F6b) (8.5.95)
Starts 3 metres right of *Ixtlan*. Climb a groove to a triangular roof with a crack in it. Cross the roof to a hard mantel and the top.

33 Famous Genitalia 10m S2 XS 5c (F6c) † (5.10.96)
The groove immediately left of *Mad about You*. At the top, take the capping roof on its left.

⭐ **34 Mad about You** 9m S2 XS 6a (F6b+) † (15.5.95)
A powerful route starting 4 metres past *Ixtlan*. Enter the groove with difficulty and continue up to the right-hand side of the capping roof. Traverse 2 metres left to finish.

The following three routes lie above a submerged ledge, and should **not** be regarded as deep-water solos.

35 Greet Flying Scotsmen 8m XS 5b/c † (13.8.98)
Long reaches between positive fingerholds on the blunt rib just right of *Mad about You*.

36 Vicious Sea Splat 10m XS 5c † (5.10.96)
The fine flowstone crack 6 metres right of *Mad About You*.

37 Shot and Wounded 12m XS 6a † (5.10.96)
The crack left of *Russion Roulette*.

⭐⭐ **38 Russian Roulette** 14m S1 XS 6a (F6b+) (11.6.95)
Not as dangerous as the name suggests! More of a gamble as to when you'll fall off. Start on *The Big Easy*, traverse rightwards to within 2 metres of the diagonal arête on the edge of the cave. Now enter the flowstone crack with commitment (crux), and climb rapidly to better holds. At the break, swing left a metre, and finish direct over the juggy roof section.

Two hundred metres south of the third crane is a depression in the grassy plateau caused by the partial collapse of the roof of a sea-cave. A metal grating fixed over the hole to protect the public has been overlaid with quarried blocks. North of these climbs the cliff juts out between two caves. *Captain*

Haddock and five other solo lines start on this arête. They are safe in all tides (except for *Up the Grotto*), and may have an *in-situ* hawser rope available for access.

Crab Party Area

39 Captain Haddock 8m S0 XS 5b (F6a+)
(19.5.95)
The bulge, wall, and capping roof 3 metres left of the arête, keeping a metre right of the descent rope.

40 Gourmet Shit Traverse 12m S0/1 XS 5c (F6a+)
(26.8.95)
From the base of *Captain Haddock*, traverse the entire arête clockwise. How's this possible? Well, after an overhanging section in the depths of the cave, a window shows the way. Crawl through it and continue back round to the starting-point.

41 Flipper Force 8m S0 XS 6a (F6b+) (19.5.95)
From the left-hand side of the arête, swing around and climb up spaced holds to the top.

42 Up the Grotto 8m E5 6a (19.5.95)
Not a deep-water solo, as there is no water under the crux roof. Climb *into* the arête, bridge up, and cross the 2-metre roof with difficulty. Swing onto the right-hand side of the arête to finish.

43 Water Wings 8m S0 XS 6a (F7a) (26.7.01)
Swing right onto the arête and make a long reach before jumping for a good flake and finishing easily.

44 Ooh, Lovely! 9m S0 XS 5c (F6b+) (19.5.95)
Sustained climbing rightwards and back leftwards up the right-hand side of the arête. Can also be finished rightwards at the same grade.

45 Out of Yer Shell 9m S1 XS 5b (F7a+) (13.3.98)
Traverse around the arête to the base of a ragged corner. Climb this to a sizeable roof, undercut right a little, and stretch over. Follow mid-air slopers leftwards for 3 metres until good undercuts allow the final roof to be climbed. Exit left

46 Crab Party 23m S1 XS 5c (F6c) (19.5.95)
A fine, pumpy route, but wait for high tide! From the arête, traverse rightwards into the cave for 12 metres. Climb up, cross the 8-metre roof on huge holds, and squirm into a small niche. From here, the optimum combination of slopers will gain good finishing holds.

From the depression, walk a few metres north and descend to the clean-cut cliff edge. The climbs are below the lowest section of this ledge, near its southern end. Abseil from a single staple bolt to some small ledges at the base of a pillar between two caves. *Intimate Dancing* moves up over the southern cave, and *Spittle and Spume* the northern.

47 Intimate Dancing 9m S2 HVS 5a (F4+) (13.6.93)
Unprotected. Climb leftwards and up to a foothold on the left arête. Bridge out leftwards on the lip of the cave and pull up on positive holds to the top.

237

Just right of *Intimate Dancing* is a fairly easy climb (8m HS † 13.6.93) and right again a groove, which has not yet been climbed.

⭐ 48 **Robertson's Jan** 8m S1 HVS 5b (F6a+)
(13.6.93)

Just to the right again, an unprotected line of flat holds leads to the cliff-top.

⭐ 49 **Spittle and Spume** 10m SO XS 5c (F6a+)
(13.6.93)

A short but exposed traverse on the very lip of the large cave which undercuts this wall. Climb up just left of the cave, traverse right for 5 metres, and make a difficult move to the top.

⭐ 50 **Bare Reputation** 18m SO XS 6b (F7a+)
(15.5.95)

The logical (but desperate!) continuation to *Spittle and Spume*. A powerful and pumpy solo, for which mid tide is necessary. From the end of the traverse of *Spittle and Spume*, continue rightwards for 8 metres until it is possible to top out.

⭐ 51 **Underbare** 18m SO XS 6b (F7b)
(1999)

Start along *Spittle and Spume*, then drop down to follow a handrail for 6 metres until it is possible to pull back up and finish up *Bare Reputation*.

⭐ 52 **Underbare Extension** 35m SO XS 6b (F7b+)
(5.05)

The footless continuation of *Bare Reputation*, finishing as for *Smile Please*.

The next collection of deep-water solos start with an F4 climb down a groove. High tide required due to submerged boulders.

⭐ 53 **Across the Water** 28m SO XS 5c (F6b)
(25.8.05)

The south-heading traverse of the lip of the roof. Descend, or abseil down, the easy finishing groove of *The Green Bearded Roof* to a small ledge. Traverse leftwards along the very lip of the cave to finish up *Bare Reputation*.

⭐ 54 **Hooked Like no Fish Before Me** 25m SO XS 5c (F6b)
(5.10.96)

The original traverse climbs as for *Across the Water*, but finishes earlier from a perched block up a prominent flake.

55 **Always the Sun** 20m SO XS 5c (F6b)
(23.8.05)

As for *Across the Water*, but at the perched block, finish rightwards up a feint rib.

⭐ 56 **Samurai in Autumn** 14m SO XS 5c (F6b)
(25.8.05)

As for *Across the Water*, but finish up the wall a few metres in, past a large stuck-on 'cornflake'.

57 **Smile Please!** 7m SO XS 5b (F6a+) (1997)
Shuffle left from the base of the descent for 2 metres and climb a thin flake back up to the ledge.

58 **Lateral Thinking** 14m S0 HVS 5a (F5+)
(8.8.05)

The obvious line immediately left of the finish of *The Green Bearded Roof*.

The next three bolted climbs require low tide and an abseil to start.

59 **The Green Bearded Roof** 10m F7a+ 5B
(6.6.96)

Start from a single bolt belay at the base.

60 **Supergeek** 10m F7b+ 5B
(28.7.96)

The best of this trio. Start from a single bolt belay at the base.

61 **Pilot of the Future** 10m F7b 5B
(18.7.96)

A very unlikely roof on which shorties may need a bunk-up to reach the holds on the lip.

Waterfall Cave

62 **Zen Zero** 18m F7c+ 10B
(28.8.96)

The challenge of the roof of the large cave taken full on. From the centre of the cave, move up and right to gain a handrail. Follow it rightwards for 8 metres and pull round the lip of the roof. Block belay.

The next collection of routes can be approached by abseil from one of the many cliff-top blocks to a large ledge (submerged at mid tide). Belay using the cliff-top blocks. Climbers have come to know the cave to the right as The Waterfall Cave, as in winter, and during heavy rain, a waterfall runs over the top of the cliff.

63 **Zombie Nation** 10m F7c 6B
(12.8.00)

An arm-stretching sister climb to *Air Hoodlum*, with a big bouldery roof to start. Undercut out 3 metres left from the start of *Air Hoodlum* and make a desperate reachy sequence to clear the first roof. Crucifix rightwards and climb straight up the juggy, bulging wall.

64 **Air Hoodlum** 10m F7b+ 4B
(7.5.95)

The grooved arête. Steep!

65 **The Cult of John Craven** 10m F7b 4B
(24.1.05)

A super little wall climb that deserves you wear your best jumper, one for the country file! Start at the base of the escape route. Climb easily to a jug and trend forcefully left on a series of sidepulls, poised above the arête on poor footholds. Better incuts gain the top.

66 **Escape Route** 9m HVS 5a
(1995)

If caught by the tide, solo out up this. Unprotected.

In the cave, 5 metres right of *Escape Route*, is a bolted project.

67 **Osaki Dolphin** 12m F7c 8B   (7.8.95)
The 8-metre roof needs very dry conditions.

To the right of *Osaki Dolphin* is a left-to-right rising traverse, another unclimbed project.

The centre of the Waterfall Cave has a supporting pillar. An old bolted project exists here, but it has a blank section, which has repelled all of the mortals who have tried it.

68 **Law of the Jungle** 12m S1 F7b+ 5B (6.5.95)
From the foot of the arête on the right-hand side of the Waterfall Cave, trend leftwards to a protruding

hold. Cross the roofs, swing right, and climb a prow to the top.

69 **King of the Swingers** 20m F7c+ 14B
                                            (27.8.95)
The biggest roof challenge on Portland with 20 metres of overhang. Start up *Law of the Jungle* but continue forever leftwards along the horizontal break to a no-hands knee-bar rest. Finish diagonally leftwards over the big roof. Block belay.

The next route starts from a ledge on the right-hand side of the Waterfall Cave – near the top.

70 **The Swinging Nineties** 8m S1/2 F7b 6B
                                            (29.5.95)
A roof-climb which starts conveniently at the top of the cliff! Descend *Law of the Jungle* for 3 metres and move left along a handrail before eventually regaining terra firma.

71 **Waterfall Wall** 7m VS 4b   (1995)
A useful downclimb for *Law of the Jungle*. Climb the wall 2 metres right of the arête. Unprotected.

Octopus Weed Area

72 CC Backstabbers 9m E2 5c   (15.7.96)
A solo across the roof 10 metres right of the left-hand arête. Swing across the roof and up the wall above. Unprotected, so watch your back.

The next five short routes are all bolted. For the full experience, top out and belay on the quarried blocks above. Mid tide required, along with low swell. Reach these routes by descending rock steps in an amphitheatre just to their north.

73 Different for Girls 9m F5 3B   (10.6.95)
The left-hand bolt line has a hard start followed by some suspect rock higher up.

74 Kisses and Lies 9m F5+ 3B   (10.6.95)
The faint flake crack is quite pumpy, with a committing finish.

75 High Klicks 9m F6a 3B   (10.6.95)
The left-hand side of the blank roof. Pull around the roof on flakes and sidepulls to easier ground above.

76 100 Reasons to be Cheerful 9m F6c+ 3B   (10.6.95)
The blank roof. Pull out of a sentry box and make a long reach to the lip of the roof. The crux is a hard slap for the ledge above.

77 Bachelor Boy and the SR 500 9m F5+ 3B   (10.6.95)
The centre of the roof. Make a long reach from a good undercut at the back of the roof – easier than it looks.

There is a very difficult bouldering project across the roof of the cave. It has several drilled holds, and is usually damp.

To the right are three caves beneath a jib crane. The first cave contains four routes, and has a full-width 'plank' along its lip.

⭐ 82 **Walking the Plank** 20m S1 E3 5c (22.7.96)
The traverse of the lip of the cave, starting on the left. Pull over a roof and swing right along the 'plank' to finish up a groove. High tide required.

83 **Staring at the Sea** 20m F7a 3B (8.96)
Low tide required. From the back of the cave, climb out past the 'plank' and up the headwall above.

84 **Underwater Love** 20m F7a 3B (8.96)
Low tide required. Start 3 metres right, and 2 metres further back, from *Staring at the Sea*. Powerful moves past the plank and roof lead to a stiff pull around onto the headwall.

85 **Leave My Sole Alone** 9m HVS 5a † (25.7.90)
Climb down from the rock amphitheatre and traverse north past a low-level roof to the first pillar (10 metres south of the jib crane). Climb the pillar and then move strenuously rightwards onto a jutting ledge. Finish straight up over bulges.

The third cave contains a number of good deep-water solos. Down-climb immediately south of the crane at Severe. This brings you to the southern end of The *Octopus Weed* Cave.

86 **The Lip Traverse** 7m S0 XS 5b (F6a+) (16.8.95)
Traverse the first half of the lip of the *Octopus Weed* Cave, starting from the left side (looking in). All moves are feet-off, but the handholds are large.

There are two climbs on the wall immediately north of the descent amphitheatre.

78 **One Cool Vibe** 9m E2 5c (11.5.89)
Escapable to the left but with good climbing. Start on the left side of the cave, below an arête with ochre lichen at its top. Pull steeply over the roof. Climb straight up, 'yarding' on jugs, with a final, committing stretch up the ochre arête to clasp the top. Block belay in the field behind.

⭐⭐ 79 **This Is the Life** 10m E3 5c (11.5.89)
A steep little route which is better than its neighbour. Start as for *One Cool Vibe*. Pull steeply over the roof and hand-traverse 3 metres right to gain a ledge beneath a shallow groove. Climb this directly on positive holds with a long reach to finish. Block belay in the field behind.

The next two routes start in a deep 2-metre-high cave.

⭐ 80 **Fly the Friendly Skies** 14m F7b+ 7B † (13.5.95)
Start 10 metres right of *This is the Life*. Climb a series of roofs to a deep break. Fingery moves up the headwall lead to an exit groove. The right-hand finish is an old, abandoned project.

⭐ 81 **Seeing is Believing** 11m F7c 7B † (31.5.95)
Starting on the right-hand side of the cave, climb over a small roof and then over an eight-footer (3 metre-er)! The line of bolts leading out left from the start is an old project, which has lost some holds.

87 **Magician's Trap** 6m S0 XS 6a/b (F7a) (9.95)
A continuation to the last route, but it can be started separately. Drop down over the lip and make powerful, bunched moves rightwards under the jutting roof to emerge 3 metres further along onto the ledge above the cave.

88 **Purple Shorts** 7m S0 XS 5a/b (F6a) (8.5.95)
The traverse of the rock bridge. Difficulty depends on how far you traverse rightwards before you bottle it and mantel!

89 **Octopus Weed** 9m S0 XS 6a (F6b+) (1.5.95)
From the right-hand end of the rock bridge, hang out backwards and launch yourself into a series of hanging heelhooks across a line of slots and jugs until a welcome foot-ledge on the far side is reached. Fantastic climbing – esoteric and a brilliant find. An essential deep-water solo tick.

90 **Tentacle Master** 6m S0 XS 6b (F7a+) (27.7.95)
A desperate boulder-problem above good water. Climb *Octopus Weed* to a protruding jug and then launch for a poor sloping side-pull; slap again for another, slightly better sloper. A final lunge gains better holds.

The following two routes are reached by walking round the back of the cave until the ledge ends. In the roof above are two hand-rails, their starts shared by reaching up to the ceiling at the end of the ledge. *Skeleton Surfers* is the most northerly handrail.

91 **Killer Loop** 7m S1 XS 6a (F6c+) (3.9.95)
Follow the left-hand hand-rail in the opposite direction (spotter advisable for the first 3 metres) until it finishes. A span backwards is required to reach an adjacent crack, which leads to the rock bridge.

92 **Skeleton Surfers** 7m S0 XS 6a (F6c+) (3.9.95)
Follow the right-hand rail skirting the wall above *Previous Tope-Rope Problem* until an undercutting move brings you to the rock bridge.

93 **Previous Top-Rope Problem** 12m S0 XS 5b (F6a+) (8.5.95)
The low-level rightward traverse of the *Octopus Weed* Cave. A fun outing taking a variable line according to water depth and how much your chalk bag gets splashed.

Beeston Cliff

OS Ref 689 695

Beeston Cliff, along with its northerly neighbour Godnor Cliff, gives routes that are short, steep, and on reasonably sound rock. In recent years several bolted routes have been climbed here on the better sections of rock. The combination of the new sports climbs, the existing trad routes and some hard deep-water solos make Beeston an interesting and varied venue. Note that several stretches of Beeston Cliff require low water for access.

Approach

There are a number of approaches, some of which require a short abseil. From the pumping-station just south of *The Eight Kings Inn* at Southwell, start by following a track to the cliff-top.

1. To reach the northernmost trad routes, walk 400 metres south along the cliff-top to the southern side of a huge conical quarry mound. Scramble down past a rusty chain to a flat ledge and continue down a ramp to the right (facing outwards). You may prefer a short abseil from bolts from the flat ledge as the final step down is onto greasy rounded boulders.

2. For the southernmost routes proceed as above, but continue south to the end of the cliff. Take your chances with collapsing earth slopes to land on the boulder beach and so reach the crag. For Sector Golden Pants it's quicker to continue along the clifftop and scramble down to the boulder beach at the southern end of the golden wall.

To the north of the earth slopes the first large corner contains *The Twist*. Then, past the arête climbed by *South Wall*, is a long section with no climbs recorded before the main easy way down is reached at the northern of two small arches. A dead

low tide is necessary to cross beneath a prominent arête beyond the boulder beach (where the '*Awkward*' climbs are) to reach Hidden Wall.

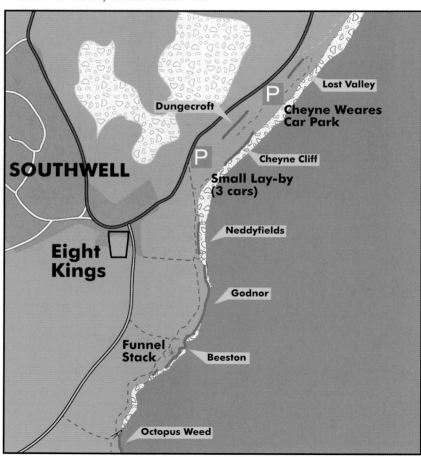

Sector Golden Pants

The following collection of short sport routes is on the flat golden wall above a boulder beach 250 metres north of the northernmost jib crane, and 250 metres south of the large conical mound. Despite being short, they all feel hard for the grade with very little to offer in the way of holds. Strong fingers are required. Scramble down ledges immediately south of the wall. The routes on the left-hand side of the wall start from a ledge at 3 metres.

1 **Always a Little Farther** 9m F6c 2B † (26.6.03)
Interesting moves between prominent jugs. Climb direct to the 'step' in the left-hand side of the cliff top.

2 **Social Lepers** 9m F7a 3B (1.97)
Much harder for the short. Climb the apparently holdless wall, starting on the left-hand side of the ledge.

3 **Suits You Sir!** 9m F6c 3B (5.96)
The first crack from the left is very hard to start.

4 **Winterset** 9m F6b 2B † (26.2.03)
The prominent crack has a testing move. Starting on the right-hand side of the ledge, follow the two diverging flake cracks. If your arms aren't long enough, select a crack and follow it.

5 **Skin Up** 9m F6a 3B (9.96)
Pull over the left-hand side of the bulge and climb the crack above. The first two bolts are poorly positioned.

6 **Sea Pink** 9m F6c+ 3B † (26.2.03)
The beautiful pink wall has a brutal move. Pull over the right-hand side of the bulge, step left, and climb the pink wall to a shared lower-off.

7 **Eva Luna** 9m F7a 3B † (12.3.03)
The faint weakness has some elegant moves. Climb the parallel blind cracks.

8 **Fight the Good Fight** 9m F7a+ 3B † (15.6.03)
An equally faint weakness, with combative moves. Climb the wall just left of the shattered cracks.

9 **Stratagem** 9m F6b 3B † (15.6.03)
The wall with an oblique move. The line up the right-hand side of the shattered cracks.

10 **Burnt Sienna** 9m F6a+ † 3B (12.6.03)
The right-hand arête has a vaguely artistic move.

The next group of climbs is approached via the collapsing slopes between the northern end of Sector Golden Pants and the main cliff. The boulder-beach at the southern end of the crag is (just) non-tidal.

1 **Verticality Plus** 6m VS †
Owing to rockfall, the small corner at the southern end of the crag is now easier-angled but loose.

2 **The Slab** 8m VD
Around the arête to the right is a wall that gives well-protected climbing. Climb the scoop, traverse left, and go up another scoop to the arête. Continue to block belays.

3 **The Twist** 6m VD   (1963)
Climb the corner and exit with a twist. Block belay.

4 **Acrobatics** 12m VS †
To the right is a deep cave with a hanging crack above it. Start just before the left arête of the deep cave by a short crack at head height. Climb strenuously up past the crack and move right to a ledge. Gain the knobbly ledge above with difficulty and climb the hanging crack to the top.

5 **South Wall** 9m S †
Low to mid tide required. Start beneath the arête. Pull up strenuously to gain the scooped arête and climb to the top.

Ben Stokes on *Return to Form* F6a (page 249). STEVE TAYLOR

The next inlet contains no climbs at present. At its northern end is an arch. The next climb takes the corner above the second arch (the buttress of which forms the main easy way down).

6 **Chimney and Traverse** 9m HS ††

The *Traverse* section of this route has now collapsed. Start immediately left of the descent. Bridge up the wide chimney, which narrows towards the top.

The right arête of *Chimney and Traverse* is the bottom of the main easy way down, a series of steps slanting up to the right. A rusty chain near the top is an identifying feature.

The first feature north of the descent is a shallow, wide cave with a large ledge above it (beneath the rusty chain). To the right is a clean wall, where the boulder beach drops in height and becomes tidal. There are seven bolted routes above the boulder beach, the first starting in the shallow cave.

7 **Flake Break** 9m F6c 4B   (16.9.04)

Start 3 metres left of the right arête of the cave. Pull over the low roof using a good flake and move right to a jammed block. Pull over the final roof to a lower-off on the ledge above.

8 **Lardman** 9m F6a+ 3B   (11.9.04)

Start at the right arête of the cave. Make a hard move to gain the arête, swing up and left to the roof, and pull up onto the ledge above. Shared lower-off.

9 **East Coast Epic** 9m F6b 3B   (16.9.04)

Start 2 metres right of the cave. Climb the slight groove past a chert slot to a chert crimp below the headwall. Difficult moves lead to the lower-off.

10 Return to Form 9m F6a 4B   (11.9.04)
Start 4 metres right of the cave, immediately left of a corner. Climb the flake crack to the headwall. Make a long stretch to a good hold and the lower-off.

11 Rusty Wall 9m F6b 4B   (16.9.04)
Start to the right of a short arête, 7 metres right of the cave. Pull into a steep groove that proves hard to leave. Continue with a long reach to a sloping ledge and a make powerful reach for the top and the lower-off.

12 Dirty Dog 9m F6c 4B   (16.9.04)
The last bolt is hard to clip. Start 3 metres right of the short arête, on top of a small boulder. Make a series of hard moves to a chert jug. Further hard moves lead to the lower-off.

13 Pavane 10m F6a 5B   (6.7.04)
The corner by the drop in height of the boulder beach. Depending on the state of the tide, either swing in to the bottom of the corner from the left, or start direct. Climb the juggy corner, with good moves to the lower-off.

14 Love of Life 10m E1 5b   (12.7.04)
The buttress immediately right of *Pavane*. Starting on a sloping ledge, romp up the easy wall to finish more pensively by a short pale groove.

The next route is 6 metres right of the drop in height of the boulder beach. This section is extremely tidal, and is approachable only for an hour or so at low Spring Tide and in calm seas (that is, about four times a year).

15 Aquaserene 10m F7a 5B †   (6.7.97)
Start just to the left of a blind crack, 2 metres right of the sloping toe of a buttress. Climb the wall past a bulge to the base of the flying arête. Fire up this to the lower-off.

★ **16 Cracked Wall** 10m F6b 4B †   (9.8.97)
The blind crack and groove 2 metres to the right.

17 Silence of the Deep 10m F6b 4B † (20.7.97)
The sustained wall midway between the blind crack and *Easy Chimney*.

★ **18 Lucky Day in Hell** 10m F7b+ 4B †   (9.9.97)
Start immediately left of *Easy Chimney*. Hard moves up the wall lead to the lower-off of *Silence of the Deep*.

19 Easy Chimney 9m HVS †
This south-facing chimney once provided a Moderate descent route but now, due to the boulders shifting, it has an unprotected, undercut start.

Steve Taylor on *Lardman* F6a+. JAMES WHARTON

The buttress forming the right side of *Easy Chimney* is severely undercut.

⭐ 20 **Heart Full of Nails** 10m F7a+ 4B † (20.9.97)
Pull onto the left-hand side of the undercut buttress and trend slightly right up a groove to an easier finish.

21 **Konked Out** 10m F7a † (9.9.97)
The arête of the undercut buttress. A very difficult start leads to easier climbing up the arête.

22 **Rags to Rags, Rust to Rust** 10m F5 4B † (9.9.97)
From the start of *Severe Corner*, trend left past two rusty pegs up the wall to the lower-off shared with the previous two routes.

23 **Severe Corner** 9m S (What else?)
Climb the corner in the south-facing wall to the right of *Easy Chimney*.

A contrived line leads diagonally rightwards up the wall: **Awkward Wall** (12m VS †)

24 **The League of Gurus** 10m F7a 3B † (27.9.97)
A steep start just to the right of *Severe Corner* leads to a groove.

25 **Awkward** 11m D
High in its grade. Climb the crack to the right of *Severe Corner* and go left at the small roof near the top. Finish up the crack.

26 **Awkward Traverse** 11m S †
Low in its grade and enjoyable. Start at the crack, as for *Awkward*, climb up, and move out rightwards beneath the small roof to a scoop, which is climbed to the top.

27 **Plain Awkward** 10m HS †
Start at the crack left of the arête before the rightward sea-level traverse to Hidden Wall.
Move up to the ledge, climb the crack, and traverse right to take in the exposed arête (*Sea of Tears*) on good holds. The overhanging continuation crack is also possible but much harder (HVS).

28 **Forever Young** 10m S2 E1 5c (F6a+) †
(26.8.04)
The left-hand side of the striking arête is similar in line to *Plain Awkward*, though it moves right to the arête at a lower, more difficult level. The first ascent was soloed, but wait for a high spring tide. Start 2 metres left of the arête. Make a difficult pull over the starting bulge, and move rightwards using a finger-pocket to finish up the arête. Fine positions.

The right-hand side of the arête is the start of The Amphitheatre area, beginning with Hidden Wall.

Tim Dunsby on *Beach Madness* F6a+ (page 255). NIGEL COE

The Amphitheatre Area

OS Ref 689 696

Movement north from Beeston to Godnor at the base of the cliffs is frustrated by two sections of cliff with a watery base, punctuated by Lime Kiln Cave and The Amphitheatre, a boulder-filled inlet rimmed by a steep, undercut wall. The steepness of the walls and the honeycombed texture of the rock give the climbs more character than would appear from above. The walls to the south of The Amphitheatre have been developed in recent years with a collection of hard deep-water solos.

Approach

From the pumping-station just south of *The Eight Kings Inn* at Southwell, follow a track to the cliff-top. Turn right and walk 300 metres south to a flat table-topped boulder atop a small mound.

1. To reach the routes on Hidden Wall, walk 70 metres further south and turn left through boulders to reach a flat cliff-top ledge, where a large flat-topped boulder can be seen 15 metres out to sea. Abseil from bolts in a block at the back of the ledge.

2. The deep-water solos are difficult to locate until you are well-acquainted with the area. Walk 50 metres south of the flat-topped boulder and abseil from one of the cliff-top quarried blocks.

3. Access to the Amphitheatre inlet and Bay of Rainbows is more straightforward. A fishermen's path to the right of the table-topped boulder leads down to a large flat ledge on the north side of The Amphitheatre. Abseil from a large block on the ledge, or from a bolt in the block. *The Great Escape* traverses the undercut southern wall of the inlet, and *Pitchfork Disney* and *Extreme Lives* climb the northern wall. Bay of Rainbows lies just to the north of the inlet and is a flowstone wall with a watery base, apart from two ledges linked by *The Bellybutton Traverse*. *Bay of Rainbows* starts from the left ledge and *Cornflake Girl* from the right.

Hidden Wall

Warning: this is not a deep water environment; at high tide, water depth ranges from one and a half to three metres (between boulders). Boulders also move around from year to year, so you'd be wise/not wise checking conditions prior to total commitment.

Near the striking arête which defines the southern end of Hidden Wall is a large round-topped boulder in the water. Abseil to this from bolts in a boulder on the large ledge above.

1 Sea of Tears 10m S1/2 F7a 4B (27.9.97)
The striking, photogenic arête, climbed on its right-hand side. From the large boulder, step onto the wall and move left to the arête. Climb it! If considering the solo, start to the left of the arête and traverse in.

2 The Underhill Mob 10m S2 F6c 4B (27.9.97)
From the large boulder, step left onto the wall, layback a flake crack into a groove, and step onto the large ledge.

The following two routes originally started from a ledge known as the Starting Block. This ledge has now disappeared, requiring a hanging stance to be taken. Abseil from the large ledge diagonally rightwards and take a hanging belay in the faultline left of the entrance to a deep chasm.

3 Easiboy 12m HS †
Easier than it looks. From the hanging belay, go up and left before traversing left to gain a sloping ledge. Climb straight up and to the right to finish.

4 Brooke's Benefit 12m VS †
A good route. From the hanging belay, move up and diagonally right. Exit to the left of the scoop on small holds.

The following three routes require an abseil to the faultline immediately right of the deep chasm. Abseil from cliff-top blocks.

5 Musclebound 12m HS †
Climb the flake-line immediately right of the deep chasm.

6 Muscleman 12m VS †
High in its grade. The second flake-line right of the deep chasm. Climb up the crack, traverse left, and gain the overhung ledge. Continue straight over the roof above.

7 Muscleman Direct 12m E2 † (7.69)
Start as for *Muscleman* but continue directly up the crack and groove, finishing to the left as for *Muscleman*.

The following routes from *Depth Gauge* to *Deep Water Drug Bust* start from a continuous break just above the high water line to the left of Limekiln Cave. There are two flakes/grooves on the left side of the face. Abseil down the right-hand of the two to gain the sloping horizontal break and the next three routes.

★ **8 Depth Gauge** 10m S3 E6 6a † (3.10.99)
A reachy eliminate up the flowstone face between the two flake-grooves. The crux is near the top (and the water is not as deep as it looks; 2 to 3 metres is what's on offer). Traverse left for one and a half metres and make a very difficult crank for better holds. Continue direct over an intricate bulge and, using the obvious layaway, go for the top.

9 Esperanto 10m S2 E2 6a (F6b+) † (3.10.99)
A good warm-up taking the right-hand flake line. Step left using finger pockets and make a long, hard move to a huge jug beneath the groove. Follow the flake-groove to an exit right onto the blocks.

★ **10 Bastinado** 10m S2 E4 6a (F7a) † (3.10.99)
One hell of a pitch that is super sustained. Move right for one and a half metres, rock up onto a good foothold and climb thinly to a position beneath a bulge, just right of the three-bolt belay. Pull through the bulge and continue on improving holds to the blocks.

For the next two routes, abseil down the face 6 metres left of the big cave to a small scoop at the break; the transfer onto rock is easy.

11 The Machine 10m S2 E6 6b (F7b) † (3.10.99)
A plum solo. Technical and unrelenting with the crux right at the top (at 9 metres above a 2.5-metre sea depth; take care). Climb the slight scoop-line on the left and so gain a good chert jug up to the right (bolts to the right and the left). Work up over the bulge onto the upper face. Proceed on spaced layaways up the flowstone wall to blocks and the top.

12 Deep Water Drug Bust 10m S2 E4 6a (F7a) † (3.10.99)
A strong line. Committing, but the crux is fairly low. Step right onto a slight rib and gain good fingerholds up on the wall. Make precarious moves right, using the arête of the cave and grope for a jam in the bottomless crack. Follow this on excellent holds to blocks and the top.

For *Borstal Bash* to *Condor*, abseil with difficulty to a jutting prow right of the cave. Note that some of these routes are **not** deep-water solos.

☆ 13 **Borstal Bash** 12m E6 6a †   (8.7.00)
☆ Traverse along the break until it is possible to step (or jump) down onto sea-washed boulders at the back of the cave. Walk around left onto a raised platform and then follow a line of jugs into a corner left of the cave. Climb the corner to a roof. Traverse right around an arête to gain solid jams in the left end of a jammed block. Hand-traverse this right, to a rest in the right-hand corner. Take the corner and finish up a steep crack above some wonky holds. Very serious.

☆ 14 **Nutter's Way** 10m E6 6b †   (3.10.99)
Effectively *Esmerelda's Monkey* pitch 2 solo, with a ground start. Forceful stuff, with a submerged boulder right where you don't want it and the inevitability of hitting the ledge if you fall off the first 5 metres. Pull over the bulge as for *The 6.03*, traverse left, and pass round a small rib with difficulty. Continue left intricately and make a powerful move to get established on the arête. Climb up and right slightly on big holds to the top.

☆ 15 **The 6.03** 10m S2 E4 6a (F6c) †   (3.10.99)
Transforms the (bulk of) the second pitch of *The Great Escape* into a deep-water solo. Make a long move over the first bulge in line with a vertical crack. Climb the narrow rib and the groove on the left to the top (passing the three bolts on *The Great Escape*).

☆ 16 **Scrubs** 10m S2 E4 6a (F6c+) †   (3.10.99)
A nice steep face, with a low crux. Step right and make a hard move past a good hold to gain a pocketed break. Climb the smooth white face and exit on white flowstone

☆ 17 **Borstal Break-in** 10m E6 6a †   (3.10.99)
Superb climbing above a submerged boulder. Traverse right along the narrowing ledge for 3 metres, and make a hard move to good flat handholds on the white wall above. Continue to an undercut, pull straight over the small chert roof above on good but questionable holds, and finish up easier flowstone.

☆ 18 **Condor** 10m E6 6a †   (9.6.01)
A downright dangerous fall-out zone – even at high spring tide. Traverse right along the narrowing ledge for 5 metres to a chert thread. Grope around the bulge for a large hold, and then spring left for a good flat hand-ledge. Move up for a rest. Climb diagonally right for 2 metres to just short of the arête. From good flowstone holds above, make a crucial long reach up a small groove, and then swing left to exit around the left-hand side of a block perched on the edge.

The Amphitheatre

19 The Great Escape 38m F6c 8B, 6B †† (19.3.94)

The traverse of the south side of The Amphitheatre and the sea wall beyond. An attractive line on a pocketed wall above a large roof leads to harder climbing which takes the easiest line across the smooth walls beyond. Start beneath an undercut flake near the back of the south wall (a metre left of the corner of *Thumbs Up*).

1 20m. F6c. Layback boldly up onto the pocketed wall and traverse leftwards to a double-bolt hanging belay on a blunt arête, the last couple of moves being the crux.

2 18m. F6b+. Climb leftwards and down slightly to good foot-ledges. Continue around the arête before trending upwards to a wall of large blocks and a twin-bolt belay.

Variations:

20 Esmeralda's Monkey 70m F7b 8B, 7B, 6B, 9B †† (16.3.96)

A tremendous and difficult continuation to *The Great Escape*. A must for any competent party.

1 20m. F6c. *The Great Escape* pitch 1.

2 16m. F7b. Climb leftwards and down slightly to good foot-ledges. Continue left around the arête (the point at which *The Great Escape* goes upwards) and make strenuous moves to gain a hanging belay just before the entrance to a large cave.

3 14m. F7b. Psyche up and then traverse the lip of the cave strenuously leftwards to the golden wall. Continue delicately at the same height to reach a bolt belay.

4 20m. F6a+. Continue more easily into a groove above a chasm. Step left onto a more featured wall and cross it diagonally to reach the commodious ledge.

21 Beach Madness 18m F6a+ 7B †† (19.3.94)

A fine and unusual VS traverse with a desperate, bold start and a hard finish. A long sling is needed

---

The level of the beach in The Amphitheatre has dropped 3 metres in the last 10 years. As a result, routes from *The Great Escape* to *Pitchfork Disney* now have difficult and unprotected starts, with no known ascents since the change.

for the last bolt but one. Layback boldly up onto the wall and traverse left to the sixth bolt on *The Great Escape*. From here, climb over a cherty bulge and up a short groove to a bolt belay. Scramble leftwards up the slope to the top of a block wall, taking special care to avoid any Portland Sea Lavender. (Coiling the ropes first will help.)

For the routes at the back of The Amphitheatre, traversing rightwards is the safest way off, although it is still worth staying roped up. (Stick to the rim of The Amphitheatre and the fishermen's path in order to avoid the colonies of Portland Sea Lavender on the slopes hereabouts.)

22 Thumbs Up 12m E1 5b †† (5.2.94)

Start 5 metres left of the left-hand cleft. Pull steeply into a corner, traverse left at the roof, and climb the flake above. From a good hold, go right to a prominent flat hold and then stretch for the top. (Continuing straight up from the good hold may be feasible in the dry.) Belay among the blocks.

The left-hand cleft (8m S ††) is easiest if started on its juggy left rib.

23 Thumbs Down 8m HVS 4c †† (5.2.94)

Start between the two clefts, to the right of a big beak at the top. Climb up to the left of a nose; then go up left to a small ledge and the top.

The right-hand cleft (8m VD ††) provides a close encounter with flowstone.

---

24 Pitchfork Disney 9m E1 5c †† (23.7.94)

This diagonal line up the north wall of The Amphitheatre has only moderate protection. Start at a short, shallow groove 5 metres right of the cleft. Move up and step right to a thin crack formed by a flake. Step right for more protection on the hidden side of the flake. Step right again and pull up steeply to easier ground.

The following four routes are reached by an easy descent down a diagonal flake to a ledge on the seaward face of the buttress.

⭐ **25 Extreme Lives** 12m E7 6b † (4.01)

An extremely bold proposition up the impressive undercut prow of The Amphitheatre. The first ascent was soloed, but this is not a deep-water solo; in fact, any waves would probably accelerate your demise should you fall. Traverse left 2 metres beyond the arête. Extend for a flat hold in the large bulge, and power up to good finger-holds. More hard locks reach a layaway and a chance to get some weight off the arms. Move up on small holds, stretch right for a good 'stuck-on' hold and crank for a flat hold on the arête. Pull up on the flake and shake away the adrenaline.

26 Staplebite 7m E4 5c † (8.7.00)

Traverse left until a metre short of the arête and take a line to the top with difficulty. Beware the hidden boulders in the water.

27 Ethical Vacuum 7m E4 6a † (8.7.00)

Step left from the descent and climb straight up the steep face to an easier finish.

28 The Portland Screw 8m HVS 5a † (23.7.94)

Step up to two short thin cracks. Continue up slightly leftwards to the top, finishing at a slight V-notch.

Bay of Rainbows Area

The following cluster of climbs is found below the northern side of The Amphitheatre's abseil ledge. Abseil from the northern side of the flat, block-strewn ledge, from bolts in blocks, or the blocks themselves, to a ledge just above the tide line. All the sport climbs here are equipped with bolt belays at their starts.

29 Krakatoa 8m F4 2B   (23.4.94)
From the widest section of the ledge, climb diagonally left to a slight depression and the top.

30 Etna 7m F3 3B   (23.4.94)
From the centre of the ledge, climb the large flake and the steep wall above to the top.

31 Popacatepetl 7m F6a 3B   (23.4.94)
A hard move at the top. From a triangular section of the ledge, climb up to the roof. Make a very long reach, *then* clip the final bolt, and pull up to finish.

32 15 Minutes to Fame 8m S2 F6a+ 3B (20.8.94)
From the right-hand side of the ledge, climb up on good but spaced holds.

33 Bay of Rainbows 11m S1/2 F7a 4B
          (10.4.94)
Strenuous and fingery climbing on very smooth flowstone, unfortunately with a resin crimp at the crux. From the right-hand side of the ledge, climb diagonally right up the undercut flowstone wall.

34 The Bellybutton Traverse 12m SO F6a+ 4B   (25.4.94)
Low swell required, otherwise the blowhole may prove troublesome! An often-soloed line, which is strenuous despite good positive handholds. Drop down from the right-hand side of the ledge and follow the horizontal break to another ledge and belay. Reverse, or escape up one of the next four routes.

The following three climbs start from a ledge on the right-hand side of the wall, just before a cave. Approach by abseil from the furthest belay bolt or, better, by *The Bellybutton Traverse*.

35 Bay of Peegs 10m SO E5 6b (F7a+) † (8.01)
A technically difficult route taking the faint groove between *Bay of Rainbows* and *Cornflake Girl*. Start at the second bolt of *The Bellybutton Traverse*. It has only had a solo ascent. A long reach from the break and a couple of stiff pulls up the groove lead to relatively easy ground and the top.

36 Cornflake Girl 9m SO F6a+ 3B   (25.4.94)
Start on the left-hand side of the ledge. Climb leftwards and then up, using calcite-cemented holds. Swing left near the top and continue up past more surprisingly well-attached 'cornflakes' to a belay bolt on the ledge.

37 Bungle, Zippy and George 8m F4+ 3B
          (20.8.94)
Start as for *Cornflake Girl* and climb the wall, to finish with a mantelshelf over a roof.

38 Gyonyuru 12m XS 5c   (8.95)
A deep cave bounds the right-hand side of the *Bay of Rainbows* wall. This route climbs the crack in the steep pillar to the right of the cave mouth. Approach by abseil. The first ascent was soloed at high spring tide, but this is not recommended as a deep-water solo.

39 Gyttja 12m E6 6a †   (8.7.00)
The impressive arête right of *Gyonuru*. A high crux and not a deep-water solo! Abseil in, as for *Gyonuru*. Stretch up to the first break (as for *Gyonuru*), and then swing right onto flat holds. Trend steeply right onto the arête to good fingerholds in the local *Gyttja*, and make a hard crank for smaller holds over a bulge - blind! Pull over and step left to the exit crack of *Gyonuru*.

Joff Cook soloing *Bay of Peegs* **E5 6b.**
DAMIAN COOK

Godnor Cliff

OS Ref 691 697

The climbs are short and steep here, and some have tidal problems. Godnor South provides predominantly traditional climbing, whilst Godnor North is mostly bolted.

Approach

1. For Godnor South, from the pumping-station just south of *The Eight Kings Inn* at Southwell, follow a track to the cliff-top. Walk south for 150 metres to the central easy way down, which starts where the track meets the cliff edge (near a large buttress of quarried blocks). A huge tank-shaped block abuts the cliff just to the south; this marks the division between Godnor South and North. Scramble carefully down, traverse southwards along a ledge, and descend carefully over spaced ledges next to a rib. This descent is extremely exposed, with a significant amount of loose material and is recommended only to the gnarliest of climbers. Those not considering themselves in this category should abseil in.

2. For Godnor North and Far North, from the end of the track from the pumping-station (or 70 metres south of the Neddyfields bouldering wall), descend next to a sewer-pipe (under Pipe Cliff – currently off-limits to climbers due to a high concentration of Portland Sea Lavender) and clamber southwards across boulders to the cliff.

Godnor South

Several stretches of this 100-metre section of cliff require low tide and calm seas for access. Although the grades are mainly VS and below, the earth slopes at the top and the occasionally suspect protection make the cliff more suitable for the experienced climber than for the novice (or the sport climber in need of a challenge.)

South of the tank-shaped block is a double-holed arch, above which *The Oh-No Variant* boldly goes. Further south an overhung bay is a scene of *Desperation*. A low tide is needed to pass the next buttress and reach a section of cliff where the boulders are piled up high. An easy, exposed escape is possible here up the short *Corner Wall*. South again, is the flake crack of *Curving Crack* just before two caves. The smooth wall beyond is sea-washed and bars easy progress southwards.

1 **Breakthrough** 15m VS ††
At the southern end of the cliff is a big cave, with a smooth wall to its left that is always awash. The crackline just right of the cave is accessible only at low tide. The start appears to have altered and the grade may well be higher than indicated. Gain the crack and climb to a ledge. Follow the steep crack above to gain another ledge. Traverse leftwards along this and finish up earth.

2 **Curving Crack** 18m VS †
Large nuts needed. Right of *Breakthrough* is a tall, thin cave with an unappetizing corner to its right. Start 5 metres further right again. Climb the long flake crack to the roof, move left on small footholds, and finish with some difficulty left of a pile of rectangular blocks.

3 **Portland Exclusion Zone** 12m F6c+ 4B
(26.3.95)
Start below a niche at 3 metres. A sustained and steep line. Climb boldly (natural protection available) up to the niche. Pull out of the niche with difficulty and move up on small holds to a flake, which leads to the large blocks and a single bolt lower-off. It is possible to abseil to a pair of bolts in the niche and start from there.

4 **The Scrog** 9m HS †
(9.69)
Start at the chimney 12 metres right of *Curving Crack*. Climb the chimney, traverse left under the roof, and continue up the crack.

Just past this point the boulders pile up high above the sea. Like many of the climbs here, the corner to the north, *Greased Lightning*, is hard to locate from above. However, once its whereabouts is known, it offers a convenient abseil descent. A rockfall in the 70s has meant that a number of routes right of *Arrowhead Crack* exist only in the memories of those who climbed them.

5 **Corner Twin** 8m S †
The slight groove just left of the blunt arête of *Corner Wall*. Climb up to a jutting ledge on the left and continue up the groove to a tricky finish over a small roof.

6 **Corner Wall** 8m VD
The blunt arête, starting from a good flake crack on its right. Unprotected.

To the right of the blunt arête, three thin cracks split the wall. The right-hand crack remains unclimbed.

7 **Bert** 8m VS †
The left-hand crack-line, with a difficult move to get over the bulge.

8 **Betsy** 8m VS †
The central crack-line, approached via a low ledge. Climb the crack, stepping left at the top to a ledge and block belay.

9 **Greased Lightning** 8m HS 4a
Climb the wide crack at the back of the south-facing corner. Block belays.

10 **Arrowhead Crack** 8m VS 4b
The undercut crack immediately to seaward is a well-protected and pleasant climb. Block belay.

To the right of a prominent flying arête is a brown wall, slabby at its base and steeper in its upper section. The wall is accessible only at low spring tides.

11 **Slab and Crack** 11m VD †
Misleadingly named. Start 2 metres right of the flying arête, on the front of the buttress, and climb the crack and groove to the top. Block belay.

12 **Crack and Wall** 11m HVS †
Start 4 metres right of the flying arête. Use a thin crack to gain the slab. Move up to a hanging crack in the headwall, which is climbed with difficulty. Block belay.

To the north is a wide bay with a smaller overhung bay in its centre.

13 **Afterthought** 12m HS †
Start at a corner-crack defining the right-hand side of the buttress. Climb the crack past a jammed block half-way up. Take care with the earth-slope finish.

14 **Desperation** 11m VS †
Start on the right-hand side of the overhung bay. Climb to the roof at 6 metres and go out right onto the face via a constricted gap. Continue steeply to gain the ledge above.

15 **Grip-Tight Gulch** 12m VS †
The wide crack 5 metres right of *Desperation*.

16 **Sidewalker** 12m HS 4a
A smooth corner provides testing jamming and leads to a ledge. Continue up a wide groove formed by two cracks. Block belay on the ledge at the top.

17 **Anvil Point** 12m HS 4b
Seaward of *Sidewalker* is a fine, half-height arête. From the left, mantel twice with difficulty onto the top of the arête and then follow the steep crack above. Block belay.

18 **Chimney Break** 12m S
Climb the wide chimney, move right to a large ledge, and follow holds up rightwards to the top. Block belay.

To the right is a wall containing a number of good routes above a tidal ledge. A straightforward abseil in from large blocks above avoids the long walk-in from Godnor Far North.

19 **The Good Life** 12m F5+ 5B   (9.6.07)
Climb the flake on the left side of the wall to a ledge. Move left, then right to cross the bulge on good, well-spaced holds. Very photogenic.

20 **Break-Over Crack** 12m E1 5b   (8.9.07)
Short-lived, but worth doing. The excellent flake crack in the centre of the wall has a tough, slightly bold finish.

21 **Enter Shikari** 12m F6c 5B   (9.6.07)
The undercut flake on the right side of the wall provides an entertaining challenge. Layback into the crack with difficulty and climb the corner above. Finish up the headwall on small holds.

22 **Shoulder Jammer** 12m S ††
Climb the chimney and finish on the left. The original finish is now unsafe due to a highly unstable rubble cornice

The next four climbs have a clean-cut ledge at the top.

23 **The Gates** 12m VS 4c
Start on the southern side of the double-holed arch 25 metres south of the tank-shaped block. Gain the small ledge between the two holes and continue up the groove above. Block belay.

24 **Dusky Corner** 12m VD
Start as for *The Gates*. Move up, go right along a ledge, and finish up the groove in the arête. Block belay.

25 **Corner Direct** 12m HS 4a
The seaward arête of the double-holed arch, starting on the north side. Scant protection but a worthwhile pitch. Move up and traverse delicately left, almost to the arête. Climb up on bigger holds to the platform. Finish up the grooved arête as for *Dusky Corner*.

26 **The Oh-No Variant** 12m E2 5b †
Very impressive positions but poorly protected; aptly named! Follow *Corner Direct* to the platform, traverse right, and step up to small ledges. Continue right to the next small corner. Move up this and then slightly right to finish steeply on large dubious holds below a large cliff-top block. Block belay.

27 Cracker's Mate 12m VS †
Move up the slab just left of *Big Slab* and step left at the bulge. Pull up into the crack and follow it to the top. (A poorly-protected start; a less serious alternative lies around the arête to the left.)

28 Short but Perfectly Formed 8m F6a 3B
(9.6.07)
Start as for *Cracker's Mate*, but climb the technical grey wall above, passing a small bulge on pockets.

29 Big Slab Variant 11m F3 4B (2001)
Start as for *Big Slab*, but continue direct up a wide scoop.

30 Big Slab 13m VD
A wall; the name refers to the jutting block on the cliff-top. Start on a ledge just left of a low-level overhang. Swing up and rightwards on chert jugs. Step right and climb a rib beneath the block. Finish leftwards.

31 Unnamed 13m F6b 7B † (2001)
This addition to the crag is in the modern mould and has immaculate rock. Start directly beneath the cliff-top jutting block, climb the wall and blunt rib with an extravagant finish onto the jutting block.

32 Crackers 18m HS 4a
Start at a thin crack 3 metres left of *Crow's Nest Corner* and follow it to a niche. Step right and climb another crack, with a hard move to exit.

33 Crow's Nest Corner 16m VD
High in its grade. Climb the corner 3 metres left of the tank-shaped block to a tiny half-way ledge. Break right and continue up a crack (on the left-hand side of a prominent chert protrusion, the Crow's Nest) to the top.

34 Crow's Nest Direct 9m HS
Technically straightforward, but the only runners, just before and after the traverse, do not protect the crux. Clamber onto the tank-shaped block. Pull onto the wall, climb up 4 metres, and traverse leftwards. Gain the Crow's Nest from the right. Finish straight up to block belays.

35 Euphemism 10m F6b 4B (9.6.07)
Step off the centre of the tank-shaped block and climb the slight groove above, using small holds to gain the finishing flake.

36 Dirty Crack 12m HS †
The seemingly rubble-filled corner-crack bounding the left-hand side of the easy way down. Better and more difficult than it looks. Exit up and to the right.

37 Godnor Buttress 12m M
The easy angled buttress provides a straightforward descent once you are used to it.

38 Monkey Business 12m VS † (6.5.79)
The small rib right of *Dirty Crack* and the piled blocks above, but they are now very unstable; not recommended!

Godnor North

A lowish tide and calm seas are required to climb here. The easy way down Godnor Buttress is 6 metres right of the tank-shaped block. From the way down, Godnor North stretches 50 metres northwards to an overhanging buttress, where *The Castle* still holds out with an aid point. The boulders at the base of the cliff are scarcer at this point, and low tide is required to reach Godnor Far North just around the corner.

39 Defiance 9m S
Climb straight up the obvious pierced arête after stepping in from the left. Poorly protected.

40 Madcap 12m HVS †
Just right of the arête of *Defiance* is a tiny through-cave. Start on the right-hand side of the cave. A hard pull over the initial roof gains thin cracks leading through three overhangs to the top.

41 Swingover 12m VS †
Start beneath a diamond-shaped overhang at half height which has a rightward-slanting crack on its left-hand side. Cross an overhang with difficulty, follow a ramp to the upper roof, and take the slanting crack to the top. A delicate and difficult finish.

42 Lucky Break 15m VS †
Start 6 metres right of the arête of *Defiance* and just right of a small cave, beneath an overhang at two-thirds height. Climb the slabby wall to the big roof, move out left, and go easily up to the top.

43 John's Corner 15m HVS †
An alternative finish to the next climb. Start to the left of a cave. A hard-looking, undercut start. Climb the steep crack in the left wall to a chert overhang. Continue straight over this and up the crack above.

44 Wrist Climb 15m HS †
Climb up to the chert overhang, step across right, and make a hard pull over into a small corner. Climb straight up and finish out right with difficulty.

45 Sunday Break 15m VS ††
Start just right of the cave at a deep corner capped by an overhang. There has been rockfall in the overhang, which has probably made this route much harder than VS. Follow the crack to a good runner at its top, move out right under the overhang to the arête, and continue steeply to a ledge above. Climb the wall and finish slightly left with difficulty.

46 Crackpot 15m VS †
Start on the left-hand side of a wide face. Climb wedge-shaped overhangs just right of the arête to a halfway ledge. Continue more easily up the crack above.

47 Middleman 15m VS †
Start at the crackline 8 metres north of *Crackpot*. Well protected. Climb up for 5 metres to gain a cramped ledge. Move up into an unattended sentry-box at three-quarter height, and continue up and right over a bulge. Beware the earth over the top and go right.

48 Hanging Crack 15m E1 5b †
This climbs the crack defining the left-hand side of the prominent overhanging buttress.
Start as for *Middleman* and follow a ramp rightwards to the crackline. Finish up it with difficulty.

49 The Castle 15m E2 5b (1 pt aid) †   (6.69)
Strenuous climbing with some dubious rock. The peg needs replacing, though natural protection may be available. Start just left of the overhanging buttress beneath the finish of *Hanging Crack*. Climb up ledges and traverse right to a small ledge.Continue to the peg in the impending wall above. Use it for aid to cross the bulge and reach the top.

Jon Howell on *The Good Life* F5+ (page 261). STEVE TAYLOR

265

Godnor Far North

This section of crag is a stark contrast to the southern stretches, having straightforward access, many bolted routes, and no tidal problems. The rock is generally sounder, but some of the routes are somewhat nondescript. A wide selection of easier sports routes ensure the continued popularity of the area.

Approach from the north by walking 60 metres south of the end of the Neddyfields bouldering wall and dropping down a steep path heading north alongside a sewer pipe. This leads to the base of a small cliff – Pipe Cliff – which is completely restricted due its profusion of Portland Sea Lavender. Walk back south along the boulders for 80 metres and you arrive at the northernmost routes of Godnor Far North.

The northern end of the cliff has an overhang at half height. A few metres south of a small north-facing corner, at a change in height of the boulder beach, is the long flake crack of *Tombstone*, which finishes up a white pillar. Twenty-five metres further on is a vague bay with a crack, *Snatch Squad*, on its left side. To the left lies a line of rotting peg stumps in the flake-line of *Harpies and Quoins*, while 10 metres south a small undercut bay gives the lines of *Remember Blair Peach* and *Cable Slab*. A boulder-hop at low tide then leads around an overhanging buttress to Godnor North.

1 **Cable Slab** 15m VS †
Start a few metres north of *The Castle*, to the left of the small bay. Climb up to roofs and then traverse rightwards before finishing up the flake crack on the left-hand side of the bay. Block belays.

The starting holds of the following two routes are not always reachable. A jump may be possible, otherwise combined tactics and/or some minor construction work may be required.

2 **Remember Blair Peach** 18m HVS 4c/5a † (30.10.88)
Difficulties are dependent on the height of the boulders. Start on the right-hand side of the bay that is undercut by a roof at 2-3 metres. Pull over the roof using a large chert hold and a flake. Step left and climb the vague corner on the right, taking care with the loose rock. Block belay.

3 **Gie It Laldy** 15m F6c 5B (15.8.97)
Start beneath the roof at 2-3 metres, 4 metres left of the once-pegged flake line. Pull onto the wall using chert jugs and climb it direct to the lower-off shared with *Harpies and Quoins*.

4 **Harpies and Quoins** 15m F6b+ 5B (22.8.97)
A good climb. Pull up to a ledge, move left into the once-pegged flake-line, and follow it to a lower-off shared with *Gie It Laldy*.

5 **Any Time, Mike** 15m F7b+ 5B (7.00)
The hanging rib above the high roof. Start as for *Harpies and Quoins*, but take the wall above direct, with a difficult move to gain the hanging rib on the headwall.

6 **One Day, James** 15m F6b+ 6B (21.9.97)
The striking crack in the high headwall. A hard start up the shallow groove leads to some barn-door type moves up the crack at the top.

7 **Pathfinder** 15m F6b 5B (14.9.97)
Start just to the right of *One Day, James*. Climb the groove to a large, loose-looking chert hold and finish up the wall above.

8 **Snatch Squad** 18m HS 4b † (15.12.85)
Start at a flake forming a short layback crack, 5 metres right of *Harpies and Quoins*. Climb the flake and crack above. Surmount a chert bulge and continue up a short corner. Either take your chance with the earth slope above and belay on a block, or move left to the lower-off of *Pathfinder*.

9 **Sidewinder** 15m F6a 5B (20.9.97)
Start a metre right of *Snatch Squad*. Follow the flake and the dusty wall above to the lower-off.

10 Dreamscape 15m F6a 5B   (20.9.97)
The rib gives a good line with some pleasant climbing. From the ledge at 3 metres, walk to its left end and pull onto the wall beneath the rib. Follow a direct line up the left side of the rib to a tricky finish to the lower-off. A direct start is possible at F6c.

11 Ben 15m F4+ 4B   (10.8.97)
Start from the ledge at 3 metres. Climb the wall to the jutting flake, step right, and continue directly to the lower-off.

12 Willem 15m F4+ 5B   (10.8.97)
From the ledge at 3 metres, climb the slight groove and wall above, 2 metres right of *Ben*, to the lower-off.

13 Jasper 15m F4+ 5B   (20.4.97)
Start at the right end of the 3-metre ledge. Make a hard move to a good hold at 3 metres and continue fairly direct up the wall above to the lower-off.

14 Jody Sunshine 15m F5 5B   (20.9.97)
Start just left of a crack. Climb up into a shallow scoop and exit with difficulty. Continue more easily to the lower-off.

15 Wave Warrior 15m F5 5B   (20.9.97)
Climb the crack past the left end of a ledge at 3 metres. Follow the groove to the pleasantly technical headwall, with a hard move to reach the lower-off.

16 Valerie's Patio 15m F3 4B   (25.8.97)
A ledge-climbing exercise, starting immediately right of the change in height of the boulder beach. The aforementioned ledges make it less than ideal for top-roping beginners.

★ **17 Starbuck** 15m F6a 3B   (25.8.97)
The left-hand side of the wide groove/bay, with difficult moves on sidepulls near the top. Climb up to a roof at 3 metres and continue up the brown streak to the lower-off.

18 Last Human 15m F6c 3B   (26.8.97)
The centre of the golden wall, again with difficult moves near the top to reach the lower-off.

19 Tin Man 15m F5+ 4B   (25.8.97)
The flowstone-streaked rib.

Barry Clarke on *The Truth is Out There* F6b (page 271). STEVE TAYLOR

23 Wedding Daze 18m F6b 5B (10.8.97)
Start on a white flat-topped boulder. Climb the wall above, following the left-hand line of bolts.

24 Future Imperfect 18m F6a+ 6B (10.8.97)
Start on a white flat-topped boulder. Climb the wall above, following the right-hand line of bolts.

⭐ **25 Jacob's Ladder** 18m F5 7B (3.5.97)
Good climbing. Start directly beneath the jutting cliff-top boulder. Climb the flakes and wall in a direct line to the lower-off.

⭐ **26 The Truth is Out There** 18m F6b 6B (20.4.97)
The flake on the left-hand side of the strip roof at 6 metres. Climb the flake easily and step left onto the more challenging wall above. Thin moves lead to the lower-off.

27 Resistance is Futile 16m F7a+ 6B (20.7.97)
Climb up to the widest part of the roof at 6 metres. Pull over and trend left to a lower-off on the rib above.

28 Car Parts, Bottles and Cutlery 15m F6b+ 5B (22.9.98)
Climb a flake to the roof, swing over, and then move up and left past an old rust stain to a lower-off in a groove. Ignore the high bolt directly above the rust stain – this is a relic of the first ascensionist's fickle mind.

29 Factor 15 15m F6a+ 4B (8.2.98)
Start 10 metres from the right-hand end of the cliff. Climb over two roofs, just left of a prominent flake at 6 metres.

20 Rubber Truncheon 18m HS 4b † (30.10.88)
Start just left of a second drop in height of the boulder beach, beneath a prominent smooth white pillar at the top of the cliff. Climb the crack, which forms the left-hand side of a large flake. Continue diagonally left and either move back right and finish over earth and blocks to a block belay, or move right to the lower-off of *Tombstone*.

⭐ **21 Tombstone** 15m F3 5B (20.7.97)
Enjoyable climbing. The prominent layback flake

above the second step in the boulder beach. Follow the rightward-leading flake over a bulge to a lower-off in the white pillar, just to the left of some flowstone trickles.

⭐ **22 Where Silence has Lease** 17m F6c 6B (31.8.97)
The groove/corner bounding the left-hand side of the highest wall. Fine climbing up the corner leads to a hard finish.

Neddyfields Cliff

OS Ref 691 700

Neddyfields has a disconcerting appearance owing to the many bands of chert nodules and a certain amount of loose stuff, though the rock is firmer than it looks. The top of the cliff is clean-cut and all the climbs have lower-offs or large belay blocks at the top. The base of the cliff is non-tidal, easy to reach, and in the sunshine all morning.

The band of rock above the cliff is a bouldering venue, see page 278.

Approach

1. From the pumping-station just south of *The Eight Kings Inn* at Southwell, follow a track to the cliff-top and go north a short distance to the top of Neddyfields. At both ends of the cliff an easy, well-worn path leads down to the boulder beach.

2. Alternatively, the cliff can be reached from a track leading from the road between Easton and *The Eight Kings*. The track starts 200 metres south of the Cheyne Weares car-park and viewpoint. There is parking for five cars at the top of this track.

Because of the grassy slopes beneath it, the left-hand end of the crag is fairly short. At the point where the grass slopes end, *Inertia* heads upwards to a recess. Far to the right is the other major feature, the easy-angled and vegetated upper section of *The Scoop*.

Just to the south of the descent path, a small solid buttress pokes out of the spoil heaps.

1 Lucy's Off the Wall 12m F4+ 4B   (13.8.97)
The broken wall on the left. Uninteresting climbing past ledges leads to a larger ledge and the lower-off.

☆ 2 **Nothing's Shocking** 12m F6a+ 5B (19.11.94)
The line slightly left of centre has an air of boldness about it, especially on the hard moves to reach the lower-off.

☆ 3 **First Contact** 12m F6b 5B   (13.8.97)
A good route which has difficult, reachy moves on the headwall to gain to the lower-off.

4 **Brace Yourself, Sheila** 12m F5 4B (13.8.97)
The right-hand line of the buttress, starting up the arête. Steep climbing on good holds leads to a tricky finish.

All the other climbs are on the main cliff.

5 Nameless 8m F6c+ 3B — (10.8.97)
The first line is a difficult proposition, with several hard moves packed into its short length.

	✓

6 The Accelerator 8m F6c 3B — (10.8.97)
Just to the right, this short test-piece is only a little easier.

	✓

7 Thick as Thieves 8m F6c+ 3B — (19.11.94)
An unbalanced route. Start half-way down the southern descent path, 5 metres right of a large flake. Climb the flat wall, with a very hard move from an undercut to gain the lower-off.

	✓

8 Frank's Effort 9m HS 4a
Next to the southern descent path, 2 metres off the ground, is an iron ring in the cliff. Start 3 metres left of the ring. Climb diagonally right and finish up the right-hand side of a slight recess at the top.

	✓

9 Three in a Bed 9m F5+ 3B — (19.11.94)
The last in this set of four sportlets proves a much more reasonable proposition, though it has a difficult start due to the loss of a hold.

	✓

10 Steve's Wall 9m VS 4b
Poorly protected but worthwhile. Start 2 metres right of the iron ring. Pull over the narrow overhang and continue direct to meet the final recess of *Frank's Effort*.

	✓

11 Inertia 21m VS 4b/c
Start at a crack just to the right of a metal spike at 2 metres (15 metres right of *Steve's Wall*). From the right-hand end of the roof, climb up leftwards over ledges, surmount an overhang, and continue to the recess above (stance possible). Climb the left wall of the recess before finishing up and rightwards.

	✓

12 Kate 24m E4 5c † (21.6.80)
A lethal route with negligible protection. Difficult and frightening climbing on dubious holds makes this a route to be wary of. Start at a blunt arête, midway between a metal spike at 2 metres and a rusty iron ring at chest height. Climb a slight nose for 6 metres and pull up left over a bulge with difficulty. Continue up the slabby wall above and trend rightwards until about 2 metres left of *Intimidation*. Finish up the headwall on very small holds (crux), moving slightly left and then straight up to a block belay.

To the right is a large, slanting corner at mid height, capped by an overhang, which is:

13 Wanderlust 20m F6a+ 7B (2000)
The main disjointed corner above the rusty iron ring. Airy moves high up and a good, clean finish make this route worthwhile. Seven bolts. Climb steeply up the corner to a resting position at 10 metres. Swing airily up and right on good, though loose holds to a position below the headwall. Step up left, then up right, to the lower-off. Award yourself an F6b tick if you reach the top of the crag.

14 Intimidation 22m E1 5b †
A dusty start and a suspect bulge rather spoil this climb, which follows discontinuous grooves and finishes up a prominent thin crack in the headwall. Start beneath the previously mentioned corner, 5 metres right of a rusty iron ring at chest height. Move up leftwards to ledges in a slight corner at 10 metres. Step left around the arête and follow the shallow corner up over a bulge to a small ledge. Finish up the thin crack to a block belay.

15 Shit Route 21m F7a 7B (7.01)
The steep wall to the right of the corner-system. A bit dusty and loose in places, but with good powerful moves over bulges to the final headwall.

⭐ **16 Julie Ocean** 21m F7a 7B (28.3.97)
The central line eclipses all other routes on this cliff. Start 5 metres right of *Intimidation*, at the base of a short corner. Climb the corner and steep wall to a half-rest beneath the headwall. Gain the headwall on small, but positive holds to reach the final, crux move.

17 Bigus Dickus 21m E3 5c † (22.6.80)
Serious on account of its poorly-protected crux and loose upper section. Start at a detached block abutting the cliff face, just as the path rises slightly. Follow a groove to gain a rightward-slanting flake at 9 metres. Climb up this for a metre to where a small break on the left leads to a pocket on the overhang. Continue straight up to a groove, which is followed to the top. Block belay.

18 Lugwiler's Dismal Itch 18m F6c+ 6B (14.2.98)
A pumpy route with a dynamic crux. Start 2 metres right of *Bigus Dickus*. Climb the lower wall direct past an overlap to the 'bubbly' section. From here, make a hard reach, or jump, to the chert fault. Continue through the bulges to the headwall and lower-off.

19 Ecosystem 17m F6b 6B (26.7.96)
Start 2 metres right of *Lugwiler's Dismal Itch*. Climb the unremarkable initial wall to the bulges, whereupon a sense of urgency is recommended due to shrinking holds.

20 Time of the Month 17m F6b 6B (18.4.99)
Start directly beneath the jutting cliff-top block. Climb the wall, trending slightly leftwards to jugs below a bulge. Gain the headwall with difficulty, just to the right of a small roof.

21 Inception 17m F6a 6B (18.4.99)
This route climbs the left-hand side of the large scoop. Start just to the right of the jutting cliff-top block. Climb up to the bulges, where a welcome weakness allows access to the headwall and lower-off.

Barry Clarke on *Brace Yourself, Sheila* F5 **(page 272).** STEVE TAYLOR

22 The Scoop 15m S
A poor route (not shown). Start beneath a wide bay in the upper part of the cliff. Climb a short, clean wall followed by the wide, vegetated scoop. Exit leftwards.

23 Better Things 15m HS 4a
Start at a shallow corner 3 metres right of a protruding girder at 5 metres. Climb the crackline with an awkward move left at its top, and exit right.

24 Ocean Boulevard 12m F5 5B   (20.7.96)
A poor route, unworthy of its name. Pull over a chest-height roof with difficulty (or step in from the right). The easy-angled wall above leads to a lower-off in the only clean rock on the route.

25 Outside Left 15m S
Start to the left of an earth mound, just right of a low overhang. Climb the corner to the top. (VS 4b if climbed just left of the arête.)

26 Crush with Eyeliner 15m E1 5b †(11.12.94)
Start 2 metres right of the corner, beneath a short groove at the top of the cliff. 'Funny-farm' protection on the lower section. Climb up to a chert thread. Move diagonally left through the band of knobbly rock to a large lump of chert, which provides a positive hold but a poor runner. Continue up the wall and groove above.

27 Sunday Rake 12m S
Start on the right side of the earth mound and climb the broken-looking rake with an awkward step half-way up. Exit right.

28 Spider Cracks 12m HVS †
Start 2 metres right of *Sunday Rake* in the middle of a bay. This climb seems to have changed and has some dubious rock near the top. Climb steeply up the leftward-slanting flake crack, go leftwards at the roof, and finish more pleasantly.

29 Butterfly Crack 8m S †
Start at steep, wide cracks 5 metres left of two sloping blocks by the path. Climb the cracks, and butterfly right on a jam for the left hand at the top. Exit earthily rightwards.

Marti Hallett on *Nothing's Shocking* F6a+ (page 272). STEVE TAYLOR

Neddyfields

The Neddyfields bouldering wall flanks the main coastal path above Neddyfields Cliff and Pipe Cliff. The wall extends for almost 100 metres and provides much interest for all standards of climber. It has an eastern aspect and provides an excellent venue with a high concentration of quality problems.

Conditions are best on cold sunny winter mornings with a light easterly breeze. The wall is shady by midday or soon after, and in summer is best left for late evening. After heavy rain many of the more classic lines are covered in wet streaks, but these dry up after a couple of days of good weather. The climbing is technical and hard on the fingers. Make sure you have a good edge on your shoes for maximum progress up the tiny edges.

The extreme left-hand end is somewhat out of character with the other sections. The rock is much less flowstone-encrusted and the problems are more powerful than the technical masterpieces further on.

1 **Foreboding V2** From a sitting start, climb the right-hand side of the arête. Poor landing.

2 **Hara-kiri V4** From a sitting start in the layback pod, climb the slim crack over a difficult landing.

3 **Psycho V4** From a sitting start, climb the centre of the face.

4 **Great Bear V1** From a sitting start, climb the left side of the arête.

5 **Little Bear V0** Climb the flowstone-encrusted blunt arête.

6 **Solar Stone V7** From the waist-height ramp, make a long move to the tiny undercut and the top.

7 **Indian Summer V3** An eliminate up the edges without the use of the flowstone pillar.

8 **Totem Pole V0-** The classic flowstone problem.

This area of Portland is an excellent place to relax and chill out. It is popular with other outdoor enthusiasts, in particular ramblers and 'twitchers'. From the main platform it is possible to see seals that regularly hang around in the cove below. It is worth taking a pair of binoculars to view them as they bask in the summer sun or swim playfully in the shallows. You can also see one of the breeding pairs of peregrine that nest over at Cheyne Cliff. Little Owls have recently been sighted in the area around the many small quarried walls and caves.

This section of wall is the centre of technical difficulty. The handholds are not usually too bad but the footholds can be shockingly poor.

9 Papoose V2 Climb the thin crack up the blunt rib.

10 Wampum V4 Various methods are possible to climb the seemingly blank wall. Very difficult for the short.

11 Vacillate V3 Balanced climbing via flowstone edges and nubbins directly above the low ledge.

12 Jimbo's Wall V8 From the undercut, reach the poor sloping pinch above with your right and levitate to the stuck-on jug via poor sloping holds.

13 Jimbo's Right-hand V8 From the undercut, make a long move to the undercut high and right before balancing left to the stuck-on jug.

14 Pock Mark V7 Make technical moves off sloping holds past the shot hole.

15 Prosthesis V3 Climb direct up the thin crack from the lowest of the pockets.

16 Colossus V4 From the start of *Prosthesis*, make a gigantic move up right to the large sloping hold and the top.

Ben Thorne on *Straight and Narrow* V4 (Page 282). JIM KIMBER

17 **Stoic Existence** V4 Climb the very blunt arête, swinging right at half height.

18 **Fontanel** V5 Balance past the two-finger undercut to climb the shallow groove.

19 **The Flake** V2 A classic line up the crack and groove.

20 **Local People** V5 An eliminate avoiding cracks to either side.

21 **Taming the Flow** V3 The crack.

22 **Fountain of Youth** V1 Follow the pinches and pockets.

23 **Stolid** V0- Follow a variety of flowstone holds.

A **Savage Traverse** V7 From the base of *Stopcock*, traverse left along the thin seam at waist height. Contorted moves after *The Flake* lead to easier ground before finishing up *Fontanel*.

24 **Stopcock** V0- Grip the flowstone pillars and pockets.

25 **Protozoa** V0- Climb under the flowstone feature.

26 **Amoeba State** V0 A rightward rising line on ever-decreasing holds.

27 **The Arête** V3 The grade applies if the conglomerate flake is used on the left. If it is not used, the grade rises to V5.

Ben Stokes on *Stairway Direct* V3. STEVE TAYLOR

16 **Detonata** 18m F7c 6B   (6.97)
Fiercely technical and fingery from the word 'go'.
From the right-hand edge of the ledge, make a series
of hard moves over bulges to an undercut 'rest'.
Now launch up the steep wall to the lower-off (crux).

17 **Illusions** 16m F7c 6B   (30.4.96)
Fine climbing to the right of *Detonata*, spoilt by the
use of resin to 'roughen-up' poor starting holds.

18 **Yesterday's Dreams** 15m F7b 7B   (4.96)
A scree fall has put paid to the route's independent
start, so start up *Illusions*. Resin was used on this
one too.

On the top of the scree to the right is a short
flowstone buttress, currently unclimbed.

Dungecroft Quarry
OS Ref 697 707

Approach
Continue south past the *Mermaid Inn* and park at the Cheyne Weares car-park and viewpoint half a mile further on the left. Walk 50 metres south to a flat quarried area atop Cheyne Cliff. The routes are on the back wall, starting in a small rift. Despite their lack of length, they each pack in a significant amount of climbing. The first area is on the left, 80 metres into the quarried area.

Tom Beaumont on *Ultrasonic Shoulder* **F6a+**. BEAUMONT COLLECTION

1 Die Screaming With Sharp Things in Your ⭐
Head 6m F5 3B   (29.4.07)
The route farthest to the left on this wall climbs good conglomerate and flowstone to finishing holds just right of the lower-off.

2 Ultrasonic Shoulder 6m F6a+ 3B   (10.4.07)
Good climbing on flowstone all the way. A reachy move at the start with a crux finish. Low in the grade.

⭐ 5 **Covert Strike** 6m F6b 3B   (29.5.07)
Start on the mini arête to reach some big flat holds.
Continue steeply up some technical flowstone to
a finishing jug left of the lower-off.

⭐ 6 **The Epicurean Paradox** 6m F6b+ 3B
(29.5.07)

The steepest route on this section, with a hard crux.
At the first bolt of *Dungecroft Delight*, reach left
to good holds in the fault. A long reach, or a small
crimp, leads up and slightly leftwards to easier
flowstone.

7 **Dungecroft Delight** 6m F5 3B   (26.5.07)
Start steeply up the stal groove and follow the tufa
to the top.

8 **The Alpha and the Omega** 6m F3+ 3B
(26.5.07)
This takes a slightly slabby wall. Climb onto the
flowstone ledge and step left to follow the flowstone
flake crack.

3 **Crazy Old Hippies** 6m F4+ 3B   (8.4.07)
Bizarre flowstone with good holds if you can find
them.

4 **Crowbar Assassin** 6m F6a+ 3B   (29.4.07)
Fingery and technical moves lead to the shared
lower-off of *Crazy Old Hippies*. Don't use jugs off
to the left for this grade and keep an eye on the
boulder to the right if you fall!

The last three routes are 30 metres to the right.

9 Truly, Madly, Steeply 6m F7b 3B   (1997)
Pull up to the break and make a desperate move to become established on the flowstone. Continue with difficulty to the lower-off.

★**10 Lifesigns** 6m F7a+ 3B   (1997)
Start 2 metres right of a cliff-high flake. Sustained!

11 Sex, Lies, and Videotape 6m F7a 3B   (1997)
Climb a tiny left-facing corner to jugs at the break, where long reaches lead to the lower-off.

Mike Robertson on *Cadwallader F6b+* (page 292).
STEVE TAYLOR

The Lost Valley

OS Ref 695 707

Approach

Continue south past the *Mermaid Inn* and park at the Cheyne Weares car-park and viewpoint half a mile further on the left. Walk 200 metres north to this short crag, which forms the western side of a chasm situated well back from the sea.

The routes reside on two cleaned areas of rock in the centre and at the northern end of the craglet; the remainder is festooned with curtains of vegetation that should be left for the birds and woodlice that nest in it. The southern end of the chasm is heavily overgrown with only a small gap between bushes and the crag.

Immediately east of the Lost Valley is a short, overhanging wall with one bolted line.

1 Enjoy My Experience 7m F6c+ 2B   (3.00)
Jamming moves gain a *hueco*, then long moves lead to a sloping ledge and a grievous mantel (crux). Lower off the second bolt runner.

The southern section consists of a number of short, difficult bolted routes, interspersed with boulder problems. In the centre of the southern section of the crag is a cliff-length vertical crack with a series of ledges on its left-hand side.

2 Quite Nice, Actually 9m F6b+ 3B   (17.3.96)
The leftmost bolted line. Climb the blind flake to a hard pull round the roof.

3 Little Pinky 9m F6b+ 3B   (14.11.93)
Start 3 metres left of the crack at a short flowstone curtain. Mantel the flowstone and make a hard undercut move to the ledge.

4 Clamped Aggression 9m F6c 3B   (9.4.94)
Start 3 metres right of the crack, by a low, shallow cave. The best route hereabouts. Powerful and reachy climbing on sloping holds and finger-pockets leads to the lower-off.

A number of difficult boulder problems exist in the small bay to the right of *Clamped Aggression*.

5 Bastard Crack 8m F7a 3B   (9.4.94)
Six metres further right, past a shallow groove, is a thin crack in a blunt arête. Climb the crack (far harder than it looks) to the breaks and finish rightwards to the lower-off.

6 Plystalker 8m F7c 1B   (2.97)
A desperate bolted boulder problem, the first bolt of which is missing. Start beneath a small overhang, 2 metres right of *Bastard Crack*.

7 No Chutney on his Ferret 8m F5+ 3B (17.3.96)
The crack immediately right of *Plystalker* is harder than it appears. Graded for those who can jam!

The next two routes start atop a small mound.

8 Chapter and Verse 8m F4+ 2B   (17.3.96)
The groove has an awkward start and an easy finish.

9 Oatsheaf Chief 8m F5+ 3B   (17.3.96)
The flake crack just left of the vegetation. Powerful starting moves lead to a ledge and an easy finish.

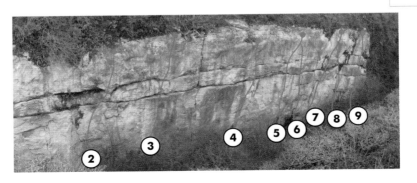

The main feature of the northern section of the crag are two converging crack-lines that are 4 metres apart at ground-level; these are *Cadwallader* and *Redundancy Crack*.

10 Training for Hubble 11m F6a+ 3B (31.7.92)
Hard for the grade, but what do you expect if you are training for *Hubble*?. Starting 6 metres left of the cracks, climb a series of jugs and layback holds and ledges to the lower-off.

⭐ **11 The Stoning of St. Stephen** 11m F7a 3B
(31.7.92)
The hardest route of the crag climbs the blank grey face 3 metres left of the cracks. A vicious boulder-problem start leads to enlarged pockets on the left. Continue on edges and 'monos' to ledges and lower-off shared with *Training for Hubble*.

12 Mono Y Mono 11m F7a 3B (5.9.96)
An eliminate up the steep wall to the left of *Cadwallader*. Start just to the left of *Cadwallader* and boulder up the steep wall on small edges.

13 Cadwallader 11m F6b+ 3B (10.4.91)
Climb the steep left-hand crack to the lower-off.

⭐ **14 Redundancy Crack** 11m E2 5b (7.90)
Worthwhile. Climb the right-hand (leftward-slanting) crack, with a big reach to finish. Lower-off shared with *Cadwallader*. Don't forget your rack on this one.

⭐ **15 The Martyr** 11m F7a+ 3B (5.7.92)
Start at the base of the slanting crack. Steep, fingery climbing with a sequence crux leads to ledges, an easy layback corner, and the lower-off.

⭐ **16 The Secret Garden** 11m F6c 3B (7.11.93)
Start beneath a shallow scoop just right of *The Martyr*. A hard crux. Climb to a good hold at 5 metres and make hard moves to the break. Finish over ledges and up an easy layback corner, as for *The Martyr*, to a shared lower-off.

17 The Beauty of Decay 11m F6c 4B (7.11.93)
Climb the faint twin cracks to the break and the lower-off of *The Martyr* up to the left.

18 Slug 9m E1 5b † (13.9.92)
To the right is some flowstone- and ivy-coated rubble at the base of the cliff. This unappealing route climbs up from its left side, finishing up grass to belay on a large number of small shrubs.

18 Bogus Roof 9m F7b 4B (4.5.98)
The big roof. Start up *The Unworthy*, step left and cross the centre of the 2-metre roof to a belay.

19 The Unworthy 9m F6c 4B (29.8.92)
The scene of many lobs, this sustained route starts beneath a leftward-slanting flake 3 metres right of *Lats, Babes 'n' Bolts*. Hardest just when you think you have arrived! Climb the flake, swing right, and go left through the bulge using calcite flutings to the lower-off.

20 The Vulcanites 9m F7a 4B (29.6.96)
A minor variation on *The Unworthy*, thought by most to be an improvement on the original line. Move right at the first bolt on *The Unworthy* and climb the steep wall to rejoin *The Unworthy*.

21 Deadlossky Must Die! 8m F7b 4B (25.2.95)
A short but uncompromising V-groove is the start of this intense, sequential problem. Enter the groove, layback wildly, and make fingery moves for the break. Trend leftwards to the lower-off of *The Unworthy*.

22 The Leer of Beethoven 8m F7c 2B (7.5.94)
To the right of the short V-groove is a very shallow groove under a flowstone roof. Climb direct up to the breaks and the belay, with desperate moves to gain the wall above the roof!

Typical January conditions on Portland; Jon Biddle on *Flowers on the Razor Wire* **F6c.** STEVE TAYLOR

297

23 Elephant on Roller Skates 12m F4+ 5B   (5.3.89)
Some large timbers are visible on the cliff-top. Start just right of these, at a calcite sheet with a crack on its right. Climb the crack to a ledge and move up left to the lower-off.

24 Limbo Dancer 12m F5+ 5B   (4.08)
Worthwhile, go-ey climbing up the arête immediately right of the calcite sheet. Pull up onto a prominent flat hold at 3 metres and move quickly to gain the ledge above. Limbo right under the roof and climb a slight rib to the lower-off.

25 Beeching's Track 12m E1 6a   (7.5.89)
Start at a thin, vertical seam. Climb the seam (difficult) to a ledge and either lower-off, or follow a short crack on the right and finish up the ivy slope. Belay on the old winding-gear over to the left.

26 Tipping the Scales 8m F7a 2B   (23.4.94)
A bolted boulder-problem 5 metres right of the calcite sheet. Climb the sequency wall to the break. A bold pull gains the lower-off.

27 Pop for the Top 8m F6c 3B   (10.5.08)
The very thin crack left of the flowstone corner packs in a lot of moves.

28 Two Nuns, a Hang-glider and Jesus 12m F4+ 5B   (7.5.89)
Start at a left-facing flowstone corner. Climb the corner to ledges, and move up to the lower-off.

The short arête to the right was drilled, and then the holes were filled in! What remains is a highball V2.

29 Nobody Runs for Free 13m E2 5c †   (1.12.94)
A shortlived and rather nondescript climb that starts just right of the once-drilled arête. Unprotected. From a minuscule left-facing corner, climb diagonally rightwards to flowstone. Stretch for large holds and finish rightwards to the lower-off of *Bend Sinister* at the horizontal breaks.

30 The Running Man 12m F6c 4B   (10.4.98)
Start as for *Nobody Runs for Free*, but take a lower line into *Bend Sinister*.

31 Bend Sinister 12m F7a+ 4B   (7.11.90)
Start 3 metres left of *Learning Curve*. Climb a blind crack to a hand-ledge and then mantelshelf past a ledge on the right to the top break and the lower-off.

32 Plyometrically Speaking 9m F7c 4B   (12.6.94)
This very powerful problem trends left up a leaning white arête, where a dynamic reach – the crux – leads to a ledge. Follow spaced-out jugs up the bulging wall above to the lower-off shared with *Bend Sinister*.

33 Learning Curve 9m E1 5c   (5.3.89)
Start 6 metres before the end of the crag. Short but sweet. Climb the thin crack in the steep thin groove and continue up over ledges. Belay on boulders down on the track.

The next two climbs are not shown:

34 The Blandford Weasel 9m F7b 3B   (28.4.96)
The short arête right of *Learning Curve*. Good climbing on rounded holds up the short arête. The lower-off has become overgrown by ivy.

35 Cold Fusion 8m E1 5b †   (7.5.89)
Now completely covered in ivy! Start below a flake 3 metres from the right-hand end of the crag. Climb up past the flake, and then via a high pocket (nut placement) to a ledge at the top. Belay as for *Learning Curve*.

The New Cuttings

This is the largest concentration of hard problems on the island. Finger strength is a must for the tiny crimps, and cold conditions for the poor sloping holds.

The Playground

The Playground area is at the south-facing wall at the southern end of the New Cuttings cliff. This area enjoys the late sun and is ideal for an evening in the summer. The more accomplished climber can use it as a good warm-up for harder things. The tops are dirty and need some care to exit. Most locals, when they've done it once, just down-climb or jump onto their pads. There used to be more climbing on the now overgrown eastern arête. The ivy is perhaps better than the problems lost.

1 **Broken Rib** **V0** Climb the arête on its right-hand side.

2 **Park Life** **V0** Flowstone-encrusted crimps and spikes lead to a dusty top.

3 **Canyon Crack** **V0** Laybacking the crack using both walls is very pleasant. Harder if climbed as an arête without the left wall: V2.

4 **Groovy** **V2** A dusty groove on suspect holds.

5 **Spare Rib** **V1** Starting on the low large rib, follow the tricky crack and groove to the top.

6 **Seams the Same** **V1** The thin finger-crack.

7 **Shot-hole Blues** **V2** An eliminate. From a low start on the large flake, reach the shot-hole and gain the high edges and jugs direct.

8 **Left Crack** **V0**

9 **Right Crack** **V0**

10 **See Saw** **V1**

11 **Swings and Roundabouts** **V4** From the deep crack, traverse left with intermittent difficulties to reach *Groovy* and exit upwards.

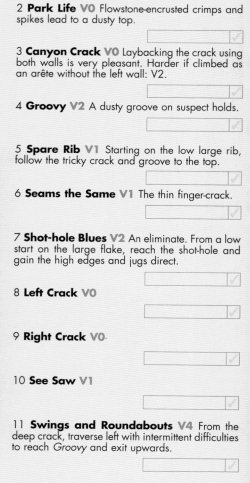

Pastoral Bay

The climbing here is fierce on the fingers and good technique is important for success. This bay is home to the original Portland hard problem, *Pastoral* and the new-wave classic, *Phat Slapper*.

1 **Loco** V1 The slab and arête.

2 **Phats and Bigs** V4 The wall is climbed direct, avoiding the large ledge to the left.

3 **Weight Watchers** V5 A harder version of *Phat Traverse* which finishes without the aid of the head-height shelf.

4 **Phat Traverse** V2 Climb left from *The Fat Controller* to exit up *Loco*.

5 **Fat Controller** V2 The crack.

6 **Phat Slapper** V5 A classic eliminate avoiding the wall and crack to the left.

7 **Phastoral** V7 A useful link-up; start up *Phat Slapper* and reach into *Pastoral*'s half-height undercut, before finishing up *Pastoral*.

8 **Pastoral** V8 The original and classic hard problem. Climb the undercuts to gain the shallow groove.

9 **Descent Horizon** V2 The crack and corner.

Sub Youth Bay

The problems around this area get harder and more highball. Good spotters and a stack of pads will help protect your head, shoulders, knees, and toes from lasting damage.

1 White Baron Left Arête V4 The highball arête is climbed on its left-hand side.

2 White Baron Sit Start V6 From a sitting start, climb the steep arête to join *White Baron*.

3 White Baron V5 From a standing start, climb the arête on its right-hand side or swing right into the groove.

4 Gunpowder Plot V5 From a standing start, finish up the groove.

5 Guy Fawkes V11 From a sitting start under the roof, climb via small crimps to finish up *Gunpowder Plot*.

6 Firestarter V5 A diagonal line via the large pocket and sloping holds.

7 Sub Youth V6+ Climb to the flowstone jug via a number of different methods.

8 Sub Youth Eliminate V6+ Climb to the flowstone jug eliminating the cracks and ribs to the left and the groove to the right.

9 **Flowers on the Razor Wire** V1 A highball crack-climb to the high ledge.

10 **Nu Skool** V5 An eliminate up the face.

11 **Stompin' With Bez** V7 A classic of the area. Climb the left face to the large pocket and traverse rightwards to the far rib via edges on the arête.

12 **My Chemical Romance** V11 The left arête of *Stompin' with Bez*. Climb the arête starting up the direct start to *Stompin'...*, to the crimp rail. Thin moves and a dramatic slap gain the upper arête.

13 **Stompin With Bez Direct** V7+ Climb to edges on the arête direct.

14 **The Fibonacci Sequence** V8+ This arête climb has since lost a hold and remains unclimbed to date.

15 **Jim's Traverse** V2 A useful traverse from beneath *Fibonacci Sequence* leftwards to *Sub Youth*.

Razor Face

As the name suggests, this face has some very small edges that can be quite painful to hold. It is the first face to lose the sun and can therefore have quite good conditions from mid to late afternoon.

⭐1 **Lats, Babes and Bolts** V8 Thin climbing up the flowstone edges and sidepulls.

2 **Mantle** V2 Mantel the sloping edge and exit into the crack.

3 **The Unworthy** V1 Highball to the break.

⭐4 **Vulcanites Direct** V4 Climb the arête directly to the high crimps.

5 **Deadloski Must Die** V4 Climb the groove and finish standing on the large edge.

6 **Razorface** V7 Traverse leftwards along the sharp edges to finish up *Firestarter*.

⭐7 **Connect 4** V5 An eliminate following the undercut and edges to finish right on the flowstone skirt.

8 **Leer of Beethoven Start** V1 Climb the groove to the flowstone skirt.

9 **Crack** V0 Layback the wide crack

Right-hand End

This section has many useful problems but by far the most popular is the rightward traverse.

⭐ 1 **Crag Traverse** **V5** A long and sustained rightward traverse following the head-height break.

2 **Seam** **V4** The thin seam provides a tricky problem.

3 **Elephant on Roller Skates** **V0** The slab.

4 **To The Left** **V2** Climb the groove to finish leftwards from the pocket.

⭐ 5 **To The Right** **V3** Climb the groove and go right to the ledge via the pocket.

⭐ 6 **Beeching's Track** **V3** A slim crack-climb. Reverse to get down.

7 **Tipping the Scales** **V5** Climb the wall on crimps to the break.

8 **Two Nuns, a Hang-glider and Jesus** **V0** The groove is interesting.

⭐ 9 **Space Manoeuvres** **V2** Climb the arête on its right-hand side. There is a single bolt at the top.

10 **Running Man Start** **V2** Climb to the flowstone skirt.

Joff Cook on *Stompin' with Bez Direct* V7+ (page 303).
STEVE TAYLOR

Adam Slater working *Firestarter* V5 (page 302).
STEVE TAYLOR

The Cuttings Main Cliff

The Main Cliff is a by-product of the quarry railway, which together with its attendant bridge has long since disappeared. This man-made face offers a different style of climbing from the rest of Portland, with grooves predominating. A less welcome feature is the top section of brittle, slatty rock and earthy slopes. Old metal fence posts, stakes, and the odd block provide adequate belays for those few routes that top out.

The first major feature of the crag is a large break in the cliff, the entrance to a sporting rift-system on two levels. This small cave is known as *Australia* or *Cherty Rift*. To the right are two walls; the second is split by the wide crack of *Jam*. Another noticeable structure is the ivy-covered mid section of *Kestrel*, which is made up of three flakes set one on top of each other. Further on, a blank-looking upper wall offers us *Haute Cuisine*, while right again two climbs make use of three short pillars: the *'Finger'* climbs. Close to the end of the crag, *Modern Nightmare* climbs an overhung open groove and the fluted wall of flowstone above, and *Shiver Me Timbers* voyages up a long thin crack.

The first fifteen routes on this cliff are extremely popular with beginner groups, and hence have become very polished. It is normal to find all the belays taken with top-ropes. Don't be dismayed – there are much better routes elsewhere on the Isle at similar grades – they simply require you to walk further. The routes here are not described in any great detail.

The first few routes are very short.

1 **Eat, Stick and Die** 6m F3 2B (1995)
A short wall and poorly-protected rightward traverse.

2 **We're Only Placing Bolts for Nigel** 5m F3 2B (1995)
Start left of the ivy and brambles and climb direct to the lower-off of *Eat, Stick and Die*.

3 **Cheese and Pickle** 5m F4+ 3B (2008)
The left-hand side of the lighter patch of rock is quite technical.

6/7/19

4 **Parsnip Soup** 5m F5 3B (2008)
The right-hand side of the lighter patch of rock is also quite technical.

5 **Corporal Punishment** 7m F5 2B (1995)
Start at the base of a small slab.

6 **On Manoeuvres** 7m F3 3B (1995)
Start to the right of the small slab and climb the left-facing corners. Shared lower-off.

6/7/19

7 **Arc Angel** 7m F3 3B (1995)
The short groove to ledges and the lower-off.

Neal Heanes on *Evening Mistress* F6a+ (page 311). BEN STOKES

8 **Charity Work, Mate** 7m F3 3B   (1995)
More or less direct up the steep wall, then ledges to the lower-off.

9 **Magical Misty Tour** 8m F4 3B   (1995)
The slight groove and ledges to the shared lower-off.

10 **Bonsai** 9m F4 3B   (1995)
Start beneath a large patch of grass at four metres. Follow a rightward trending line to the shared lower-off.

11 **Sting in the Tail** 9m F5+ 3B   (1995)
Climb the groove and wall to the shared lower-off.

12 **Baron's Revenge** 9m F3 4B   (2008)
Climb past a ledge, a corner and more ledges to a steep finish.

13 **Chicken Boy** 9m F3 4B   (2008)
Pull onto the ledge then use sloping holds to gain a higher ledge, finishing steeply to the lower-off.

14 **Tantrums and Tiaras** 9m F4 4B   (2008)
The tight groove left of the shattered groove is hard to enter and a little sustained.

15 **100 Sunny Days** 9m F3 4B   (2008)
Very pleasant climbing up flakes on the right of the shattered groove.

6/7/19

16 **Juggernaut** 12m F5 3B
(1995)

Start beneath a large, light brown rock scar at 3 metres. Make a difficult move to gain a ledge and trend rightwards across the slab to the lower-off.

17 **Rock Lobster** 12m F4 3B
(1995)

Climbs the groove to the right of *Juggernaut*. Pull onto a flake that leads to a lower-off shared with that route.

18 **Amazonia** 12m F4+ 4B
(1995)

The groove just right again. Pull into the groove on jugs and follow the flake above to a ledge, before moving up and right to the lower-off.

19 **The Great American Hamburger Disaster** 12m F5 4B
(29.10.88)

The thin crack just right of *Amazonia*. Harder than it looks. Climb the crack to the ledge and move up to the lower-off shared with *Amazonia*.

20 **Definitely Maybe** 12m F6a+ 4B
(1995)

Particularly eliminate in nature – blinkers might be useful. Climb the tricky wall between the two flake lines and trend slightly right to the shared lower-off. Hard for the grade.

21 Little Chef 12m F5+ 4B
From the start of *The Sod*, move steeply left into a groove containing a peg. Follow the groove and gain a prominent foothold on the right with difficulty. Continue to the break and either finish up left to the lower-off, or scramble up the corner on the right to the top.

22 Little Sod 13m F6b+ 5B   (2.2.07)
An eliminate, starting as for *The Sod*. Pull up left to gain a small flake on the left wall of the groove. Continue direct, keeping right of the arête.

23 The Sod 13m F6a 5B
Start below the groove, opposite a manhole cover and a couple of large boulders. After a difficult and polished start, climb the bolted groove to its top. Finish either up the wall above to a lower-off on a protruding shelf, or top out as for *Little Chef*.

24 Mindmeld 13m F7a 4B   (19.7.95)
A good eliminate (i.e. keep out of the corner) up the arête right of *The Sod*. Pull onto the arête and follow it until it is possible to lean left to a thin handrail on the right wall of the groove. Make a high step (avoiding the groove) and then join *The Sod* to finish.

25 Sign of the Vulcan 11m F7b+ 3B   (4.9.94)
An intense and powerful line straight up the blunt rib, where passing the 'Vulcan pocket' is the crux. It has been soloed!

Dave Stringfellow on *Hillman the Hunter*
F6b+ (page 310). RON KENYON

The next two routes start behind a large flake, near a cave entrance.

26 Hillman the Hunter 13m F6b+ 4B (13.1.91)
Start beneath an obvious bricked-up section. Move up to undercuts (crafty bridging should help) and make a hard move using a crack in the bulge. Continue more easily over a small roof and up the brick wall to a lower-off above its left-hand side.

27 Hole in the Wall 15m E1 5c † (22.5.77)
Climb the crack in the shallow groove past an overlap to the overhang. Move delicately leftwards across the brick wall and up to the lower-off of *Hillman the Hunter*.

The starting-point for the last two routes is an entrance to Australia Rift; the other entrance is reached by a scramble up the centre of the bay, leading to the next two routes, both of which have been bolted to avoid the obvious natural challenges:

28 Flying Peach 10m F6b 3B (31.7.07)
The wall to the left of the left-hand flake has clean rock and pleasant moves.

29 Grapefruit Takes a Whipper 9m F6b 3B (31.7.07)
The wall to the left of the right-hand flake also has clean rock and pleasant moves.

30 The Cutting Edge 12m F6c 4B (18.12.88)
The fine, sharp arête on the right-hand side of the bay. Struggle up onto the ledge, move left, and follow the arête to a ledge. Reach right and clip the lower-off of *Dumbfounded!* The direct start warrants F7a.

31 Dumbfounded! 12m F7a+/7b 3B (15.4.90)
The blank white wall provides a problematic route, the difficulty of which is highly dependent on reach. Claim at least F7b if you are 178 centimetres (the author's height!) or less. Start as for *The Cutting Edge*. The climb has two drilled pegs as well as the bolts. Clamber up onto the ledge. Climb the wall direct to a lower-off on its left side.

32 Chalkie and the Hex 5 13m F5+ 3B (1981)
Short-lived, but excellent. Climb the fine finger-crack on the right side of the wall. Lower off, or continue to the top.

33 The Ramp 13m F5 5B
Start just right of *Chalkie and the Hex 5*. Follow the flake ramp in the corner to its top and continue up to a roof. Either turn the roof on the right past an ancient bolt, and step up and left to the lower-off, or traverse leftwards and climb the wall and groove to the top.

Between the corners of *The Ramp* and *Evening Mistress* is a slight buttress. Two climbs have been crammed onto it.

34 Lusty Wedlock Needs Coil of Prevention

11m F7b 4B   (27.10.94)

A short, intense eliminate up the left rib of the buttress. Scramble leftwards above the brambles and move up to a ledge. Step right and climb the right-hand side of the arête on very small holds to a hand-ledge. Go easily rightwards to the lower-off.

35 Rusty Chublock Seeks Oil of Lubrication

12m F7b 4B   (15.4.90)

A fascinating sequence up an overhanging black arête. Climb easily to the base of the right-hand arête. Climb its right-hand side and then its very edge on flowstone crinkles to ledges above. Shared lower-off.

36 Evening Mistress 13m F6a+ 3B (18.12.88)

Technical groove climbing. Climb the next corner and surmount the roof on its left side. The lower-off is on the left. Alternatively, on natural gear, move back above the corner and finish up the corner on the right.

37 Amen Corner 15m F5 5B

Start below the left arête of a slight bay. Very pleasant climbing up the groove with some hidden flowstone thrown in for good measure, though there are a couple of difficult (for the grade) clips.

38 Mousefolk 15m F6c 5B (15.4.90)

Start 2 metres right of the grooved arête. Climb diagonally leftwards to the obvious projecting foothold and move up past the horizontal crack. Now layback up the right-hand side of the arête and go for the lower-off.

39 Too Many Cooks Spoil the Broth 15m F6a+ 5B   (5.11.90)

The centre of the wall right of *Mousefolk* requires a long reach. The wide crack of *Jam* is off limits. Follow a vague crackline to the horizontal crack. Make a series of mantelshelves to the breaks and lower-off bolts shared with *Mousefolk*.

40 Jam 14m F4 3B

Low in its grade. Start below the prominent vertical fist-crack in the left wall of the slight bay. Climb the crack to the faultline. Either move left and up to the lower-off or traverse right and climb a corner to the top.

41 **Chips with Everything** 15m F5 4B (21.6.80)
A good route which starts 2 metres right of *Jam*.
Climb the pleasant flake/crack to a tricky rockover
beneath a small roof. Finish up the corner above to
a lower-off.

42 **Quality Family Day** 15m F5 5B (16.02.08)
Good climbing up the flowstone flake, though loose
to start. Step up onto the grassy ledge left of the
flake and climb the wall, avoiding the loose initial
section of the flake. Climb the remainder of the flake
and flowstone to finish at a worryingly-placed lower-
off.

43 **True Love** 15m F6b+ 5B (16.02.08)
The blunt arête left of *Bridget Riley* has a difficult
finish.

44 **Bridget Riley** 21m E2 6a (6.10.91)
Excellent technical bridging. Start 5 metres right of
Jam, below a smooth, wide groove. Gain the
groove from the right and follow it with increasing
difficulty to a peg. Reach for the 'swallow's nest'
and pull out rightwards. Use the lower-off nearby
or climb up over ledges to the top bolt of *The Mind
Terrorist*. Step right and finish up the earthy slope.
Post and block belays.

45 **The Mind Terrorist** 15m F7c 3B (11.90)
The flying arête just right of *Bridget Riley*. Climb
straight up past the ledge to the break and go
leftwards onto the arête. Keeping on the right-hand
side, slap away until a long reach rightwards gains
a flowstone boss. Use this and hidden pockets to
reach the ledges. Move right to a lower-off.

46 **Knockout Punch** 15m F7b+ 5B (2.10.96)
Technical climbing up the thin seam. Low in the
grade. Scramble up the easy wall. Make a hard
reach to a small finger jam (or use small pockets on
the right) and power up to a good flowstone sidepull
and easier climbing.

★ 47 **Spicer** 24m E2 5c/6a (1986)
One peg. Climb to a thin crack and follow it to the
horizontal break. Hand-traverse left for 3 metres
and finish direct.

48 **That Chill Divine** 21m E2 6a † (20.1.90)
An obtuse technical problem up a seemingly-bare,
square-cut groove. Reasonable protection from
smallish wires. Start 3 metres right of *Spicer*. Go
straight up to a good ledge. Climb the right-hand
of two small corners, swing up rightwards onto the
arête, and gain easier ground above. From the
scoop, finish out rightwards as for *Kestrel*.

49 **Kestrel** 21m VS 4c (22.5.77)
Start beneath a groove containing a flake broken
into three parts. Climb the wall and then the tripartite
flake. At the top of the flake make a difficult
move to reach a horizontal break before going left and
finishing out right. Block belay far back.

50 **Looking for Love** 21m E2 5b † (29.4.90)
Sparsely protected. Start under the right arête of
Kestrel. Climb the wall directly below the arête to
Friend 4 and *Hex 11* placements at the break.
Follow the stepped arête to the top, moving slightly
right when difficulties occur. (Hidden nut-pocket to
the left at the first ledge.) Block belay far back.

**Unknown climber on *The Cutting Edge* F6c
(page 310).** PAUL BELFIELD

51 Dee 21m HS †
Look for the large block to find this overgrown route. Secateurs required to prune the bushes! Gain the block perched 8 metres up the wall via the right-hand crack and climb to the top trending left. Block belay far back.

The blank face right of *Dee* has two routes.

52 Blowing the Gimp 18m F7a+ 6B (23.11.94)
A tricky number with short-lived difficulties. Climb a slight groove to jugs and a short vertical crack at the base of the headwall. Trend slightly rightwards on layaways (crux), and make a long reach to the lower-off.

53 The Sears Tower 18m F7b+ 5B (4.11.90)
Start 5 metres right of *Dee*. Climb straight over a small roof and up a blind crackline to reach the centre of the grey sheet. Move right before teetering up to juggy ground and the lower-off.

54 The Holy Hand Grenade 12m F7a 5B (26.11.95)
Start beneath a groove, 3 metres left of *Brief Encounter*. Climb the steep wall to enter the groove with some difficulty. Climb this groove for a few moves until it is possible to pull into the crack on the left and mantel onto the ledge.

55 Brief Encounter 21m F6b 7B (6.10.91)
The left-hand of two wide grooves has become difficult due to the loss of a large flake in the central section. From the boulder problem start (no cheating stones), climb straight up to the right-hand side of the ledge at the base of the groove. Follow the right-hand side of this (pumpy) to a ledge on the right. Pull over a bulge to the lower-off.

56 Infernal Din 21m F7b+ 8B (15.4.90)
The narrow pillar between the two wide grooves. A strenuous pitch: reachy, sustained, intricate, and with its crux at the top. Climb the steep wall 3 metres right of *Brief Encounter* to reach the foot of a thin crack. Follow the crack with difficulty to a ledge on the right and continue to the lower-off above the top break.

57 European Flavour 18m F6b 6B (2.10.96)
The left-hand side of the wide groove is accessed via a very hard, undercut start. Boulder over the low roof to reach a ledge. Climb diagonally leftwards to the base of a flake crack, which is climbed via a series of long reaches. Pull up to the roof and swing leftwards to a short finishing corner.

58 Gourmet 18m E1 5b (7.5.79)
Start below the right-hand side of the wide groove. Ivy is gradually obscuring this line. Climb the initial wall to the base of the groove. Traverse left and make one move up the left-hand side of the groove to a hidden hand-ledge before crossing to its right-hand side. Climb up to the roof and exit rightwards.

James Dunlop on *The Mind Terrorist* F7c (page 313). MIKE ROBERTSON

Rob Lamey on *Mousefolk* F6c (page 311). ANDY LONG

59 The Breathing Method 23m F8a 8B   (24.4.94)
A ferocious line which takes an uncompromising, flowstone-encrusted groove. Low in the grade, but testing nevertheless. Start just right of the wide groove of *Gourmet*. Climb the wall to chert jugs and move slightly left to reach a short, vertical crack. Move up to the bulge, switch on the power, and continue up the groove to flowstone. At the break, step right and trend right to the lower-off of *Hall of Mirrors*.

60 Hall of Mirrors 21m F7c 7B   (3.11.90)
An impressive route with good moves, climbing the bulging prow 5 metres right of *Gourmet*. Low in the grade. Climb steeply up juggy bands, over a chert bulge, and then use flakes to reach a short, bottomless V-groove. The crux follows: precariously palm up the rib to a deep horizontal crack. Cross a flowstone bulge to ledges and the lower-off.

61 Want Out 21m F7b+ 7B   (24.3.91)
A sustained line. Follow *The New Saladin* to the small ledge beneath its deep crack. Step left and climb creaking flakes to a bulge underlying a groove. Go up the left wall of the groove and pull over the capping roof to a sloping ledge. Continue to the lower-off shared with *The New Saladin*.

62 The New Saladin 21m F6c 8B   (13.1.91)
A rewarding pitch up a steep groove. Climb straight up the juggy lower wall and make a long reach to good flakes. The crux consists of reaching right to an overhanging crack and laybacking strenuously for the breaks. The lower-off is up and left.

63 Hurricane on a Mill Pond 21m F7c+ 6B   (2.11.96)
The exceptionally technical wall right of *A New Saladin*. Climb the initial wall to a ledge. Pull into the bulge and cross it using an extremely complex sequence (impossible to on-sight) to gain the faultline and the lower-off.

Mark Glaister crimping the crux of *Live by the Sword* F7a+ (page 321). KEITH SHARPLES

64 Consommé 21m F6a+ 7B
The long, thin, layback flake in the white wall 10 metres right of *Gourmet*. Climb the steep wall (crux) to a resting ledge below the flake. Climb the fine flake to its end and the lower-off.

65 Haute Cuisine 21m F7a+ 6B   (16.4.90)
Start beneath a grey face immediately left of the block-choked gully which forms the left-hand side of a vegetated terrace. Climb straight up to the roof beneath the grey face. Delicately surmount this and proceed slightly leftwards to foot-ledges. Follow a vertical hairline crack to good ledges above.

66 The Mouth Waters 22m F7a+ 7B   (16.4.90)
This good eliminate up the right-hand side of the grey face has a continental flavour. Bon appétit! Follow *Haute Cuisine* over the roof but then swing right to a projecting handhold. Now climb straight up the face on small holds to reach a break and ledges on the left. Shared lower-off.

The '*Finger*' climbs, together with *Opus* and *Wallflower*, were originally approached by scrambling up a block-choked gully formed by a huge flake and traversing right along the loose, vegetated terrace. Direct, bolted starts have now been added.

67 Two Fingers 20m F6a 6B   (16.10.83)
Above the terrace are three finger-like pillars of rock. Start on the left-hand side of a huge flake, beneath the fingers. Scramble up to a ledge at 6 metres and pull into the base of a crack in a groove on the left of the fingers. Climb to a sloping ledge and make a difficult move to a ledge and the lower-off.

68 Three Fingers 21m F6a 6B
Start 2 metres right of *Two Fingers*. Climb to the ledge at 6 metres and pull onto the headwall on the right-hand side of the fingers. Climb to a sloping ledge and pull up rightwards to the break and lower-off.

69 **Opus** 21m F5 6B

The chimney/groove 10 metres right of *Consommé* gives elegant bridging. Start 2 metres right of *Three Fingers* and climb up to the base of the chimney. Bridge elegantly up the groove to the lower-off.

70 **Rusty the Redneck Takes One for the Team** 21m F6a+ 7B (24.4.04)

Start as for *Opus*. Climb to a ledge at the base of the chimney and make an exquisite rockover rightwards towards the arête. Climb the pocketed wall above on good holds to the lower-off of *Opus*.

71 **Perihelion** 25m F6a+ 7B (7.5.79)

The undercut crack 3 metres right of *Opus* gives a good pitch. Start at a crack beneath the main crack. Climb up a crack to the terrace. Move up to the bulge and pull over into the crack above. Continue to the top of the crack and the lower-off.

72 **Disobedience Contest** 20m F6b 6B (17.11.95)

This route is centred on a clean, roof-capped V-groove. Climb straight up to the groove, which is entered with difficulty. Make crimpy moves up and left over the triangular roof and finish up the wall above.

73 **The Potting Shed** 21m F6a 7B (6.10.91)

This climbs the concretion-capped groove 5 metres right of *Perihelion*. Climb up and rightwards up steps before assailing the groove. Pull rightwards around the bulge and gain the lower-off with difficulty. Alternatively step rightwards and finish up the ivy-clad corner of *Wallflower*.

Neal Heanes on *Rusty the Redneck Takes One for the Team* F6a+. STEVE TAYLOR

74 Wallflower 21m VS 4c   (2.4.77)
At the right-hand end of the vegetated terrace is a very large flake below a wide, left-facing crack. Climb up to the ledge and flake and follow the wide crack to the top.

75 Old Buffer 21m F6b 7B   (2.11.91)
Climb past ledges to a chert overhang. Swing rightwards along it and layback up to a ledge. Make tricky moves up and left to a ledge on the arête before stepping back right. Follow the crack, moving left to the lower-off.

76 Live by the Sword 21m F7a+ 7B   (5.2.94)
Good climbing on the white headwall. Start beneath a high jutting block. Strenuous climbing up the lower wall leads to a scoop and a rest. Pull over a small bulge and continue to the headwall, where a succession of extending moves on positive incuts leads to a break. Trend right to the shared lower-off.

77 Another Notch in the Gun 21m F6a+ 7B   (14.1.91)
An enjoyable, pumpy route. Start at a flake in the cherty wall beneath the centre of a smooth face. Climb the steep flake to chert bands. Continue straight up and climb a finger-crack to the break. Use jugs on the left to reach the lower-off.

The following three climbs start from a raised ledge to the right of *Another Notch in the Gun*.

78 Figgy Dropwise 18m F6c+ 6B   (23.11.95)
Start from the left-hand side of the raised ledge. Swing left and climb the steep lower wall. From a series of small incut holds, work out with which hand to start the difficult crux sequence! If lucky, continue up the wall on large, sloping holds.

79 Dusty Fred's Winter Collection 18m F6b 6B   (23.11.95)
A difficult start leads to some enjoyable climbing higher up. From the right-hand side of the raised ledge, make a very difficult move up to the bulge. Pull over to a ledge, and then climb the rib on the right to the lower-off.

Aperitif (28m HVS) climbed to the prominent overhang left of the rib on *Dusty Fred's Winter Collection*. No ascents are known of since excavations left 6 metres of friable wall at its base.

80 Ectomorph 25m E1 5b †   (21.5.77)
Start below the conspicuous crack with an overhung base that leads out leftwards from a cave. High in the grade and plastered in ivy. Move up to the big roof and climb the crack to a chockstone. Follow the crack straight up and trend leftwards past a peg to finish up a corner.

81 Unknown Arête 20m F7a+ 5B †   (1997)
The interesting climbing is all based around the flying arête. Climb *The Bournemouth Flier* to the base of the corner and step left onto the arête, which is climbed on shallow pockets to a ledge.

82 The Bournemouth Flier 20m F6a+ 5B   (29.4.90)
Good climbing, which starts at the left-hand end of the cave. Climb up steeply over ledges to the corner. Follow the corner with hard moves to reach its top. Traverse right and step up to the lower-off.

83 Hors d'Oeuvres 27m E1 5c †
Start in the cave at the lowest point. A poorly-protected upper section. Climb a flake crack from the cave to the foot of the corner climbed by *The*

Mark Williams powering up the crack of Another Notch in the Gun F6a+. STEVE TAYLOR

Bournemouth Flier (peg). Traverse left for 3 metres (peg). Climb a pedestal and move onto the ramp above (peg). Follow the ramp to the roof, traverse right to the break, and finish straight up.

The next four routes are somewhat in conflict. *Bad Dream* was climbed using natural gear. Later, its three neighbours were bolted and climbed. *Modern Nightmare* follows the left side of *Bad Dream*'s groove and *Fighting Torque* shares its finish.

84 **The Nightmare Scenario** 23m F7b+ 9B
(25.2.95)
Excellent climbing in the upper half, though spoilt by suspect rock. Follow *Modern Nightmare* to its fourth bolt before heading up a fractured section on the left. Complicated crux moves up a blind crack in a vague rib lead to the break, and steep stretches to the lower-off.

⭐ 85 **Modern Nightmare** 22m F7a+ 9B (29.4.94)
The start is technically the hardest section, but the crux is right at the top, when one is pumped stupid – most failures have occurred with the leader staring at the lower-off. Start a metre right of the cave. The first bolt is best threaded with a sling; a deckout occurred here when a short fall by a heavy climber broke the back of a karabiner. Climb through bulges with difficulty and trend right to the base of the corner. Follow the corner (mostly on its left side) and continue over its capping roof. Make hard moves up the groove above to reach the lower-off.

86 **Bad Dream** 25m E4 6a (1.5.81)
The original route up the groove was serious and is still strenuous. The grade assumes that one shuns the bolts. Traverse left onto the wall and climb up to ledges. Bear rightwards into the corner above and climb it with increasing difficulty to the large roof. Make a strenuous traverse out right to avoid the roof, and continue up the wall above (passing the lower-off of *Fighting Torque*) to the top.

87 Fighting Torque 22m F7c+ 7B   (14.4.94)
The front of the rightmost pillar of the crag. Pull up to a large slot and climb a vague groove to a blind horizontal break. Swing 2 metres left and climb the right-hand side of the arête to the breaks, before finishing up flowstone pipes to the lower-off.

88 Shiver Me Timbers 20m F7a 5B   (7.12.85)
Near the right-hand end of the cliff is a thin crack. The difficulty of the crux is proportional to finger size. Climb straight up to the crack before jamming and spragging your way to the top break. The lower-off is above and left.

89 Weird Shit – Keep Drilling 14m F6b+ 6B   (14.3.94)
Worthwhile climbing which is low in its grade. Start close to the right-hand end of the crag. Start up the open groove and then use the sharp arête to reach a ledge by the roofs. Swing left and pull up through the top roof using a deep hole, before making a difficult move to the lower-off. (Sticking solely to the initial groove, avoiding the sharp arête is worth F6c+. Blinkers required).

The Cuttings Lower Tier

Below the track in front of the main cliff lies a small, unquarried crag. The first two climbs here are best approached from the southern end of the crag. Each requires a further 15 metres of scrambling to reach their shared belay. They have now fallen into neglect, are blanketed in ivy, and require a machete approach. They are not pictured.

1 Hot Flush 8m HVS 5a †   (29.4.90)
Start 3 metres from the left end of the crag at a weathered crack. Climb to the roof, pull up left, and complete the difficulties using a suspect flake.

Scramble to the grassy summit and belay on a horizontal stake 2 metres down the other side.

2 Xerdna 8m VS 4c †   (27.1.90)
Well protected. Start at a corner formed by a flake 2 metres right of *Hot Flush*. Climb the corner and crack, and then scramble over the top of the whaleback to a horizontal belay stake 2 metres down the other side.

Two sports routes on the Lower Tier are approached from the north.

⭐ 3 Up the Junction 17m F6b+ 7B   (3.08)
A good route up the left-hand bolted line. Easy climbing leads to a crux bulge, where a positive approach pays dividends. Easier climbing on fine rock leads to the lower-off.

4 Round the Bend 17m F6b+ 7B   (2.11.91)
The right-hand bolted line. Climb easily up to and over a small roof . Enter the slight groove above using a small undercut to reach good holds. From here make a difficult move on hard-to-spot edges, followed by easier climbing to the lower-off.

To the north of The Cuttings is the unattractive and loose Grove Cliff. Limestone blocks have been cemented across some of the chimneys and gullies, and these artificial walls could possibly give better climbing than the cliff proper.

Much further to the north, the cliffs forming part of the defences of The Verne have some climbing interest, as do the walls surrounding a sunken football pitch. Unfortunately, The Verne is a prison and the football pitch is part of The Grove Youth Custody Centre, so scaling the walls, even from the outside in, could give you a short sharp shock! Definitely not recommended!

Finally on Portland is a pinnacle with a view at OS reference 698 732. Left over from quarrying activity, Nicodemus Knob has a name that is much better than the short scramble to its summit.

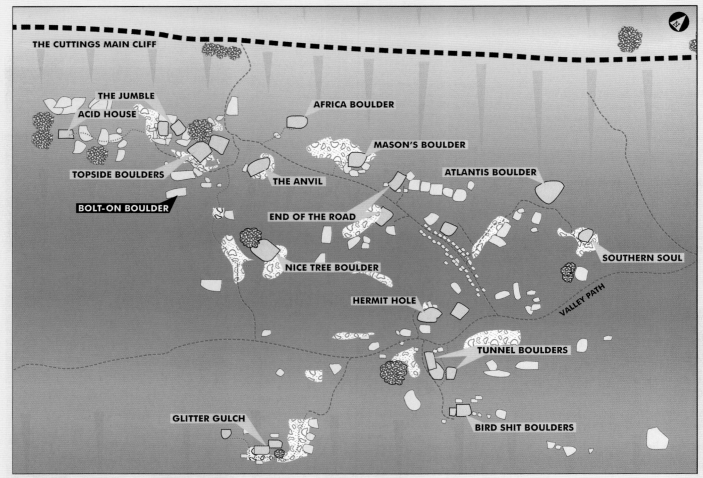

THE CUTTINGS MAIN CLIFF

THE JUMBLE

ACID HOUSE

AFRICA BOULDER

MASON'S BOULDER

ATLANTIS BOULDER

TOPSIDE BOULDERS

THE ANVIL

BOLT-ON BOULDER

END OF THE ROAD

SOUTHERN SOUL

NICE TREE BOULDER

HERMIT HOLE

VALLEY PATH

TUNNEL BOULDERS

GLITTER GULCH

BIRD SHIT BOULDERS

The Boulderfield – Southwestern Section

The Boulderfield

Since the turn of the new millennium, the sprawling mass of boulders beneath The Cuttings have been explored and developed, playing host to more than 100 individual problems. The development was the subject of scepticism and negative comment from some local climbers, these comments being occasionally reiterated in the climbing press. Whilst some of the problems are rather nondescript, a significant number are of genuinely high quality, and would have classic status in any of the more established bouldering venues in the UK. The boulders may be generally short in stature, but the problems pack a punch and the rock is compact, solid limestone with a wide variety of holds and features. A bouldering mat is needed for all the problems.

Gain an overview of the area from the maps opposite and on page 340.

Sector Top Side

The boulder problems nearest to The Cuttings Main Cliff are found at Sector Top Side. Here, a jumbled mass of boulders lies on a terrace 10 metres below the Cuttings track and above the infamous Bolt-on Boulder. Sector Top Side is home to some highly entertaining boulder problems and provides a convenient first stop for a day's antics in the Boulderfield.

TOPSIDE BOULDERS   THE JUMBLE

THE ANVIL

VIEW FROM THE CUTTINGS TRACK

Approach

The first descent from the Cuttings track into the developed area of the Boulderfield is situated 25 metres beyond the far right-hand end of The Cuttings Main Cliff. A steep path descends immediately to the north of a group of large bushes on the right edge of the Cuttings track. Follow the descent until a squeeze between rocks leads one to a tree. Beneath its branches nestle a pair of boulders – the Top Side Boulders. Between these boulders is a narrow tunnel. The descent takes you to the landward side of the smaller Top Side Boulder. This is where you will find the classic *Rocky and Diesel*.

1 **Made in the Shade** V4 Start from edge A and pinch B. Move leftwards using reasonable edges.

2 **Rocky and Diesel** V2 The arête to the right of *Made in the Shade* is a quality problem on mainly sloping holds. Start from a pinch B and sidepull C.

3 **Slim Shady** VB Under the tree, at the entrance to the tunnel, is a slab with a huge jug at its base. A good beginner's problem starts with hands on the jug.

BOULDERING The Boulderfield

On the seaward side of the Top Side Boulders is a prominent arête above a smooth rock platform. This is *Jo's Arête*. The following boulder problems may be started from a variety of holds, giving various levels of difficulty.

4 **Blue Skies** **V1** To the left of the prominent arête is a scooped wall. Start from a standing position in the trench with both hands on ramp D. Rock over onto the ramp and use shallow pockets to reach the top of the boulder. Eliminating the big pocket on the right of the wall makes for a better problem.

5 **Blue Skies – Sitting Start** **V3** Start from a sitting position *à cheval* the arête using sidepull E and pinch F; lunge for ramp D. Finish as for the parent problem.

6 **Jo's Arête** **V0** The left side of the prominent arête is a good problem. A standing start in the trench with both hands on ramp D. Move right to the arête.

7 **Jo's Arête – Sitting Start** **V3** A sit-start *à cheval* the arête, using sidepull E and pinch F is worthwhile but not as good as the parent route.

8 **Old Codes, New Chaos** **V2** A nice link-up of established problems. Start on ramp D as for *Jo's Arête*, cross *Nu Breed* using ledge G and finish up the slab on good holds to the left of *Global Underground*.

9 **Nu Breed** **V1** The right side of the prominent arête may be started from a standing position with both hands on sloping ledge G. A tricky rock-over gives access to the finishing slab.

10 **Nu Breed – Sitting Start** **V4** Starting from a sitting position using sidepull E and pinch F is very powerful and is one of the best problems of the grade in the Boulderfield. A series of hard moves using a nose of rock above pinch F and arête itself lead to sloping ledge G. A tricky rock-over gives access to the finishing slab.

11 **Pleasant Greetings** **V6** Start as for the last problem. Gain ledge G with your left hand and stretch right to good holds as for *Old Codes...* Somewhat contrived, but good climbing nonetheless.

12 **Global Underground** **V4** The face to the right of *Nu Breed* gives a good problem with a powerful sit-start. Start near the entrance of the tunnel with your left hand in the very small pocket I and your right hand on a pinch H. Grit your teeth and power up to a good ledge. Rock over onto the slab with difficulty.

The Jumble

Immediately to the south of the Top Side Boulders is a jumble of blocks and boulders. Nearest the Top Side Boulders is a conspicuous cube-shaped block supported by, and overlooking a rock corridor.

13 **Hard Porn** **V5** This poor problem starts from a sitting position under the small roof of the left-hand supporting boulder. Make a couple of campus moves up the supporting boulder before using the left arête of the cube-shaped block to finish.

14 **Porn** **V4** Supporting the cube-shaped block are two boulders. This problem starts from a sitting position at a projecting edge on the left arête of the right-hand supporting boulder. Follow the arête and move onto the cube-shaped block. The finish is on sloping edges.

On the south side of The Jumble is an eye-catching rising traverse above a horrifying pit.

15 **Filth** **V4** The supported boulder provides a left-to-right lip traverse above the pit. The left-hand end of the lip is horizontal – start here. Shun the traverse and make a horrendous mantelshelf direct onto the slab. Watch your back!

16 **Glue** **V5** The lip traverse itself is a much more enjoyable problem. Start at the left-hand end, where the lip of the boulder is horizontal. Follow the lip rightwards to the apex of the boulder.

VIEW FROM THE JUMBLE

THE ANVIL

The Anvil

Immediately to the north of the Top Side Boulders is The Anvil. The main face of The Anvil is tall and unusually featured. A plethora of pockets, chicken heads and flakes create interesting climbing. Unfortunately, less than ideal landings necessitate a bold approach and prevent the problems on this face from attaining classic status. The Anvil is best approached by walking north-east (parallel to the Cuttings track) from the foot of *Jo's Arête*. After 6 metres, you ascend a short gully of scree between boulders. At the head of the gully is a small cairn. The boulder under the cairn is The Anvil. All the climbing is on the heavily-featured seaward face.

There is one more boulder problem in this area and arguably it is the best. Approximately 30 metres to the south over a jumble of boulders is a traffic cone on top of a boulder. This rather unsightly example of littering provides a useful reference point, for underneath the cone is a steep and undercut face. Whilst the photo indicates the recommended approach, the problem may still be hard to locate. Don't be discouraged - it is worth it!

⭐⭐ 17 **Acid House** V6 Make a sitting start at the bottom of the face using a pinch and a sidepull. The steep face above succumbs to a fusion of power and technique.

⭐ 18 **Hammer Time** V0 The main face of the boulder has three vertical pocket veins. This pleasant problem follows the leftmost pocket vein from a sit-down start. The last move is a long reach to a hidden jug on the lip of the boulder.

⭐ 19 **The Anvil** V1 This bold problem follows the middle pocket vein from a sit-down start to a thought-provoking final move off an undercut.

22 **The Rift** V1 This problem climbs the right arête of the boulder from a standing start. It's just as scary as the previous problem.

The Ramp

From the top of The Anvil, a ramp descends north-eastwards into the heart of the Boulderfield. The ground to the left of the ramp (as one descends) rises steeply to the Cuttings track and is densely vegetated. The ground on the right of the ramp drops off gradually into a shallow basin. A number of worthwhile problems are found on either side of this ramp.

Approach

Enter the Boulderfield by following the approach for Sector Top Side as far as the tree. From this point, walk north-eastwards, parallel to the Cuttings track. The top of The Ramp is between The Africa Boulder and The Anvil.

20 **Breaking Rocks** V1 The furthest right pocket vein gives similar climbing to the other problems on this boulder – a sit-down start on flakes and a tricky last move.

The Africa Boulder

Overlooking The Anvil is the aptly named Africa Boulder. From the cairn on the top of The Anvil, walk towards the Cuttings track aiming slightly to the left of the Africa Boulder. Surmount a waist-high block and scramble to the foot of the boulder.

21 **Africa** V4 From a standing start, climb the face immediately to the right of the undercut section. With the right arête out-of-bounds, technical moves lead past an obvious boss to the apex of the boulder. The landing zone is small and the descent is tricky.

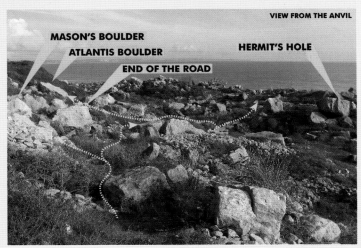

VIEW FROM THE ANVIL

MASON'S BOULDER

ATLANTIS BOULDER

END OF THE ROAD

HERMIT'S HOLE

The Mason's Boulder

This boulder remained hidden for a number of years before an observant Jimbo Kimber spotted the face that would subsequently yield *Mason's Handshake* and more recently *Hot Ride*. As you descend the ramp, the path is blocked by a square block. A scree slope reaches the ramp from above a few metres further on again. A traverse from this point will bring you to the somewhat hidden Mason's Boulder.

The left arête has been climbed at V2 but is not really worth the effort.

⭐⭐ 23 **Mason's Handshake V5** The problem up the hidden face is both devious and powerful. Make a sit-down start using pinch J low down and edge K in the centre of the face. The left arête is out of bounds.

⭐⭐ 24 **Hot Ride V7** The arête to the right of *Mason's Handshake* is a fine problem. Start from a sitting position *à cheval* the arête using holds L and M. Hard moves up the arête lead to a pair of desperately sloping holds. Trend slightly leftwards into *Mason's Handshake* to finish.

The following problems are found near the lowest point of the ramp. As you descend past the *Mason's Boulder* there is a large boulder with a low shallow cave to the left of the ramp. This is known as the *End of the Road*, although *Bottom of the Ramp* would be more appropriate. If you have reached parallel lines of quarried blocks, you have gone too far. The first problem 'weasels' out of the cave.

25 **Gasoline and Apple Pie** V4 A poor problem. Start at the back of the cave with both hands in a deep pocket. Reach for the lip and rock over onto the slab with difficulty. Rather contorted and unpleasant.

26 **Off to Cham** V3 To the right of the cave, facing the path, is a scoop flanking an arête. From an awkward crouching start at the bottom of the scoop, make a hard move to gain good holds on the arête. Finish more easily.

The opposite side of the boulder to *Gasoline and Apple Pie* is blank and leaning. The landing zone under the face is flat but surrounded on all sides by boulders. Take a spotter.

27 **Tim's Traverse** V2 The left-to-right lip traverse of the leaning face is strenuous and rewarding. Make a sit-down start on top of a block on the left side of the face. Rock over onto the slab at the extreme right of the lip using tufa pinches.

28 **Jump and Mantel** V1 Start under the centre of the leaning face. Jump to the lip and mantel on jugs.

29 **Days of Colour** V2 On the other side of the path to *Tim's Traverse* is a half-buried boulder with a steep north-east face. This problem traverses the lip of the boulder from left to right. Start on the far left where the lip protrudes slightly. Finish up the rock steps on the far right.

331

The Block Road Area

At the foot of the ramp that descends from The Anvil are a large number of quarried blocks neatly arranged in parallel lines. At the far end of these blocks, providing a useful landmark is the conspicuous arête of The Toll Booth. Midway along the lines of blocks is the steep and juggy Halfway House. A ridge of scree reaches the lines of blocks just beyond the Halfway House. This marks the approach to the Atlantis Boulder and *Southern Soul*.

Approach

To reach the Block Road either descend into the Boulderfield as for Sector Top Side and the Ramp or use the valley path from the north-east. To reach the valley path, follow the Cuttings track for one kilometre to the north-east of The Cuttings Main Cliff. Here a distinct path leaves the main track, turning back on itself as it descends. As the descent levels out the path splits into two; the right-hand fork leading into a shallow valley. From here, the valley path may be followed to the Toll Booth.

The Halfway House

The side of the Halfway House which faces away from the Block Road is littered with good holds. Both the following problems sport good landings and

VIEW FROM THE HERMIT HOLE

ATLANTIS BOULDER   SOUTHERN SOUL

HALFWAY HOUSE

are excellent for limbering up on or for introducing beginners to the Boulderfield. Approach the Halfway House by making your way to midway along the lines of quarried blocks. A ridge of scree reaches the blocks on the Cuttings track side. A path leads west towards the Halfway House from the foot of the scree.

★ 30 **Thrupenny Bits** **V0** Climb the left arête of the juggy face from a sit-down start.

★ 31 **Bristol Cities** **V0** From a sit-down start, climb anywhere up the centre of the juggy face.

The undercut slab to the left provides further scope for beginners and children.

34 Minimum Rage V3 From a sit-down start using positive edges, climb the left side of the prow by means of good sidepulls.

35 Waiting for the Day to End V4 From the start of *Minimum Rage*, use a mono pocket to gain the right arête; finish up this.

A path leads east from the face of the Atlantis Boulder and then north past a short slab. The right flank of this slab is a steep face that has recently been excavated.

36 Southern Soul V4 An excellent hidden traverse that follows a rising line from right to left along the lip of the boulder. Start at the far right of the steep face. Follow the lip leftwards to a hard finishing rockover left of the sharp nose.

The Atlantis Boulder

The large but unfortunately squat Atlantis Boulder provides a handful of problems that can be adequately described as one-move wonders. Approach the boulder along the ridge of scree that marks the approach for the Halfway House. The ridge of scree is flanked on the right by three boulders; turn right after the third. The Atlantis Boulder is found on the left after a short tramp through knee-high vegetation. The climbing is on the north-east face.

32 Genedefekt V1 Start from a sitting position under a projecting ledge just left of the arête. Gain the ledge, then the lip, and mantel with surprising difficulty.

33 La La Land V2 A metre to right of *Genedefekt* is a blunt arête. Make a sit-down start using poor holds and reach for a deep pocket. The projecting ledge on *Genedefekt* is not to be touched.

To the right of *La La Land* is a shallow groove. This groove had been climbed from a sit start but is of little worth. Further right is a prow-like feature that provides two worthwhile problems.

Steve Taylor on *Southern Soul* V4. BEN STOKES

HERMIT HOLE

The Toll Booth

At the seaward end of the lines of quarried blocks is a tall boulder with a striking undercut arête – *Toll Booth Arête*. See the approach for the Block Road.

37 **The Sentinel** **V0** The left arête is pleasant and blessed with good holds. From a sitting start climb the arête on the left side.

38 **Tommy Cliffhanger** **V3** The face left of *Toll Booth Arête* is home to a contorted eliminate. An awkward sit start on the left side of the face leads to flowstone ripples and the top. At this grade, neither arêtes should be used.

⭐ 39 **Toll Booth Arête** **V7** The dominating undercut arête is a brutal proposition. Start from a sitting position using holds on the lip of the roof.

40 **The Dominator** **V3** Start to the right of *Toll Booth Arête* with your hands in pockets just above the lip of the roof. The roof is usually turned without elegance. Use small edges in a blind crack and then finish more easily.

The Hermit Hole

Named after the deep cave under the west face, the Hermit Hole lies immediately to the south-west of the Toll Booth. This cave is the starting point for the classic *Lightning Strike* and *Relativity*. Facing the Toll Booth is a short sharp prow – the home for the *Doogy Howser* problems.

41 **Doogy Howser Gets Laid** **V3** This is a short but sharp problem up the undercut prow facing the Toll Booth. Start lying on your back with both hands on edge N at the very bottom of the prow. Follow pinches on the prow before making a tricky move onto the left face.

⭐ 42 **Doogy Howser Gets VD** **V5** This hard eliminate has a trick move. Make the same lying-down start as *Doogy Howser Gets Laid*. Move up onto the right face with difficulty and use sloping holds around a rib to gain the top.

43 Lightning Strike V7 This problem is undoubtedly the classic of the Boulderfield and would not be humbled in any world class location. Start with both hands on good jugs at the back of the cave. Steep moves across the roof lead to a hard pull around the lip. Gain the flat edge on the nose and finish more easily. It is worth remembering that this problem receives sun later in the day than any other in the Boulderfield.

44 Relativity V4 This is another classic, but at a slightly more amenable grade. Start at the same holds as *Lightning Strike*. Follow a jug rail rightwards and make a long stretch around the right lip of the roof.

Ben Stokes on *Collo Della Terra* V7 (page 348).
JAMES WHARTON

335

The Tunnel Boulders

On the opposite side of the valley path to the Toll Booth are two large boulders separated by a narrow corridor. The larger of the two boulders supports a slab of rock creating a tunnel betwixt them. The northern end of this tunnel is regarded as the entrance and the southern the exit. The classic *Pornographic Beats* traverses through this tunnel.

⭐ 45 **Streamline V2** The left-hand of the two large boulders (looking from the Toll Booth) leans over the narrow corridor. The left arête of this face gives a fine problem. Start from a sitting position and follow the steep side of the arête to a jug at the very apex.

46 **Tunnel Slab VB** The highest problem in the Boulderfield is up the centre of the taller of the two large boulders. Start with your hands on the good ledge.

47 **Bling, Bling V4** At the entrance to the tunnel is a short, bulging arête. Start from a sitting position using a rough sloping hold on the left and a split four-finger pocket on the right. The supported slab is out of bounds at all times – and that includes for hand jams!

48 **Pornographic Beats V4** The left wall of the tunnel provides an excellent and unusual lip traverse. Reach the lip of the boulder by starting up *Bling, Bling*. Once at the lip, traverse rightwards through the tunnel and around the back of the boulder only using holds on the lip itself – no hand-jams.

49 **In Ya Face V4** At the exit of the tunnel the supported slab forms a steep roof. The roof can be climbed from a sit-start at the left arête using holds on the arête itself. Just before you run out of roof, make a strenuous rock-over onto the left face. The boulder behind you is out of bounds.

The Bird Shit Boulders

To the east of the Tunnel Boulders, overlooking the densely vegetated valley is a tall, conspicuous boulder. Beneath it, pointing south, is a squat boulder with a jutting lip. These are the Bird Shit Boulders. Approach directly from the southern exit of the Tunnel Boulders.

50 **Achilles Heel** V3 A traverse of the jutting lip of the smaller boulder is a strenuous encounter. Start on the left-hand side of the boulder, with one hand on the lip and the other on a good pinch on the left face. Traverse rightwards along the rail and finish by standing on the slabby right face.

51 **The Scene, Revisited** V3 The south-eastern arête of the taller boulder is one of the classic problems of the Boulderfield. Start from a sitting position *à cheval* the arête. Stand up to pinch the arête and move onto the right face. A dynamic move gains the ledge just below the top.

52 **Hello Sailor!** V2 A worthwhile eliminate up the face to the right of *The Scene, Revisited* without using the right arête. From a sit-down start close to the right arête, trend diagonally leftwards on small edges to the ledge on *The Scene, Revisited*.

53 **The Fear** V0 The arête that *Hello Sailor* avoids is a fine problem. From a sitting start, follow the arête and then the lip of the boulder. Mantel once you have reached the apex.

Tim Crawshaw on *The Scene, Revisited* **V3.** BEN STOKES

Glitter Gulch

The Bird Shit Boulders overlook a densely vegetated valley – Glitter Gulch. Hidden at the foot of this valley is a handful of quality problems.

Approach

Follow the valley path south from the Toll Booth. Pass the Tunnel Boulders and then, after 10 metres, branch off left on a clear track. Follow this track until you overlook the shallow, heavily-vegetated valley. Walk south along the top of the slope for a few metres to a small cairn and follow a scree fan past another small cairn down to the valley bottom. The boulders face downhill and are on your right as you descend.

The Jelly Boulder

This is the first boulder you reach following the descent to Glitter Gulch. Overlooking a neat, man-made landing area is a leaning face, the main feature of which is the central groove of *Lemon Jelly*. For the first two problems, only footholds on the main boulder are allowed.

54 Neil Armstrong V6 The slight rib to the left of the central groove. Start with your right hand on the positive hold at the base of the groove and make a wild swing left, around the rib, to an obvious sidepull. Make a tenuous move to gain the sloping lip and mantel with difficulty.

55 Lemon Jelly V3 The central groove feels desperate for the grade until you spot the trick. Start from the positive hold at the base of the groove and power your way up to poor holds on the lip. Search frantically for the hidden slot and pull over onto the slab.

56 Bag o' Shite V3 The right arête of the leaning face (from a crouching start) is poor by comparison to the rest of the problems on this boulder.

57 The Death of Kings V5 A superb leftward traverse along the sloping lip of the boulder. Start from a good hold above the right arête and follow the lip past *Lemon Jelly* and *Neil Armstrong* to jugs around the left arête. Step off onto the pile of rocks.

58 Grafenberg V7 Uphill and to the right of the main boulder, behind bushes, is a 45-degree face, home to a brutal, if slightly contrived problem, using the conspicuous split central pocket. Make a sit start with the left hand in the split pocket and the right hand on the arête. Keeping the left hand in the split pocket bring the right hand up the arête to a dish on the lip of the boulder. Match the lip, and mantel using a large flake.

TO THE JELLY BOULDER

Silent Hill

Fifteen metres up the valley from the Jelly Boulder is another leaning, though somewhat smaller boulder.

59 **First Impressions** V2 The sharp southern arête from a crouching start is relatively straightforward until the desperate mantelshelf finish.

60 **Silent Hill** V4 A devious problem up the blunt arête facing the Jelly Boulder. Start from a crouching position using an edge for the left hand and a sidepull for the right.

The Nice Tree Boulder

Underneath the Ramp, alongside a nice tree, is the Nice Tree Boulder. This is where you will find the hardest and best traverse in the Boulderfield – *Liquid Sun.*

Approach

Either make your own way to the boulder down the slope from beneath the Anvil, or approach from the north using the valley path. Follow the valley path 200 metres south of the Tunnel Boulders. At a small cairn a path branches rightwards through bushes to a wide expanse of scree. The Nice Tree Boulder is situated just to the north of this scree.

61 **Pinky Power** V6 From a powerful sitting start using a small undercut, climb the leaning wall under the 'nice tree' on small flakes to a jug just below the lip. The finishing mantel is frustratingly problematic.

62 **More Power** V7 An eliminate breaks out rightwards from Pinky Power at the undercut, using only a sloping edge to gain the lip.

63 **Liquid Sun** V7 The compelling rising lip of the boulder provides one of the best problems in the Boulderfield. Start on the nose of the prow on the far right and strenuously traverse leftwards on sloping holds to the finishing mantel of *Pinky Power.*

64 **The Prow** V4 Beneath the start of *Liquid Sunshine* is a steep prow. Start from sitting position using a good sidepull on the left side of the prow and a

low pinch on the right side. A couple of powerful moves lead to a good jug on top of the prow. Much harder if the trick is missed.

65 **Liquid Sunshine** V8 The combination of *The Prow* and *Liquid Sun* provides the stiffest challenge in the Boulderfield.

To the right of *The Prow* are a number of eliminates, the best of which are described here. The photo topo indicates the 'in' holds. The landings are poor and more than one mat is recommended.

66 **Rain Dodging** V3 A metre right of *The Prow* is a slight rib. Make a sit start to the left of the rib using edge O and pinch P. Move to sloper Q just right of a wide pinch. Now reach or lunge for the top.

67 **A Bracing Dampness** V4 Follow *Rain Dodging* to sloper Q, but this time grab the wide pinch R with the left hand and reach right to sidepull S. Finish rightwards up the slab.

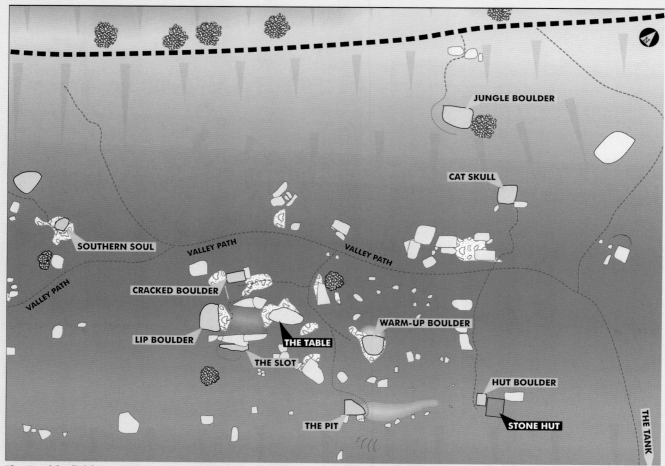

JUNGLE BOULDER

CAT SKULL

SOUTHERN SOUL

VALLEY PATH

VALLEY PATH

VALLEY PATH

CRACKED BOULDER

WARM-UP BOULDER

LIP BOULDER

THE TABLE

THE SLOT

HUT BOULDER

THE PIT

STONE HUT

THE TANK

The Boulderfield – Northeastern Section

THE STONE HUT

90 **Southeast Arête** **V2** The south face of The Hut Boulder consists of quarryman's roach. This rock is crusty and sharp. Fortunately the right arête of this face is not so unpleasant. Start from a sitting position.

91 **Jurrassic Slab** **VB** Outside the entrance to the hut is an east-facing slab liberally encrusted with fossilized shells. This provides an interesting beginners' problem.

The Cat Skull

Named after the cat skull found in the bushes, this once hidden face provides good, steep climbing.

Approach

Take the northern descent into the Boulderfield: follow the Cuttings track for one kilometre to the north-east of The Cuttings Main Cliff. Here a distinct path leaves the main track, turning back on itself as it descends. As the descent levels the path splits into two; the right fork leading into a shallow valley. Follow the valley path for 30 metres to a knee-high walled-up cave. From here, a path leads inland through bushes to the Cat Skull. Alternatively, if you are approaching from the heart of the Boulderfield, follow the valley path 40 metres

beyond the Table. Here, on the left, a path leads between bushes to the Cat Skull.

92 **Eco Terrorists** **V3** The steep side of the left arête is a good problem. Watch your back on the rock behind.

93 **Cat Killer** **V3** A simple problem – sit start, gain the lip, and mantel – although surprisingly difficult to execute. Start from a sitting position using the two big slots in the centre of the face. Reach directly for the lip of the boulder and mantel with a struggle.

94 **Nine Lives Lost** **V2** A leftward lip traverse with a difference. To the right of the main face is a chest-high boulder – start with both hands on top of this. Reach out behind you and traverse leftwards along the lip. Turn the left arête and step off.

95 **Tour de Bloc** **V4** An interesting link up of existing problems: Start from a sitting position with both hands on the left arête. Traverse rightwards, using the big slots of *Cat Killer* to join the lip of the boulder at the far right-hand end. Traverse back across the boulder using the lip. Turn the left arête and step off.

The Jungle Boulder

Nestling under the northern approach into the Boulderfield, the Jungle Boulder gives a handful of worthwhile problems. Unfortunately, infrequent use leaves it overgrown for much of the year.

Approach

Three metres before the northern descent path into the Boulderfield is an earthy gully. Scramble down this and the rock step beneath. Skirt round to the right (looking out to sea) of a large boulder and descend a shallow grassy gully to the start of some serious vegetation. The main face of the Jungle Boulder is found on the left.

96 **Hope Slide** V5 The left side of the bulging section is a Boulderfield classic. From a sit-down start using big flakes, gain the sloping flowstone ledge. Either use a sharp crimp to reach the top or leap!

97 **Cheese Grater** V6 At the right-hand side of the bulging section is a very slight rib. This rib is overcome by powerful moves starting from a crouching position at an obvious two-finger pocket. The name comes from the texture of the sloper near the top of the problem.

Jon Howell on *Made in the Shade* V4 (page 325). BEN STOKES

98 **Grate Escape** V4 Start at the two-finger pocket as for *Cheese Grater* and stretch rightwards for a pocket.

99 **Napalm** V1 Starting just to the right, the juggy scoop, climbed using all the holds available, is a good warm-up for the other problems on this boulder.

The remaining three problems on the Jungle Boulder. They are of an eliminate nature and share a sit-down start at the big low flake a metre right of *Napalm*. The landings are sloping and rather awkward.

100 **I'm a Swinger Baby, Yeah** V2 Make a wild swing leftwards to a distant jug. Mantel easily.

101 **Tripomatic Fairytales** V4 Not pictured. Tackle the rounded arête direct on poor holds.

102 **Downwards Spiral** V4 Not pictured. Move rightwards to a wide sloping pinch. Gain the lip and mantel with difficulty.

The Tank

If the northern descent into the Boulderfield is followed down to the coast you come across a second stone hut. Near here, an isolated boulder of unusual rock provides good steep climbing on small jugs and pockets. Be warned: this venue is quite exposed and in the winter is often very cold.

Approach

Use the northern descent into the *Boulderfield*: Follow the Cuttings track for one kilometre to the north-east of The Cuttings Main Cliff. Here a distinct path leaves the main track, turning back on itself as it descends. As the descent levels, the path splits into two; the left fork leading down towards the coast. When you reach the coast, head right along the wide path. After 25 metres the path passes a steep pocketed boulder – the Tank. All but one of the problems start from a squatting position on the supporting boulder.

103 Pocket Traverse V2 Not pictured. Traverse the low, east wall without using the lip of the boulder, starting on the left from a standing position. Finish as for *Tufty*.

⭐ **104 Tufty V2** The left arête of the steep face is overcome by a long reach or a slap. Start on the supporting boulder, lean back, and gain a good ledge at the base of the left arête. Move directly to the top of the boulder.

⭐ **105 Christopher Columbus V5** A fantastic rightward traverse of the steep face, starting up *Tufty*, following the low lip, and finishing up the right arête. Unfortunately, you cannot award yourself the V5 tick if you use the deep break above *Crouching Start, Hidden Agenda*.

⭐⭐ **106 Crouching Start, Hidden Agenda V4** The centre of the steep face has a hard start, which is easier for the tall. Start on the supporting boulder and use small pockets and edges to reach the deep break. Finish direct on jugs.

⭐ **107 Hard Labour V1** Start on the supporting boulder, one metre to the right of *Crouching Start, Hidden Agenda*. Use positive edges over the first lip to gain a good flake (the crux) and then a jug. Mantel easily.

⭐ **108 Captain Cook V2** Start on the right end of the supporting boulder. Reach round to the right arête and prepare yourself for a huge reach to a distant jug near the lip of the boulder on the landward face. If you reach the jug, gather your wits and mantel easily.

⭐ **109 The World's Best Mono II! V4** From the start of *Captain Cook*, swing round onto the landward face using the obvious mono pocket and small edges. Grab the top of the boulder with relief and mantel without further difficulty.

The Collo Boulder

The final documented problems of the Boulderfield are found along the coast, a kilometre to the south of the Tank. The Collo Boulder sits precariously on the cliff edge and will undoubtedly tumble to the beach one day. Whilst the south and seaward faces of the Collo Boulder lean horrifyingly over crumbling cliff edges, the landward face offers some worthwhile climbing, with one excellent problem in particular.

Approach

Follow the cliff edge south from the Tank for one kilometre. Look for a tall boulder right on the cliff edge where a short hanging valley meets the coast.

⭐ 110 **Ménage à Trois** V2 The left-hand side of the landward face is bounded by a rock step. Start sitting on the quarried step. Keep to the right side of the arête and mantel with interest.

⭐⭐⭐ 111 **Collo Della Terra** V7 The landward side of the right arête gives a superb problem. Start from a sitting position *à cheval* the right arête. Move up to a small edge on the arête before swinging leftwards onto the landward face. Finish directly using an assortment of sloping holds.

⭐ 112 **The Cutting Room** V6 Start as for *Collo Della Terra* and climb the southern side of the right arête direct. Try to ignore the nagging presence of the collapsing slope behind you.

Ben Stokes on *Lightning Strike* V7 (page 335). TIM CRAWSHAW

Additional problems

A number of new problems have been unearthed in the Glitter Gulch Area (page 338). The first boulder is down the vallley from *Lemon Jelly* (Problem 55).

113 **Shark Bait** **V2** Down the valley, 12 metres northeast of *Lemon Jelly*, is a man-made pit beneath the south face of a small boulder. From a sit down start in the pit make your way up the leaning face by a series of aesthetic moves.

114 **Dug** **V0** A further 12 metres down the valley from *Shark Bait* is a large boulder with a relatively tall north face. The left arête of the face is a pleasant problem. From a sit down start climb the right side of the arête using prominent flakes and the arête itself.

115 **Dig** **V2** Immediately to the right of *Dug* a series of horizontal pockets and slots provide an interesting eliminate. The sit down start is hard for the grade and the prominent flakes and arête are out-of-bounds at all times.

116 **Big Wall** **V2** A traverse of the face from left to right without using the top. Start as for *Dug* and turn the right arête to finish.

117 **T.T.T.** **V2** The right arête has a hard sit down start involving a tough pull on a small crimp.

The Lulworth Area

The Weld estate owns the whole of the Lulworth area. In 1995, they announced a total ban on climbing on their land, apparently for conservation as well as public safety reasons. However, low-profile climbing has continued in some areas since then. **Please check the situation with the BMC before climbing here.**

The Lulworth area consists of a number of distinct crags, each with its own character, with all crags containing a healthy mix of sport and trad climbing. **Durdle Door** is a sea-arch familiar to many, having been photographed for dozens of coffee-table landscape books. The few routes on the promontory are in stunning locations, with a couple of world-class lines to boot, though they are difficult to access. **Dungy Head** and **Church Rock** have an eclectic mix of routes, ranging from loose and esoteric to worthwhile clip-ups. **Stair Hole** is perhaps the deep-water solo capital of Dorset, combining arm-wrecking sports routes and stunning solos, with a few minutes walk to pubs, cafes and beaches. At **Arthur's Mount**, however, you will feel a million miles from civilisation, with difficult access, some loose rock and a worrying feeling of isolation. **Lulworth East** has long traverses and hard, horizontal sports routes but these are interspersed with very worthwhile trad routes. **Worbarrow Tout** stands alone as a pure trad venue, with the accent on adventure climbing, with the interesting 'lost' village of Tyneham giving an added bonus to visitors.

The one thing these cliffs have in common is their location within a nationally-known tourist area (several climbs having been established within picture-postcard views). This brings many benefits, including easy access, good pubs and cafes and several family-friendly beaches. However (as well as the total climbing ban) there are disadvantages

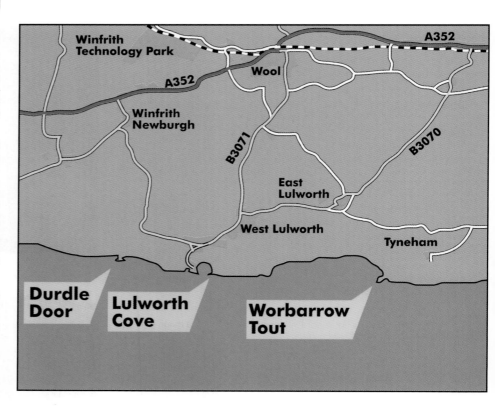

too. Car parking is expensive and traffic congestion in summer is a problem. The most prominent issue is that our actions as experienced climbers may attract tourists into dangerous situations. Please gently discourage all members of the public from approaching areas where falling climbers and rocks could endanger them, but most of all, remember that they have as much right to be there we do!

Why we all climb at Lulworth! Clockwise from top left: Divers watching climbers at Stair Hole, Joff Cook on *Window of Opportunity* F7b (page 364), Leo Houlding slacklining across Stair Hole Entrance.
STEVE TAYLOR, MIKE ROBERTSON, STEVE TAYLOR

Durdle Door

OS Ref 806 802

Half a mile or so west of Lulworth Cove, a distinctive T-shaped promontory projects from the chalk beds to form the subject of many a postcard. Although an impressive formation, the limestone arch of Durdle Door has produced a varied bag of climbs, the rock being loose in places. Whilst the ban on all climbing within the Lulworth Estate would seem to be harsh, the ban on climbing at Durdle Door has slightly more validity as it is far too easy to dislodge rocks onto tourists on the beach and in the water beneath the promontory. Extra care should be taken if holiday-makers or divers are in the vicinity and the sports-plan changed if they are anywhere near the chosen route.

Approach. From Wareham take the A352 west towards Wool. Two miles after leaving Wareham, turn left on the B3070 towards East Lulworth. Continue through East Lulworth to a T-junction, turn left, and follow the B3071 to West Lulworth. Here, turn westwards and head uphill to Newlands Farm caravan site. This has a public car-park for which a charge is made. A track leads down the hill to Durdle Door. Alternatively, continue through West Lulworth to reach the car-park at Lulworth Cove. From here, follow the well-trodden path over the hill. The first route described lies a kilometre to the west of Durdle Door, just before the end of the beach at Batt's Head.

Butterfingers 8m S 4a † (31.3.90)
Butter Rock is the chalk stack on the east side of Batt's Head. The rock and protection is poor, but it is a near-virgin summit. Low tide required. Climb the south-west face to the top.

On the right-hand side of the Durdle Door promontory lies the big arch. Two routes climb its landward side: *Archway* takes the supporting column while the rightward diagonal of *Country Girl* finishes above the apex of the arch. *Sardine Liberation Front* sneaks through the arch, a manoeuvre that seems to have paid off, as apparently nothing but solid rock is encountered. *Arcwelder* and *Riding to Babylon* are the undisputed crag classics, following converging lines on the seaward side of the arch. *Unleash the Veins* tackles the leaning wall to their right, looking landward. To the left of the ridge connecting with the mainland is the smooth sweep of slab climbed by *Exfoliator*.

1 **Country Girl** 30m HVS 4c (1.83)
An exposed route in an impressive situation, marred by loose rock near the top and poor protection.

Start at low tide where the beach meets the foot of the arch, at the seaward end of a reef. Climb up for 3 metres, move right a touch, and continue up towards a small overhang, avoiding the unpleasant terrain on the left. Move right and then downwards to a position above the arch. Go up rightwards on more definite holds and belay on solid blocks and several metal stakes.

2 **Sardine Liberation Front** 20m E2 5c (2.7.89)
Effectively retro-bolted with the bolting of *Riding to Babylon*. Follow *Riding to Babylon* to the sloping ledge at the top of the narrow white rib. Make a long reach leftwards to a jug on the arête, swing out and up, and finish more easily up the slab and cracks on the right. Scramble to the ridge.

3 Archway 27m S   (16.1.83)

This ascends the landward side of the outermost limb of the arch. Well positioned but fairly serious, as the climb has some loose rock. Approach by abseiling from blocks and stakes down to ledges on the landward face. From beneath a small overhang, climb up and right, reaching the arête at half-height. Move left along a line of ledges to the top of the arch.

Before climbing *Archway*, you could warm up on the tramontane traverse of **Durdley Doodle** (9m S † 8.9.91). From the belay of *Archway*, step down and traverse left, strenuously at first, with a final committing move to gain another belay ledge. Continue by scrambling around to your starting-place.

4 Arcwelder 23m F7b 10B   (4.93)

The inner wall of the outermost limb of the arch and the leaning south-facing wall above. Reach by abseil down the landward face of the outermost limb to a small ledge inside the archway. From a bolt belay on the small ledge, climb steeply leftwards into a snaking groove (crux) and follow it to a shakeout near the base of a long flake/groove. Swing diagonally right on the very lip of the arch to its centre. Continue up the steep headwall to a thread belay on the ridge.

5 Riding to Babylon 23m F7a+ 10B   (22.12.92)

Highly photogenic, very overhanging, and on good rock throughout, though it incorporates a significant section of *Sardine Liberation Front*. From the end of the reef, traverse rightwards along the landward side of the arch to a small alcove and a large nut belay. Swing out left and climb the apex of the narrow white rib on hidden jugs to a perched ledge hard under the arch. Pull around the roof on good holds to gain a large handrail and then move 3 metres left. Continue straight up the leaning wall

past the left side of a big shield of rock to a shakeout. Sustained moves lead past a large undercut to a pumping final move and a belay on the ridge.

6 They Call Me Tall Man 10m F6b 3B (13.12.92)

Fifteen metres right of the arch itself, on the seaward face of the promontory, is a steeply overhanging wall; climb this, with a mid-height crux, to the lower-off.

7 Scott's Escape 18m HS †   (11.7.93)

Start beneath a V-shaped inset wall of chert nodules. A poorly-protected middle section. Enter the cleft and climb its left wall. Traverse left to the end of the ledge (close, but not close enough, to the previous route's belay bolts). Continue up to the ridge.

8 Unleash the Veins 16m F7b+ 4B   (16.10.92)

Very steep climbing situated 10 metres right of the last route. Start at the leaning white wall just left of a slabby corner. An abseil approach is possible from a good block in the col before the arch. Four bolts. From good holds, climb up and then slightly right with increasing difficulty to buckets in a small recess. More large holds lead steeply to the lower-off.

Starting at the eastern end of the promontory, the two pitches of **Slanting Slab** (S) traversed a short distance along the seaward face before a scramble to the ridge. A variation, **Wet Feet** (VS 5a 6.11.84), continues the traverse right around the promontory. Calm seas necessary.

To the left of the ridge connecting Durdle Door with the mainland is a clean sweep of slab, rising direct from the beach in Man o' War bay.

9 **Stormbringer** 35m E2 5b †   (1985)

A serious line up the left side of the slab. The rock is loose and friable and the protection very poor. Start about 2 metres left of a large flake. Pegs required. Pull up on a finger-pocket to reach small fingerholds and a good hold above. Move left for 3 metres past an *in-situ* peg and then back up rightwards, placing a peg. Continue up to the right to the grass ledge. Pull through the overlap immediately above and continue to the top. Multiple belay.

10 **Exfoliator** 40m E2 5b   (1.6.76)

A serious route as its name might imply, with both poor rock and poor protection. Pegs required. Follow *Stormbringer* to the grass ledge. Move right along the ledge until 2 metres from its end, move up, place a peg above the overlap, and pull over. Move up and right to the tottering corner. Follow this with care for 3 metres and then continue up a crack in the slab, trending slightly left to the top. Multiple belay.

Dungy Head

OS Ref 816 799

Dungy Head is the headland between Lulworth Cove and Durdle Door. Although broken rock abounds, there are some solid sections.

Approach. Park at Lulworth Cove (parking fee charged). Walk to the seaward side of the car-park and turn right. Follow a road up a hill, amongst some impressive houses, until a hidden, narrow footpath on the left (behind a double garage) can be taken to the cliff-top. Follow the path along the cliff-top to the west to reach a collection of pinnacles; the House Boulder is below and requires a careful descent down a grassy slope. For the first route only, follow the footpath up the hillside towards Durdle Door. After the first stile, walk down a valley to the sea. The picturesque Man o' War bay is to the west and Dungy Head lies to the east, with *Pickpocket* being the first feature at beach level.

Pickpocket 24m HVS 5a †   (5.4.87)

Not shown on topo. Rather crunchy. Start on a pedestal abutting the westernmost wall of the cliff. Climb up and then rightwards for 3 metres on the lip of the overhang. Trend leftwards and climb a shallow corner past two very thin *in-situ* threads. Swing right and climb another corner and the steep earth above to stake belays. A direct start is available at E1 5b, starting 5 metres right of the pinnacle.

All but two of the following climbs tackle the two pinnacles situated high above the beach, far to the right of *Pickpocket*. They are best approached from above. The ground is steep and has some loose rock. The first two climbs lie on the cliff just to the left of the pinnacles. Twenty metres west of the two pinnacles, on top of the cliff, is a stake. Abseil from here to a twin-bolt belay at the base of the buttress.

1 **Vixen** 22m S †

Step left from the belay to enter the chimney on the left side of the clean-looking – appearances can be deceptive – face. Climb the chimney to a large recess. Use blocks in the crack above with care to

exit left. Alternatively, finish out left from the recess and climb the steep wall above.

2 Morris the Carnivore 18m F6a 7B † (24.4.94)
From the belay, climb a loose wall, a bulge, and a slab to arrive back at the abseil stake.

3 Beavis and Butthead 13m F6a+ 4B (19.2.94)
A poor, loose route based (loosely!) on the western arête of the western pinnacle. Climb up and move slightly right to clip the third bolt, which is almost on the front of the pinnacle. Continue up, using a chert sidepull to cross a bulge. Lower-off on the pillar above.

4 Beers, Steers and Queers 14m F6c+ 5B
(19.2.94)
The left-hand line on the front face has a grip-clip at the crux. Cross the low-level roof with difficulty to a recess. Continue up a faint crackline on the left-hand side of the face to the shared lower-off.

5 Dungeons and Dragons 14m F7a 5B (27.9.87)
Start at the centre of the western pinnacle. Steeper than it looks and high in the grade. Pull strenuously over the roof and climb the centre of the wall, with some perplexing moves on the mid-height blank section. Lower-off on the pillar above.

6 Exposed Slab 14m VD
Start in a gully to the left of the easternmost pinnacle. Move up and right onto the slab and climb this to a grassy terrace. Surmount the short wall to multiple belays in the depression.

7 Lost Souls 15m F6b 4B (5.12.93)
Start 3 metres left of the easternmost pinnacle's arête. Some loose rock! Climb gradually leftwards up the wall, through a niche, and over a bulge to the lower-off.

8 Looking through the Infinity Window
18m E3 5c † (23.12.88)
Four worn-out *in-situ* threads. Climb the sensational exposed arête of the easternmost pinnacle, with a diversion to the left and back at a flake. Multiple belays in the depression, though it may be possible to use the lower-off of the following route.

9 Closing Time 16m F7a+ 5B (27.3.94)
A good route up the imposing east-facing wall of the eastern pinnacle. Start at a single-bolt belay in a corner at the base of the pinnacle. Steep, sustained climbing up the centre of the face leads to a crux reach from two vertical slots to gain the lower-off. Avoiding the crux by moving left to the arête reduces the grade to F7a.

Dungy Head

The House Boulder (local name Church Rock) is a huge block on the boulder beach, one hundred metres east of the pinnacles. This compact craglet has six routes, and is worth the effort involved in the approach. In recent years, locals have added many boulder problems on the smaller boulders around the House Boulder. Bring plenty of mats though, as the landings can be terrible.

'[The boulder] seems inaccessible without mechanical aid; perhaps Dorset's last great problem.' (Hugh Nelson 1961) Perhaps Hugh was responsible for the six-inch nails in the boulder! It is now possible, however, to pull onto the boulder from a smaller boulder on its seaward side at about Difficult.

10 The Debt Collector 13m F6b+ 4B (10.7.93)
Low in the grade, but more sustained than it looks. Start in the middle of the northern face. Climb the steep wall via a scoop to the lower-off.

11 Wall of Feedback 13m F6b+ 4B (13.12.88)
Hard to leave the ground! Start in a shallow scoop 3 metres left of the arête. Step leftwards and up to reach pockets. Follow disjointed cracks rightwards to the lower-off.

12 Oh Blow You 14m F7a 4B (5.9.07)
The wall left of *Blow Daddy-O*.

13 Blow Daddy-O 15m E3 5c (20.11.88)
Difficult to protect. Climb the obvious arête via a boulder-problem start. Thread belay at sea-level on the other side of the boulder.

14 House Nation 13m F6b 4B (13.12.88)
Start 2 metres right of the arête. Low in the grade. Climb rightwards across the smooth, pocketed wall and up to the lower-off.

15 B-Boys Rock 13m F6b+ 4B (5.9.07)
Link the start of *Jugmaster...* with the finish of *House Nation*.

16 Jugmaster Funk Featuring M C Lane 12m F6a+ 3B (13.12.88)
Start 5 metres right of the arête. Climb steeply up on a profusion of pockets and slots, pull over a small roof to reach large jugs, and gain the slab. Lower-off on the right.

17 Turn It On 11m F7a+ 4B (4.7.93)
The right side of the westward-facing wall is very powerful and sustained.

Lulworth Cove

OS Ref 824 798

None of the climbs in this area is in the cove proper. Indeed the loose, vegetated, and fairly easy-angled slopes behind Lulworth Cove do not offer a worthwhile challenge, and climbing them would pose extreme stonefall danger to holiday-makers on the beach; these cliffs should be **avoided completely**.

As well as the two through-caves at Stair Hole and the dramatic folding of the strata nearby, the rock at Lulworth has other peculiarities. A first impression is of a chaotic jumble of broken rock. This proves to be fused and cemented together and is often more solid than it looks, although great care should still be taken. The better climbs are on the more homogeneous lower layers of rock, and the many large sloping roofs near sea-level have been exploited. The Stair Hole and Lulworth East areas hold a concentration of sport climbs. The remaining areas provide traditionally-protected routes where, despite their lower grades, the accent is on adventure. Note that Lulworth East is an agreed bolt-free area, so don't rely on the bolts being there.

In view of the large numbers of tourists and school parties in the area, climbers should try to keep a low profile to avoid emulation by the inexperienced. Calm seas are required to approach the vast majority of routes hereabouts.

Approach. From Wareham, take the A352 westwards to Wool. Turn left 2 miles after Wareham, following signs to East Lulworth. Follow the B3070 through East Lulworth then turn left onto the B3071 towards West Lulworth and Lulworth Cove. This road ends at a large (expensive) car-park at Lulworth Cove.

The cliffs on the west of the cove are sub-divided into three parts: Stair Hole Bastion, the seaward side of the cliff enclosing Stair Hole; Intermediate Slabs, below the tourist telescope; and Arthur's Mount, further to the east. The sea-cliff east of the cove has a few very long traverses, a number of illicitly-bolted roof climbs, and a recent selection of trad climbs.

357

Stair Hole Bastion

This is the ridge pierced by two sea-filled through-caves which forms the inlet of Stair Hole, south of the car-park and west of the cove proper. Climbing on the unusual rock architecture of Stair Hole has come into its own with the advent of several hard roof-climbs. Nowadays, many climbers shun the rope, as most of the routes here are soloable, with deep water beneath at all tides. Even the crag's hardest route, *Adrenochrome*, has been soloed.

The accessible pebble beach, calm water, wonderful swimming and snorkelling (and the sheer

Jon Biddle on *Sliding Down the Banister* F6c+ (page 365). STEVE TAYLOR

Ben Stokes on *Despicable Terrier* F7a+ (page 364). STEVE TAYLOR

358

quality of the climbing) have made Stair Hole the deep-water solo venue of choice for locals and travellers alike, surpassing Conner Cove at Swanage, the original deep-water solo venue. At the end of 2005, the raw-sewage outlet beneath Arthur's Mount was finally diverted to the treatment works at Wool. It is no longer necessary to keep your mouth closed on a splashdown!

The first three routes traverse the cliff on the west side of the Stair Hole inlet.

1 The Laws Traverse 18m SO XS 6a (F6b) (1993)
A deep-water solo on good rock. The leftward low-level traverse of the east-facing wall of Stair Hole. Swing underneath a hanging slab and ape to the back of a cave (crux). A leftward traverse, sustained at around F6a, leads to the arête. You are then faced with a swim, the route in reverse, or a long walk out via Dungy Head!

⭐ **2 The Walkin' Dude** 13m S2/3 XS 6a (F6b)
(26.6.93)
Start as for *The Laws Traverse,* the start of that route being the technical crux; the rest of the climb is never harder than F6a. This route has only ever been soloed, and always on a high spring tide due to submerged boulders beneath the higher section of the route. Follow the overhanging crack up and out of the cave and diagonally leftwards to the southern face. Traverse leftwards and descend an easy arête. Now reverse the *Laws Traverse* to finish.

3 Skillfish 13m S2/3 E2 5b (F6a+)   (1.9.07)
The higher diagonal above *The Walkin' Dude,* starting from the top of the hanging slab. Descend the seaward face and finish as for *The Walkin' Dude.*

4 Thieving Gypsy 7m SO XS 6b (F7a+)   (2004)
A solo from the beach into the west side of the eastern cave. Downclimb a series of flakes to enter the eastern cave. From an undercut just above the high-water line, make a blind reach left to a pocket and the start of *Window of Opportunity.* From here, the most logical option is to climb *Window of Opportunity,* but it is possible to traverse beneath *Anarchy Stampede* to escape.

⭐ **5 Imp of the Perverse** 12m SO XS 6b (F7b+)
(6.06)
A hard solo through the centre of the arch. From the start of *Thieving Gypsy,* move left on very steep ground to swing under the arch, eventually reaching the hands-off rest on *Horny L'il Devil,* finishing as for that route.

Routes between *Bastion Traverse* and *Herbert the Turbot* are best approached along *The Maypole.* The buttress to the right on the skyline as the arête is rounded is the *Lewis* buttress.

⭐⭐⭐ **6 The Maypole** 80m SO XS 5b (F6a+) (23.5.90)
A traverse from the pebble beach to the Stair Hole entrance and back through the western cave - the tourists will wonder how you managed to stay dry! From the beach on the landward side of Stair Hole, traverse rightwards just above the water-line, generally on easy ground, to the entrance to Stair Hole. Continue into the western cave, where things get more interesting. Drop down until your feet are almost in the water and make some long stretches between good holds until a prominent flake crack is reached. Continuing at this level to the beach is very pumpy. Moving up and over a hanging slab is easier, but risks a greater fall.

☆ 7 **Bastion Traverse** 35m S
The compelling rising traverse linking the extreme western edge with the finish of the next route. Start near sea-level on a sloping ledge.
1 15m. Take the vertical crack to where the angle eases below the overhang and continue along sloping ledges to a recess. Peg and nut belay.
2 20m. Move out of the recess, and by a slowly ascending hand-traverse beneath the overhang, follow the crack around the top of the bay to the finish of *Slab and Corner*.

8 **Slab and Corner** 17m S   (1962)
Low in its grade. Follow the gully left of the *Lewis* buttress (or the groove in the centre) to a ledge below the slab. Move onto the slab, traverse right, and go up the steep wall. Move around the arête to a good belay on top.

9 **Lewis** 18m VD
High in its grade. This climbs the buttress at the point where the high overhang peters out. Start on the left of the buttress. Follow good holds to an awkward little wall and move into a small scoop. The loose stuff above is best avoided by climbing two small ribs of rock immediately in front. Finish up the slab to the right.

10 **Cheddar** 18m VS 4b   (1962)
The sharp arête. Start below some overhanging flakes on the right-hand side of the *Lewis* buttress. Climb the flakes to a small scoop and move out left to the arête. Follow the natural line up and over on the right of the overhang with difficulty and continue straight up across friable rock. Step left eventually onto the finish of *Lewis*.

A direct start beneath, and slightly left of the arête is possible at HVS 5b. Swing rightwards along a vein of pockets and pull direct onto the arête.

11 **Truth, Justice and the Ragamuffin Way**
18m S1/2 E2 5c (F6a+) (20.7.91)
Similar to some climbs at Conner Cove, above a deep-water landing. Start 3 metres right of the corner. Follow a V-groove slightly rightwards, and climb a wall steeply to the roof. Pull through from hand-jams at the notch to easy, though slightly friable, ground.

12 **Crazy Notion** 16m S1 E5 6b (F7a) (22.8.95)
The steep wall to the left of *Animal Magnetism*. Climb *Animal Magnetism* to its second bolt, and then continue directly up the 45-degree face on pockets to arrive at the base of a groove. Swing left into this and continue to easier ground.

13 **Animal Magnetism** 18m S1 F7a+ 4B (4.6.92)
A safe but hard deep-water solo. Climb a corner to the roof, where a jammed boulder in a pod marks the start of a ramp leading rightwards. Follow this through the 8-metre overhang, past a number of hidden holds, to enter a slabby V-groove on the right with difficulty. Scramble up to a bolt belay. The grade is for the on-sight. The route becomes much easier with experience, and is generally soloed in the summer.

Dave Pickford cutting loose on *Burning Arms* F7c (page 366). STEVE TAYLOR

Lulworth Cove

⭐⭐ **14 Journey To Eternia** 20m S1 F7c+ 5B (09.02)
'The best route in the western cave!' One of many hybrid routes on the Lulworth roofs. Start up *Animal Magnetism* and reverse *Magnetic Gates*, to finish up *The Gates of Greyskull*. Three routes in one – superb.

15 Last Season's Loozas 30m S1 HVS 5b (F6a)
(21.7.91)
A traverse of both walls of the western cave, which is escapable halfway. Lovely moves with spooky lighting. Recommended only as a deep-water solo, as a rope would prove a hindrance. Start from sea-level ledges on the western side of the seaward entrance of the cave. Traverse the western wall of the cave (towards the beach), heading upwards. Make a hard move down to sea-level and follow the rising bulge using holds on its top. Descend to sea-level again, where a squat move gains the landward entrance. Traverse across the lip of the cave before moving back in and around a pillar to the rock window. Gain the groove in the eastern wall, move diagonally up and down the slab, and continue at low level to the seaward entrance.

⭐⭐⭐ **16 Never Kneel to Skeletor** 18m S1 F7c+ 6B
† (5.9.92)
Yorkshiremen would die for this! The central line above the cave features particularly powerful pulls and novel footwork. Start at a twin-bolt belay beside a pedestal in the mouth of the cave. Undercut out and use deep slots and fins to reach a hidden jug at 6 metres. Hard moves on poor holds lead to slopers, before a finger-ledge on the left allows entry leftward into the V-groove of *Animal Magnetism*. Scramble up to a bolt belay.

17 Route 66 10m S2 XS 5b (F6a+) (30.7.94)
A short cut between the two walls traversed by *Last Season's Loozas* via the roof of the cave. Start on a ledge above a prow halfway along the western wall. Best soloed. Pull up and mantel onto a shelf with difficulty; don't fall here or the prow you have just vacated will bite you! Crawl along the slot in the roof, continue across the rest of the roof (now safe, high above the water), and descend a juggy chimney to sea level. Escape along *Last Season's Loozas*.

18 Escobar 6m S0 XS 6b (F7a) (1.8.95)
A tricky solo across the inner lip of the 'door', requiring a little tenacity and a blind reach. Check out the holds from the hanging slab up and beyond the route. Traverse in from the beach to start. Launch onto the hanging wall and traverse rightwards until it's possible to climb down to the pillar.

19 Contortions 8m S1 E4 6b (F7a) (1.8.95)
This one goes in! Start from inside the finish of *Escobar*. A spotter is required in-situ on the hanging slab due to the closeness of the slab and your head. Climb up and steadily outwards on very steep ground until you reach the roof fault. Finish along *Route 66*.

⭐ **20 Showtime** 8m S1 E5 6b (F7a+) (5.8.95)
Take your spotter again and make sure you give him your camera. This one starts from inside the pillar – but not as for *Contortions*. Start beneath the blank-looking, overhanging face just inside the 'window'. It's not blank! Make desperate moves off a good starting jug to negotiate several small pockets, hit a sidepull on the left and then dyno wildly for a big flat hold. Continue up to the roof fault and finish along *Route 66*.

⭐ **21 El Guapo** 10m S0 E6 6b (F7b) (19.9.95)
'The Beautiful'. Where *Showtime* trends leftwards slightly up to the sanctuary of *Route 66*, El Guapo continues up and ever rightwards on sidepulls, pockets and jugs to finally step onto the small hanging slab on the far side of the cave. Steep and powerful, with a pumpy finish.

22 Rebirth 12m S0 XS (F7a) (2000)
A solo 'climb' along the passageway connecting the two caves. Should be attempted only at low tide and in calm seas. Much of the effort expended is in keeping one's feet dry!
1 6m 5c. Enter the cleft from the western cave with difficulty and bridge/squirm along the tunnel until it is possible to exit onto the landward slab through a hole.
2 6m 6b. Re-enter the hole (hard) and continue to the start of *I Love Ezster*.

23 Old Timers 12m S1 XS 6b (F7a+) (2003)
A traverse across the southern wall of the inside of the west cave. Start as for *Rebirth*. Climb diagonally left up into the roof. At the apex of the roof launch rightwards with a series of blind stretches to reach the start of *Herbert the Turbot*.

⭐⭐ **24 Herbert the Turbot** 15m S0 E4 6a/b (F7a+)
(22.7.91)
Lulworth's answer to *The Conger* is shorter than that route but has wilder moves. The route crosses the seaward entrance of the western cave. Start from sea-level ledges on the western side of the seaward entrance of the cave as for *Last Season's Loozas*. Swing onto the cave's sidewall and hand-traverse rightwards to a niche. Move up slightly rightwards and make a strenuous stretch to fall across onto a tiny hanging slab (hard for shorties). Make a full body-bridge to reach the obvious jug and swing

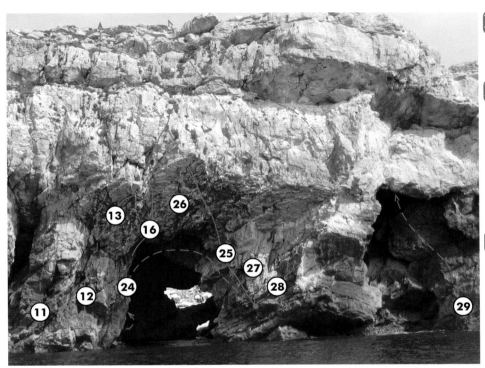

26 **Magnetic Gates** 19m S1 F7b+ 5B (07.00)
Another hybrid route. Start up *The Gates of Greyskull*, move left across *Never Kneel to Skeletor*, and finish as for *Animal Magnetism*.

27 **The Honourable Society of Self-Publicizing Water Rats** 18m S1 E4 6a (F7a) (7.96)
An enjoyable deep-water solo taking in the bulging territory to the right of *The Gates of Greyskull*. Start as for *The Gates of Greyskull* at the twin-bolt belay. Climb up the wall and tackle the ever-steepening section on slopers and jugs by a series of powerful lock-offs to arrive at a jug, where a rockover leads to easy ground. Continue up the slab to the top of the ridge.

28 **The Hairy Clamber** 20m S2 VS 4c (F5) (7.00)
Another enjoyable route, which is just about a deep-water solo. Start at the twin-bolt belay of *The Gates of Greyskull*. Follow the slabs diagonally rightwards until beneath the narrowest section of the strip roof. Pull over on jugs and follow the brittle slab leftwards to the top of the ridge.

29 **Curtain Call** 14m HS 4a (23.10.88)
A unique route. Start between the two through-caves, in a cave with a blowhole at its top. Climb up, exit through the blowhole, and take your bow to the tourists on the far side of the cliff.

wildly across. Move rightwards through the roof with difficulty to gain a jug and easier ground on the other side. Descend a slab to sea level.

25 **The Gates of Greyskull** 18m S1 F7b+ 6B (4.6.92)
A counter line to *Animal Magnetism* tackling the 10-metre upper roof. Start at a twin-bolt belay on the east side of the western cave, reached by abseil from the ridge. Climb a slight corner and stretch leftwards for good holds in a recess. Continue directly out on hidden jugs until some powerful locks lead to buckets at the apex of the prow. Pull around and scramble leftwards to a bolt belay.

Lulworth Cove

The roof of the eastern cave catches all the sun going, dries quickly, and is criss-crossed with hard, bolt-protected climbs. It also offers many of the hardest deep-water solos around.

The following routes are all in the eastern cave, and their approaches are described from The Grotto, a commodious ledge 12 metres above the sea. To reach The Grotto, walk eastwards along the path on the top of the ridge to a conglomerate pillar. Drop carefully down the seaward side of the ridge for 5 metres, step right and down-climb an easy wall to The Grotto. This gives a fine view of the goings-on on the steep roofs.

The following six solos are reached from The Grotto by down-climbing an easy groove leftwards (facing in) to sea level.

30 The Ringfinder 14m S2 VS 4b (F4) (28.7.04)
From the base of the easy groove, step left and climb the right-hand side of an arête on good holds. Pull onto a slab beneath a roof and move left. Climb the groove above and scramble up the slab to the ridge.

⭐ **31 Captain Bastard Got There First** 8m SO E1 5c (F6a) (21.7.91)
The overhanging corner directly beneath The Grotto. Follow the pockets and move leftwards around the big bulge at the top to The Grotto.

⭐ **32 Despicable Terrier** 9m SO XS 6b (F7a+) (24.7.04)
The hanging arête right of Captain Bastard... From the starting holds of Captain Bastard..., move up and right onto the arête. A series of hard moves lead to The Grotto.

⭐ **33 Anarchy Stampede** 9m SO E3 6a/b (F7a) (6.9.88)
The overhanging buttress on the western, seaward side of the eastern cave gives powerful climbing with a deep-water landing. Stretch right from the starting holds of Captain Bastard..., to a large sloping hold on a block. Jump up to a horizontal slot and make a strenuous move to a good pocket above. Hand-traverse the ledge and climb the corner-crack to The Grotto. Often slightly damp and graded for such conditions.

34 I Love Eszter 9m SO XS 5c (F6a+) (4.97)
A line of unbridled passion taking the chimney to the right of Anarchy Stampede. A deep-water solo which is approached most easily at low tide. From the start of Anarchy Stampede, traverse rightwards low down until you find yourself below a left-slanting chimney. Climb this until it is possible to step left on to a big sloping ledge. Continue up to The Grotto, an easy exit, and a nice cuddle. Not shown.

⭐ **35 Window of Opportunity** 10m SO XS 6b (F7b) (8.8.98)
A fine, steep deep-water solo from sea level to the aven on Horny L'il Devil. Approach as for I Love Eszter. Launch rightwards onto the overhanging wall and climb up through a recess, past two poor knee bars, to arrive, pumped, at the 'Horny' knee-bar rest. Finish as for that route.

36 Stagedivin' 9m S1 F7a+ 3B (5.92)
A short but hard route starting at a bolt belay in The Grotto. It can be soloed, but needs spotters for the initial moves. Swing out rightwards on a huge hold and make hard moves to gain a small 'trench' full of buckets. Trend rightwards over the lip with more difficulty.

Horny Lil' Devil and the remaining lines based on the eastern through-cave are approached by walking eastwards along the ridge, skirting to the right of the conglomerate pillar along a path. This path becomes a horizontal scramble until it is possible to down-climb easily to a slab. Traverse left (facing in) along this slab until beneath the routes.

⭐ **37 Hornier than Thou** 12m SO XS 6b (F7b) (8.1998)
The pumpy and powerful traverse line underneath Horny L'il Devil. Only viable as a deep-water solo. Start at the base of Horny L'il Devil. Make a very hard move leftwards to gain a jug-rail 3 metres above mean water level. Make footless moves leftwards then pull into the groove above. Bridge up until it is possible to swing across into Window of Opportunity. Reverse this route to the start of I Love Eszter. A good variant, (**Z Carz** F7b SO 1999), makes a big jump from the top of the groove to gain a pocket on Horny Li'l Devil and finishes as for that route.

⭐⭐ **38 Horny Lil' Devil** 10m SO F7a 4B (19.5.92)
Start at the end of the traversing, on the eastern side of the eastern through-cave, directly above the water. A fantastic deep-water solo on divinely ordained jugs. The first two bolts are shared with Adrenochrome. Enter the short groove and swing left a couple of metres along the break running above the through-cave. Continue leftwards above the water, passing a spectacular knee-bar rest in an aven. Finish up the corner-crack of Anarchy Stampede. Bolt belay in The Grotto.

40 Mark of the Beast 15m S3 F7c 7B (22.10.87)
A contender for the best, and most sought after, route in Dorset. It has been on-sight soloed, though failure on a long move right at mid-height could result in you hitting the slab below. Start as for *Horny Lil' Devil*. Follow a faint runnel on good holds to a small recess two-thirds of the way up. The crux moves lead to the lip and a pull round on good holds to easy ground.

41 Lord of Darkness 13m S1 F7c 5B (01.99)
Another traverse line, this time above *Horny L'il Devil*. Start up *Mark of the Beast*. At the third bolt, move left across the wall with difficulty, with a very hard move to gain The Grotto.

42 Sliding Down the Bannister 10m S0 XS 6a (F6c+) (23.5.92)
An unusual solo. Drop down from the start of *Horny Lil' Devil* and move strenuously through the roof of the through-cave. Having emerged on the landward side, pull onto the slab and scramble up rightwards to the ridge.

43 Does Leviathan Plop Float? 10m S0 E1 6a (F6b+) (7.91)
This low-tide solo traverse, beneath *Sliding Down the Bannister*, of the through-cave's eastern sidewall is a limbo dance just above the water, moving around a bulge and pulling blindly but on big holds onto the slab on the other side.

39 Adrenochrome 16m S1 F8a 9B (20.5.92)
An immaculate test-piece up a smooth, leaning line above the through-cave. High in the grade. The hardest independent deep-water solo to date. Enter the short groove and swing left 2 metres along the break, as for *Horny Lil' Devil*. Jump for a bucket and gain holds on the left. From a shallow porthole, dyno for a jug and crucifix back right for a huge pocket. Continue up a slight rib, sustained and hard, to some deep pockets. Gain the lip more easily.

A link from *Window of Opportunity*, reversing *Horny L'il Devil* and into *Adrenachrome* has been soloed. Christened **Windowchrome**, (5.9.07) the grade is probably S1 F8a+

⭐ **44 Burn Hollywood, Burn** 14m F8a+ 7B   (10.5.92)

This power climb is low in the grade (F8a for the tall). Yard up on three huge pockets to a blank bulge. Very hard, reachy slaps rightwards gain a big sidepull and a line of jugs above. From a large handrail, reach a sharp pocket and make hard stretches diagonally left on three 'portholes' to exit just right of the *Mark of the Beast*.

⭐ **45 Lulworth Arms Treaty** 13m F7b 5B   (23.10.87)

This take the line 2 metres right of *Burn, Hollywood, Burn*. High in its grade, especially for the short. Climb dynamically past a short crack (crux) and follow good holds past an *in-situ* thread. Move rightwards to a hole. Now go leftwards to a scoop and cross the lip to easy ground and a single-bolt belay.

⭐ **46 Burning Arms** 14m F7c 5B   (23.10.97)

A difficult hybrid, connecting the start of *Lulworth Arms Treaty* with the finish of *Burn Hollywood, Burn*, making the switch left at the thread on *Lulworth Arms Treaty*.

⭐ **47 Freed From Desire** 13m F7b 5B   (4.12.97)

A tight bolt line between *Lulworth Arms Treaty* and *Grimly Fiendish*. Good steep climbing leads to the finishing moves of *Lulworth Arms Treaty*. Easily identified by the *Petzl* hangers used.

⭐⭐ **48 Roof Predator** 18m F7c 10B †   (28.12.92)

An absolute animal, which feeds off the other routes here, traversing leftwards at three-quarter height and taking in the cruxes of *Grimly Fiendish* and *Mark of the Beast*. Follow the 'trench' of *Grimly Fiendish* to the holes by the threads and swing left into *Lulworth Arms Treaty*. Use a sloping handrail to cross *Burn, Hollywood, Burn* and gain the juggy recess on *Mark of the Beast* with difficulty. Follow that route diagonally left for 3 metres to a flake. Power left to a big sidepull on *Adrenochrome* before continuing left on pockets to *Stagedivin'* and a 'Thank God' hold. Step down into The Grotto to finish. Bolt belay.

49 Grimly Fiendish 11m F7a 3B   (23.10.87)

Start 3 metres right of *Lulworth Arms Treaty*. As well as the bolts there are three *in-situ* threads. High in the grade, and quite fierce. Pull up into the obvious 'trench' and follow it leftwards to its end. Continue direct on deep pockets and cross the lip to easy ground. Single-bolt belay.

50 Omega 8m VS †

Five metres left of the descent is a flake in the roof. Climb the flake to the path beneath the conglomerate.

Dave Pickford **relishing the rest on** *Horny L'il Devil* **F7a (page 364).** SIMON CARTER

To the right of *Grimly Fiendish*, and the descent, are a series of walls topped by small roofs. Routes have been recorded across these roofs, but they are not long enough to warrant detailed description and are left for exploration on calm, sunny days. They range in difficulty from Difficult to Very Severe. Further right the lines become more substantial.

A very orderly queue, lining up for the crux of *The Maypole* **F6a+ (page 359).** MIKE ROBERTSON

Intermediate Slabs

Approach. From the westerly viewing point and tourist telescope (not always in place), scramble as inconspicuously as possible down the grass to seaward for several metres, then follow a horizontal vegetated ledge leftwards (east) for 25 metres. Finally descend broken rock to reach a conglomerate ledge above the slabs. Either abseil to sea-level (using the most solid rock-mix) or, when familiar, down climb. All the routes described finish on the conglomerate ledge.

51 **Good Start** 10m VD †

Start beneath a triangular roof at 8 metres. Move right to pass a large flake, then up to a bulge. Step right and climb direct up to the ledge.

The following five routes all start from a common point, a ledge 10 metres left of a cave protected by a reef 6 metres out to sea.

52 **Pitted Slab** 12m D †

From the ledge, move left and over a block into a shallow cave. Pull out of the left of the cave and climb the slab on the left to the large ledge.

53 **Triple Overhang** 14m VD †

From the shallow cave of *Pitted Slab*, climb the centre of the slab above.

54 **Cheater** 12m M †

Exit the cave on the right and climb the slab above.

55 **Hypothesis** 11m VD †

From the ledge, traverse right and move up the steep wall above. Surmount the bulge to gain the ledge.

56 **Conclusion** 11m S †

Follow *Hypothesis*, but where that route moves up, step right and climb a groove to the ledge.

The next four routes are reached by following the conglomerate ledge eastwards until above a zawn. Descend the slab via a stepped crack (*Corner Climb*) to reach a rock bridge by the entrance to the zawn

57 **Hanging Slab** 8m S †

Start 3 metres left of the sharp arête and climb the slab to the large ledge.

58 **Corner Climb** 9m D †

The stepped corner 3 metres left of the arête. Climb the corner to the large ledge.

59 **Hanging Wall** 8m HVS 4c

The prow overlooking the west side of the zawn has an overhanging crack on its left side. Climb it.

60 **The Rouble** 22m VS 4b S1 † (20.10.03)

A right-to-left traverse on juggy rubble across the back wall of the zawn. A worthwhile, but mercifully short piece of esoterica. Cross the rock bridge and step onto the wall. Move left at sea-level and step up onto the lip of a small roof. Follow this line leftwards into the zawn recess. When you bridge across to gain the approach slab, you have finished.

Mark Williams on *Hornier Than Thou* F7b (page 364). STEVE TAYLOR

Nigel Coe on *Windy Corner Variation* VS
(page 370). PAM HOLT

369

Arthur's Mount

Approach along the ridge past the point where a coastguard hut slipped off several years ago (try not to do the same). Continue down the exposed ridge past The Haven – a large scooped recess on the seaward side – until a downward break occurs near the end of the ridge. This gives access to a large ledge at the tip of the headland. This ledge may be reached more easily by boulder-hopping out of the western side of the entrance to Lulworth Cove itself. The climbs start at sea-level to the west. The main features as one moves westwards from here are a large overhang with a narrow but deep sea-cave on its far side, a small sea-level platform (the Luncheon Shelf), a large tiered overhang, and a disused sea-level sewer-pipe which impedes progress towards Intermediate Slabs. The westernmost group of climbs take in the full height of the cliff. The steep grass and loose rock at the top are 'an acquired taste'.

61 **Martinetros** 13m D †

Shown on the previous topo. Approach by traversing at sea-level from the large ledge at the tip of Arthur's Mount. Where the traversing ledges end, step left onto the wall and traverse until beneath a buttress. Climb more or less direct up the buttress to the intermediate ledge and traverse off leftwards.

62 **Gangway** 50m HS †

From the end of the traversing ledges, step onto the wall and traverse 5 metres left to belay at the foot of a wide, recessed groove. Low tide and calm seas required.

1 18m 4a. Climb the groove to the 'gangway' and follow this dark shelf rightwards to a sloping platform.

2 32m. Go rightwards from the belay block and over the bulging wall above. Pull onto the grass

with difficulty and continue upwards. Belay on the remains of the coastguard hut.

Variations:

63 **Commando Crack** VS †

1a 18m. Start below the prominent crackline immediately west of the large tiered overhang. Climb the crack and escape right at the top. Move up to belay on the sloping platform.

64 **Zig-Zag** HVS †

1b 15m. A good pitch, sustained, technical, and exposed. Start on the wall to the right of the large tiered overhang. Climb steeply for 5 metres, make an awkward move left under the protruding roof, and make an airy 8-metre traverse along the lip of the overhang. Move up and left with difficulty to a sloping ledge.

65 **Windy Corner** 45m VS   (1962)

Exciting and varied situations, and quite serious. Start 10 metres to the left of the Luncheon Shelf.

1 14m 4a. Climb the recess on big holds and continue on up, keeping slightly left to reach a sloping platform beneath a steep wall.

2 9m 4b. Move up the corner above to the second of two holes. Traverse left under a roof past an old peg. Continue leftwards around the undercut arête to small ledges and belay.

3 22m 4c. Climb up leftwards and then back right to a peg on a steep wall. Overcome this by a delicate traverse left before moving up to steep earth and grass. Ascend this with much fear and loathing to a belay on the remains of the coastguard hut.

An exciting variation is to traverse left beneath two roofs from the first belay to a very exposed belay on two pegs. Climb straight up to join the third pitch.

Beneath The Haven is a shelf at sea-level, the Luncheon Shelf, which is protected to some extent from the waves by a detached reef out to sea, providing a fine swimming and diving spot. It is best reached by traversing westwards beneath a large roof and over the sea-cave from the easy way down at the tip of Arthur's Mount.

66 Haven Ordinary 18m VD
Start 3 metres left of the Luncheon Shelf. Follow a hold-littered slab leftwards to a niche. Climb up and right to a large thread on an overhung ledge. From the left-hand side of the ledge, move up and then go diagonally rightwards over ledges to belay just below The Haven.

67 Haven Direct 18m VD †
From the Luncheon Shelf, move diagonally leftwards and up to the left side of a high, wide bulge. Step left over this and move easily up to The Haven.

68 Haven Twin 18m VD †
Climb straight up from the Luncheon Shelf, passing the left side of a roof at 8 metres, Move up to the wide bulge and cross it to reach The Haven.

69 Haven Variant 18m S †
As for *Haven Twin*, but move right after the roof at 8 metres. Pull over the right side of the bulge above and climb to The Haven.

70 Sideshow 30m E1 †   (16.5.92)
Belay beneath the niche under the left-hand side of the large overhang, 10 metres before the sea cave, and at a higher level. The rock is better than it looks.
1 12m 5c. Climb the overlaps left of the niche to the roof. Move left and up onto a prominent block. A harder move leads to a slab and ledge above.

Imaginative multiple belays.
2 18m. Traverse easily rightwards to the large ledge.

71 Triple Traverse 28m HS
Start as for *Sideshow*. A well-positioned first pitch slightly marred by the 'terrors' above.
1 15m. Bridge up and step left onto a hanging slab. From here, carry on leftwards, gradually being forced downwards until a nose is reached. Move around this and belay on the ledge 5 metres above.
2 13m. It is possible to escape left along the horizontal band but the route proper takes in the rock above, which is broken in appearance but firmer than it looks. Climb up 6 metres above the stance and traverse left to an earthy ramp. Use this to exit into The Haven. Block belay.

72 The Safety Rail 10m E4 5c †   (31.5.92)
Eight metres of eminently protectable roof make this a strenuous delight. From the left-hand side of the overhang follow the rail rightwards until it eventually meets the lip. Pull over. Multiple belays on the ledge a metre or so above.

73 Gorgonzola 13m E2 5b †
Start at the rib below the right-hand side of the large overhang. Climb the rib to the overhang, stretch over, and traverse 3 metres right. Exit via a groove. Belay immediately and then scramble off rightwards.

74 Warmer 6m VD †
The short sharp overhang on the western tip. Move right and down onto the beach to finish.

371

Lulworth East

Warning. The eastern stretches of this cliff lie within the danger area of the Army Tank Ranges, which are open to the public only at specific times. Details of when the range walks are open are published in the local press or can be obtained from the Range Officer by phoning 01929 462721 ext. 819 or 824. Red flags flying at the perimeter of the range area are also used to indicate when entry is prohibited.

There are three types of climb at Lulworth East. The original explorations resulted in three long traverses following the two main lines – a sea-level line, and a line immediately beneath the roofs. Later additions include a concentration of excellent, hard, pure roof climbs, all of which have the added advantage of lying outside the Army Tank Ranges. However, the latter are bolted climbs in a no-bolt area and they may be debolted. Finally, in recent years, local climbers have expoited the high-quality virgin rock between Lulworth Cove entrance and the Fossil

Forest to climb some very good trad lines, mostly on-sight.

Unfortunately, the descriptions of the long traverses are for the record only, as even when firing is not taking place the public are not permitted to stray from footpaths delineated by yellow marker posts. The bye-laws **forbid climbing inside the Lulworth firing ranges**, and the Army state that people found off the marked paths may be liable for prosecution. This is a great shame as the long

View across Lulworth Cove to Lulworth East. STEVE TAYLOR

traverses detailed below are worthwhile expeditions and almost worth the risk of a short appearance in front of a magistrate.

1 Lulworth Cove – Mupe Bay Traverse
1,300m Very Difficult

The grade refers to the easiest alternative and presupposes ideal conditions: a warm sunny day, calm seas (the difficulty is very dependent on tide and waves), and lots of friends (friends, not *Friends*). A long, fairly sustained traverse on firm rock all the way: a fine but committing expedition. Start on the eastern side of the mouth of Lulworth Cove. The final 200 metres are possible only within a few hours of low tide but may be avoided. A rope is advised for the vertical finishing pitches.

1 D. Traverse east at sea-level. After about 200 metres the cliff-top is clear and escape is easy; this is the Fossil Forest, an internationally important geological site. Continue below overhangs for a long way to a slight bay. (Beyond are some wide ledges and two hundred yards past these are the pinnacles in the sea which mark Mupe Bay.)

2 HS 4b Approx. 200m. At low tide continue east, only hard at the start, to the final zawn before Mupe Bay.

3 D 15m. Start beneath a low overhang a short distance back from the final zawn. Climb diagonally right and up to a ledge. Continue up the crack above and exit rightwards onto an easy north-slanting slab. Follow this past a cave into Mupe Bay.

Variations

2a VD 12m. Start just to the east of the slight bay on pitch 1. Climb the wall just to the left of the nose of the buttress and belay in a corner.

3a VD 12m. From the corner, traverse 10 metres left and finish straight up on sound rock.

3b HVS 50m 6a. A contentious grade maybe, but the technical section is not long, and nothing more harmful than deep water awaits a blunder. Hardest

at the start. After pitch 2, traverse at low level around the final zawn and continue around the headland into Mupe Bay.

⭐ 2 Traverse of the Fossils 305m E2 † (5.9.93)

A high traverse on good rock, this climb follows twin horizontal cracks, which have a roof above them for most of the way. It is impossible to get lost! For this reason a detailed description is superfluous. Escape onto an easier climb is often possible by descending to the Mupe Bay Traverse. Start on the eastern side of the mouth of Lulworth Cove.

1 15m. Scramble rightwards to a prow and belay.

2 30m 4b. Traverse right,…

3 15m 4c. …further right,…

4 30m 5b. …and right again to a small bay.

5 10m 5a. Cross the bay; easier than it looks.

6 30m 5b. A strenuous pitch.

7 15m 4b. Continue to a belay in a grotto. The cliff-top can be reached easily from here. (E1 so far.)

8 30m 4b. Continue…

9 20m 5b. …to a hanging belay on a prow.

10 25m 5a. Carry on rightwards…

11 35m 5a. …to a hanging belay just past a bird's toilet and vomiting-spot!

12 25m 5c. The route's strenuous crux consists of passing a projecting block. Belay just beyond.

13 25m. Continue rightwards and then finish upwards into the Fossil Forest.

3 Back to the Future 275m E1 † (3.10.93)

A continuation climb along the same pair of parallel cracks as the last route. Start at the eastern end of the Fossil Forest, by a concrete cube in the middle of a cliff-side bowl. Some hanging belays.

1 30m. From the concrete cube, climb down and scramble eastwards to an overhung bay.

2 45m 4c. Traverse right and belay just before an arête.

3 40m 4c. Continue and belay just before a deep cave.

4 40m 4c. Belay on an undercut arête.

5 10m 5a. A short loose section leads into a corner and out onto another undercut arête.

6 35m 4c. Continue around a wide bay to a commodious ledge.

7 25m 5b. Traverse around an overhung bay to a small ledge.

8 30m 4a. Continue until beneath the left-hand side of a large depression in the broken rock and grass above. This is the point at which the wide ledges mentioned in the *Mupe Bay Traverse* description start.

9 20m 4a. Traverse across a smooth wall and scramble up to the cliff-top.

The roofs west of the MoD fencing and the Fossil Forest have provided the scene for some excellent bolted roof climbs and somewhat easier traditional climbs. The bolts routes are steeper and even more intimidating than their counterparts at Stair Hole though somewhat shorter. However, the moves are outrageous and the rock quality is faultless.

To approach these routes, walk around the eastern side of Lulworth Cove and follow the path up a short hill to a small monument. Walk 50 metres east along the cliff-top path then descend to a cliff-top grotto, which has loose, shale roofs above. Beneath this grotto is a straightforward descent (VD) leading to the first of the climbs. *Bad to the Bone* starts 10 metres east (right) of the descent and climbs up to, and across the first large roof. Note that these climbs should be avoided in anything but calm seas, as the belayer is at risk of a soaking.

The routes between *Plwmp* and *Ghost of You* are best accessed by abseil from a dodgy stake (backed up with wires) in an alcove approximately 100 metres west of the normal descent. The line of the abseil is the grey wall of *Evening Slab*.

☆ 4 **Plwmp** 12m S † (15.9.07)
Not pictured. Start beneath the left end of the triangular strip roof, 10 metres left of the foot of the abseil. The left arête of the slab beneath the roof is split by an easy groove. Climb this with a tricky move at half-height.

5 **Lesbian Spank Inferno** 12m E3 6a † (15.9.07)

The triangular strip roof contains a striking diagonal crack. Climb the delicate arête, 2 metres left of the crack, to the roof and arrange bomber gear. Make a powerful move out to a jug on the lip, followed by a hard, bold rock-over to gain the wall above. Finish to the left.

6 **Recursion** 12m HVS 5a † (15.9.07)
Climb the deep corner left of *Evening Slab*. An exposed move right onto the face gains a deep break, where a stiff pull leads to easy ground and the alcove.

7 **Ouzo Envy** 12m VS 4c † (15.9.07)
The grooved arête left of the foot of the abseil. Climb the groove past a bulge to the deep break. Move up the compact wall to the alcove.

☆ 8 **Evening Slab** 12m S † (20.4.07)
☆ Excellent climbing with adequate protection from small wires. From the foot of the abseil, ascend the broad, easy rib, with a tricky move from a supect block immediately below the alcove.

9 September Sessions 12m VS 4b † (29.9.07)
The slabby rib between *Evening Slab* and *Lulworth New Order* gives some great climbing, though take care with the loose finishing moves to the alcove.

10 Lulworth New Order 12m VS 4b †
(20.4.07)
Climb the tricky thin flakes to the right of *Evening Slab* to the edge of a strip roof. An awkward move left leads to an easy finish and the alcove.

11 Cuzco 12m E1 5b † (20.4.07)
Start beneath the alcove, under a strip roof. Move up and squeeze through some prominent flakes to reach the roof. Arrange lots of protection – it's quantity rather than quality here – prior to making a hard pull around the roof. Easy ground leads to the alcove.

12 Ghost of You 12m VS 4b † (20.4.07)
Above and right of *Cuzco* is an 'Africa'-shaped flake in an overhang. The break in the roof to the left is taken by this route. From beneath the break, climb the wide corner until a move right gains some large jammed blocks. Trend left over the strip roof to the alcove.

Tim Dunsby pioneering the first ascent of *Traverse of the Fossils* E2 (page 373).
NIGEL COE

The remaining routes are reached via the approach described on page 373. From the base of the descent, traverse left at sea-level for 30 metres to a deep alcove formed by two flakes.

⭐ **13 Stalinist Regime** 13m HVS 5a † (23.7.06)
Climb the left-hand flake until it is possible to move left onto the face and follow a thin seam up to the deep break beneath the roof. Climb this on large holds to reach a cliff-top ledge. Nut belays.

☐ ✓

14 Southern Stutter 13m E1 5a † (23.7.06)
Belay at the base of the right-hand flake. Move out right onto the slab and climb a short flake up to the deep break. Make thin moves up and right, with scant protection, and mantel onto the cliff-top ledge. Stake and flake belays.

☐ ✓

⭐ **15 The Poet and the Thief** 13m VS 4b † (24.7.06)
The slab right of the flake. Climb the slab, with good small wires all the way. Load the break with gear and head over some beautiful coral 'fangs' to the unprotected headwall. Stake and flake belays above.

☐ ✓

⭐⭐ **16 Mojo-Pin** 13m VS 5a (30.6.06)
A quality steep slab climb - recommended. Climb up the right-hand side of the slab (slightly bold) to the break. Finish as for *The Poet and the Thief*. Stake (the Mojo-Pin) and flake belays.

☐ ✓

17 4 Years, 5 Months and 15 Days and Still Missing You... 14m E2 5b † (30.6.06)
A bold route, 15 metres left of the descent. Start immediately left of a small alcove and climb a protectionless slab to a steepening. Pull up to the deep break (crux – bold), where the small roof can be climbed on good holds. Nut belays on the wide ledge above.

☐ ✓

18 Extraordinary Rendition 14m E1 5c †
(13.5.06)
Start 6 metres left of the descent. Climb easily up the slab to jugs on the lip of a small roof. A long reach gains small crimps and the top.

19 Hyperbole 14m E1 5a
(13.5.06)
A good, varied climb, taking in some interesting geological features. Start just left of the descent route, just right of an arête. Climb to a prominent cave; pull leftwards out of the cave via thin cracks to gain a niche (good but hard-won protection), from which tricky moves gain the left-hand tree-bole and the top.

20 MC Hammer 14m VS 4c †
(24.6.06)
An easier finish to *Hyperbole*. Climb that route to the roof, before moving right and up using an obvious undercut. Finish easily to the ledge above.

The descent route down-climbs the flakes to the right, beneath the lowest point of the amphitheatre.

21 Too Driven 12m HS
(17.6.06)
A pleasant though escapable climb immediately right of the descent route. Follow a thin flake until it fades. Tricky moves lead slightly right then left to the deep break. Step left, and pull over the small roof using the first of two flakes. Finish easily on slightly dubious rock.

22 Pussy Galore 12m VS 4b
(13.5.06)
Start 4 metres right of the descent route, in a right-facing corner that forms the left-hand side of a bay. Climb easily up the corner on very rough rock to the small roof. Steep moves on suspect jugs gain a rest before the final move to the amphitheatre.

Steve Taylor looking apprehensive on the second ascent of *Hyperbole* E1.
ROB KENNARD

★ **23 Bad to the Bone** 13m F7b+ 8B   (1990s)
From a single-bolt belay directly beneath the widest part of the roof, climb easily up to the roof. Pull across a world of steepness slightly leftwards to a lower-off just over the lip.

★★ **24 Il Pirata** 13m F7a+ 7B   (1990s)
Start as for *Bad to the Bone*. Climb the centre of the massive roof on good holds to a lower-off just over the lip.

A bolted project (F8b-F8c) moves out rightwards from the base of the roof.

★ **25 Jurassic Coast Pimp** 13m E1 5b † (17.6.06)
This well-protected route tackles the right side of the huge *Il Pirata* roof at a surprisingly amenable grade. Roughly in the centre of the *Il Pirata* bay is a deep, blocky flake. Belay 2 metres right of the flake at good foot-ledges. Follow thin flakes and a slab to the breaks. Lean out and follow a line of huge jugs to the lip of the roof. Pull over using undercuts. Finish with care on slightly dubious rock. Stake belay.

26 Svengali 11m E3 6a †   (24.6.06)
Difficult moves through the roof make this the hardest trad route hereabouts. Climb *Jurassic Coast Pimp* to a crack in the roof formed by a 'pancake' feature. Make a hard rock-over onto the wall above (*Rock 1*) and finish easily.

27 Bolt Free 12m VS 4b †   (17.6.06)
The obvious weakness through the narrow section of roof 4 metres right of *Jurassic Coast Pimp*. Climb the easy slab to the roof. Pull over past a small niche (good wires) to a solid finish. Stake belay.

Steve Taylor on the first ascent of *The Gift* **HVS.** BEN STOKES

28 **Carbon Footprint** 12m HVS 5b † (17.6.06)
The deep cleft on the right-hand end of the bay.
Climb the easy right-facing corner to the fissure
through the roof. A combination of thrutching and
gurning gains the upper groove and the top. Stake
belay.

29 **The Gift** 13m HVS 5b (5.11.06)
The buttress and hanging arête give excellent
climbing in a great situation. Start on the right side
of the white buttress and climb thin flakes to the
roof. Step left and enter the well-protected hanging
groove with difficulty. Climb this to the top.

**Ben Stokes pulling through the roof on the
first ascent of *Jurassic Coast Pimp* E1.**
STEVE TAYLOR

Right of the white buttress, two bolted lines start from a single-bolt belay by a niche. The left-hand line is still a project.

30 Dry Your Eyes Mate 13m F7c+ † 6B (4.05)
The right-hand bolt line. From the single-bolt belay, climb easily up to the roof and make a series of desperate moves to link the pockets.

31 Jay Kay 16m HVS 4c † (5.11.06)
The flake 4 metres right has an airy feel higher up. Climb the left-facing flake to the roof and move airily right and up to a deep break. Make tricky moves up and right to the roof where a long traverse left leads to easy ground. Nut belays.

After a further 20 metres, in a deep groove with a deep flake crack at the back, three routes share a common start from a single bolt.

32 The Lemon Express 14m F7b 7B (1990s)
Climb the deep groove to the roof. Stretch out and clip the first bolt in the roof, move left 2 metres, and pull across the roof on big, well-spaced holds.

33 Breathe the Pressure 14m F7b+ 7B (1990s)
Start as for *The Lemon Express*, but take the line of round pockets across the centre of the roof. Superb.

34 Ramases Cubed 14m F7b+ 7B (23.1.05)
Start as for *The Lemon Express*, but move right across the flake to the roof. Climb this with some very inventive footwork.

Ten metres to the right, passing some slightly less impressive roofs, is a larger roof with a recess on its lip.

35 Granny Lifts Car 18m F7b+ 6B † (23.1.05)
The strange alien face formed by tree-bole holes gives an innocuous-looking route that packs some explosive moves. Swing out right and up an easy white scoop left of a flying buttress to a rest beneath a roof aven. Lean out from the aven and make reflex power pulls to gain juggy pockets halfway. More positive holds lead with sustained interest over the lip.

36 Let Ya Bones Hang 13m F7a 7B (18.2.01)
The easiest roof-climb hereabouts. *Start* from a bolt belay on a square ledge, down to the right of the flying buttress. Climb a groove in a rib to the roof, and ape across on large pockets to a lower-off above the lip.

☆☆ 37 **Rigor Mortis** 14m F7a+ 8B　　(1990s)
Another roof-climb at an amenable grade. Climb
to the recess in the roof, swing left, and climb the
roof on good holds, past a halfway niche, to a
lower-off above the lip.

☆☆ 38 **A Storm in Heaven** 15m F7c 7B　　(1990s)
The hardest route on the roofs. From the recess,
climb across the central part of the roof to a difficult
transition at the lip and the lower-off.

☆☆ 39 **Eye of the Storm** 14m F7b+ 7B　　(25.2.01)
From the niche in the roof, pull out rightwards along
a handrail to finish up a groove.

Right of *Eye of the Storm* is a bolted project across
a blank-looking section of the roof.

☆ 40 **Language of Nature** 13m F7b 7B (25.2.01)
Eight metres right of the start of *Rigor Mortis* is a
deep flake. From the flake, pull up to the roof and
climb the roof-crack leftwards to finish as for *Eye of
the Storm*.

41 Lewd's Mother 14m F4+ 5B (1990s)
The escape route! Climb the rib right of the flake of *Language of Nature* to a slab and an abseil stake.

To the right of the rib is yet another roofed bay, above and right of which lies the MoD fence.

⭐⭐ **42 Monolith Monsters** 14m F7b+ 6B (1990s)
The blank-looking roof. Climb a crack up to the left-hand side of the roof. Pull across on good, but spaced holds to the lower-off on the lip.

⭐⭐ **43 Mirrorball** 14m F7c 7B (4.01)
Links the start of *Monolith Monsters* with the finish of *Shining Path* via some outrageous footless moves. Reachy, steep, and with a difficult finish.

⭐ **44 Shining Path** 14m F7a+ 6B (1990s)
Climb the wall and attack the roof with some long reaches to a hard rockover at the lip.

Ben Stokes on *Shining Path* F7a+ STEVE TAYLOR

Worbarrow Tout

OS Ref 869 795

Worbarrow Tout is the rocky promontory topped with grass, which protrudes from the eastern corner of Worbarrow Bay. Mud and vegetation appear to predominate and the area of overlapping slabs on the northern side of the promontory, whilst reminiscent of the Culm Coast, is of too low an angle to offer any challenge. The climbs, however, are all on the southern face, a 400-metre long cliff ranging in height from a few metres to 35 metres plus scrambling. The routes at the western end of the Tout finish on top of a clean rocky ridge, whereas those on the central and eastern end finish up steep vegetation with no known stakes for belays.

Approach. Turn off the A351 at Corfe Castle and follow the road through the villages of Church Knowle and Steeple. Two miles before East Lulworth, turn south and park in the deserted village of Tyneham (this is possible only when the firing ranges are open to the general public). Fifty metres south of the car-park follow a signposted path to Worbarrow Bay (about a kilometre).

Warning. Worbarrow Tout lies within the danger area of the Army Tank Ranges, which are open to the public only at specified times. Details of when the range walks are open are published in the local press or can be obtained from the Range Officer on 01929 462721. Red flags flying at the perimeter of the range are also used to indicate when entry is prohibited.

Unfortunately, the following descriptions are for the record only, as even when firing is not taking place the public are not permitted to stray from footpaths delineated by yellow marker posts. The by-laws **forbid climbing anywhere within the Lulworth firing ranges**, and the Army state that those found off the waymarked paths may be liable for prosecution.

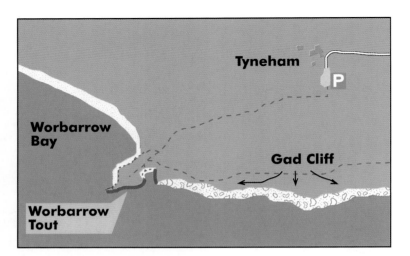

The sea-level traverse of the promontory requires calm seas and goes at Difficult in either direction. The exploratory feel is often lost, however, owing to the fishermen encountered *en route*!

To access to the routes at the western end of the Tout follow the tourist path to the base of the Tout (Gad Cliff is now on your left). Walk around the right hand side of the Tout across flat boulders (mid to low tide only) to a large shallow cave. Cross the small beach and scramble up and over the clean ridge to reefs below the cliff.

1 West Kante 200m D   (09.2003)
Scramble to the most westerly part of the ridge. From here, climb over a squat pinnacle, and then follow the clean-cut ridge direct. Scrambling follows with some nervous steps up conglomerate walls, where the climb degenerates into a path.

2 West Corner 8m E(asy)
The first feature on the seaward side of the ridge is a shallow angled west-facing corner. Useful as a descent for the other routes.

3 Ticket Tout 10m HS 4b   (09.03)
The face directly above *West Corner* contains three bottom-right to top-left diagonal cracks. This route combines the lower two to give a pleasant introduction to the climbing hereabouts. Good wire belays on the landward side of the ridge.

The next three routes start on the clean slab about 4 metres above sea level, 8 metres right of *West Corner*, beneath a conspicuous 3-metre roof crack.

4 Eleanor 10m VS 4c   (4.10.03)
Climb up to the corner crack above the right hand side of the slab. Pull over the first bulge and then

move left under the large roof. Step left again into a left facing corner to finish easily.

5 Samuel 12m HVS 5a (4.10.03)
Takes the 3-metre roof crack at an amenable grade. Start as *for Eleanor*. After the first bulge pull over a second bulge to get established at the base of the roof crack. Climb the crack using layaways and jams until it is possible to pull right into a groove – finish up this.

6 Ricochet Wall 14m E1 5b (4.10.03)
The bullet-riddled wall right of *Samuel* is harder than it looks. Start in the cleft beneath the clean slab. Move up and right then follow the leftwards-slanting crack until a finger traverse right across the bullet scarred wall leads into a large niche. Move up slightly left for a metre then finger traverse rightwards again (crux) to reach a small groove. Climb the crack on the left for 2 metres before a stretch rightwards leads to the rubbly final groove. Small belays up the ridge on the right.

7 Scuba 73m S † (10.6.78)
Follow the traverse eastwards beneath the cliff until a crackline is reached which leads up past two overhangs to a third overhang with a prominent left lip about 22 metres up.
1 45m. A fine pitch with good rock, excellent protection, and positive holds. Climb the crack passing the first two overhangs direct. Climb the third overhang and move left under a prow of rock onto the lip. Traverse delicately left along this past two grooves to a third groove and a stance.
2 28m. Scramble up the loose rock and earth above, and belay on the other side of the ridge.

8 Centre Line 20m VDiff † (1979)
Three-quarters of the way along the eastwards traverse of the cliff is a cleft with a noticeable

hanging chimney above it. Start 6 metres above the sea on a large ledge. Climb up and follow the chimney. Exit to the right when forced to do so and follow an easy corner to an obvious ledge.

9 The Pony 20m HVS 5a † (25.4.04)
Excellent climbing on good rock, with a steep start and a sound exit. The bottom belay is well above the sea. Climb the wall to the right of *Centre Line*. Belay on the last good rock (stakes may be in-situ).

The final route on this cliff is best reached from the east (Gad Cliff) by traversing in from a small, pebbly cove.

10 White Line 16m VDiff † (1979)
Follow the low level traverse leftwards (Severe at high tide) to where a small channel has to be negotiated. Start 5 metres left of the channel. Move easily up to a small overhang and climb this on good holds. Continue rightwards and up across some slabs to gain a small cleft. Belay here, or continue 5 metres further back to a curious hole, which takes a *Hex 11*.

Gad Cliff

To the east of Worbarrow Tout lies the unmistakable limestone precipice of Gad Cliff. Reaching approximately 65 metres in height at its western end, it is unfortunately as loose and unstable as it looks. The cliff finishes in a 12-metre band of vertical earth, grass, and assorted choss, making the top of any new route rather unpleasant. However, a few rock buttresses do intrude through this band and have been inspected by abseil. The only attempted ascent on the main section of cliff, by local loose-rock afficionados, was swiftly repulsed. No need to be brave, however, as nesting birds mean this cliff should not now be climbed upon; no great loss. The western end of

Gad Cliff, however, presents a buttress of Dorset's finest limestone, very similar to the best parts of Pembroke in quality. Undercut by a deep cave, however, the scope for "straight up" lines is limited, but a number of fine traverse lines (bottom left to top right) are possible, only one of which has been recorded.

11 Blubbered 32m E1 5a † (13.7.91)
Fairly solid and definitely worthwhile. Start on pointed rocks to the left of the cave. Go easily along to ledges and an obvious block (old peg) and swing round this. After 2 metres, step up a little then back down and continue above the cave past a few steep moves. Keep going in the same line on easier but less solid ground past a possible stance in a niche to finish on the skyline. A pre-dangled rope on a stake (removed) was used on the FA to make the finishing rubble less exciting.

Brian Watson on *The Pony* HVS. SCOTT TITT

First Ascents

The number of any aid points used on the first ascent, for resting or for progress, is detailed after the names of the first ascensionists; (aid) means that a climb was originally ascended as an aid route or with a long aid section. (AL) or (VL) indicate alternate or varied leads respectively.

Before the 1980s, few records were kept of activities on the eastern side of Portland, though the Reverend Bob Shepton is accredited with the majority of the routes here. Ian Kestin and Steve Jones produced a number of the harder early Portland climbs. Most of the early routes in The Cuttings were the work of Messrs Dyke, Northcote, McCombie, Whiteley, Hirst and Hubble.

Portland

1963	**The Twist** R Shepton	
1967 Aug	**Vesuvius** R Shepton, S Jones	

The first venture onto cliffs which Bob Shepton, in a Mountain Craft magazine article, had once considered 'far too loose for ordinary mortals'. Ian Kestin took a 40-footer when attempting the second ascent as he had no written description to follow – he'd be spoilt for information nowadays.

1968 April   **Amateur Dramatics** R Shepton, S Jones
'Extra pegs were used on the final wall on the first ascent due to falls sustained by the leader finding no holds in the grass over the top. An earth-axe would be useful.'

1968 Aug   **Faceache** R Shepton, S Jones
Destroyed by rockfall.

1968 Aug   **Lucky Dip** S Jones, R Shepton
Variation climbed by R J Crewe, K Winkworth, E Butt in May 1973.

1968   **Jutland** J Whiteley

1969 June   **The Castle** I Kestin, I Mitchell (1 pt aid)
Still awaiting a free ascent (or even a repeat?)

1969 July   **Muscleman Direct** I Kestin, I Mitchell

1969 Aug   **Smugglers' Stairs** R Shepton
Destroyed by rockfall.

1969 Aug   **The Gash** R Shepton, I Kestin

1969 Sept   **The Scrog** I Kestin S Jones

1970 April   **Samson** I Kestin

1970 April   **McKenna's Cleft** R Shepton, I Kestin

1970 Aug   **Half-Way House** R Shepton, A Miller

1970 Aug   **Ferocity** R Shepton

1970 Aug   **Lacerations** R Shepton, F Walshe, I Kestin

Ian Kestin running it out in style on the first ascent of *Plain Awkward* HS (page 251). KESTIN COLLECTION

1970	**Lotus Eater** J Whiteley, R Whiteley

Destroyed in a massive rockfall in 2001.

1971 Aug 13 **Persistence** R Shepton, D Wragg
1971 Aug 13 **Insistence** D Wragg, R Shepton (AL)
1971 Aug 30 **Blockhead** R Shepton
1971 **Dee** T Hubble
1972 May 19 **Port Wine** C McCombie, M Hodgson, T Hubble
1972 June **Scoop, Scoup, The Devil** M Hodgson
*Scoup was retrobolted in April 1995 by D B Cook and had a
hold chipped to make the crux easier.*

1972 June **String of Pearls** M Hodgson, T Hubble
1972 June **Reunion** M Hodgson, D Chapman
1972 Aug 5 **The Worm** R Shepton, I Kestin
1972 Aug 7 **Big Corner** R Shepton, C McCombie
1972 Aug 8 **Flake Out** R Shepton, I Kestin
1972 Aug 12 **Light Relief** C McCombie, J Graveling
1972 Aug 23 **Wallsend Wall** R Shepton, M Hodgson
1973 Aug 14 **Sea Saga** R Shepton, J Coote
1973 Aug 24 **Stylus** C McCombie, R Shepton
1973 Aug 31 **Slim Jim** R Shepton
1974 Aug 29 **Bolder Crack** R Shepton
1974 Aug 31 **Ammonite's Tooth** R Shepton, A Dutton
Destroyed by rockfall.

1975 Feb 9 **Bag End** P Northcote, P Sommerill, A Boldeno
Retrobolted without the first ascentionist's permission in 2008

1975 July 31 **Dirt Track** R Shepton, J Tookey
1975 Aug 3 **The Curler** A Dutton, R Shepton
1975 Aug 4 **Kraken** R Shepton, A Dutton (AL)
1975 Dec 31 **Slings Shot** J Tookey, C Hubbard
*The second's first and only climb. First free ascent N A Coe,
N Weymouth on 24 September 1988. Controversially retroed
and renamed by P Oxley in 1995.*

1976 Aug 3 **The Prow** R Shepton, I Kestin
1976 Aug 9 **Family S** R Shepton, D Shepton
1976 Aug 10 **Hangman's Loose** A Dutton, R Hughes
1977 April 2 **Wallflower** G Hounsome, J L Titt, S L Titt
1977 April 23 **Struggling Jim** R Wallbridge, J Cohen
1977 May 14 **Nomad** P Northcote, T Taylor (AL)
1977 May 14 **Dreamer** T Taylor, P Northcote
1977 May 21 **Ectomorph** D Gumn, G Hounsome (1 rest pt)
First free ascent T Dunsby, S L Titt on 25 October 1992.

1977 May 22 **Hole in the Wall** G Hounsome, D Gumn
1977 May 22 **Kestrel** D Gumn, G Hounsome, K Winkworth, R J Crewe
1977 July 4 **Fond Farewell** R Shepton, A Monument, C Gonzales
*The last of Bob Shepton's large number of pioneering first ascents
on the Isle, on which he pulled off a block and took a 10-metre
fall.*

1977 Sept 17 **Mirage** P Northcote
*A top-rope was employed on the slat band. First complete ascent
(as Lesser Evil) by P R Littlejohn, C King on 28 February 1979.*

1979 Feb 28 **Faceache Direct** P R Littlejohn, C King (AL)
Destroyed by rockfall.

1979 Feb 28 **Poison Tip** C King, P R Littlejohn
*Second's Swing variation had previously been climbed by
G Ratcliffe, W Waterfield in June 1977.*

1979 May 6 **Monkey Business** D Jones, A Monument
1979 May 7 **Perihelion** G Hounsome, S L Titt
1979 May 7 **Gourmet** First free ascent G Hounsome, S L Titt
c.1979 **U-143** G Hounsome (solo)
1980 June 21 **Chips with Everything** D Jones, J Kenton
1980 June 21 **Kate** D Jones, J Kenton
The crux headwall was practised on a top-rope.

**George Hounsome on the first ascent
of Gourmet E1 (page 315).** SCOTT TITT

First Ascents

1980 June 22 — **Bigus Dickus** D Jones, J Kenton
After top-rope practise.

1981 May 1 — **Bad Dream, Divine Madness, Slice of Life** P R Littlejohn, H Clarke

1981 — **Chalkie and the Hex 5** C Ellison, H Venables

1983 Oct 16 — **Two Fingers** First free ascent P Oxley, T Dunsby
Oxley's first new route.

1985 Dec 7 — **Shiver Me Timbers** P Oxley, N A Coe (2 rest pts)
Previously an aid climb known as Peggler. First free ascent D Goddard in 1986 by an unintentional on-sight solo!

1985 Dec 15 — **Snatch Squad** N A Coe, S L Titt
Climbed in the last five minutes before dark.

1986 July 6 — **No Lion, No Tiger** N A Coe, S L Titt

1986 — **Spicer** First free ascent A Legg, D Goddard

1987 Aug 8 — **Inchworm** C Waddy (on-sight solo)
The first route of the cliff. A bold effort indeed.

1987 Aug 8 — **Medusa Falls** C Waddy (on-sight)

1988 June 1 — **Equinox** C Crowther, R White
Almost climbed on-sight by H Venables several years before. However, he 'decked it' from the final mantel and was promptly carted away by a nearby team of squaddies!

1988 Aug 8 — **Superfly Guy, Nothing but the Groove, Oblivion Is Forever** P Oxley, J Williams

1988 Aug 8 — **Jezebel Spirit** J Williams, P Oxley

1988 Aug 10 — **The Mystical Gill** P Oxley (solo)

1988 Aug 15 — **The Man Who Never Found Himself** P Oxley (roped solo)

1988 Aug 21 — **Last Rose of Summer** P Oxley

1988 Aug 21 — **Inch Perfect** P Oxley (solo with a hanging rope)

1988 Aug 21 — **Pinch an Inch** P Oxley (solo)

1988 Oct 15 — **The Vertical Thrill** N A Coe (on-sight solo)
Subsequently bolted, against the wishes of the first ascensionist.

1988 Oct 29 — **The Great American Hamburger Disaster** W Brown, J Haine
Probably climbed before.

1988 Oct 30 — **Remember Blair Peach** S L Titt, N A Coe

1988 Oct 30 — **Rubber Truncheon, Speleo Joy Toy** N A Coe, S L Titt

1988 Nov 5 — **Lord Stublock Deepvoid Breaks the Chain of Causation** P Oxley, H Venables

1988 Nov 8 — **Colors** P Oxley, H Venables

1988 Nov 8 — **Trance Dance** P Oxley

1988 Nov 8 — **One for the Gipper** P Oxley

1988 Nov 13 — **Out of Reach, Out of Mind, Barbed Wire Kisses** P Oxley, H Venables

1988 Nov 19 — **President Elect** P Oxley

1988 Nov 19 — **Humanoid, Judge Jeffreys, Serious Music, Rêve d'un Corbeau** P Oxley, H Venables

1988 Nov 19 — **Eighth Wonder** N A Coe, H Venables

1988 Nov 26 — **On the Wall** P Oxley, H Venables

1988 Dec 10 — **Keyboard Wall** P Oxley

1988 Dec 10 — **Stripped for Action, Kicking Steps, The Sheer Weight of Prague** N A Coe, H Venables, P Oxley
The name refered to the climb not the climbers!

1988 Dec 17 — **Evening Falls** P Oxley, N A Coe

1988 Dec 17 — **Sugar 'n' Spikes** N A Coe, H Venables

1988 Dec 17 — **Borstal Breakout** H Venables, N A Coe

1988 Dec 18 — **The Cutting Edge** P Oxley

1988 Dec 18 — **Evening Mistress** First free ascent P Oxley

1988 Dec — **Monoculture** P Oxley (1 rest pt)
First free ascent P Oxley on 17 April 1993 (after retrobolting).

1989 Feb 4 — **Undercut Arête** N A Coe (solo)

1989 Feb 11 — **Silent Boulder** S L Titt, N A Coe

1989 March 5 — **Zeno, Deception** D Sealy, E Waters

1989 March 5 — **Elephant on Roller Skates** S L Titt, N A Coe

1989 March 5 — **Descent Horizon** N A Coe

1989 March 5 — **Learning Curve** N A Coe, S L Titt

1989 March 26 — **Rhyme Intrinseca, The Strobolising Scyphostoma** M J Crocker

1989 March 27 — **Sparkling Bone Chamber** M J Crocker, N A Coe

1989 March 27 — **The Enema Within, Good Lay** M J Crocker, N A Coe
Good Lay was bolted and claimed by G Gibson in 2005.

1989 March 27 — **Blood and Chocolate** N A Coe, M J Crocker
Led in poor style on account of all the blood after a foothold broke! Reascended properly a month later when the scars had healed. Retrobolted without the first ascensionist's permission by N Heanes.

1989 April 1 — **Bawdy House, Wind in the Riggin', Silage Clamp** M J Crocker

1989 April 1 — **The Misanthrope** M J Crocker

1989 April 9 — **Eyes in Your Navel, Nigel** M J Crocker
Bolted and claimed as Meet the Manatees by G Gibson in Summer 2003

1989 April 9 — **Citizen Dust** N A Coe, S L Titt, M J Crocker
Direct, bolted start by S Taylor, June 1996

1989 April 9 — **Skateboard to Oblivion** S L Titt, N A Coe

1989 April 9 — **Wurlitzer Jukebox** M J Crocker, H Venables

1989 April 9 — **Choco Loni** M J Crocker, N A Coe

1989 April 9 — **Bilboes** M J Crocker, N A Coe, H Venables

1989 April 15 — **Slumberland** N A Coe, T Dunsby, S L Titt
Later compromised by the bolts of Slumberland Direct and Reality Bites.

1989 April 15 — **Sacred Angel** H Venables, N A Coe, T Dunsby (1 rest pt)
First free ascent S Taylor in 1993 (after retrobolting).

1989 April 22	**Turned to Stone** P Oxley, M J Crocker

1989 April 22 **Turned to Stone** P Oxley, M J Crocker
1989 April 22 **Master of Ape Science, Gratuitous Lies Here** M J Crocker, P Oxley, H Venables
1989 April 22 **Hipnition, Margaret on the Guillotine, Come Armageddon, Come** P Oxley, H Venables, M J Crocker
1989 April 23 **Bum Droplets** M J Crocker
1989 April 23 **Master of the Rolls, So Special** M J Crocker, P Oxley
1989 April 23 **Think Black** P Oxley, H Venables, M J Crocker
1989 April 23 **Mechanoids** M J Crocker, P Oxley, H Venables
1989 April 29 **Organic Snail Farming** M J Crocker, P Oxley
1989 April 29 **Halfway to Heaven** P Oxley, M J Crocker
1989 April 30 **Stalker's Zone** P Oxley, M J Crocker
1989 April 30 **Great Barrier Reef** M J Crocker, P Oxley
1989 May 6 **Dial a Cliché** P Oxley, M J Crocker
1989 May 6 **Come In Alone, Go Out Alone** P Oxley (solo)
1989 May 6 **The Right Mix** M J Crocker, P Oxley
1989 May 6 **Topsy Turvy Land** M J Crocker
1989 May 6 *RP Screamers* M J Crocker
A hold broke and Crocker kissed the ground from 8 metres, held by a solitary RP 3! A later solo attempt by Damian Cook resulted in a groundfall and damaged ankle.
1989 May 7 **Puffin Billy** T Dunsby, S L Titt, N A Coe
1989 May 7 **Beeching's Track** N A Coe, T Dunsby
1989 May 7 **Two Nuns, a Hang-glider and Jesus** S L Titt, N A Coe
1989 May 7 **Cold Fusion** S L Titt, N A Coe, T Dunsby
1989 May 7 **Kendo Nagasaki, Cliché upon Cliché, Wax on Wheels** M J Crocker, P Oxley
1989 May 8 **Lazy Days and Summer Haze** P Oxley, J Williams
1989 May 10 **Victims of Fashion** P Oxley, J Williams, H Venables
1989 May 10 **Weakest to the Wall, No Soft Option** P Oxley
1989 May 11 **So Hardcore** P Oxley
1989 May 11 **This Is the Life** P Oxley (solo), J Williams
1989 May 11 **One Cool Vibe** P Oxley
1989 May 11 **Black, Layback Chimney** J Williams (on-sight solo)
1989 May 11 **Cocteau Phenomena** P Oxley
1989 May 13 **Desireless, Loco** N A Coe, T Dunsby, S L Titt
1989 May 13 **Zit** T Dunsby, N Coe (both solo)
1989 May 13 **On the Boil** S L Titt, N A Coe
1989 May 13 **The Fat Controller** T Dunsby, N A Coe
1989 May 14 **My Love of This Land** P Oxley
1989 May 14 **Portland Heights** P Oxley
1989 May 19 **Nobody's Hero, Chaos UK** M J Crocker
1989 May 19 **Senseless Thing** M J Crocker
1989 May 20 **Acid Jazz Disco, The Montreal Protocol** M J Crocker
1989 May **Midnight Oil** B Tilley, N Willit
Originally had improved holds, which were later repaired.
1989 May **Gunbarrel Highway, Boys from the Loose Stuff** B Tilley

A pioneering Portland team! Martin Crocker, Pete Oxley and Gordon Jenkin showing off their sartorial elegance NIGEL COE

1989 May **Explorator Motivator** R White, B Tilley
1989 June **Cunning Lingo** J Williams (solo)
1989 June **San Andreas** T Dunsby, H Venables
1989 July 2 **Shatter My Illusions but Don't Break My Heart** S L Titt, N A Coe
1989 July 5 **Reverence, Outside the Gate** P Oxley, B Tilley
1989 July 8 **Poppadom** T Dunsby, H Venables, N A Coe
1989 July 8 **Pining for Glossop** H Venables, N A Coe, T Dunsby
1989 July 11 **1789** P Oxley
1989 July 11 **Best Fingers Forward** P Oxley
1989 July 11 **China White** B Tilley, P Oxley
1989 July 11 **Sink the Bismark** P Oxley, M Williams
1989 July 13 **The Enchanted Path** B Tilley, P Oxley, M Williams
1989 July 13 **Hawaiian Pipeline** P Oxley, B Tilley
1989 July 13 **Troll Team Special** P Oxley
1989 July 15 **Accordions Go Crazy, Laughing Peter** M J Crocker
1989 July 16 **On a Desert Island Beach, Coconut Milk** M J Crocker
1989 July 16 **ZumZeaux** M J Crocker, P Oxley
1989 July 27 **Frenzied Detruncation** P Oxley
1989 July 27 **Wave Graffiti** P Oxley (1 rest pt)

First free ascent P Oxley, J Williams on 24 September 1989

Date	Route	Climbers
1989 Aug 5	**Dripping with Blood**	G A Jenkin
1989 Aug 12	**My Dog's Got Fleas, Poop Scoop**	M J Crocker
1989 Aug 13	**The Bigger Piece, Blue Faced Booby, Gossip and Drool** M J Crocker	
1989 Aug 20	**Come Hell or High Water**	P Oxley

Destroyed by rockfall.

1989 Aug 20	**Van People**	B Tilley, P Oxley
1989 Aug 20	**Shining Heart**	P Oxley

Formerly Don't Let the Teardrops Rust Your Shining Heart.

1989 Aug 25	**High on the Richter Scale**	T Dunsby, R Mardon
1989 Sept 1	**Grip '89 (Audi 80 v. The Law)**	P Oxley, M Williams

Destroyed by rockfall.

1989 Sept 1	**Face the Truth**	P Oxley
1989 Sept 1	**Bob's Gold Run, Running down a Dream**	P Oxley
1989 Sept 7	**Heatstroke Groove**	P Oxley

Formerly Do We Learn From All the Pain?

1989 Sept 24	**Realm of Chaos**	P Oxley
1989 Sept 25	**Disintegration**	P Oxley
1989 Dec 27	**Eternity's Toothpaste**	N A Coe, N Holley, S L Titt, T Dunsby
1989 Dec 31	**The Watchman, Peace in the Nineties**	P Oxley
1990 Jan 20	**That Chill Divine**	G A Jenkin, N A Coe
1990 Jan 27	**Xerdna**	N A Coe, S L Titt
1990 March 27	**A Shadow on Mankind**	P Oxley
1990 March 27	**Ecstasy**	P Oxley
1990 April 1	**The Wax Museum**	M J Crocker
1990 April 15	**Dumbfounded!**	M J Crocker
1990 April 15	**Rusty Chublock Seeks Oil of Lubrication**	M J Crocker
1990 April 15	**Mousefolk, Infernal Din**	M J Crocker
1990 April 16	**Haute Cuisine, The Mouth Waters**	M J Crocker
1990 April 29	**Looking for Love, Hot Flush**	S L Titt, N A Coe, T Dunsby
1990 April 29	**The Bournemouth Flier**	T Dunsby, N A Coe, S L Titt
1990 April 30	**A Mask of Self Hate**	P Oxley
1990 May 11	**Sweet Smell of Success**	P Oxley
1990 May 11	**Precious to the Last**	P Oxley
1990 June 10	**Running It In!**	M J Crocker
1990 June	**Scapa Flow, Chappaquiddic**	P Oxley, M Ford
1990 July 10	**No Man's an Island, Always Have the Edge, Buoys Will Be Buoys**	P Oxley
1990 July 11	**Psychic EMF**	P Oxley
1990 July 11	**Searing Tunnel of Re-Injury, God Told Me to Skin You Alive**	P Oxley
1990 July 13	**The Price of Potatoes**	G Jefferies (solo)
1990 July 13	**Screaming Toilet Fish**	G Jefferies
1990 July 13	**Oscourt**	G Jefferies
1990 July 17	**Twistin' My Melon, Man**	P Oxley (solo)
1990 July 17	**So You Want to Be Happy?, Stay Golden, Hallelujah!, Def Con One**	P Oxley
1990 July 18	**Info Freako**	P Oxley

A two-day ascent.

1990 July 22	**This Is This, Wake Up, Time to Die, Like a Drowning Man, Listing Badly, She's Going Down!**	P Oxley, C Appleby
1990 July 25	**Zinc Oxide Mountain**	P Oxley
1990 July 25	**Leave My Soul Alone**	P Oxley (on-sight solo)
1990 July	**Redundancy Crack**	J Haine
1990 Aug 19	**Breakbeat**	M J Crocker
1990 Sept 16	**After the Goldrush**	N A Coe
1990 Sept 23	**Saskatchawan Uranium Miner**	M J Crocker
1990 Sept 23	**The Bad Seeds**	M J Crocker
1990 Oct 14	**Rag 'n' Bone Man**	P Oxley
1990 Oct 20	**Maud in Memoria**	M Ford, P Oxley
1990 Oct 21	**End of the Pier**	T Dunsby, N A Coe
1990 Nov 3	**Hall of Mirrors**	P Oxley
1990 Nov 4	**The Sears Tower**	P Oxley
1990 Nov 5	**White Baron, Gunpowder Plot**	P Oxley (both roped solo)
1990 Nov 5	**Too Many Cooks Spoil the Broth**	P Oxley
1990 Nov 7	**Sub Youth, Flowers On The Razor Wire**	P Oxley.
1990 Nov 7	**Stompin' with Bez, Bend Sinister**	P Oxley (both solo)
1990 Nov	**The Mind Terrorist**	P Oxley (1 rest pt)

First free ascent P Oxley on 13 January 1991.

1990 Nov	**Head of Steam**	P Oxley (on-sight solo)
1990 Dec 16	**Electrically Injected Shed Head**	M Ford, P Oxley
1990 Dec 16	**Splat the Cat**	P Oxley
1990	**Mr Angry**	M Hamblin (on-sight solo)
1991 Jan 13	**Hillman the Hunter**	S Taylor, E Flood, P Oxley
1991 Jan 13	**The New Saladin**	P Oxley, S Taylor
1991 Jan 14	**Another Notch in the Gun, Driven Like the Snow**	P Oxley
1991 Jan 27	**Dreams Burn Down**	P Oxley
1991 Feb 2	**Spontaneous Cattle Combustion**	P Oxley, P Cummings
1991 Feb 2	**UK Subs**	P Oxley
1991 Feb 2	**Fear's Younger Brother**	S Taylor, E Flood

"It's not that scary. It's like, well, Fear's Younger Brother" Eamonn Flood.

1991 March 24	**Want Out**	M J Crocker
1991 March 25	**Junk Gun Fever**	P Oxley

Destroyed by rockfall.

1991 April 10	**Cadwallader**	S Taylor, S Kerr
1991 April 12	**Bad Moon Rising**	P Oxley

Spring-tides cut off the whole team; one of the problems with lower-offs!

1991 April 13	**What Gives My Son?**	P Oxley

1991 April 13	**The Feedback Monster, Full Fathom Five** P Oxley, M Ford
	The former has been destroyed by rockfall.
1991 May 11	**Smashing Orange, Drive Blind** P Oxley, P Cummings
1991 May 11	**Pastoral** P Oxley (on-sight solo)
1991 June 22	**Snorkelling amongst Sharks** M J Crocker
	Destroyed by rockfall.
1991 June 29	**Brooklyn Bimbo** M J Crocker
1991 July 17	**Quick as Rainbows** P Oxley
1991 July 17	**Aeon Flux** P Oxley
1991 July 17	**Under the Sky, inside the Sea** P Oxley
1991 Aug 8	**Fleshworld** P Oxley
1991 Aug 8	**Gedge** P Oxley
1991 Oct 6	**Bridget Riley** N A Coe, T Dunsby, S L Titt
1991 Oct 6	**Brief Encounter** T Dunsby, S L Titt, N A Coe
1991 Oct 6	**The Potting Shed** S L Titt, N A Coe, T Dunsby
1991 Oct 12	**Overture Chimney** S L Titt, N A Coe
1991 Oct 12	**Resurgent Spirit of Loose** N A Coe, S L Titt
1991 Oct 12	**Enlightenment** N A Coe, S L Titt (VL)
1991 Nov 2	**Old Buffer** T Dunsby, N A Coe, S L Titt
1991 Nov 2	**Round the Bend** T Dunsby, N A Coe, S L Titt (VL)
1991 Nov 10	**Broadway** M J Crocker
1991 Nov 10	**Manhatten Skyline** M J Crocker, P Oxley
1991 Dec 1	**Arc of a Fridge** P Oxley
1991	**The Cruel Sea** S Taylor
	On sight solo in the dark! Kindly bolted by M Ward, 2003.
1992 April 12	**Going Blank Again** P Oxley, D B Cook, D M Cook, J M Cook
1992 April 12	**Useless Generation** P Oxley, D M Cook
1992 April 12	**Teenage Lust** P Oxley
	The staple makes its first appearance on Portland.
1992 April 19	**Catatonic** P Oxley, M J Crocker
1992 April 19	**Mr Natural, Downhill Spiral** P Oxley, M J Crocker
1992 April 20	**Moan, Moan, Moan** M J Crocker
1992 April 25	**Injury Encyclopedia** M J Crocker
1992 April 26	**Son of Mustang Ford** P Oxley, M J Crocker
1992 April 26	**Million Watt Marshalls** P Oxley, M J Crocker
1992 April 26	**Spinal Tap** P Oxley, M J Crocker
1992 May 2	**Cool to Be Uncool, Mick Lovatt Stole My Trousers** M J Crocker
1992 May 2	**Summer Babe, Slavestate** P Oxley
1992 May 2	**Opposites Attract, No Place for Mambas** M J Crocker, P Oxley
1992 May 30	**The Treacle Factory** A Cook, D B Cook
	A fourth Cook brother joins the new-route scene.
1992 May 30	**Old Painless** J M Cook

1992 June 7	**John Craven's Jumper Contest** P Oxley
	John Craven stated that he was pleased to be honoured in such a way on the BBC TV programme Countryfile. No-one thought to mention the other route named after him at Dancing Ledge – John Craven's Willy Warmer!
1992 July 2	**Never Loose That Feeling** P Oxley
1992 July 5	**The Martyr** S Taylor, P Oxley
1992 July 5	**Live Now, Pay Later** P Oxley
1992 July 5	**They Walked in Line** P Oxley, S Taylor
1992 July 8	**The Watchmaker's Hands** P Oxley
1992 July 12	**Headwall Emptiness** P Oxley
1992 July 17	**Lost in Rock** P Oxley
1992 July 25	**Hot Pants Explosion** N Heanes
1992 July 31	**The Stoning of St Steven** P Oxley, J Gandy
	Originally Taylor's project. The pockets were modified to make a dyno less painful.
1992 July 31	**Training for Hubble** P Oxley, J Gandy
1992 Aug 15	**Youth Body Expression Explosion** P Oxley
1992 Aug 18	**Unsung** P Oxley, D B Cook
1992 Aug 29	**Breakfast of Champions** D B Cook
1992 Aug 29	**Jungle Drums, The Unworthy** J M Cook

Joff Cook on a very early repeat of *Wolfgang Forever* F7a (page 41). COOK COLLECTION

First Ascents

1992 Aug 29	**Lats, Babes 'n' Bolts** P Oxley	
1992 Aug 31	**Subterfuge** N A Coe, J Walmsley	
1992 Sept 4	**Seattle Be the Day, Ironhead** P Oxley, J Williams, M Dutson	
	The flowstone revolution begins.	
1992 Sept 4	**England's Dreaming** P Oxley	
1992 Sept 5	**Onto the Icefloe** D B Cook, N A Coe	
1992 Sept 5	**Ximenesque** J M Cook, N A Coe	
1992 Sept 12	**Reptile Smile** P Oxley, D B Cook	
	Thought by many to be the best route on the island.	
1992 Sept 12	**Downtown Julie Brown** P Oxley, D B Cook, J M Cook	
1992 Sept 12	**Henry Rollins for President** P Oxley	
1992 Sept 12	**Very Sleepy River** D B Cook	
1992 Sept 13	**Slug** N A Coe, C Dunsby, T Dunsby	
1992 Sept 20	**Beer and Corruption, The Death of Cool** P Oxley, S Taylor	
1992 Oct 3	**Gaze of the Gorgon** T Dunsby, N A Coe	
	Mistakenly retrobolted and renamed Vaci U, by D B Cook.	
1992 Oct 3	**Is Vic There?** S Taylor, J M Cook	
1992 Oct 4	**Wolfgang Forever, Quakin' in My Bones** P Oxley	
1992 Oct 10	**Last of the Summer Wine** T Dunsby, S L Titt, R Elder, N A Coe	
1992 Oct 10	**Bob's Big Mistake** S L Titt, R Elder, N A Coe	
	The mistake involved a large poorly-attached block.	
1992 Oct 10	**Klepto Krack** N A Coe, T Dunsby, S L Titt	
1992 Oct 10	**Cakewalk** S Taylor, J M Cook	
1992 Oct 11	**Appleturnoverload** J M Cook	
1992 Oct 31	**Suck, Don't Blow** A Cook	
1992 Oct	**Meg's Got Leukaemia** S Vaughan	
1992 Nov 3	**Freaky Ralph** P Oxley	
	Over five days.	
1992 Nov 7	**Trad Free World** P Oxley, S Taylor, S Vaughan	
1992 Nov 8	**Mother's Milk** S Cook	
	Portland is overrun by the Cook brothers; a fifth becomes a first ascensionist.	
1992	**Lost Army Expedition** B Tilley	
	Retrobolted and straightened by S Taylor, 1994.	
1993 Feb 7	**Imbolc** N White, C Alston	
	A single, important, addition from the author of the Devon guide. 7b or 7b+? – the debate continues.	
1993 Feb 7	**No Me Comas el Coco** J Biddle, P Oxley, D B Cook, S Taylor	
1993 Feb 13	**Hot from the Forge** P Oxley, D B Cook, S Taylor, J M Cook	
1993 Feb 14	**Boilermaker** P Oxley	
1993 Feb 16	**Keelhaul** D B Cook	
1993 Feb 17	**Actually (Shit Happens), 21½ Weeks** M Robertson, P Oxley, D B Cook, J M Cook	
1993 Feb 20	**Hysterical Solitude** M Robertson	

Mike Robertson making the second ascent of *Forget Columbus* F7a+ (page 199). STEVE TAYLOR

1993 Feb 20	**Kit Kat** J Walker	
1993 Feb	**Protein Delta Strip** J M Cook	
1993 March 6	**Crucifix Kiss** P Oxley	
1993 March 6	**Twangy Pearl** D B Cook, P Oxley	
1993 March 6	**Nothing Is Cool** S Taylor, P Oxley	
1993 March 7	**Retaining the Ashes** S Taylor, P Oxley	
	Nicked from Aussie Simon Vaughn.	
1993 March 13	**Apfelstrudel** Ms A Jende, C Guter	
1993 March 20	**Captain Klutz and the Sailors of Fortune** S Taylor, P Oxley	

1993 April 14	**Pump Hitler** P Oxley, S Taylor	
1993 April 16	**Jurassic Shift, Nihil** P Oxley	
1993 April 17	**Never Drive a Car When You're Dead** S Taylor, P Oxley	
1993 April 18	**Eternal Spider** P Oxley	
1993 April 20	**Walking the King** P Oxley	
1993 April 28	**Drag Racing Underground** P Oxley	
1993 April 28	**Dr Phibes** P Oxley, S Taylor	
1993 May 28	**Fantasy Island** M Higgs, P Oxley	
1993 May 28	**In on the Kill Taker** P Oxley, M Higgs	
1993 May 28	**Paint a Black Picture, Prison Sex** P Oxley	
1993 June 6	**Forget Columbus** P Oxley, J Boyle, M Robertson	
1993 June 13	**Intimate Dancing** M Robertson, S Taylor (both solo)	

The introduction to deep-water soloing on Portland for Robertson and Taylor.

1993 June 13	**Spittle and Spume** M Robertson, S Taylor (solo)
1993 June 13	**Robertson's Jan** S Taylor (solo)
1993 July 10	**Fat Falling Pigs** G A Jenkin, G Gibson

Gibson's only contribution to the island. That is, until 2002!

1993 Aug 26	**The Bolt Factory** S Taylor, M Bateman
1993 Aug 28	**Edgehog** S Taylor, G Fitch
1993 Aug 28	**The Last Suitcase Before the Holocaust** S Taylor
1993 Sept 4	**Raising the Titanic** S Taylor, M Bateman
1993 Sept 18	**Coming Unstuck, Hang On to Your Ego** S Taylor, M Williams.
1993 Sept 18	**Braer Rabbit** S Taylor (solo)

Named in memory of the shipwrecked oil tanker.

1993 Sept 25	**Wave Dodging** J M Cook, M Higgs, S Taylor

The name refers to a game played by the Cook Clan on Boscombe Pier in heavy seas.

1993 Oct 9	**Dirty Cow** D B Cook, J M Cook
1993 Nov 2	**Buried Violence** P Oxley
1993 Nov 6	**Hate the Sin and Love the Sinner** N A Coe (on-sight solo)

Ghandi's dictum seemed appropriate for a line climbed in a knee-jerk response to the unnecessary bolting of the neighbouring crack. Bolted without the permission of the first ascensionist by G Gibson May 2006.

1993 Nov 7	**The Secret Garden** S Taylor, M Williams
1993 Nov 7	**The Beauty of Decay** M Robertson, S Taylor, M Williams
1993 Nov 14	**Little Pinky** M Robertson, M Higgs, M Williams
1993	**Price of Silence** M Bateman
1993	**Pregnant Pause** J Courtier, J Robertson

Robertson's last route prior to giving up climbing for 10 years!

1994 Jan 16	**The Cones of Stress** P Oxley
1994 Feb 5	**El Poder de un Coño** M Robertson, D M Cook
1994 Feb 5	**Live by the Sword** P Oxley, D Ardron
1994 Feb 8	**Thumbs Up, Thumbs Down** S L Titt, N A Coe
1994 Feb 13	**Doolittle** E de Stefani

1994 March 14	**Weird Shit – Keep Drilling** J M Cook.

Cook witnessed a strange procession re-enacting an ancient ritual in the boulder field while bolting this line. The name comes from Oxley's comment at the time.

1994 March 19	**The Great Escape, Beach Madness** M Robertson, M Williams
1994 March 20	**Hong Kong Phooey** D B Cook
1994 March 26	**Diamond Boulder** S L Titt, Miss P Holt
1994 April 9	**Bastard Crack** S Taylor, M Williams
1994 April 9	**Clamped Aggression** M Williams, S Taylor
1994 April 10	**Bay of Rainbows** D M Cook

Still sporting a resin crimp 10 years later.

1994 April 14	**Fighting Torque** P Oxley

On day four.

1994 April 16	**Snakes Alive** P Oxley, B Tilley, Ms J Rostron
1994 April 18	**To Wish the Impossible** P Oxley
1994 April 23	**Krakatoa, Etna** S Taylor, M Williams, M Robertson, G Fitch
1994 April 23	**Popocatepetl** S Taylor, M Williams, M Robertson
1994 April 23	**Tipping the Scales** S Taylor, G Fitch
1994 April 24	**The Breathing Method** P Oxley
1994 April 24	**Cosa Nostra** E de Stefani
1994 April 25	**The Bellybutton Traverse, Cornflake Girl** M Robertson, M Williams
1994 April 28	**Stay on Target** J M Cook
1994 April 29	**Modern Nightmare** P Oxley, M Ryan, M Radtke, M Johnston
1994 May 7	**The Leer of Beethoven** M Robertson
1994 May 8	**The Web** E de Stefani
1994 May 8	**Can't Stop the Bosch, So Shoot Me** J M Cook
1994 June 12	**Plyometrically Speaking** P Oxley
1994 June 12	**Kill a Gent's Tart** P Oxley, B Tilley

Can you work out the anagram?

1994 June 13	**Obscene Gesture (Part 2), Sad Young Biscuits** M Robertson, M Williams.

Development of White Hole begins.

1994 June 26	**Splendid Isolation** S Taylor, G Dixon.
1994 June 26	**The Codebreaker and the French Teacher, The Skin Trade** M Robertson, M Williams
1994 June	**Mirthmaid** D B Cook
1994 July 10	**Kamikaze Moped** P Oxley
1994 July 10	**Cute Ass, The Oldest Profession** P Oxley, Ms J Rostron
1994 July 14	**The Erogenous Stone** N A Coe (on-sight solo)
1994 July 16	**Faceache** (White Hole) M Robertson, M Williams
1994 July 18	**Road Rage** P Oxley
1994 July 22	**Rocket from the Crypt, Coralized** P Oxley
1994 July 22	**The Pigskin Bus Pulls In to Tuna Town** P Oxley, Ms J Rostron
1994 July 23	**Pitchfork Disney, The Portland Screw** N A Coe, T Dunsby

First Ascents

1994 July 31	**Temporary Lifestyle** M Robertson (on-sight solo)	
1994 Aug 5	**Streaky, Walking on Sunshine** M Robertson, M Williams	
1994 Aug 5	**The Great Pretender** M Robertson, D B Cook	
1994 Aug 6	**Dead in Europe, Too Funky (For Me)** M Robertson, M Williams	
1994 Aug 6	**Memory Lane** M Williams, M Robertson (alternate pitches, both on-sight solo)	
1994 Aug 6	**The Big Easy, Foxy Chicks, Babes and Bedsheets** M Robertson (on-sight solo)	
1994 Aug 8	**Toothless Vampire** W Jones	
1994 Aug 19	**We Are Not Men, We Are Roto** N Heanes, W Jones	
1994 Aug 20	**15 Minutes to Fame** S Taylor, M Robertson (both solo). *Taylor couldn't wait for the glue to dry on the bolts, so the route was soloed.*	
1994 Aug 20	**Bungle, Zippy and George** M Williams, M Robertson, S Taylor (last two solo)	
1994 Aug 20	**Penny Lane** M Williams, M Robertson, S Taylor (all solo)	
1994 Aug 29	**Pandemonium** P Oxley	
1994 Sept 4	**Sign of the Vulcan** P Oxley	
1994 Sept 5	**Run, Rabbit, Run, Wafer Thin, Tickled Pink, Red Raw** P Oxley	
1994 Sept 16	**The Reign of Steel, End of Season Sale, Funnel Web, The Pipers of Portland** P Oxley	
1994 Sept 18	**Mid-Strife Oasis** P Oxley	
1994 Sept 21	**Xavier's Wall** P Oxley, Ms J Rostron	
1994 Sept 21	**Actions Speak Louder** P Oxley	
1994 Sept 27	**The Empire State Arête** P Oxley	
1994 Sept 30	**Biscuits for Smut** P Oxley	
1994 Sept	**Frazzled** D B Cook	
1994 Oct 1	**Vespasian** P Oxley *Portland's hardest route required six days of effort and waited 9 years for a repeat ascent.*	
1994 Oct 1	**Staple Diet, The Feather** S Taylor, Ms M Huisman	
1994 Oct 27	**Lusty Wedlock Needs Coil of Prevention** P Oxley	
1994 Nov 1	**Magical Mr Mephistopheles** P Oxley, Ms J Rostron	
1994 Nov 6	**Razzamatazz** P Oxley	
1994 Nov 15	**Drowning on Dry Land** M Robertson, D B Cook	
1994 Nov 19	**Thick as Thieves** S Taylor, M Williams	
1994 Nov 19	**Nothing's Shocking** S Taylor, M Williams, M Robertson	
1994 Nov 19	**Three in a Bed** G Dixon	
1994 Nov 23	**Blowing the Gimp** P Oxley, Ms J Rostron	
1994 Nov 26	**California Hot Licks** G A Jenkin, A March, K Marsden	
1994 Dec 1	**Nobody Runs for Free** P Oxley (on-sight solo)	
1994 Dec 11	**Crush with Eyeliner** N A Coe, I Birch	
1994 Dec 17	**Found under Carnal Knowledge** M Robertson	
1994	**Sergeant Ford's Roving Truncheon** J M Cook, D B Cook (AL)	

1994	**Jane Says** J M Cook	
1994	**The Route With No Name** M Robertson (solo)	
1995 Feb 25	**The Nightmare Scenario, Deadlossky Must Die!** P Oxley	
1995 Feb 26	**Cerebellum, Crown of Thorns** P Oxley	
1995 March 4	**Mexican Stand-off, Natural Born Drillers** P Oxley	
1995 March 26	**Portland Exclusion Zone** S Taylor, M Robertson. *The name alludes to the evacuation of much of Portland due to the disarming of an unexploded bomb.*	
1995 April 9	**Diamond Solitaire** S Taylor (on-sight solo – in trainers)	
1995 April 23	**Bar Room Brawl** P Oxley	
1995 April 30	**Wharfedale Boyz** P Oxley	
1995 April 30	**Do Ixtlan** D B Cook *Two drilled holds were created to ease the finishing moves. The first ascentionist was more than capable of doing the route clean, but wanted to make the route more do-able by less talented climbers.*	
1995 April 30	**Imperfect** D B Cook *Sadly containing drilled holds to maintain a consistent grade of climbing throughout. The belay was lowered several months after the first ascent as the chipped finish was believed to be too hard.*	
1995 April 30	**It's My Life** Ms J Wylie	
1995 April	**Ixtlan** D B Cook (on-sight solo) *The start of a prolific deep-water solo summer on Portland.*	
1995 May 1	**Shades of the Deep** M Robertson	
1995 May 1	**Octopus Weed** D M Cook, J M Cook, M Robertson, G Dixon	
1995 May 6	**Aaron the Aardvark, Bladerunner** M Robertson, S Taylor. *Robertson makes a play to be first in the alphabetical list.*	
1995 May 6	**Spare Rib, Ausfahrt** M Robertson	
1995 May 6	**Go With The Flow** M Robertson	
1995 May 6	**Law of the Jungle** P Oxley	
1995 May 7	**No Victory in Europe** P Oxley	
1995 May 7	**Boiled Lobster** Mrs H Heanes, N Heanes. *The neglected Pit Prop Crag gets a dusting off.*	
1995 May 7	**Another One for the Pot, Reinheitsgebot** N Heanes, Mrs H Heanes	
1995 May 7	**Slim Fingers' Revenge** N Heanes	
1995 May 7	**Air Hoodlum** P Oxley	
1995 May 8	**Twisting by the Pool, Reservoir Dogfish** D B Cook	
1995 May 8	**Jaws, Karma** M Robertson (second route on-sight solo)	
1995 May 8	**Previous Top-rope Problem** D B Cook. *A dig by the first ascentionist at an over-used put-down in the Rockfax guide.*	
1995 May 8	**Purple Shorts** G Dixon, T Dunsby, M Robertson	
1995 May 13	**Niagara Wall** M Robertson	
1995 May 13	**Fly the Friendly Skies** P Oxley	

1995 May 14	**Forensic Scene** P Oxley, D Ardron
1995 May 14	**Red Medicine** P Oxley
1995 May 15	**The Little Hard** M Robertson (on-sight solo)
1995 May 15	**Mad about You, Bare Reputation** M Robertson (on-sight solo)
1995 May 17	**Read the Small Print** S Taylor, M Bateman.
1995 May 19	**Blame it on the Drain** D B Cook
1995 May 19	**Captain Haddock, Up the Grotto** M Robertson (on-sight solo)
1995 May 19	**Flipper Force** D B Cook (on-sight solo).

A later repeat attempt by Joff Cook ended with a soaking following the loss of a hold. While falling, he was heard to scream "Take, take,… shit!"

1995 May 19	**Ooh, Lovely!, Crab Party** M Robertson (on-sight solo).
1995 May 19	**Blame it on the Drain** D B Cook
1995 May 21	**Reel 'em In** D B Cook (on-sight solo)
1995 May 27	**Losing My Sad Tomato** M Robertson
1995 May 27	**La Cranium Cassé** D B Cook
1995 May 28	**Six Good Biceps** J Cook
1995 May 29	**The Swinging Nineties** P Oxley
1995 May 29	**Cybernetic Orchard** P Oxley
1995 May 31	**Seeing is Believing** P Oxley
1995 June 1	**Bushwacked** D B Cook

Another drilled route. Oxley abseiled the line to smash off the improved holds, but unfortunately removed some natural holds instead. The drilled undercut remains.

1995 June 6	**Ausfahrt** M Robertson
1995 June 9	**Godzuki, Lick of the Cat** D B Cook
1995 June 9	**Desperado** M Robertson
1995 June 9	**Pirates of the Black Atlantic** D B Cook

Soloed first as a downclimb.

1995 June 10	**Different for Girls, Kisses and Lies, High Klicks, 100 Reasons to be Cheerful, Bachelor Boy and the SR 500** M Robertson

Roberton develops a new sector, including his 100th recorded new route.

1995 June 10	**Doughnuts and Duvets** S Taylor, M Robertson
1995 June 10	**Psycho Man, Marine Boy** M Robertson
1995 June 10	**Slumberland Direct** S Taylor

Taylor straightens up an existing trad line against the wishes of the first ascensionist.

1995 June 11	**Russian Roulette** M Robertson

A 30-minute epic.

1995 June 11	**Skank Central** D B Cook
1995 June 11	**Aeroforce** J Cook
1995 June 16	**Shoobedoobabada** S Taylor, M Bateman

1995 June 18	**Burning Skies** P Oxley

One of Portland's best routes is climbed on a cliff previously thought to be worked out.

1995 June 25	**The Jewel of the Isle** P Oxley
1995 June 25	**Project A** D M Cook
1995 June 25	**Flowstone Shuffle/Unstuck on You** J Cook/P Oxley

A highly controversial route which contained two glued-on pieces of flowstone to ease the crux. The resulting discussions were extremely heated. The offending holds were subsequently removed and the route reascended by P Oxley on the date above.

1995 June	**Zimmerframe with Attitude** N Heanes
1995 June	**Ninth Wave** L Percival
1995 July 2	**Meltdown** N Heanes

The upper half of this route is a retrobolt of High on the Richter Scale.

1995 July 8	**Limpet-Fest** J Cook

'Tap them, then crimp on them'

1995 July 9	**The Fabulous Bakery Boys, Sandcastles** P Twomey, N Heanes
1995 July 9	**Captain Lob Meets the Nipple Pincher** N Heanes, P Twomey, Mrs H Heanes.

The consequences of holding a belay device too close to your chest!

1995 July 19	**Wynona's Big Brown Beaver** P Twomey
1995 July 19	**Mindmeld** M Vaicaitis
1995 July 23	**Mike's Free Willy** D B Cook
1995 July 27	**Tentacle Master** J Cook

Two splashdowns before eventual success.

1995 Aug 3	**In Dust We Trust** P Twomey
1995 Aug 4	**Surface Tension** M Robertson
1995 Aug 5	**Makin' Bacon** M Robertson
1995 Aug 7	**Osaki Dolphin** P Oxley
1995 Aug 11	**Aquamarina** S Taylor

Taylor's second of three deep-water solo contributions to the Isle, but certainly one of the most technical.

1995 Aug 11	**Trashy's Traverse** M Robertson

Soloed on the highest spring-tide of the summer.

1995 Aug 13	**Corinthian Spirit, Return to Roissy** P Oxley

The one natural line on this face finally gets an ascent.

1995 Aug 16	**The Lip Traverse** D M Cook
1995 Aug 19	**Draper's Henchmen, Silent But Deadly** P Oxley

Oxley nips in to claim the line right of The Devil, bolted and failed on by Damian Cook.

1995 Aug 21	**An Ideal for Living, Time Bomb** P Oxley
1995 Aug 21	**Winning at Rodeo** M Higgs
1995 Aug 24	**The Lizard of Oz** Ms J Rostron
1995 Aug 26	**Gourmet Shit Traverse** M Robertson

First Ascents

1995 Aug 27	**King of the Swingers** P Oxley
1995 Aug	**Gyonyuru** D B Cook
1995 Aug	**My Little Buddha** Ms K Little
1995 Aug	**Sunday Swing** S Taylor
1995 Aug	**Suburban Dave** M Bateman
1995 Aug	**Sketchtastic** J Fletcher
1995 Sept 3	**Skeleton Surfers** M Robertson

Success came after splashdown when attempting the line from the far corner of the cave.

1995 Sept 3	**Killer Loop** J Cook

Three spotters on the first ascent.

1995 Sept 16	**Once Were Warriors** P Oxley.

Harder and now bold since the loss of a large block in the roof.

1995 Sept 17	**Fireblade** G Dixon
1995 Sept	**Magician's Trap** D M Cook

Dominic's initial attempts were captured on film for the programme Under the Sky, Above the Sea.

1995 Oct 1	**The White Unconquerable** P Oxley
1995 Oct 14	**Trent Reznor** P Oxley
1995 Nov 17	**Disobedience Contest** M Robertson

Robertson uses the new CC guide to identify one of several gaps at The Cuttings.

1995 Nov 23	**Figgy Dropwise** M Robertson
1995 Nov 23	**Dusty Fred's Winter Collection** J Cook
1995 Nov 26	**The Holy Hand Grenade** M Robertson
1995 Dec 1	**Toe the Line** J Cook
1995 Dec 8	**The Long Walk** M Robertson
1995 Dec	**Resisting Mutiny** G Wright
1995	**The Singing Bush, Pitch in the Ditch, Rock Logs, Dump Pump, This Shit's Something, Eight Bar Blues** J Cook
1995	**Bushwacked, Gold Dust, Ditch the Bitch** D B Cook
1995	**Up, Up and Away, Escape Route, Waterfall Wall** P Oxley (last two solo)
1995	**We're Only Placing Bolts for Nigel, Corporal Punishment, Eat, Stick and Die, On Manoeuvres, Arc Angel, Charity Work, Mate, Magical Misty Tour, Bonsai, Sting in the Tail, Juggernaut, Rock Lobster, Amazonia, Definitely Maybe** N Heanes, Mrs H Heanes and members of Basingstoke Mountaineering Club
1996 Feb	**Flickhead Goes Boing Boing, Hats off to the Insane, Trashcan Man, Setting the Date, Champagne Supernova** S Taylor
1996 Feb	**Andy Wallhole** J Waddington, S Taylor (both led)

Taylor gets a whole crag to himself, bar one route!

1996 March 16	**Esmerelda's Monkey** M Robertson, N Heanes

Robertson climbs the longest route, to date, on Portland. Most of the line was soloed by Crocker on 9.6.2001!

Pete Oxley on the first ascent of Honorary Froggatt F7b+ (page 231). HELEN HEANES

1996 March 17	**Quite Nice, Actually, No Chutney on his Ferret** N Heanes
1996 March 17	**Chapter and Verse, Oatsheaf Chief** Mrs H Heanes
1996 March 19	**Honorary Froggatt, Pocketful of Shells** P Oxley
1996 March 24	**Into the Sun** N Heanes
1996 March 27	**Burbage Belle** P Oxley (solo)
1996 April 4	**L'Eau Profile, Private Dancer** P Oxley
1996 April 4	**Thirty Years Young** P Oxley (solo)
1996 April 7	**Nightmirth** P Oxley
1996 April 28	**Left Little Slapper, Right Little Slapper** J Kimber

Both subsequently soloed by Kimber, though one fall resulted in a broken ankle.

1996 April 28	**The Blandford Weasel** P Oxley
1996 April 30	**Illusions** J Cook
1996 April	**Yesterday's Dreams** M Roberston
1996 May 9	**Ariane V** P Oxley
1996 May 11	**Genuflection** P Oxley
1996 May 21	**Teacakes Calling** P Oxley
1996 May 28	**Blackthorn Winter** S Taylor, D M Cook (both led)
1996 May	**Suits You Sir!** N Heanes
1996 June 2	**The Singing Bush** J Cook

1996 June 6	**The Green Bearded Roof, Hombre Solaire** P Oxley
1996 June 27	**Do You Like Our Owls** N Hellyer
1996 June 29	**The Vulcanites** P Oxley
1996 June	**The Ghost of Saturday Night** S Taylor
1996 June	**The Best Men** S Taylor, M Williams

Both ascentionists had recently been asked to do the honours.

1996 July 15 **CC Backstabbers** P Oxley
Oxley was mightily aggrieved at the perceived anti-bolt stance of the 1995 CC guide.

1996 July 18 **Pilot of the Future** P Oxley
1996 July 20 **Ocean Boulevard** B Slattery
1996 July 22 **Walking the Plank** P Oxley
1996 July 25 **Glamour Cat** Ms J Rostron
1996 July 25 **Lifeline** D Glover
1996 July 26 **Ecosystem** M Vaicaitis
1996 July 28 **Supergeek** P Oxley
1996 July 30 **Spare the Fern** J Leonard
1996 July **Toes Curl** W Jones
1996 Aug 4 **Another Stone on the Pile of Choss** J Kimber
Kimber steals Hellyer's project and makes a personal statement.

1996 Aug 15 **Where's Blue Hippo** N Heanes
1996 Aug 28 **Wiggy and Mopokes Excellent New Hilti, A Dream of White Porsches** N Hellyer
1996 Aug 28 **Zen Zero** P Oxley
1996 August **Staring at the Sea, Underwater Love** P Oxley
1996 August **Talking Smack, Spanner Eyes** W Jones
1996 Sept 5 **Mono Y Mono** J Kimber
Project stolen from Vaicaitis.

1996 Sept 8 **Bermuda Triangle, Sale of the Century** P Oxley
The second line was 'gifted' by Taylor to Oxley.

1996 Sept 8 **Coming of Age** Ms J Rostron, P Oxley, M Higgs
1996 Sept 14 **A Bird in the Hand, Magnetic Pull** P Oxley
1996 Sept 15 **No Survivors, A Meeting of Minds, Lip Service** P Oxley
1996 Sept 28 **Dead by Sunset** P Oxley
1996 Sept **Skin Up** A Ashmore
1996 Sept **Indian Summer** H Heanes
1996 Oct 2 **Knockout Punch, European Flavour** P Oxley
1996 Oct 5 **Hooked Like no Fish Before Me, Vicious Sea Splat, Shot and Wounded, Famous Genitalia, Lunge or Plunge, Mad in Me, Huge Reaches, Massive Amounts of Strength** M Crocker (solo)
1996 Oct 6 **The Devil's Work** N Burton
1996 Oct 14 **Greasepaint and Monkey Brains** N Burton
1996 Oct 19 **If You Should Go Skating...** N Hellyer
1996 Oct 26 **The Big Blue** L Percival
After a long period of failed attempts, Percival finally gets the big tick.

1996 Nov 2 **Hurricane on a Millpond** P Oxley
1996 Dec 7 **The Loneliness of the Long Distance Driller** N Hellyer
Hellyer makes a weekend visit from the big city

1996 **The Unknown Soldier** Unknown
No-one has owned up to this rather fine climb.

1996 **Skating on Thin Ice** N Hellyer
1997 Jan 26 **Error 404, Still My Bleeding Heart** N Hellyer
1997 Jan **Social Lepers** N Heanes
1997 Feb **Plystalker** D Henderson
Henderson nicks Percival's project

1997 March 14 **Blowing Chunks** N Heanes
1997 March 16 **Roadkill on the Information Superhighway** N Hellyer
1997 March 28 **Julie Ocean** M Vaicaitis
1997 March **While the Cat's Away** N Heanes
1997 April 4 **Aim High, Shoot Low** N Hellyer
1997 April 5 **The Sound of One Hold Snapping, Dwarf Lops** N Hellyer
1997 April 19 **Even Better than the Beatles** S Taylor
1997 April 20 **Jasper** P Cunningham
1997 April 20 **The Truth is Out There** M Vaicaitis
1997 May 2 **Punter's Way** S Taylor, G Dixon, M Campbell (All led)
1997 May 3 **Jacob's Ladder** M Vaicaitis
1997 May 23 **Darkest Before Dawn, Vampire Killers** P Oxley
1997 May 23 **Space Shanty** C Parker, P Oxley
1997 May 23 **Astra Blaze, Azymuth** P Oxley
1997 May 28 **L'Esprit du Vent** P Oxley
1997 May **Underage** Ms J Rostron
1997 May **Young at Heart** P Oxley
1997 June 4 **The Fun Factory, The Racing Line** P Oxley
1997 June 22 **Bring on the Night** G Jenkin
1997 June 22 **Monsoon Malabar** G Jenkin, M Robertson (both led)
1997 June **Detonata** G Dixon
Taylor finally gives up his project from 1994!

1997 July 1 **Trance Mission** P Oxley
1997 July 5 **Come in and Burn** P Oxley
1997 July 6 **Aquaserene** P Oxley
A neglected area gets the Oxley treatment!

1997 July 20 **Silence of the Deep** P Oxley
1997 July 20 **Tombstone** S Robbins
1997 July 20 **Resistance is Futile** M Vaicaitis
1997 July 23 **Seaman Staines** N Heanes
1997 July 29 **Captain Pugwash** N Heanes
1997 Aug 1 **Master Bates** Mrs H Heanes
1997 Aug 1 **Roger the Cabin Boy** N Burton
1997 August 9 **Te Taniwha** J Dunlop
Probably previously climbed (trad) as Cracked Wall by R Shepton

1997 August 10 **Ben, Willem** P Cunningham
1997 August 10 **Wedding Daze** J Parsons

1997 August 10	**Future Imperfect, Nameless, The Accelerator** M Vaicaitis
1997 August 13	**Lucy's off the Wall, Brace Yourself Shiela** P Cunningham
1997 August 13	**First Contact** M Vaicaitis
1997 August 15	**Gie it Laldy** G Ridge
1997 August 22	**Harpies and Quoins** Ms J Horrocks
1997 August 25	**Valerie's Patio** P Cunningham
1997 August 25	**Starbuck, Tin Man** M Vaicaitis
1997 August 26	**Last Human** M Vaicaitis
1997 August 31	**Where Silence Has Lease** M Vaicaitis
1997 Sept 4	**Cutthroat Jake** Mrs H Heanes
1997 Sept 9	**Lucky Day in Hell, Konked Out, Rags to Rags, Rust to Rust** P Oxley
1997 Sept 14	**The Lost Buoys** P Oxley
1997 Sept 14	**Pathfinder** M Vaicaitis
1997 Sept 20	**Heart Full of Nails** P Oxley
1997 Sept 20	**Sidewinder, Dreamscape** M Vaicaitis
1997 Sept 20	**Jody Sunshine** P Cunningham
1997 Sept 20	**Wave Warrior** S Robbins
1997 Sept 21	**One Day, James** A O'Boyle
1997 Sept 27	**The League of Gurus, Sea of Tears, The Underhill Mob** P Oxley
1997 Sept 28	**Welcome to the Gravity Programme** N Hellyer
1997 Oct 4	**Black Pig** N Heanes
1997 Nov 3	**The Shallow End of the Gene Pool** N Hellyer
1997 Dec 12	**Happy to Go Blind** P Oxley
1997	**Smile Please** S Taylor (solo)
1997	**Unknown Arête** Unknown
1997	**Sex, Lies and Videotape, Lifesigns, Truly, Madly, Steeply** M Vaicaitis
1998 Feb 8	**Factor 15** P Church
1998 Feb 14	**Lugwiler's Dismal Itch** N Hellyer
1998 Feb 22	**Talk** N Hellyer
1998 Feb 25	**Karate Kid, Bar Bar Black Sheep, Excalibur's Edge** P Oxley
1998 Feb 28	**Crossing the Boundaries of Affection** J Dunlop
1998 Feb 28	**Memories** J Kimber
1998 April 6	**Reality Bites** Ms J Horrocks, G Ridge
	An excellent climb using some of the existing line of Slumberland.
1998 April 10	**The Running Man** M Williams, G Symonds
1998 April 19	**Through the Barricades** M Robertson
1998 April 26	**Coastguard Ron** M Williams
1998 April	**Where's Me Washboard** N Heanes
	Once one of Portland's more notorious undergradings, leaving many an HVS leader swinging under the final roof.
1998 April	**An Arse With a View** N Heanes
1998 April	**Ocean Drive** Mrs H Heanes
1998 May 2	**Tarquil's Trollies** M Robertson

1998 May 2	**Lefty Hoot 'n' Annie** N Heanes
1998 May 2	**The Sex Cauldren** J Cook
1998 May 2	**Guardian Angel** P Oxley
1998 May 3	**Witchdoctor** D Pickford
1998 May 4	**Bogus Roof** P Oxley
1998 May 9	**New York Dolls** P Oxley, C Collins
1998 May 9	**Chevette de la Mer** A Bell
1998 May 9	**Swimsuit Issue** P Oxley
1998 May 9	**Hate Crime** N Heanes
	For once, a route on Portland which is harder for the tall.
1998 May 16	**Psychosomatic Addict** M Hallett
1998 May 18	**The Font of Knowledge** P Oxley
1998 May 27	**Seat of Learning, Reactor Meltdown, Small Talk Costs Walls** P Oxley
1998 May	**Castle Anthrax** G Symonds
	Symonds climbs his first new route.
1998 June 4	**The Nth Degree** P Oxley
1998 June 19	**My Two Left Feet** P Oxley
	Climbed by Oxley with two left-footed boots.
1998 June	**Crack My Bitch Up** M Hallett
1998 July 25	**I Love the Smell of Resin in the Morning** N Hellyer
1998 July	**Loose Cannon** M Robertson
1998 July	**Tennessee** A Long
1998 Aug 3	**Beefcake, Beefcake** N Heanes
1998 Aug 7	**Second Attention, Kinaesthesia** J Dunlop
1998 Aug 13	**Out of Yer Shell, Greet Flying Scotsmen** M J Crocker
	Followed by Paul Savage and Neil McGinty – the Flying Scotsmen!
1998 Aug 16	**Choc Speedway** G Jenkin
1998 Aug 16	**The Stal's on Me, Pal** F Haden
1998 Aug 16	**Inbreeding** F Haden, G Jenkin (both led)
1998 Aug 16	**Falling With Style, Screw You, Hippy, Gay Dog** N Heanes
1998 Aug 16	**Tanya's Sex Pot, Lay Back and Take It, Blackwind Fire and Steel** N Burton
1998 Aug 18	**Stone Cold Sober** M Robertson
1998 Aug 24	**Intricacies of Dreaming** J Dunlop
1998 August	**The Big Boss** P Savage
1998 Sept 22	**Car Parts, Bottles and Cutlery** N Hellyer
1998 Sept 23	**Zero Tolerance** P Oxley
1998 Oct 3	**Meridian Line** P Oxley
1998 Oct 17	**Glycerine** P Oxley
1998 Nov 7	**Ming the Merciless** P Oxley
1998	**Steve's Route** C Cubitt
	Not yet climbed by 'Steve', though others have succeeded where he has failed.
1998	**Until the End of Man** P Oxley

1998	**Screw the Roses, Send Me the Thorns** N Hellyer

Hellyer's hardest contribution to date. Several flyers were made on earlier attempts.

1998	**Babelicious Redhead** M Robertson
1998	**Girl Power** D B Cook
1998	**Dutch Courage** M Hallett
1999 Jan 10	**Hung, Swung and Zawned Out** P Oxley
1999 Jan 11	**The Drill Sergeant** P Oxley
1999 March 20	**Dudas Sin Nombres** N Hellyer
1999 March 28	**Wasted** N Heanes
1999 April 2	**Tunnel Vision** P Oxley
1999 April 8	**Escape from the Dwaffee Room** Ms A Newcombe
1999 April 18	**Time of the Month** N Hellyer, Ms C Forkin
1999 April 18	**Inception** B Slattery
1999 April 18	**Isle of Slingers** N Hellyer

Portland was once called this by Thomas Hardy due to the fact that strangers were often stoned. The practise has reappeared in recent times, though is reserved mainly for visiting climbers.

1999 April 20	**Dyno-Mite** P Oxley

An abandoned Vaicaitis project.

1999 April	**Clockwork Orange** G Symonds
1999 May 10	**Last Orders** P Oxley
1999 May 17	**Lolita** P Oxley
1999 August	**Aphasia** C Weedon
1999 Sept 14	**The Launch** J Dunlop
1999 Sept	**The Pickford Files** D Pickford

This time Pickford climbs a route before it has been properly cleaned – a dangerous flake awaits.

1999 Oct 3	**Depth Gauge, Esperanto, Bastinado, The Machine, Deep Water Drug Bust, Nutter's Way, The 6.03, Scrubs, Borstal Break-in** M Crocker

A most productive day! Crocker adds 9 hard deep-water solos to Portland's itinerary.

1999 Oct	**Relax** N Hellyer
1999 Nov 21	**Balance of Power** P Oxley

Oxley waits for good, cold conditions to complete his hard White Hole project. Soloed in 2007 by G Symonds.

1999 Dec 10	**Screaming Skulls** P Oxley
1999 Dec 23	**Fibonacci Sequence** J Kimber
1999 Sept	**Grand Larceny** D Pickford

Pickford, keen as ever for a new challenge, steals Hellyer's project.

1999	**Look on the Bright Side** P Oxley
1999	**Underbare** D Henderson

The Devon raider makes his mark on the Dorset deep-water solo scene.

2000 Jan 23	**El Scorchio** R Godfray
2000 Jan 23	**Maximum Grrr...** P Oxley

2000 Jan 26	**Dawn of a New Age** P Oxley
2000 Feb 2	**Paraphilias** C Weedon
2000 Feb 12	**Down to the Wire** P Oxley

The last route climbed before the appearance of the 2000 Rockfax.

2000 Mar 19	**100% Columbian, Gun Runner, Hang 'Em High** P Oxley
2000 Mar	**Enjoy My Experience** J Kimber
2000 May 1	**Pure Shores** P Oxley
2000 May 9	**One Life** G Symonds
2000 May 17	**Heartland** P Oxley
2000 May 25	**La Usurpadora** P Oxley
2000 May	**American Beauty** G Symonds
2000 May	**Californian Dreams** A Betts, A Long
2000 June	**H'Electric Boogaloo** N Heanes
2000 June 15	**Siurana** C Weedon (solo)
2000 June 15	**Just for a Day, True to the Game, On with the Games, Unnamed 5** P Oxley (solo)
2000 June 24	**Sister of Night, Spanish Air, Totally Stoked, Tiny Smiles** P Oxley (first two solo)
2000 June 24	**Pedriza, Chorro, Penon, Sella** C Weedon
2000 June 25	**Tombstonin'** P Oxley (solo)
2000 June 25	**The Red Crane Traverse** M Stammers, B Stokes
2000 July 2	**Razor Laugh** T Dunsby, S Titt, B Wilkinson, Ms M Broere
2000 July 2	**Hell Razor** T Dunsby, S Titt

The Swanage old boys make their mark in traditional on-sight style. The names are a reference to the nearby Razorbill colony.

2000 July 8	**Staplebite, Ethical Vacuum, Gyttja, Bortsal Bash** M Crocker
2000 July	**Any Last Requests, Dragon's Lair, End of the Land** P Oxley (solo)
2000 July	**Any Time Mike** J Kimber
2000 August	**The Labyrinth** P Oxley
2000 Oct 17	**Extreme Lives** M Crocker

Portland's hardest non-bolt route. An audacious solo above a deadly landing.

2000	**Into the Groove** P Oxley
2000	**Wanderlust** P Church
2000	**Red Crane Wall** P Harris
2000	**Wall of Squares** Ms. K Dominey
2001 June 9	**Condor** M Crocker (solo)
2001 July 26	**Water Wings** G Symonds
2001 July	**Shit Route** A Long

Unwilling to give it a name, Long was less than complimentary about his own route. The description stuck!

2001 August	**Bay of Peegs** J Cook

Cook originally drilled a hold on this route in 1995, but still failed to climb it. He later returned, repaired the damage and soloed the line. A reformed character?

2001 Sept 9	**Existenz** G Symonds
2001	**Solar Flare, Sun Spot, Sea of Tranquility, Moonshine, Walking on the Moon, Dark Side of the Moon, Lunar Eclipse, Half Moon, Full Moon** J Kimber

A new sector provides some pleasant short sports routes.

2001	**Big Slab Variant** Unknown

Martin Crocker risking all on the first ascent of *Extreme Lives* E7 (page 255). CARL RYAN

2002 March 16	**Carlos Fandango Belay** N Heanes
2002 March 16	**Paying it Forward** H Heanes
2002 March 22	**Hollow Ground** B Stokes

The deadly flowstone flake, avoided for years, is finally climbed.

2002 March 29	**Flipper's Revenge** G Gibson

Gibson finally arrives, drill in hand, and spearheads the new-route boom for the next three years

2002 March 30	**And the Boat Sails By** G Gibson
2002 April 1	**Everything's Eventual, More Than a Legend, Under Crimson Skies** G Gibson

Cleaned by Mike Robertson many years before, Everything's Eventual put up little resistance to the Gibson bolting machine.

2002 May 3	**The Man Who Wasn't There** G Gibson
2002 May 4	**Fatal Fibre, Billy Bob's Way** G Gibson
2002 May 7	**The Bronx, L'Odyssee Noire** G Gibson
2002 May 9	**Major Mushrooms and that Mentally Muffled Mentality, Wavewatch** G Gibson
2002 May 11	**My Figure Head, Laid Black** G Gibson
2002 June 1	**Wonderful, Wonder-bra** G Gibson
2002 June 3	**The Shipping News, Five Easy Pieces** G Gibson
2002 Aug 24	**Skids of Mark** G Gibson
2002 Aug 26	**From a Buick Eight, Skyscraper** G Gibson
2002 Sept 15	**Marshalling Amps, September Mourning, A Ship Load of Moonies** G Gibson
2002	**Valerian, One Fine Day, Ocean Rock, Best Destiny, Chasing the Sun, Absolute Beginners, The Black Spot, Cinema Paradiso, Mirror of the Sea, Silver-Studded Blue, Raptor** M Ward

Another new name to new-routing on Portland!

2002	**Dogtown Skate Team, Rush, Beautiful South** A Long
2003 Feb 23	**The Angry Sea** M Ward
2003 Feb 26	**Winterset, Sea Pink** M Ward
2003 March 12	**Eva Luna** M Ward
2003 March 31	**Immaculata** M Ward
2003 May 4	**Norfolk Coast, Blood Simple, Hasta la Vista** G Gibson
2003 May 6	**Face in the Chert** G Gibson, P Gibson
2003 May 7	**Steptoe and Son** G Gibson, P Gibson, Mrs H Gibson
2003 May 8	**Xavier Zoo** G Gibson (solo)
2003 May 9	**AKA UK OK** G Gibson
2003 May 9	**Critical Mass** G Gibson, Mrs H Gibson, M Ward
2003 May 9	**Rapid Response** G Gibson, M Ward
2003 May 10	**Black'll do Nicely, Chert Noble** G Gibson
2003 May 25	**Scoobydoobydoo, Scooby Snacks, Up on the Hill** G Gibson
2003 May 27	**Hen's Tooth** G Gibson
2003 May 27	**Yikes Shaggy, Old Speckled Hen** G Gibson, P Gibson
2003 May 27	**Das Boot** G Gibson, Mrs H Gibson, P Gibson

2003 May	**The Heanous Quest**	N Heanes
2003 June 12	**Burnt Sienna**	M Ward
2003 June 14	**Basra Blues Band, Sang Chaud**	N Heanes
2003 June 15	**Fight the Good Fight, Strategem**	M Ward
2003 June 16	**Vin Chaud**	N Heanes
2003 June 20	**The Parkhurst Dozen**	B Stokes
2003 June 23	**Sans Frontiers**	Mrs H Heanes
2003 June 26	**Always a Little Farther**	M Ward
2003 July 5	**Garstang**	M Ward
2003 July 7	**Olympus Mons**	G Gibson, P Gibson
2003 July 17	**The Bog Man**	M Ward
2003 July 22	**Alpenglow**	M Ward
2003 Aug 9	**Painted Lady**	M Ward
2003 Aug 15	**Adonis Blue, Chalk-hill Blue**	M Ward
2003 Aug 17	**Get Some Air, Fatso**	B Stokes, M Williams (both solo)
2003 Sept 6	**To Hungary, for Love**	G Symonds

Symonds climbs Damian Cook's old project, making it the first 8th grade climb on Portland by someone other than Oxley.

2003 Sept 27	**Holding the Zero**	M Ward
2003 Oct 4	**Dark Play, Eternal Peace**	M Ward
2003 Oct 17	**Sniper in the Brain**	M Ward
2003 Oct	**Dead Man's Click**	M Ward
2003	**Underlife**	G Symonds (solo)

A similar line has been reported by M J Crocker.

2004 April 24	**Rusty the Redneck Takes One for the Team**	N Heanes

Even The Cuttings gives up new lines.

2004 May 12	**Chymerie**	M Ward (solo)
2004 May 13	**The God of Sleep**	M Ward (solo)
2004 May 16	**Edge of Beyond**	M Ward (solo)
2004 May 17	**Rapture of the Deep**	M Ward (solo)
2004 May 19	**Swirling Pool**	M Ward

A series of daring solos on Pulpit Rock for Ward.

2004 May 20	**Sing Something Simple**	G Gibson
2004 May 22	**Calcichew**	G Gibson, Mrs H Gibson
2004 May 22	**Calcite Compliment, Jazz it Up, Totally Foo to You**	G Gibson
2004 June 19	**Bevis, Moonfleet**	M Ward
2004 July 6	**Pavane**	M Ward (solo)

Mistakenly retrobolted later the same year by M Williams. A section of crag which had seen no attention for almost 30 years is suddenly in vogue.

2004 July 6	**Shibumi**	M Ward
2004 July 12	**Love of Life**	M Ward (solo)
2004 July	**Dizzy up the Girl**	G Symonds
2004 Aug 26	**Forever Young**	M Ward (solo)

Named in memory of the late Will Perrin.

2004 Aug	**Athenian Tactics**	S Golley

Gav Symonds on *To Hungary, for Love* F8a (page 131). NEAL HEANES

2004 Sept 11	**Lardman**	M Williams

Named in memory of the late Brian Tilley.

2004 Sept 11	**Return to Form**	S Taylor

Climbed quickly to escape an incoming tide.

2004 Sept 14	**Another Trojan Horse, The Black Pariah, The Barton Fink, Big Fish**	G Gibson
2004 Sept 15	**No Ifs, No Butts**	G Gibson
2004 Sept 16	**How Now, Brown Cow, The Shells, The Shells**	G Gibson
2004 Sept 16	**East Coast Epic, Dirty Dog, Rusty Wall**	S Taylor, B Stokes (both led)
2004 Sept 16	**Flake Break**	M Williams

Taylor and Williams return mid-week to complete their routes, worried that Gibson might nip in before the weekend to take the remaining lines.

2005 Jan 24	**The Cult of John Craven** P Oxley	

John Craven made a visit to the Island and met Pete during a TV programme, to discuss the naming of The John Craven *Jumper Contest!*

2005 Feb 27	**Diamond Geezer, Diamond Edge** S Taylor
2005 Feb 27	**Portland Snowshine** S Taylor (solo)
2005 July 22	**Eight Inches** J Woods (solo)
2005 Oct	**Pulling Daisies, Hello Sailor, The Sponginess of the Wrong Mixture Filler, Crocadilia, Kite Marks, Sanfet Kuss, Chin Reaction, Sellerfield** G Gibson
2005	**By Mistake** A Long
2006 April 4	**Shape of Tomorrow, Michèle, Will** M Ward

A previously neglected area of Wallsend moves into the 21st Century.

2006 April 13	**River of Dreams** M Ward
2006 April 30	**Boom-Boom Boom Box** G Gibson
2006 April 30	**Ghetto-Blaster Master** G Gibson, H Gibson
2006 May 2	**Sniffin' Glue, The Chronicles of Vladimir, Slither** G Gibson
2006 May 3	**The Kane Mutiny, No Smears Here** G Gibson, H Gibson
2006 May 4	**Sueños con España** J Pickles
2006 May 4	**I Walk the Line, Dusty Bedrock in Need of Careful Preparation** G Gibson
2006 May 5	**The Viper's Tale** G Gibson
2006 June 10	**Charlton Mackerel, the World's Strongest Fish** N Heanes
2006 June 27	**Bleeting Nincompoops** M Robertson (on-sight solo)
2006 June	**Random Texter** G Symonds
2006 June	**Taking Advantage** A Long
2006 July	**Cloud Atlas** G Symonds
2006 Sept 5	**Faith, Hop and Charity** T Beaumont

Tom Beaumont completes his first new route, and soon becomes Portland's most active new-router.

2006 Sept 23	**Gravity Epiphany** Miss J Weir
2006 Dec 12	**Short 'n' Sexy** T Beaumont
2006	**A Nugget of Purest Green** T Beaumont
2007 Jan 29	**Pixie and the Milford Powerhouse** T Beaumont
2007 Feb 2	**Little Sod** S Muncaster
2007 March 17	**French Connection** Y Genoux
2007 March	**Popeye Doyle** A Long
2007 April 8	**Crazy Old Hippies** T Beaumont
2007 April 10	**Ultrasonic Shoulder** T Beaumont
2007 April 29	**Crowbar Assassin** T Beaumont
2007 April 29	**Die Screaming With Sharp Things in Your Head** J Whittles
2007 May 22	**Grapefruit Takes a Whipper** S Muncaster
2007 May 26	**Dungecroft Delight** T Beaumont
2007 May 26	**The Alpha and the Omega** J Whittles
2007 May 29	**The Epicurean Paradox, Covert Strike** T Beaumont

2007 June 9	**The Taylor Show, The Good Life, Short, but Perfectly Formed, Euphemism** S Taylor
2007 June 9	**Enter Shikari** G Symonds
2007 July 31	**Flying Peach** J Leonard
2007 Sept 8	**Break-Over Crack** S Taylor, J Howell

First Free Ascent. Previously VS & A1.

2008 Jan 31	**Van Life** G Symonds
2008 Jan 31	**Heartbeats** A Long
2008 Feb 16	**Quality Family Day, True Love** M Hallett
2008 March	**Up the Junction** N Heanes, Mrs H Heanes
2008 April	**Baron's Revenge, Chicken Boy, Tantrums and Tiaras, 100 Sunny Days** S Taylor (solo)
2008 April	**Parsnip Soup, Cheese and Pickle** N Hellyer
2008 April	**Limbo Dancer** J Howell
2008 May 10	**Pop for the Top** M Ward

The Lulworth Area

Bob Shepton put up the majority of the early routes at Lulworth.

1962	**Cheddar, Windy Corner, Slab and Corner** R Shepton
1976 June 1	**Exfoliator** J L Titt, F Farrell

After top-rope practice.

1978 June 10	**Scuba** C Mellor, P Smethurst
1979	**Centre Line** J L Titt, S L Titt
1979	**White Line** S L Titt, J L Titt
1983 Jan 16	**Archway** C Mellor, B Simmons

Must be a good route: Mellor repeated it with his daughter.

1983 Jan	**Country Girl** J Godding, Ms L Heinemann, T Daniells
1984 Nov 6	**Wet Feet** A Palmer, N Moriarty
1985	**Stormbringer** C Ciumui, D Sharman
1987 April 5	**Pickpocket** T Dunsby, N A Coe

Unintentionally stolen (with apologies) from whoever placed the thread runners and stakes. Direct start added 4.96 by M Robertson, M Williams.

1987 Sept 27	**Dungeons and Dragons** P Oxley, S Williams
1987 Oct 22	**Mark of the Beast** P Oxley, S Williams, J Williams (yo-yoed)

Attempted solo by J Dawes, who reversed down from two-thirds height. Subsequently soloed by P Oxley.

1987 Oct 23	**Grimly Fiendish** P Oxley
1987 Oct 23	**Lulworth Arms Treaty** P Oxley (yo-yoed)
1988 Sept 6	**Anarchy Stampede** J Biddle (on-sight solo)

A route which has claimed many splashdowns, despite it's relatively low grade.

1988 Oct 23	**Curtain Call** J Williams, P Oxley
1988 Nov 20	**Blow Daddy-O** C Alston, N White, B Wilkinson, E Heslam
1988 Dec 13	**Wall of Feedback, House Nation, Jugmaster Funk Featuring M C Lane** P Oxley

1988 Dec 23	**Looking through the Infinity Window**	P Oxley
1989 July 2	**Sardine Liberation Front**	A Donson (on-sight solo)
1990 March 31	**Butterfingers**	D J Felce
1991 July 13	**Blubbered**	J Biddle, J Cook

On sight on a single 9mm in the drizzle! An old peg 10 metres along the traverse suggested a previous attempt, but no record has been found.

1991 July 20	**Truth, Justice and the Raggamuffin Way**	J Biddle

(on-sight solo)
A bold effort, considering the friable nature of the finishing moves.

1991 July 21	**Captain Bastard Got There First**	J M Cook (on-sight solo)
1991 July 21	**Last Season's Loozas**	D B Cook, D M Cook (solo)

The first half was climbed as The Maypole by J Williams on 23 May 1990.

1991 July 22	**Herbert the Turbot**	J Biddle (on-sight solo)
1991 July	**Does Leviathan Plop Float?**	D B Cook
1991 Sept 8	**Durdley Doodle**	K Balfour, M Goulding
1992 May 10	**Burn, Hollywood, Burn**	P Oxley (redpoint)
1992 May 16	**Sideshow**	S L Titt, N A Coe (on sight)
1992 May 19	**Horny Lil' Devil**	P Oxley, D B Cook.

A sport route which sees far more solo attempts than roped ones.

1992 May 20	**Adrenochrome**	P Oxley (redpoint)

Ascent over three days. Soloed by Richard Bingham.

1992 May 23	**Sliding down the Bannister**	P Oxley (on-sight solo)
1992 May 31	**The Safety Rail**	T Dunsby, S L Titt, N A Coe (VL)
1992 May	**Stagedivin'**	P Oxley (redpoint)
1992 June 4	**The Gates of Greyskull, Animal Magnetism**	P Oxley

(redpoint)

1992 Sept 5	**Never Kneel to Skeletor**	P Oxley (redpoint)
1992 Oct 16	**Unleash the Veins**	P Oxley, J M Cook (redpoint)
1992 Dec 13	**They Call Me Tall Man**	J M Cook
1992 Dec 22	**Riding to Babylon**	P Oxley, D B Cook, J M Cook (redpoint)
1992 Dec 28	**Roof Predator**	P Oxley (redpoint)
1993 April	**Arcwelder**	P Oxley, S Taylor (flashed)
1993 June 26	**The Walkin' Dude**	M Robertson (on-sight solo)
1993 July 4	**Turn It On**	S Taylor, M Higgs
1993 July 10	**The Debt Collector**	M Robertson
1993 July 11	**Scott's Escape**	S L Titt, Miss P Holt, N A Coe
1993 Sept 5	**Traverse of the Fossils**	T Dunsby, N A Coe (AL) (flashed)
1993 Oct 3	**Back to the Future**	T Dunsby, N A Coe (AL) (flashed)

The initial 60 metres were climbed by an unknown party as Forester's Traverse prior to 1961.

1993 Dec 5	**Lost Souls**	M Robertson, M Williams
1993	**The Laws Traverse**	P Oxley, M Robertson, G Fitch, M Higgs

(all solo).
All four were jockeying for position at the start, but it was Oxley who was first past the winning post.

Steve Taylor on an early attempt of *Turn It On* F7a+ (page 356). MARK HIGGS

1994 Feb 19	**Beers, Steers and Queers**	S Taylor, M Robertson
1994 Feb 19	**Beavis and Butthead**	M Robertson
1994 March 27	**Closing Time**	S Taylor, G Fitch
1994 April 24	**Morris the Carnivore**	M Robertson, M Williams, G Fitch
1994 July 30	**Route 66**	M Robertson (on-sight solo)
1995 Aug 1	**Escobar**	J Cook (solo)
1995 Aug 1	**Contortions**	M Robertson (solo)
1995 Aug 5	**Showtime**	J Cook (solo)
1995 Aug 22	**Crazy Notion**	M Robertson (solo)
1995 Sept 19	**El Guapo**	J Cook (solo)
1996 July	**The Honourable Society of Self-Publicising Water Rats**	D B Cook (solo)

Damian Cook takes a sideways view of the Dorset deep-water soloing scene.

1997 April	**I Love Eszter**	D B Cook (solo)
1997 Oct 23	**Burning Arms**	P Oxley

1997 Dec 4	**Freed From Desire**	J Kimber
1998 Aug 8	**Window of Opportunity**	M Robertson (solo)
1998 Aug	**Hornier than Thou**	J Cook (solo)
1999 Jan	**Lord of Darkness**	P Oxley
1999	**Z Cars**	J Cook
1990s	**Shining Path**	D B Cook
1990s	**Monolith Monsters, Lewd's Mother**	D M Cook
1990s	**Bad to the Bone, Il Pirata, The Lemon Express, Breathe the Pressure, Rigor Mortise, A Storm in Heaven**	P Oxley

2000 July	**Magnetic Gates, The Hairy Clamber**	D B Cook (solo)
2000	**Rebirth**	M Glaister, M Williams, S Taylor (solo)

Williams was the only one who succeeded on the second pitch.

2001 Feb 18	**Let Ya Bones Hang**	P Oxley
2001 Feb 25	**Eye of the Storm, Language of Nature**	P Oxley
2001 April	**Mirrorball**	P Oxley
2002 Sept	**Journey to Eternia**	P Oxley
2003 July	**Thieving Gypsy**	G Symonds (solo)

A project stolen from Stokes.

2003 Sept	**West Kante, Ticket Tout**	B Clarke (solo)
2003 Oct 4	**Samuel, Eleanor**	S Taylor, B Clarke
2003 Oct 4	**Ricochet Wall**	B Clarke, S Taylor

Damian Cook on *Monolith Monsters* **F7b+ (page 382).** JOFF

2003 Oct 20	**The Rouble**	B Clarke
2003	**Old Timers**	M Robertson (solo)
2004 July 24	**Despicable Terrier**	M Williams (solo)

Both Williams and Stokes were in the rush to steal this project from J Cook. Williams won the race, but objected to the route being called Dirty Dog *by the others and settled on this name.*

2004 April 25	**The Pony**	S Titt, B Watson
2004 July 28	**The Ringfinder**	S Taylor (solo)

Probably done before.

2004 Aug 14	**Cheddar (Direct Start)**	S Taylor, M Hallet (solo)

Probably done before.

2005 Jan 23	**Granny Lifts Car**	P Oxley
2005 April	**Dry Your Eyes Mate**	D Kennard
2005 July 17	**Rameses Cubed**	P Oxley
2006 May 13	**Hyperbole, Extraordinary Rendition, Pussy Galore**	R Kennard, A More

Seasoned sport climber Kennard puts up his first trad routes in Dorset!

2006 June 17	**Too Driven**	B Stokes, S Taylor (both solo)
2006 June 17	**Jurassic Coast Pimp**	B Stokes, M Williams
2006 June 17	**Bolt Free**	S Taylor, M Williams
2006 June 17	**Carbon Footprint**	R Kennard, J Dunlop, J Howells
2006 June 24	**MC Hammer, Svengali**	R Kennard, J Dunlop
2006 June 30	**Mojo-Pin**	R Kennard, M Hallett, A More
2006 June 30	**4 Years, 5 Months and 15 Days and Still Missing You**	M Hallett, A More, R Kennard
2006 June	**Imp of the Perverse**	G Symonds
2006 July 23	**Southern Stutter**	D Simmonite, S Taylor

Photographer David Simmonite got a thorough soaking in the rush for new routes at Lulworth.

2006 July 23	**Stalinist Regime**	S Taylor, D Simmonite
2006 July 24	**The Poet and the Thief**	A More, R Kennard
2006 Nov 5	**The Gift**	S Taylor, S Titt
2006 Nov 5	**Jay Kay**	R Kennard, S Titt
2007 Apr 20	**Evening Slab, Lulworth New Order**	S Taylor, R Kennard
2007 Apr 20	**Cuzco, Ghost of You**	R Kennard, S Taylor
2007 Sept 1	**Skillfish**	J Biddle

On-sight solo.

2007 Sept 5	**Windowchrome**	G Symonds

A ground-up solo (with several splashdowns prior to success) resulting in Dorset's hardest deep-water solo to date. Repeated immediately by D Pickford.

2007 Sept 5	**B-Boys Rock, Oh Blow You**	M Hallett
2007 Sept 15	**Lesbian Spank Inferno, Recursion**	R Kennard, J Howell
2007 Sept 15	**Plwmp, Ouzo Envy**	J Howell, R Kennard
2007 Sept 29	**September Sessions**	A More, I Gamblin

Index of Climbs

Due to space constraints, boulder problems are not
included in the index.

Index

406

Index

Index

Index

Index

First Aid

• If spinal or head injuries are suspected, do not move the patient without skilled help, except to maintain breathing.

• If breathing has stopped, clear the airways and start artificial respiration. Do not stop until expert opinion has diagnosed death.

• Stop bleeding by applying direct pressure and elevate injured limbs, where possible.

• Summon help.

Rescue

In the event of an accident where further assistance is required, DIAL 999 and ask for the COASTGUARD. The Coastguards are responsible for the co-ordination of all sea-cliff rescues, and will co-ordinate the other services such as helicopters, lifeboats, cliff rescue teams, etc.

It is important to report the exact location and details of the accident and also to have someone meet the rescue team to guide them to the spot.

Nearest Phone Points

Portland & Lulworth Cove – Both within easy reach of a phone.

Durdle Door – At the top of the hill behind the arch is a phone box by a caravan park; this is closer than Lulworth Cove itself.

Helicopter

In the event of a Helicopter evacuation **all** climbers on or off the cliff should take heed. A helicopter flying close to the cliff will make verbal communication very difficult and small stones will be dislodged by the rotor downdraught. All loose equipment should be secured and climbers in precarious positions should try to make themselves safe.

The people with the injured person should try to identify their location. **No** attempt should be made to throw a rope at the helicopter, but assistance should be given to the helicopter crew if requested. **Do not** touch the lowered crew member or his winch wire until the trailing wire has earthed the helicopter's static electricity.

Local Hospitals

The walking wounded can receive treatment in the casualty departments of the following hospitals:

• Weymouth & District Hospital, Melcombe Avenue, Weymouth. (01305) 760022.

• Dorset County Hospital, Williams Avenue, Dorchester. (01305) 255541

• Poole General Hospital, Longfleet Road, Poole. (01202) 442202.

Follow-Up

After an accident a written report should be sent to the Mountain Rescue Committee Statistics Officer, Mr Ged Feeney email ged@gfeeney.demon.co.uk tel. 01228 525709, giving details of: date, extent of injuries, and name, age, and address of the casualty. Normally this will be done by the police or local rescue team involved, who will also require the names and addresses of those climbing with the injured party.

If unreasonable equipment failure is suspected then the British Mountaineering Council's technical committee may wish to investigate; contact the BMC at 177-179 Burton Road, West Didsbury, Manchester, M20 2BB.

Portland Coastguard rescue helicopter Whiskey Bravo performing a rescue at Battleship. STEVE TAYLOR